INFORMATION POLITICS, PROTESTS, AND HUMAN RIGHTS IN THE DIGITAL AGE

We live in a highly complex and evolving world that requires a fuller and deeper understanding of how modern technological tools, ideas, practices, and institutions interact and how different societies adjust themselves to the emerging realities of the digital age. This book conveys such issues with a fresh perspective and in a systematic and coherent way. While many studies have explained in depth the change in the aftermath of the unrests and uprisings throughout the world, they rarely mentioned the need for constructing new human rights norms and standards. This edited collection provides a balanced conceptual framework to demonstrate not only the power of autonomous communication networks but also their limits and the increasing setbacks they encounter in different contexts.

INFORMATION POLITICS, PROTESTS, AND HUMAN RIGHTS IN THE DIGITAL AGE

MAHMOOD MONSHIPOURI

San Francisco State University

CAMBRIDGE
UNIVERSITY PRESS

CAMBRIDGE
UNIVERSITY PRESS

32 Avenue of the Americas, New York NY 10013

Cambridge University Press is part of the University of Cambridge.

It furthers the University's mission by disseminating knowledge in the pursuit of
education, learning, and research at the highest international levels of excellence.

www.cambridge.org
Information on this title: www.cambridge.org/9781107140769

© Cambridge University Press 2016

First published 2016

A catalogue record for this publication is available from the British Library.

Library of Congress Cataloging-in-Publication Data
Names: Monshipouri, Mahmood, 1952– editor of compilation.
Title: Information politics, protests, and human rights in the digital age /
edited by Mahmood Monshipouri.
Description: New York, NY : Cambridge University Press, 2016. |
Includes bibliographical references and index.
Identifiers: LCCN 2015037453 | ISBN 9781107140769 (Hardback)
Subjects: LCSH: Information technology–Political aspects. | Human rights. |
Social media–Political aspects. | Political participation–Technological innovations. |
Protest movements. | Social movments. | BISAC: Political science /
Political Freedom & Security / Human Rights.
Classification: LCC HM851.I53174 2016 | DDC 323–dc23 LC record
available at http://lccn.loc.gov/2015037453

ISBN 978-1-107-14076-9 Hardback

CONTENTS

Contributors   vii
Acknowledgments   xii
*Foreword: reflections on protests and
human rights in the digital world*   xiii
DAVID P. FORSYTHE

1   Introduction: protests and human rights in context   1
MAHMOOD MONSHIPOURI

PART I   Framing the digital impact: information society, activism,
and human rights   21

2   Social movements in the digital age   23
JACK J. BARRY

3   What does human rights look like? The visual culture of aid,
advocacy, and activism   50
JOEL R. PRUCE

4   Activism, the Internet, and the struggle for human rights:
youth movements in Tunisia and Egypt   73
MAHMOOD MONSHIPOURI, JONATHON WHOOLEY,
AND DINA A. IBRAHIM

PART II   Digital dissidence and grassroots politics   99

5   Grassroots sanctions: a new tool for domestic and
transnational resistance for Palestine   101
SHANE WESBROCK, MAHMOOD MONSHIPOURI,
AND JESS GHANNAM

6   Social media, Kyiv's Euromaidan, and demands
for sovereignty in Eastern Ukraine   127
BRYON J. MORASKI

7   Networks of protest in Latin America   151
     JUANITA DARLING

PART III   Network politics and social change   175

8   Iran's Green Movement, social media, and the exposure of
     human rights violations   177
     ELHAM GHEYTANCHI

9   The politics of protest and repression in the digital age:
     Turkey during and after the Gezi Park protests   196
     IHSAN DAGI

10   Social media and the transformation of Indian politics in the
     2014 elections   221
     SANJOY BANERJEE

11   Promises to keep: the Basic Law, the "Umbrella Movement,"
     and democratic reform in Hong Kong   239
     MICHAEL C. DAVIS

12   Conclusion: the quest for human rights in the digital age: how
     it has changed and the struggle ahead   267
     MAHMOOD MONSHIPOURI AND SHADI MOKHTARI

     Selected bibliography   294
     Index   302

CONTRIBUTORS

SANJOY BANERJEE is Professor of International Relations at San Francisco State University and teaches courses on international relations theory and methodology as well as on South and Southeast Asia. His research interests include the same topics. He has publications in historical structural analysis, the role of national identity and narratives in foreign policy, artificial intelligence in international politics, and political economy. His articles have appeared in *International Studies Quarterly*, *European Journal of International Relations*, *International Relations of the Asia-Pacific*, and elsewhere. He received his PhD in Political Science from Yale University in 1982.

JACK J. BARRY recently received his PhD in Political Science from the University of Connecticut. His most recent publication include "A Digital Sublime or Divide?" in Anita Breuer and Yanina Welp, eds., *Digital Technologies for Democratic Governance in Latin America: Opportunities and Risks* (2014). His journal publications include: "Microfinance, the Market and Political Development in the Internet Age," *Third World Quarterly*, and "Democracy Promotion and ODA: A Comparative Analysis," *Contemporary Politics*. He has taught courses at various institutions of higher education including University of Connecticut, University of Rhode Island, and Trinity College (Hartford, Connecticut).

IHSAN DAGI is Professor of International Relations at the Middle East Technical University, Ankara, Turkey. His publications have appeared in *Journal of Democracy, Turkish Studies, Critique: Critical Middle Eastern Studies, Mediterranean Quarterly: Journal of Global Issues, Journal of Southern Europe*, and *Black Sea Studies, Middle Eastern Studies, and Perceptions: Journal of International Affairs*. He is the author of *Turkey between Militarism and Democracy* (2009).

JUANITA DARLING is Associate Professor and Director of the Latin American Studies Minor at San Francisco State University. She leads the Latin America and Alternative Research Methods in International Relations seminars and teaches undergraduate classes in Latin American Policy, US–Central America Relations, International Relations Analysis and Application, and International Media Politics. She is active in the Latin American Studies Association, International Communications Association, Red de Historiadores de la Prensa y el Periodismo en Iberoamérica, and American Journalism Historians Association.

MICHAEL C. DAVIS, a professor in the Law Faculty at the University of Hong Kong, has held visiting chairs in human rights at Northwestern University and Notre Dame as well as the Schell Senior Fellowship in Human Rights at the Yale Law School. As a public intellectual, Professor Davis has contributed to the debate over constitutional reform and human rights in Hong Kong for over two decades. In the recent debate over political reform, Professor Davis has offered an open letter and a series of commentary in the press on various proposals and government reports relating to political reform. His work has highlighted the importance of democratic reform to Hong Kong's rule of law and promised autonomy.

DAVID P. FORSYTHE is Emeritus University Professor and Charles J. Mach Distinguished Professor of Political Science at the University of Nebraska–Lincoln. Mr. Forsythe has been a consultant to the International Red Cross and Red Crescent Movement, as well as to the United Nations Office of the High Commissioner for Refugees. He has also served as President of the Human Rights Committee of the International Political Science Association, as Vice President of the International Studies Association, and as a member of the Committee on Scientific Freedom and Responsibility of the American Association for the Advancement of Science. He has published more than two dozen books, including *The Politics of Prisoner Abuse: The United States and Enemy Prisoners after 9/11* (2011). He is currently a Senior Fulbright Chair in Denmark.

JESS GHANNAM is Clinical Professor of Psychiatry and Global Health Sciences at the University of California, San Francisco, School of Medicine, and Adjunct Professor of Ethnic Studies at San Francisco State University. He is a psychoanalyst and practices in San Francisco and the East Bay. Dr. Ghannam specializes in working with chronic illness, including chronic pain and cancer. He also works and does research in the area of global health and post-traumatic stress disorder. He is also a founding member of the US Campaign for the Academic and Cultural Boycott of Israel (USACBI).

ELHAM GHEYTANCHI teaches sociology at Santa Monica College. Her research focuses on media, online activism, and civic engagement. Her scholarly articles, opinion columns, essays, and book reviews on the impact of digital media on women's rights movements in the Middle East and North Africa have appeared in academic journals as well as a host of online and print media. She has previously collaborated on programming for *To the Point*, a popular show on National Public Radio, as an associate producer.

DINA A. IBRAHIM is Associate Professor of Broadcast and Electronic Communication Arts at San Francisco State University and the Director of the California State University Entertainment Industry Initiative. She teaches broadcast news production and media performance. Her articles on the framing of Arab countries and Islam post-9/11 have appeared in the *International Communication Gazette* and the *Journal of Arab & Muslim Research*. She is the coauthor of *Television and Radio Announcing* (2013). Her research interests include the psychological impact of television news on audiences, analyzing American television representations of the Mideast, and the post–Arab Spring role of journalists in Egypt.

SHADI MOKHTARI is Assistant Professor in the School of International Service of American University. Her teaching and research focuses on human rights, Middle East politics, and political Islam. She is the author of *After Abu Ghraib: Exploring Human Rights in America and the Middle East* (2009), which was selected as the co-winner of the 2010 American Political Science Association Human Rights Section Best Book Award. From 2003 to 2013, she served as Editor in Chief of the *Muslim World Journal of Human Rights*. She holds an LLM and PhD from Osgoode Hall Law School, York University, and a JD from the University of Texas.

MAHMOOD MONSHIPOURI is Professor of International Relations at San Francisco State University. He is also a visiting professor at the University of California, Berkeley. He is author of *Democratic Uprisings in the New Middle East: Youth, Technology, Human Rights, and US Foreign*

Policy (2014), *Terrorism, Security, and Human Rights: Harnessing the Rule of Law* (2012), and editor of *Human Rights in the Middle East: Frameworks, Goals, and Strategies* (2011). His new edited volume is entitled *Inside the Islamic Republic: Social Change in the Post-Khomeini Iran* (forthcoming, 2016).

BRYON J. MORASKI is Associate Professor of Political Science at the University of Florida. His articles have appeared in *The American Journal of Political Science, Government and Opposition, The Journal of Politics, Party Politics,* and elsewhere. His current book manuscript (coauthored with Bill Reisinger at the University of Iowa) considers the links between federal elections and gubernatorial selection in Russia and their influence on the country's post-Soviet trajectory. While much of his work focuses on Russia, he has also conducted research in Armenia, Georgia, and Ukraine.

JOEL R. PRUCE is Assistant Professor of Human Rights Studies at the University of Dayton. He recently served as a postdoctoral fellow in human rights studies and joined the faculty as an assistant professor in the fall of 2014. His publications have appeared in *Human Rights & Human Welfare, Journal of Human Rights,* and *Millennium: Journal of International Studies.* He has contributed several book chapters, including "Spectacle of Suffering and Humanitarian Intervention in Somalia" in *Media, Mobilization, and Human Rights: Mediating Atrocity,* edited by Tristan Anne Borer (2012), and "Constituencies of Compassion: The Politics of Human Rights and Consumerism" in *Uses and Misuses of Human Rights,* edited by George Andreopoulos and Zehra K. Arat (2014).

SHANE EDWIN WESBROCK has been involved in social justice activism for many years, most recently conducting research for If Americans Knew, an NGO concerned with the special relationship between the United States and Israel. In March 2014, he also participated in organizing the National Summit to Reassess the US–Israel Special Relationship. He has closely studied the relations between the US, Israel, and the Palestinian territories since living in Israel and working with Palestinians in the West Bank in the 1990s. Currently, he is a graduate student in the Department of International Relations at San Francisco State University and serves as research assistant and teaching assistant in courses such as International Political Economy.

JONATHON WHOOLEY, PhD, is an adjunct lecturer at the University of San Francisco and San Francisco State University, where he teaches human rights, strategy and war, American foreign policy, gender, and global politics. His research interests include the historical construction of American foreign policy related to the Middle East, identity, gender, human rights, and conflict. His articles have appeared in the *Journal of Women, Politics, and Policy* and the *International Studies Journal.* He has also coauthored book chapters with Laura Sjoberg in *The Arab Spring and Arab Thaw: Unfinished Revolutions and the Quest for Democracy* (2013), and with Mahmood Monshipouri in *Human Rights in the Middle East: Frameworks, Goals, and Strategies* (2011).

ACKNOWLEDGMENTS

Since the 2011 uprisings in the Middle East and North Africa, I have worked on the idea of editing a book on the emancipatory potential of the digital media as well as its limits, even as I have struggled to keep my optimism concerning the empowering tools that social media and new technologies have offered us. I have also incurred enormous intellectual debts. Let me start by acknowledging how much I have learned by putting this volume together and how much I have benefited from the contributors to this volume and their unique perspectives and experiences regarding this globe-spanning subject matter. I could not have assembled a better team of supremely competent, knowledgeable, and able teachers and scholars in the field with whom to work.

I would also like to extend special words of thanks to Professor David P. Forsythe, who graciously consented to write the Foreword to this volume. Throughout the past four decades, Professor Forsythe has been an inspiration not only to his students and colleagues, but equally to the human rights community at large. The comments made on the final revisions of the conclusion by my extraordinary colleague Professor Juanita Darling were truly invaluable. Equally important was Professor Shadi Mokhtari's participation in finalizing this project. Her comments throughout this project considerably boosted the quality of this volume.

Finally, I give a special thanks to my former student, now a PhD holder at the University of Florida and adjunct professor at the University of San Francisco as well as San Francisco State University, Jonathon Whooley, for sharing his sharp intellectual insights and offering generous assistance along the way, without which this project would not have moved along smoothly. I owe an especially deep intellectual debt to John Berger, Senior Editor at Cambridge University Press, and Ezhillmaran Sugumaran, Senior Project Manager at Cambridge University Press, whose enduring feedback and systematic communication helped me to improve this project. Most of all, I offer gratitude to several anonymous reviewers for providing eminently helpful suggestions and comments by raising relevant and substantive questions.

FOREWORD

Reflections on protests and human rights in the digital world

It seems clear that all inventions carry within themselves the potential for positive or negative developments. The telephone can be used to call for help in an emergency, and it can be used by commercial enterprises to invade your privacy and try to get you to buy something you don't want and don't need. Television can be used to spread high culture as well as important news, and it can be used to disseminate cultural garbage as well as falsehoods. Airplanes can be used for family reunions and relaxation or turned into weapons to attack civilians and to make a political point. So it is with the digital world and computerized electronics.

There is no doubt, as the following pages make clear, that computerized social media can be a great asset to those who are politically active and seek to mobilize in order to advance human rights and democracy. Examples are abundant – from Turkey to Hong Kong and from Egypt to Ukraine. But threatened elites are not oblivious to developments, and they take steps to control and coerce in defense of their power, as this book also shows. One could use the very same examples to demonstrate elite efforts to block Internet usage and/or spy on progressive activists.

Other negative examples of contemporary digital politics can and should be mentioned. The Islamic State (ISIS or ISIL) uses slick propaganda through electronic journals on the Internet to recruit alienated and atomized individuals from around the world to fight in its campaign of total war in a woefully misguided effort to create a multinational Islamic caliphate. This bloody movement, abjuring all human rights and humanitarian limitations, has been successful in its digital reach. It has found ways to appeal to those who feel marginalized and disinherited, despite its policies of murder, rape, extortion, and so on in a litany of true atrocities. Since ISIS is supported by no government anywhere, its ability to recruit adherents is crucial to its continued existence and success, along with other factors such as its effective hard power and ability to raise money through capturing banks, levying "taxes" on road and water use, and obtaining ransom payments for hostages. But the Internet remains a crucial playing field for ISIS.

Unfortunately, the misuse of electronics is not limited to ISIS, al-Qaeda, and other armed nonstate actors. The US government, supposedly democratic, committed to human rights, and endorsing the rule of law, has collected massive data on its citizens and others who have no links to terrorism or other legal violations. At Guantanamo Bay, military authorities, having promised the International Committee of the Red Cross (ICRC) confidential interviews with detainees, almost certainly listened in by electronic means when prisoners described their abusive interrogations. Some prisoners were sanctioned for what they said, with the result that other prisoners refused to talk to ICRC delegates. It seems highly probable that this pattern of electronic violation of confidentiality is not limited to the United States.

There is no doubt that cyber war will be a feature of any future armed conflict between or among technologically sophisticated fighting parties. Already, various states use electronic means not only to spy on each other but also to hack into various databases and computer systems in order to steal information, perhaps for potential blackmail or worse. In the future, it is almost certain that a sophisticated belligerent will try to disrupt an enemy's banking system, and/or electrical grid, and/or water supply by electronic means. There will be damage to civilians and civilian structures, not just to combatants and their weapons. Various weapons systems, themselves highly computerized, will be attacked by electronic means. Already, if press reports can be believed, the Americans and Israelis tried to destroy Iranian energy-related systems with a computer virus. If one destroys a weapons-related system by electronic means rather than by kinetic (explosive) means, does that constitute an armed attack?

Second, in all these examples and many others that could be cited, as this fine book makes clear, digital politics is not so much the new controlling feature of political struggles as it is a new dimension to old and pervasive features. The Internet and computerized connections provide something new that was not there about twenty-five years ago. But rather than something completely sui generis and all controlling, digital space provides a new extension of controversies we have already faced.

There was already a search for information by governments hyper-concerned about security and stability versus a claimed right to privacy by citizens fearing an overreaching public authority. There was already hijacking of airplanes by those trying to find a way to publicize their cause, even before al-Qaeda-central and its various franchises took airplane suicide bombings to a new level. There was already humint (human intelligence) or human spying before electronic eavesdropping. There was already governmental disruption of peaceful protests before electronic tracking and blocking. There were already court cases about governmental searches and seizures before the issue arose of electronic searches and storing of presumably private information.

This book does a good job of reminding readers that digital developments, whether positive or negative, have to be placed in political context. NATO takes satellite photos and collects other evidence by electronic means, showing Russian military involvement in Eastern Ukraine. Yet as long as the Putin regime is in search of respect from NATO powers and determined to build a non-Western *cordon sanitaire* in its near abroad, it will continue with its deceptions and intervention. The existence of NATO evidence, collected in sophisticated ways, is only one factor in the political big picture.

Likewise, one can observe and protest against China's censoring of Internet sites via the Great Firewall. But as long as Chinese elites are preoccupied with that country's past instability, and as long as they view human rights norms as something imported from the West and dangerous to future stability, it is unlikely that China will soon prioritize individual freedom of thought, speech, and assembly. The 1948 Universal Declaration of Human Rights may speak about an individual right to seek and receive information across borders, but those words are likely to have little impact on a Chinese ruling elite consumed by fears of loss of control (especially after Gorbachev tried to expand civil freedoms in the old Soviet Union but wound up presiding over the implosion of that country).

Various persons and groups in Syria use their cell phone cameras to send pictures to the rest of the world about that humanitarian disaster. But as long as the United States is war weary after long involvements in Afghanistan and Iraq, and as long as European military powers are less interested in action there as compared with Libya in 2011, and as long as Russia and Iran (and Hezbollah) continue to back the Assad regime, those computerized photos, while important, are not likely to push outside powers into decisive intervention to end the atrocities. The broader context must indeed be understood for a proper understanding of digital developments.

Third, it seems clear enough that persons will differ in their approach to the proper regulation of digital politics. Disagreement seems the pervasive human condition. It has been noted in the following pages that certain UN circles have pushed for the idea of a human right to Internet access. Others have expressed opposition, however, because such a right would be dependent on an antecedent right – not mentioned in international documents – to adequate electrical energy. And at the moment, this antecedent right would itself be dependent on more burning of fossil fuels, which is not easily compatible with an asserted right to a safe and healthy environment. Even the discourse about human rights and Internet access leads to varying views. While the more affluent among us debate the Internet and rights, most of the world's population continues to scratch out a subsistence living without adequate food, shelter, and health care.

One might also note that in 2014 the European Court of Justice, part of the European Union, declared a right to be forgotten as a dimension of an individual's right to privacy. In the Costeja case, the Court affirmed that a Spanish citizen was within his legal rights to demand that Google remove his name from the Internet in conjunction with a property foreclosure case. Since the financial matter had been resolved, the Court held that Internet information should not be posted ad infinitum, which otherwise constituted a negative stigma for individuals. Other courts in other jurisdictions, however, had reached different conclusions about a right to personal privacy versus the public's right to know various facts.

All sorts of digitized electronic developments led down the road of inherent and inescapable debate about proper public policy, whether the subject was drone strikes, cyber war, automated or automatic weapons, laser weapons, and so on. Needless to say, the views of ICRC lawyers were not often the same as Pentagon lawyers as to the proper international law on these matters. If we take the issue of international drone strikes, as for now we do not even have full access to still-classified information about the process. It will be some time before we are in a position to evaluate the use of weaponized unmanned aerial aircrafts (UAVs). Perhaps when numerous powers possess this capability to kill from half a planet away via UAVs, reciprocity will propel us to agreement on regulation. In the meantime, we continue to debate.

As a final observation, one might be excused for thinking that we might be headed for an Orwellian world in which "Big Brother" is always watching and listening and perhaps photographing on the basis of digital developments. Yet the various court cases here and there, such as *Costeja*, the fact of democracy demonstrations in places like Hong Kong, the outcome of elections in Turkey, the evolution of politics in Tunisia, and other factors serve to remind us of broad and continuing concern for individual human rights. There are courageous people, organizations, and social movements across various nations determined not to let science lead us into that Orwellian world. What is clear is that, as before, the protection of human rights will occur to the extent that people of good will are prepared to struggle for that rights-based outcome. Some elites pushed back against a US policy of torture after 9/11 (e.g., John McCain, Diane Feinstein). They were joined by various organizations (e.g., the American Civil Liberties Union), journalists (e.g., Jane Mayer of the *New Yorker*), and others. Without doubt, various persons will contest to the misuse of digital developments. Human rights principles will be of great use in that struggle. The outcome is not certain. But that has always been the case with the struggle for human rights.

David P. Forsythe
Lincoln, NE

1

Introduction

Protests and human rights in context

MAHMOOD MONSHIPOURI

As the public discourse of the global normative order unfolds in the context of modern communications technology, two contradictory tendencies are worth noting: While human rights are compromised in some circumstances, they are widely regarded as a common moral language in others.[1] The aggressive digital surveillance of governmental authorities has undermined and continues to eclipse the most basic rights and civil liberties, including the right to privacy. These and similar abuses have resulted largely from domestic and extraterritorial surveillance, the interception of digital communications, and the collection of personal data.[2] At the same time, the increasing demand for information and the ensuing need for anonymity, security, privacy, and the protection of other civil liberties have particularly contributed to the heightened public awareness by the news media of the potential abuse of digital communications, most notably the Internet.[3]

In the face of current deployment programs that principally use smart surveillance technology and cyberspace, legal safeguards to ensure individual privacy are not capable of creating ironclad systems free of error. Moreover, because technology has evolved so quickly, the risk to personal privacy protections has significantly increased. This and similar trends only serve to further undermine such basic rights, especially when the

---

[1] Charles R. Beitz, *The Idea of Human Rights* (New York: Oxford University Press, 2009), p. 1.

[2] Report of the Office of the United Nations High Commissioner for Human Rights, "The Right to Privacy in the Digital Age" (June 30, 2014), available at www.ohchr.org/en/hrbodies/hrc/regularsessions/session27/documents/a.hrc.27.37_en.pdf. Accessed on September 30, 2014.

[3] Joseph Migga Kizza, *Ethical and Social Issues in the Information Age*, 5th edn. (London: Springer, 2013), p. 78.

quest to minimize criminality and terrorism becomes the normative goal in domestic and international politics.[4]

At the same time, the emancipatory power of the Internet and other modes of digital communication has drawn attention for its unprecedented potential for social change. The expansion of global communication technologies has opened the possibility for collective mobilization and communication for change both within and across sovereign states.[5] Arguably, a *smart* use of technology can help expand and guarantee human rights, especially freedom of expression or the right to culture and access to knowledge on the Internet in those places where they are repressed.[6] Access to the Internet is generally understood to mean access not only to the medium (technology) but also to the content (the right to speak).[7] Equally important is the extent to which citizens can participate in shaping the governance of new technologies from a human rights perspective.[8] Emancipative values emerge, insists Christian Welzel, in response to the growing popular control of action resources – namely, their material means, intellectual skills, and connective opportunities.[9] "It is safe to conclude," Welzel observes, "that technological advancement is a formidable indicator of the combination of all three types of action resources."[10]

More than just a communication medium, the Internet fosters the spread of liberty and the exchange of ideas, both of which go hand-in-hand with democracy.[11] The power of the Internet lies in its ability to "feed a process that prepares people for an open and civil society."[12] Unlike more traditional media, however, the Internet does the job in real time with interactivity and concurrently in text, images, audio,

---

[4] Mathias Klang, "Privacy, Surveillance and Identity," in Mathias Klang and Andrew Murray, eds., *Human Rights in the Digital Age* (London: The Glasshouse Press, 2005), pp. 175–89; see esp. pp. 188–89.

[5] Karin G. Wilkins, "Mobilizing Global Communication: For What and For Whom?," in Karin G. Wilkins, Joseph D. Straubhaar, and Shanti Kumar, eds., *Global Communication: New Agendas in Communication* (New York: Routledge, 2014), pp. 100–18; see p. 101.

[6] Giovanni Ziccardi, *Resistance, Liberation Technology, and Human Rights in the Digital Age* (Dordrecht and New York: Springer, 2013), p. 126.

[7] Ibid., p. 129.   [8] Ibid., p. 126.

[9] Christian Welzel, *Freedom Rising: Human Empowerment and the Quest for Emancipation* (New York: Cambridge University Press, 2013), p. 113.

[10] Ibid., p. 120.

[11] Gary W. Selnow, "The Information Age Is Fostering the Spread of Freedom and Democracy," in James D. Torr, ed., *The Information Age* (Farmington Hills, MI: Greenhaven Press, 2003), pp. 31–34.

[12] Ibid., p. 32.

and video.[13] Not only has the digital revolution in the Middle East and North Africa (MENA) provided an impetus for nonviolent modes of public action, but perhaps more fundamentally, new technologies have in fact changed the concepts of democracy and citizenship held by a younger generation keen on pursuing a more civil, inclusive, and liberating form of democracy.[14]

By making information more accessible than ever before, digital technologies have come to shape societies and cultures in many respects. These technologies also offer tools for resistance and change that can be effectively deployed to influence existing power relations. People around the world have increasingly used digital media to present political reactions against authoritarian rule or to speak out against failed policies. In contrast to the all-too-familiar centralized, vertically integrated social movements, theories of new social movements (NSMs) argue for a new way of doing politics – namely, through "network politics." More importance is attached to social and cultural concerns in these movements, and the focus of politics shifts away from recruiting members toward establishing informal, loosely organized social networks of supporters.

Critics of NSMs have noted that change in the MENA region transpires through movements that typically lack an ideological framework, designated leadership, and the formal structure of protest organizations. Asef Bayat describes this phenomenon as social "nonmovement," involving street protests and political activism directed at the state. Bayat argues that the discontented subaltern groups – the poor, the youth, women, and the politically marginalized – have not been passive or obeying the diktats of their repressive states, nor have they been fatalistic in their beliefs and attitudes. Far from it, they have always been engaged, albeit in mostly scattered and diffused struggles. By engaging such social "nonmovement," they have been able to take advantage of movements to turn mishaps into the path of resistance and shift their mostly quiet and individual struggles into discernible and collective defiance.[15] Such movements, Bayat goes on to argue, expose the inapplicability of Western mainstream social movement theories to the MENA region.

---

[13] Ibid., p. 33.

[14] Linda Herrera and Rehab Sakr, "Introduction: Wired and Revolutionary in the Middle East and North Africa," in Linda Herrera with Rehab Sakr, eds., *Wired Citizenship: Youth Learning and Activism in the Middle East* (New York: Routledge, 2014), pp. 16–26; see esp. p. 20.

[15] Asef Bayat, *Life as Politics: How Ordinary People Change the Middle East*, 2nd edn. (Palo Alto, CA: Stanford University Press, 2013); see pp. x–xi.

Today's social movements, such as feminism, the environment, and human rights, are organized around flexible, dispersed, and horizontal networks.[16] By promoting horizontal links and providing a method for communication across space in real time, new technologies have bolstered decentralized network constellations, facilitating informal or underground transnational coordination and communication.[17] This network politics involves the creation of inclusive spaces where diverse movements converge around common goals while still maintaining their autonomy.[18]

These technologies have allowed communities, groups, and individuals "to unite around shared grievances and nurture transportable strategies for mobilizing against dictators."[19] The information and communication technologies (ICTs) of our modern online age bring new perspectives on how to target structures of power at both national and transnational levels. The adoption of new methods and strategies to affect power relations has added fresh urgency to our need to understand how societies are responding to the more permeable forms of information flows. At the same time, Internet penetration of societies and the spread of social media offer a new platform for discussion of government policies and performance and spur intense debate about domestic revolts and related violence.

Experts of contemporary networked society, such as Manuel Castells, have demonstrated the speed at which more empowering opportunities emerge and grow exponentially. Castells argues that the development of autonomous networks of horizontal communications, free from the control of those holding institutional power, has led to new forms of social change and political democracy.[20] "The autonomy of communication," Castells posits, "is the essence of social movements because it is what allows the movements to relate to society at large beyond the control of the power holders over communication power."[21]

---

[16] Jackie Smith et al., *Global Democracy and the World Social Forums* (Boulder, CO: Paradigm Publishers, 2008), pp. 28–29.

[17] Ibid., p. 29.   [18] Ibid., p. 29.

[19] Philip N. Howard and Muzammil M. Hussain, "The Role of Digital Media," in Larry Diamond and Marc F. Plattner, eds., *Democratization and Authoritarianism in the Arab World* (Baltimore, MD: Johns Hopkins University Press, 2014), pp. 186–99.

[20] Manuel Castells, *Networks of Outrage and Hope: Social Movements in the Internet Age* (Cambridge, UK: Polity Press, 2012), p. 9.

[21] Ibid., p. 11.

Our conceptual framework is grounded in human empowerment theory. This theory is based on three interrelated propositions: (1) that technology has rendered the costs of an unmitigated state restriction on modern means of communication economically and politically exorbitant and, even more importantly, technically impractical; (2) that human empowerment relates to norms, values, and beliefs held by individual members of a society; and (3) that those individuals' access to modern communications technology is all too likely to affect the allocation of power in that society.

This volume's central argument is that the potential for civil disobedience and protest embedded in contentious politics has been facilitated by various modes of interactive technology, challenging the claims of many states to absolute sovereignty and making global nonintervention a less clear-cut stance for the international community. There is broad consensus among social scientists that the power of human rights more generally – and that of national human rights institutions in particular – is often better measured through the politics of contention than by the state's compliance with evolving standards.[22]

A state's official adoption of international legal and human rights covenants and instruments may not necessarily change state practice. It is through protesting against state violations of human rights norms that social forces can fundamentally alter state actions. The activities of autonomous, mobilized, and digitally interconnected social actors – through individual or collective means – are likely to weaken the control of those holding institutional power. How and under what conditions such empowering tools can be successfully utilized remains open to debate. The critical matter is that the emancipatory theory of power and social change in the digital age is bound up with internal and external systems of support and incentives.

This book is thus motivated by the broader theme of exploring networked social movements and the ways in which the growing digital diffusion of images and ideas helps shape the political and social landscape at the local, national, regional, and global levels. This is also an inquiry into seeking ways to build democratic and just societies around the world by promoting dignified living conditions for all. The context is varied – from the Occupy Wall Street movement to the Arab uprisings to

---

[22] This point is well illustrated by Sonia Cardenas, *Chains of Justice: The Global Rise of State Institutions for Human Rights* (Philadelphia: University of Pennsylvania Press, 2014), pp. 356–58.

other social movements across the world – as is the nature of such movements: sometimes spontaneous, sometimes premeditated. In general, however, we are interested not so much in the evolution of these movements as in their dynamics and the ways in which they may precipitate social change – technologically and from a normative standpoint.

Emancipatory potential of the digital age

The Internet has become a key enabler of human rights activities, allowing individuals, no matter where they reside, to receive information and redirect it to others. By confronting repressive regimes that persistently restrict such freedom of information, Internet users have a significant newfound tool at their disposal. Several studies have shown that the Internet has become a key to improving civic engagement and social connectedness. Studies have also illustrated that political blogs have upended the prevailing notions of participation and that blogging has revolutionized civic engagement in a networked society.[23] But as the information explosion becomes a defining paradigm of our time, it is important to acknowledge that the emergence of a digital world is no guarantee that its dark side will be minimized and that its benefits will trickle down to humanity at large.

The Internet has become a natural and dynamic platform and meeting point for mobilization and discussion.[24] Technology has empowered the demand for a more accountable governance, especially in the twenty-first century when we may see a real blossoming of more sophisticated and organized nonviolent social movements.[25] Digital technology has come to mean having a video camera anywhere – a tool of empowerment and agency that has fundamentally altered the game. Consider, for example, how a group of black social-media activists built the first twenty-first century American civil rights movement. A systematic effort to quickly mobilize protests in several US cities where a police shooting had

---

[23] Antoinette Pole, *Blogging the Political: Politics and Participation in a Networked Society* (New York: Routledge, 2010), p. 4.

[24] Gary R. Bunt, "Mediterranean Islamic Expression: Web 2.0," in Cesare Merlini and Olivier Roy, eds., *Arab Society in Revolt: The West's Mediterranean Challenge* (Washington, DC: Brookings Institution Press, 2012), pp. 76–95; see p. 87.

[25] Kenneth E. Boulding, "Nonviolence and Power in the Twentieth Century," in Stephen Zunes, Lester R. Kurtz, and Sarah Beth Asher, eds., *Nonviolent Social Movements: A Geographical Perspective* (Oxford, UK: Blackwell, 1999), pp. 9–17; see p. 17.

occurred showed how online activism – supported by the broad networks that allowed for the easy distribution of documentary photos and video – became not just the site of uprising but the conduit for the spread of ideas.[26] From Ferguson to Staten Island to Baltimore, the so-called Black Lives Matter movement demonstrated how the speed with which such movements now act as well as the large number of people they can draw to every protest has "turned every police killing into a national referendum on the value of black lives in America."[27]

Throughout the world, the Internet and social media have enabled the youth movement to collectively voice their frustration with the state and its repressive apparatus. Without romanticizing or fusing the many-sided culture of youth in this wired revolutionary generation, as Linda Herrera and Rehab Sakr posit, it can be argued that "growing numbers of youth in the MENA [region] are pursuing a more civil, inclusive, and liberatory form of democracy."[28] Similarly, the resurgence of the political Green Movement in Iran following the disputed 2009 presidential elections gave voice and membership to previously excluded students, women, and exiles.[29] The movement's nonviolent orientation marked a clear historical break from the violent past and gained from the universal appeal of many great emancipatory events such as the anticolonial movement in India, the African American struggle for civil rights, and the antiapartheid struggle in South Africa.[30] Despite its delayed – and apparently ineffectual – impact in the face of the regime's widespread physical repression, the ensuing internal power struggle between reformists and conservatives adversely affected the Iranian political landscape by undermining the government's proclaimed exclusive legitimacy and religious mandate.[31]

Likewise, prodemocracy, student-led protests that have gripped Hong Kong, which since its return to Chinese rule in 1997 has been stable and

---

[26] Joy Caspian Kang, "The Witnesses," *The New York Times Magazine* (May 10, 2015), pp. 34–39 and 52–53.

[27] Ibid., pp. 52–53.

[28] Herrera and Sakr, "Introduction: Wired and Revolutionary," pp. 1–16; see p. 4.

[29] Alison Brysk, *Speaking Rights to Power: Constructing Political Will* (New York: Oxford University Press, 2013), p. 145.

[30] Nader Hashemi, "Strategies of Hope: Edward Said, the Green Movement and the Struggle for Democracy in Iran," in Nader Hashemi and Danny Postel, eds., *The People Reloaded: The Green Movement and the Struggle for Iran's Future* (New York: Melville House, 2010), pp. 397–407; see esp. p. 406.

[31] Brysk, *Speaking Rights to Power*, p. 145.

calm, have attracted an unknown number of mainland participants and pose one of the biggest challenges in years to Communist Party rule.[32] These protests, which have been directed at Chinese-imposed limits on voting rights, have prompted a heightened resistance to mainland China and have essentially become a battle over the text (Basic Law) that focuses on Beijing's failure to fulfill its commitments. Thus, unlike struggles in Egypt and Ukraine, for example, these protests have not been a struggle to overthrow the regime. Instead, they have been a struggle demanding compliance.

Similarly, blogs have become key tools for dissident activity in states that control the mainstream media. While the Internet may not be widely accessible across socioeconomic classes, it has created a new ecology of participation in a world of collective action without traditional formal organization. The unfolding, open-ended uprisings in the MENA region have caused the collapse of regimes in Egypt, Tunisia, and Libya, and may do so in other countries of the region in the not-too-distant future. While traditional party politics and power relations within the region failed to produce any democratic change, a combination of youth and technology facilitated a revolutionary change unprecedented in the region's history.

To be sure, the old US bargain with local Arab autocrats has unraveled, making it more difficult for the United States and the broader West to work with authoritarian, yet pro-West, regimes. Instead of focusing on the "high politics," that is, the national and international security concerns, some analysts have noted that we should consistently observe "micropolitics" of social struggles and contentious politics, including prosaic strategies of resistance and "low key politics," as well as the invisible movements and "nonmovements" that influenced protesters' strategies as they poured into Tahrir Square.[33] To gain a better understanding of the ramifications of these democratic changes, it is also important to contextualize the mobilizing impacts of the information technology explosion.

Underlying the current political "clash of ideas" is a competition between different knowledge structures and worldviews (paradigms)

---

[32] Neil Gough and Austin Ramzy, "Mainland Chinese in Hong Kong See Protests as Inconvenience and Inspiration," *The New York Times* (October 2, 2014), p. A12.

[33] Fawaz A. Gerges, "Introduction: A Rupture," in Fawaz A. Gerges, ed., *The New Middle East: Protest and Revolution in the Arab World* (New York: Cambridge University Press, 2014), pp. 1–38; see esp. p. 23.

among many actors on the global scene. This contest over worldviews has intensified with the drift to the post–Washington Consensus.[34] Rather than a single alternative to neoliberal views, there is a wide array of opposing views and philosophies. For the indigenous, or the "localized," knowledge is a viable alternative. The struggle over worldviews and knowledge can no longer be separated from technological resources. Worldviews, knowledge, and technology have become interwoven. Yet the fact remains that political freedom has to be accompanied by a civil society that is literate and densely connected if it is to be protected and sustained in the long term.

Limits of modern technology

As previously shown, different communication technologies and software applications can help spark and accelerate protests, uprisings, and social movements by empowering citizens to stand up to despotism. Similarly, as many observers have pointed out, the Internet's disruptive impact, as a source for both tremendous good and potentially worrisome problems, has only just begun, and citizens throughout the world will have more power than at any time in history.[35] As a result, authoritarian governments will find their digitally connected population more difficult to control, repress, and even influence, while democratic states will be compelled to include many more voices – including individuals, organizations, and companies – in their affairs.[36]

Yet virtually all experts simultaneously point to the potential and limits of this so-called liberation technology, warning against troubling implications stemming from the exploitation of such technologies by authoritarian and repressive regimes.[37] The impact of the new technologies and social media platforms on abusive governments remains

---

[34] Robert O'Brien and Marc Williams, *Global Political Economy: Evolution and Dynamics*, 4th edn. (New York: Palgrave Macmillan, 2013), p. 276.

[35] Erich Schmidt and Jared Cohen, *The New Digital Age: Reshaping the Future of People, Nations, and Business* (New York: Alfred A. Knopf, 2013), pp. 3–11; Klang and Murray, *Human Rights in the Digital Age*; and also see Giovanni Ziccardi, *Resistance, Liberation Technology, and Human Rights in the Digital Age* (Dordrecht and New York: Springer, 2013).

[36] Schmidt and Cohen, *The New Digital Age*, p. 7.

[37] For an illuminating account of the most dramatic recent instances of global mobilization and protests facilitated by the digital revolution, as well as coercive reactions to these protests, see Larry Diamond, "Liberation Technology," *Journal of Democracy*, 21, 3 (July 2010), pp. 69–83; see esp. pp. 78–80.

uncertain.[38] Under such circumstances, we should distinguish between social media–inspired empowerment as a current state of affairs and as an ideal. While the current state of affairs may be progressive and forward looking insofar as the power of new media is concerned, and while some changes have transpired as a result, we cannot avoid the reality of powerful institutions and organizations that have a longstanding history of survival and perseverance. Although Internet access is sharply increasing, governments and transnational corporations are becoming more and more capable at using the Web to undermine people resisting injustice and calling for change, as Symon Hill contends.[39]

At a time when most societies encounter rapid technological change and persistent instability across social structures, the notion of promoting social media as an instrument of progressive sociopolitical change should be cautiously approached. Some scholars such as Robert D. Putnam have made the case that technology may lead people to stay at home rather than join established organizations. Modern technology, asserts Putnam, comes at the expense of social connectedness and civic engagement.[40] As a result, civic life, which represents collective and social space to protect the individual and community from the intrusive powers of the state and the market, has increasingly grown weaker. The decline in associational life on the one hand and the heavy reliance on technology-at-home on the other has proven to be mutually reinforcing.[41]

Technology may, in some ways, be undermining the influence of some organizations while making it easier to organize demonstrations. It is strikingly clear now that liberal-secular students and groups in Egypt, for instance, learned this lesson the hard way as they lost elections to the more organized Muslim Brotherhood in the aftermath of the 2011 uprisings. Ultimately, however, whether social media will prove to be influential will depend on the leaders' long-term commitments to political change. At this point, experts argue, it appears that social media will continue to play a mostly transitory role – that is, they will help to galvanize protesters to rise up against their governments while failing

---

[38] Eric B. Shiraev and Vladislave M. Zubok, *International Relations* (New York: Oxford University Press, 2014), p. 412.

[39] Symon Hill, *Digital Revolutions: Activism in the Internet Age* (Oxford, UK: New International Publications Ltd., 2013), pp. 118–19.

[40] Robert D. Putnam, *Bowling Alone: The Collapse and Revival of American Community* (New York: Simon & Schuster, 2000).

[41] Ibid.

to give rise to the vibrant political leadership necessary to sustain and promote these revolutionary tools and upheavals.[42]

Critics also argue that, in some cases, technology has failed to fundamentally alter certain factors on the ground, such as the power drive and hard resources at the disposal of autocrats. The Saudi state, the Syrian regime, the Chinese Party, and the Putin administration in Russia have all used numerous tactics to blunt the sharp edge of technology, suppressing the flow of information and fending off opposition, popular unrest, or calls for political reform.[43] Technology may change certain aspects of how the game is played, but the autocratic drive for power remains a difficult problem to tackle – as is often the case with dictatorial regimes around the world. In a larger sense, we see the old tension between liberal and illiberal forces, with both camps utilizing modern communications simultaneously.

In general, three types of limits can be acknowledged: (1) timing, (2) context, and (3) strategy. In terms of timing, it should be noted that throughout the protests, social media play a key role, especially at the earlier stages of instigation and mobilization. Social media, for example, played a crucial role in forcing Ukraine's beleaguered President Viktor Yanukovych to flee the country and Egypt's Hosni Mubarak to step down. In the post-upheaval period, in the face of fractured politics, the issue of organizations and institutions tends to return to the forefront. In Egypt, the Muslim Brotherhood under the guise of the Freedom and Justice Party was able to elevate its candidate, Mohammad Morsi, to the country's first popularly elected president. They did it in large part with their organizational prowess and reach.

Tempting as it is to treat the Arab Spring as a single progressive social change, there are broad variations within the Arab countries' historical and modern contexts. Uprisings in Tunisia, Egypt, and Libya took different directions due in large part to their different historical and modern contexts: The military acted professionally in Tunisia; in Egypt, the army was so embroiled in politics and the economy that it could not extricate itself from revolutionary changes; in Libya, by contrast, the military lacked

---

[42] Steven C. Roach, "Critical Theory," in Tim Dunne, Milja Kurki, and Steve Smith, eds., *International Relations Theories: Discipline and Diversity* (New York: Oxford University Press, 2013), pp. 171–86; see esp. p. 181.

[43] For an interesting account of the state strategies to blunt protest and opposition in Saudi Arabia, see Gwenn Okruhlik, "Saudi Arabia," in Michelle Penner Angrist, ed., *Politics and Society in the Contemporary Middle East*, 2nd edn. (Boulder, CO: Lynne Rienner Publishers, 2013), pp. 417–43; see esp. pp. 436–39.

an established and centralized army, which made the removal of the regime possible and speedy. Having crushed the 2009 Green Movement, a year and half later the Islamic Republic of Iran found itself in the ironic position of heaping praise on all but one country (Syria) entangled in the 2011 Arab uprisings.

Equally important in the postrevolt era are cultural and political contexts in which traditional actions (such as those via labor unions, peasant associations, and non-governmental organizations (NGOs) become far more important than digital actions. In hybrid cases, where online and offline activities are blended, the situation can be even more dynamic. Traditional actions are more sustainable and can last longer through time in some societies. In some parts of Latin America, they have transformed collective action into social movements, demonstrating that institutions and politics are often beyond the reach or influence of social media. One key question that persists is: Why are traditional organizations at times still more impactful despite the penetration of social media in a society?

From a strategic standpoint, there is widespread agreement that social media cannot create social change and revolution by itself. One media critic rightly argues that social media cannot effectively provide what social change has always required – that is, strategy, activism, and personal connection.[44] Technology as such is not a remedy; it is a tool. Another critic has noted that the use of digital technology to support a humanitarian cause or protest injustice has led to "slacktivism" – a form of social media activism that is low cost, as low as clicking the mouse button or sending a text.[45] Further, such activism is unlikely to lead to sustainable ethical commitment and individual accountability.[46] Still another social media activist writes that "history is made on the street, not on the Internet."[47]

These reservations are most aptly captured by one prominent historian who has asserted that just as young people "could mount marches and sit-ins in the physical world, so they could create internet traffic and use

[44] Malcolm Gladwell, "Small Change: Why the Revolution Will Not Be Tweeted," *The New Yorker* (October 4, 2010), available at www.newyorker.com/magazine/2010/10/04/small-change-3. Accessed on August 15, 2014.

[45] Stephen Hopgood, *The Endtimes of Human Rights* (Ithaca, NY: Cornell University Press, 2013), p. 106.

[46] Ibid., p. 107.

[47] Wael Ghonim, *Revolution 2.0: The Power of People Is Greater Than the People in Power: A Memoir* (Boston, MA: Houghton Mifflin Harcourt, 2012), p. 190.

their websites for protests and strikes."[48] Critical though as virtual space was for contentious politics – a space for many vigorous discussions that could never have been held in meatspace – the Internet's relative accessibility to all and transparency had the disadvantage of rendering it vulnerable to the secret police.[49] Despite the fact that cyberspace provided an outlet and a key medium for youth social movements and dissidents to express their legitimate frustration and grievances against the government, the revolution's most triumphal moments transpired in the sphere of physical efforts – that is, where a whole range of NGOs, organizations, and associations operated.[50]

Contextualizing a different but related concern, Ian Bremmer points out that the Internet promotes calls for democracy where there is already a demand for basic freedoms and democracy.[51] If modern technologies have helped citizens to pressure authoritarian governments in several countries, it is not because these tools have created a demand for change. That demand must come from public resentment toward authoritarian regimes itself.[52] Innovations in modern communication, as Bremmer reminds us, may help undermine authoritarian power over time. But for the time being, their impact on global politics is not so easy to predict.[53] As tools, social media and the information and communication technologies have been most effective in those countries where there is already a modicum of freedom and independence.[54]

The danger of technological determinism is in giving the tools more credit than the activists. It is important to bear in mind, as most experts in the field suggest, that revolutions have been occurring prior to the Internet. People protested and brought down governments before Facebook was invented. They did it before the Internet came along. Along these lines, critics point out that there is no such thing as "virtual revolt." The metaphor of a digital revolt tends to confuse the medium with the

---

[48] Juan Cole, *The New Arabs: How the Millennial Generation Is Changing the Middle East* (New York: Simon & Schuster, 2014), p. 48.

[49] Ibid., p. 62.   [50] Ibid., pp. 63 and 83.

[51] Ian Bremmer, "Democracy in Cyberspace: What Information Technology Can and Cannot Do," *Foreign Affairs* (November/December 2010), available at www.foreignaffairs.com/articles/66803/ian-bremmer/democracy-in-cyberspace. Accessed on September 2, 2014.

[52] Ibid.   [53] Ibid.

[54] Michael S. Doran, "The Impact of New Media: The Revolution Will Be Tweeted," in Kenneth M. Pollack et al., *The Arab Awakening: America and the Transformation of the Middle East* (Washington, DC: Brookings Institution Press, 2011), pp. 39–46.

message.[55] During the January 25–27, 2011, demonstrations in Tahrir Square in Cairo, neighborhood-level interpersonal networks, largely fostered through cell phones and face-to-face conversations, proved far more effective than hierarchical organizations.[56]

On the pessimistic side, a critique of cyber-utopianism has shown us that the Internet is not always what we think and that it is not going to magically transform dictatorships into democracies. The Internet almost as often constricts or even prevents freedom.[57] Some experts, such as Charli Carpenter and Daniel W. Drezner, have argued that social media and the Internet are the greatest intervening variables.[58] They have lowered the transaction costs of collective action and organizing, as well as the cost of monitoring and control. They have equally dramatically increased contagion effects and information cascade.[59]

Structure of the book

In considering the politically emancipatory potential of these tools, several core questions arise: Are these tools inherently democratizing or contingent upon the intentions and attitudes of the agents using them? Under what conditions and how might the Internet foster these democratizing efforts? How do individuals use social media differently in diverse contexts? Have the Internet and social media enabled activists, NGOs, and other advocates of human rights to better mobilize their activities? And what are the promises and limitations of digital media in asserting human rights? To address these questions, this volume is organized into three parts. Part I, "Framing the digital impact: information society, activism, and human rights," deals with wide-ranging issues – including social movements, nonviolent resistance, the visual culture of activism and advocacy, and the youth movements in Egypt and Tunisia prior to and following the 2011 Arab uprisings – with an eye to explaining the possibilities and the limits of social change in the information age.

---

[55] Sheila Carapico, "Egypt's Civic Revolution Turns 'Democracy Promotion' on Its Head," in Bahgat Korany and Rabab El-Mahdi, eds., *Arab Spring in Egypt: Revolution and Beyond* (Cairo: The American University in Cairo Press, 2012), pp. 199–222; see p. 212.

[56] Ibid., p. 213.   [57] Evgeny Morozov, *The Net Delusion* (New York: Public Affairs, 2011).

[58] Charli Carpenter and Daniel W. Drezner, "International Relations 2.0: The Implications of New Media for an Old Profession," *International Studies Perspectives*, 11, 3 (August 2010), pp. 255–72.

[59] Ibid.

The authors in this section make clear that "network politics" are particularly well suited for the human rights movement because of their ability to spread ideas rapidly across borders and also due to their contribution to the idea of a "cascade of rights" leading to a progressive realization of human rights. Capturing the effectiveness and essence of visual culture also has become crucial to protecting human rights. This is particularly the case, as the chapters on social movements in the digital age and visual culture in aid, advocacy, and activism in this volume demonstrate, for the dynamic power of informational politics is not confined to mere words or slogans; pictures can convey powerful and meaningful messages as well. A combination of nonviolent protests, online communication and activism, and the organizational skill of the youth movement in Egypt and Tunisia in 2011 resulted in an unprecedented cascade of falling regimes across the MENA region. Although these uprisings in most cases have failed to prevail over well-entrenched institutions and foreign policy meddling by powerful outside actors, they have left a lasting impact on the region's political landscape.

Part II, "Digital dissidence and grassroots politics," provides a systematic analysis of online struggles for rights in the cases of Palestine and Ukraine. Also in this part, special attention is given to the issue of human rights and ICTs in Latin America. In the case of Palestine, as the contributors to this chapter make clear, social media and ICTs have been utilized to support sanctions against the Israeli policy of occupation, yet sanctions have proven limited in their application, even when they are grassroots sanctions. The chapter on the Ukraine crisis shows that the overthrow of an existing regime might create a power vacuum where uncertainty, along with prior grievances, may very well fuel regional tensions.

The chapter on Latin America shows that social media have drawn considerable attention to human rights abuses but nevertheless have failed to counter them. Throughout the world, new technologies have been effective when they have taken the state by surprise, but on balance, the state has figured out ways to mitigate their effects. This is especially the case in Latin America where a deep digital divide has characterized the boundaries of access and corporatist states have carefully and methodically co-opted leaders of dissident movements. In all these case studies, our authors demonstrate the promise and limitations of digital media in asserting human rights. The fact remains that social media can call attention to abuses but cannot single-handedly prevent them. To be sure, for activists, success in using social media and ICTs has yet to fully translate into dramatic, longstanding change in the real world.

Part III, "Network politics and social change," demonstrates the crucial role that new media and technologies play in revealing public dissidence. In the case of Iran, social and political networking has proven ineffective, particularly in determining outcomes, as secret police have often employed social media to track and arrest dissidents. In the case of Turkey, digital media has been successfully utilized to influence – though not dictate – state policies. The authors in this part describe the growing use of digital media in generating social change and deepening the viable level of engagement in populist electoral politics. This trend has resulted in enforcing the rule of law in the evolving political contexts of India and could potentially bring about change in Hong Kong. In both cases, as the contributors to this part have revealed, the free exchange of ideas in an informed society, facilitated by the Internet and social media, has led to the creation of a citizenry who can no longer be kept in the dark about the real or potential pledges that governments make.

The book's concluding chapter expounds on the ways in which new technologies have led to new opportunities and demands, weakening some despotic systems while strengthening others. While it is true that social media and ICTs, used by activists, assisted in mobilizing the 2011 uprisings in the MENA region, these digital tools also were used effectively by repressive regimes. The speed with which information is communicated exceeds the state's capacity to adjust, hence compelling the government to constantly adapt to new changes in order to gain technological prowess. This process is likely to lead to a struggle for the control of the public sphere, frequently pitting the society against the state. The issue of how to alleviate the tension between freedom of information and government regulation remains open to debate. These squabbles aside, exploring the ways in which social media can potentially strengthen collective action continues to be of obvious importance and worth further scrutiny. In the end, it is difficult to escape the conclusion that digital technology can indeed become one of the most liberating tools of our time only if state policies, as well as the international community, allow that to happen.

Method of analysis and conceptual framework

This volume focuses on such issues as interactivity, agency, structure, and social networking; it is also organized around several thematic issues, including the global justice movement, network politics and freedom of information, individual empowerment, and gender inequality. It blends theoretical research with normative analysis. It features chapters analyzing the processes of change and human rights demands in the global network society. Our case studies (Egypt, Hong Kong, India, Iran, Tunisia, Turkey, Ukraine, and Latin America) demonstrate the impact of social movements, collective action, protests, and uprisings in a variety of different contexts, while challenging conventional theories of the persistence of authoritarianism in the some parts of the world, including the Arab world.

While individual chapters rely on each contributor's conceptual or theoretical framework, the book's overall approach incorporates a synthesis of theoretical perspectives, including realism, liberalism, constructive critical theory, and feminism. We organize our discussions and interpret our facts by looking at them through various theoretical lenses, while utilizing various practical and moral conceptions associated with such perspectives. The contributors also examine various strategies that rely on digital tools for social mobilization in order to gain political power in various political contexts. To that end, these chapters focus not only on how technology is used but also on what limits the use of technology entails. In what ways is technology changing the nature of resistance and protests or shaping the behavior of states? Given the limits to technology and its pervasive use for surveillance purposes by the governments, what consequences might that incur? Addressing these and other related questions requires a thorough examination of not only the benefits of the Internet and digital media but also the negative consequences of the cyberspace in terms of the deception, control of the flow of information, the violation of privacy laws, and surveillance.

Significantly, this volume demonstrates that living in a hyperconnected world is likely to change the relationship between the individual and the state in ways totally unlike in the past, posing new challenges and risks in terms of individual rights such as the right to privacy and freedom of information, most notably the right to Internet access. Creating and protecting the right to privacy, for example, is particularly difficult in light of new surveillance technologies. There cannot be unlimited or absolute privacy given the necessity of balancing the right of the individual to privacy with the needs of the state.[60] While the quest to minimize criminality and terrorism are worthy causes, there is a growing

---

[60] Mathias Klang, "Privacy, Surveillance and Identity," in Klang and Murray, *Human Rights in the Digital Age*, pp. 175–89; see esp. p. 186.

consensus that they should not become ultimate goals in themselves, thereby overriding individuals' privacy.[61]

The significance of the project

The lackluster commitment to human rights norms and values resulting from the post-9/11 dramatic turn in US foreign policy away from personal security and toward a renewed emphasis on national security has had grave consequences for promoting human dignity globally. In many respects, fighting terrorism and protecting basic laws and liberties have not comfortably sat together. At the present stage of world history, one observer notes, it is not clear that law and legal conventions can prevent or even control torture.[62] This departure from conventional US foreign policy has rendered the revival of internationally recognized human rights contingent upon the reopening of the political space largely preempted by the war on terrorism.[63]

We submit that the digital age has facilitated the beginning of such a reopening. The Internet's defining feature, experts remind us, is its interoperability – that is, information can cross geographic and techno-logical boundaries.[64] New forms of social media have likely punctuated the strength and speed of the boomerang effect on news, and, most notably, the graphic display of state repression can now be transmitted broadly across the globe instantly.[65] Given the increased importance of digital media and ICTs, and the mind-boggling pace with which change is unfolding on the global scene, these issues deserve more critical scrutiny and examination. Increasingly, the new media, including the Internet, Facebook, Twitter, and interactive blogs, have had a constrain-ing impact on governmental authority and control. The worldwide spread of democratic values and norms has further intensified the

---

[61] Ibid., p. 189.

[62] David P. Forsythe, *The Politics of Prisoner Abuse: The United States and Enemy Prisoners after 9/11* (New York: Cambridge University Press, 2011), p. 230.

[63] Jack Donnelly, *International Human Rights*, 4th edn. (Boulder, CO: Westview Press, 2013), pp. 239–41.

[64] Neil Gerschenfeld and J. P. Vasseur, "As Objects Go Online: The Promise (and Pitfalls) of the Internet of Things," *Foreign Affairs*, 93, 2 (March/April 2014), 60–67; see esp. p. 67.

[65] Jeffry A. Frieden, David A. Lake, and Kenneth A. Schultz, *World Politics: Interests, Interactions, Institutions*, 2nd edn. (New York: W. W. Norton & Company, 2013), pp. 444–45.

struggle over who gets to define modernity, authenticity, legitimacy, and rationality.

International relations experts as well as laymen will find this volume helpful in gaining a better understanding of how a quiet revolution from below spreads throughout the world. This book will also appeal to scholars with interests in international and area studies. The study will be of particular interest to policymakers who have seen the dramatic changes ushered in during the digital age – a period of extraordinary change in the world, especially since the 2011 Arab uprisings. We live in a highly complex and evolving world that requires a fuller and deeper understanding of how modern technological tools, ideas, practices, and institutions interact and, better yet, how different societies adjust themselves to emerging realities of the digital age. We shall try in this book to convey such a new understanding in a timely, systematic, and coherent way.

Many others have addressed the issues of technological revolution and their impact on political stability and autocratic regimes. Although they have explained in depth the change in the aftermath of the unrests and uprisings throughout the world, they have rarely if ever mentioned the need for constructing new human rights norms and standards. Today, we face a startling paucity of knowledge – in the form of comparative analysis and case studies – that can help identify and mitigate threats to human rights in the digital realm. There have been only a handful of studies that have pointedly demonstrated and captured the complexity of processes of social change in the face of rapid technological deployment. The chapters in this volume intend to provide a balanced conceptual framework to demonstrate not only the power of autonomous communication networks but also their limits and the increasing setbacks they encounter in different contexts. There are still many unanswered questions about the new tools and forms of social change and the process of democratization in a globally interconnected world. Our hope is to answer some of these questions with this volume.

PART I

Framing the digital impact

Information society, activism, and human rights

2

Social movements in the digital age

JACK J. BARRY

Introduction

In the fall of 2010, conspicuously on the eve of the unpredicted Arab Spring protests, Malcolm Gladwell published a piece in *The New Yorker* titled "Small Change: Why the Revolution Will Not Be Tweeted,"[1] which sparked a now-infamous debate between Gladwell and Clay Shirky about the role of new digital technologies on political action. Neither Shirky nor Gladwell could have foreseen the political upheaval that was about to engulf the Middle East, but their disagreement began yet another round of debate about the *extent* that new digital technologies influence political action, participation, human rights, and social movements.

A prelude to their debate began in 2009 when reports surfaced of the momentous role Twitter was playing in the Green Movement in Iran by helping to ignite, and mobilize, a larger than anticipated movement against the ruling government. However, Gladwell did not agree with the media's take on the impact of Twitter, and the Internet more broadly, in fueling and sustaining the nascent Green Movement. In his article in *The New Yorker*, Gladwell discounted so-called weak ties formed on the Internet, particularly social media, instead positing that effective social movements in the past exhibited "strong ties" at their heart. His article prominently featured the example of a tightly knit group of four friends from North Carolina Agricultural and Technical State University, all freshmen at the black college, in 1960 wanting to be served at the lunch counter at the Woolworth department store in downtown Greensboro, at risk to life and limb, to protest the segregation of blacks in the South.

For Gladwell, this story illustrates that without strong ties, personal sacrifice, and eventual organizational structures, there will not be much

---

[1] Malcolm Gladwell, "Small Change: Why the Revolution Will Not Be Tweeted," *The New Yorker* (October 4, 2010), available at www.newyorker.com/magazine/2010/10/04/small-change-3.

salience to movements. He proceeds to argue that these characteristics are lacking in the "weak tie"–oriented, so-called clicktivism he saw as prevalent yet championed across social media. Gladwell states that "digital evangelists," his term for scholars and activists aligned with Shirky's perspective, proclaim rather impetuously: "The new tools of social media have reinvented social activism. With Facebook and Twitter and the like, the traditional relationship between political authority and popular will has been upended, making it easier for the powerless to collaborate, coordinate, and give voice to their concerns." Yet Gladwell does not agree with this perspective, instead purporting, "These are strong, and puzzling, claims . . . Are people who log on to their Facebook page really the best hope for us all?"[2] However, as was soon to be on full digital display for all to see, Gladwell may have been the one making the more "puzzling" claims in the end.

Clay Shirky, specifically called out by Gladwell for writing *Here Comes Everybody*, which Gladwell described as the "bible of the social-media movement," responded to Gladwell's critique convincingly by claiming that new technologies are critical "tools" for political participation in the digital age for both armchair activists and true believers alike; yet also perhaps most important in refuting Gladwell, they are vital tools for organizations as well. Their exchange, which took place in a back and forth in *Foreign Affairs* and *The New Yorker*,[3] ignited strenuous debate, ironically across the Internet and Twitter, that lasted through the subsequent large-scale protest events that were concurrently unfolding such as the Arab Spring, Occupy Wall Street, and protests in Brazil.

To be sure, the response was devastating for Gladwell, as elucidated by Jen Schradie:

> Activists, new media pundits, and techno-enthusiasts of all stripes delved into this debate that eventually framed formal strong-tie organizations as passé and individualized weak tie digital networks as the new movement prototype. If you believe the blogs and the tweets, Gladwell was taken down in this tête-à-tête as an old school movement analyst. His name often brings derision at tech conferences: organizations = bad; digital networks = good.[4]

[2] Ibid.

[3] For Shirky's article in *Foreign Affairs*, responding to Gladwell's *New Yorker* one, see www.foreignaffairs.com/articles/67038/clay-shirky/the-political-power-of-social-media.

[4] Jen Schradie, "Bringing the Organization Back In: Social Media and Social Movements," *Berkeley Journal of Sociology* (2014), www.berkeleyjournal.org/2014/11/bringing-the-organization-back-in-social-media-and-social-movements/#note-539-2.

Despite the overwhelming support for Shirky's perspective among the so-called digerati as well as many social movement scholars, it is still worth keeping Gladwell's critique in mind as this chapter unfolds. Here I will explore the social movements literature, with a focus on the human rights movement, to elucidate what is new, what is not, and what might be overblown in an exploration of the complex, yet intriguing world of social movements in the networked twenty-first century. In doing so, my central argument will come shining through: On balance, despite the limitations of information and communication technologies (ICTs), the digital age remains bright for social movements, activists, and organizations as they employ the connective tools ICTs offer in new and always evolving ways. I will argue, through my primary example of the human rights movement, that the diffusion of new digital technologies to societies around the world has led to positive changes in the sociopolitical environment for the spread of human rights norms and standards, helping the movement gain momentum in various ways.

Social movements: a brief history

If casually reading *The New York Times* or steeped deep in esoteric academic journal articles on the topic, one would be struck by the many proclamations that new ICTs, especially mobile phones and the Internet, are proving to be extremely effective political mobilization tools. However, as the Shirky versus Gladwell debate displayed, there are widely differing views on the *extent* of their impact on social movement mobilization. Some scholars[5] proclaim they are unprecedented "game changing" tools; others[6] are less willing to crown ICTs king of political and social mobilization, or pro-poor economic development, instead purporting that they are

---

[5] See work by Joe Trippi, *The Revolution Will Not Be Televised: Democracy, the Internet and the Overthrow of Everything* (New York: Harper, 2005), p. 4; Thomas L. Friedman, *The World Is Flat* (New York: Farrar, Straus and Giroux, 2006); Esther Dyson, *Release 2.0: A Design for Living in the Digital Age* (New York: Broadway Books, 1997); Schradie, "Bringing the Organization Back In"; and of course the articles by Clay Shirky mentioned in the introduction.

[6] See Charles Kenny, *Overselling the Web?: Development and the Internet* (Boulder, CO: Lynne Reinner Publishing, 2006); N. H. Nie, "Sociability, Interpersonal Relations, and the Internet: Reconciling Conflicting Findings," *American Behavioral Scientist*, 45, 3 (2001), 420–35; N. H. Nie and L. Erbring, *Internet and Society: A Preliminary Report* (Stanford, CA: Stanford Institute for the Quantitative Study of Society, 2000), www.stanford.edu/group/siqss/Press_Release/press_release.html; and of course the articles by Malcolm Gladwell mentioned in the introduction.

only contributing factors, and in some cases a negative influence. Although it is safe to say there are *not many* scholars currently staking the claim that ICTs play a minuscule role in influencing political mobilization, communication, and movements in the modern world. On balance, I argue that it is hard to deny that ICTs are playing an important role; the debate should be more focused on the *extent* of their influence, instead of whether or not it exists at all in the modern world. To that end a primary goal of this chapter is to explore the findings of the literature about the *extent* that social movements are influenced by ICTs and to evaluate theories proposed by new social movements (NSMs), which today argue for new approaches to politics and contestation taking place through "network politics." Before proceeding any further, it is worth defining ICTs in broad terms as technologies that *enhance communication processes* over great distances specifically measured by Internet, mobile phone, computer, radio, and television penetration rates (per capita).

At first glance, it appears that ICTs, often steeped in dubious content, should not be mentioned in the same sentence as human rights or in the same arena as other grave political and economic issues. It is hard to imagine how online content, such as video games à la Angry Birds, or the commercialism of TV's "Vast Wasteland," at least in the words of former FCC chairman Newton Minow, should be promoted and championed by human rights or social movement scholars. Do people in areas of the world where grave abuses of human rights are commonplace really care about access to and the content on the Internet? The issues regarding their relevance notwithstanding, ICTs are undoubtedly in greater demand around the world today than ever before – people from all classes, political affinities, and nationalities want access to them, and just as in other areas of the information-gathering component of their lives, some of the content they consume will be politically relevant, yet most of it will not. Before we can attempt to evaluate the impact of this new digital age on social movements, we must begin with a brief history of the social movement literature, and the human rights movement will serve as a prime example throughout.

Also, skeptics and their critiques must be addressed – for instance, how could one tell if ICTs were actually *causing* anything new without investigating past scholarship? Do the rise of ICTs merely correlate with recent developments in the social movements field? Perhaps there is nothing *causal* about their impact at all? How can we evaluate their impact without a counter factual? In grappling with these questions, I will begin by outlining important definitions and concepts employed in the literature.

Conceptually, social movements arise out of some kind of group dissatisfaction with a sovereign political authority, almost always the state or government. For Charles Tilly and Sidney Tarrow, perhaps two of the most prominent scholars in the field, social movements can be defined as follows: "a sustained campaign of claim making, using repeated performances that advertise the claim, based on organizations, networks, traditions, and solidarities that sustain these activities."[7]

I find their popular definition a bit broad for my purposes in this chapter. Instead, I adhere more closely to a targeted conception offered by Cyrus Ernesto Zirakzadeh, who, in contrast to Tarrow and Tilly, defines social movements as having three primary characteristics: (1) "a social movement is a group of people who endeavor to build a radically new social order"; (2) movement participants are not elites – "they normally lack political clout, social prestige, and enormous wealth, and their interests are not routinely articulated or represented in the political system"; and (3) movement participants usually employ "confrontational and disruptive tactics" in a manner unlike those utilized by traditional political parties or interest groups.[8]

From these two definitions, we can distinguish social movements from other political phenomena, such as various kinds of protests, by imagining one or more underrepresented and non-elite groups challenging the state in a sustained and confrontational manner. Furthermore, social movements are not flash mobs, smart mobs, or other various types of quick political flashes in the pan; they usually need a longer time frame to achieve their objects. Social movements also cannot be easily put into a conceptual box post maturation either – sometimes they turn into interest groups or a persistent part of civil society, and sometimes they take a long time to mature, gnawing away at the edges of power, or they may even fade away when their objective is met or permanently failed.

In general, according to movement scholars such as Zirakzadeh and David Meyer, literature on social movements has gone through three generations, or distinctive "waves." Meyer identifies the first wave of the literature in the 1950s,[9] as sociologists and political scientists investigated

---

[7] Charles Tilly and Sidney Tarrow, *Contentious Politics* (Boulder, CO: Paradigm Publishers, 2007).

[8] Cyrus Ernesto Zirakzadeh, *Social Movements in Politics: A Comparative Study*, expanded edn. (New York: Palgrave Macmillan, 2006), pp. 4–5.

[9] David S. Meyer, "Protests and Political Opportunities," *Annual Review of Sociology*, 30 (2004), 126.

the political protests happening at the time and writing with fascism and its derivatives in mind.[10] They tended to see movements as dysfunctional, irrational, and inherently undesirable, and described those who joined them as disconnected from intermediate associations that would link them with more productive, and less disruptive, social pursuits.[11] In this older, more classical view of social movements, scholars tended to see movement emergence as the product of structural, often economic, historical processes, which manifest themselves in mass mobilizations of people who had previously repressed their frustrations.[12]

The second wave of social movements was shaped by the protests of the 1960s, which were blossoming across industrialized countries. As these countries had more of a variety of pluralist political systems, scholars were forced to examine movements with a less critical eye. This second wave rejects the historical and psychological foundations of the first wave; in its place is a vision sensitive to political, economic, and social inequality, and emphasizing participants' rationality and choice.[13]

During this second wave, NSM theory also came into prominent existence. Two changes in society help elucidate the assent of NSM in the 1960s: (1) The development of the postindustrial economy in rich countries was primarily responsible for the emerging NSMs; and (2) the new movements of the 1960s were significantly different from previous social movements of the industrial economy. These new movements were more issue focused and often dealt with social and cultural concerns such as environmental protection, anti–nuclear power, civil liberties, and human rights. Furthermore, NSM made the case for a new way of doing politics that will come to play a prominent role in the debate over the influence of ICTs: *network politics*. In creating effective grassroots networks the focus of politics shifts away from recruiting "members" toward establishing informal, loosely organized social networks of supporters. Further on, I will argue that this network politics approach has been greatly complemented and expanded by the new "tools" that digital ICTs bring to the table.

---

[10] See work by Seymour Martin Lipset, Eric Hoffer, Hannah Arendt, and William Korrnhouser.

[11] Meyer, "Protests and Political Opportunities."

[12] See Hannah Arendt, *The Origins of Totalitarianism* (New York: Schocken, 1951, 1968, 1972); Eric Fromme, *Escape from Freedom* (New York: Henry Holt and Company, Owl Books Edition, 1941).

[13] Zirakzadeh, *Social Movements in Politics*, p. 9.

At the individual level and fully complementing NSM during the second wave was the rise of empirically oriented ethnographic studies and interview-based analyses of the activists who undermined the premises of anomie and political disconnection extolled by first-wave scholarship. For instance, Kenneth Keniston found through interviews that leaders of activist student groups in the United States were psychologically better adjusted than their less active peers.[14] Fran Parkin's examination of the British Campaign for Nuclear Disarmament found that members of this activist organization were likely to be involved in many other social and political organizations.[15] This second-wave tradition (largely identified with the renowned social movement scholars Sidney Tarrow, Charles Tilly, and Doug McAdam) further noted that for those left outside of the pluralist political opportunity structure, protest was a "political resource" to be used to influence policy.[16] The vindication of protest strategies as politics by this literature shifted the research focus from *why* movements emerge to *how* they did so.[17]

The second wave is a primary forerunner to understanding how ICTs will influence movements in the digital age and thus requires in-depth elucidation. Zirakzadeh identifies three distinctive traditions of theorizing in the second wave of social movement literature: "resource mobilization theorizing," "indigenous community theorizing," and "political-process theorizing."[18] Although all three emphasize different aspects of the political process, they point to the significance of the political process, plus the economic and social inequalities behind social mobilization, and the practical yet also "wise" nature of movement participants. Some of the distinction was that the "resource-mobilization" approach highlighted the role of leadership in the movement, while "indigenous-community" explored how local-level social institutions, such as neighborhood clubs, unions, and local community churches, provided organizational structures, communication networks, tactical ideas, and leadership for later social movements. In turn, the "political-process" tradition held that constitutions, national-level policy-making process,

[14] Kenneth Keniston, *Young Radicals: Notes on Committed Youth* (New York: Harcourt, Brace & World, 1968).

[15] Fran Parkin, *Middle Class Radicalism* (New York: Praeger, 1968).

[16] See Michael Lipsky, *Protest in City Politics* (Chicago, IL: Rand-McNally, 1970). Also see J. D. McCarthy and M. N. Zald, "Resource Mobilization and Social Movements: A Partial Theory," *American Journal of Sociology*, 82 (1977), 1212–41.

[17] Meyer, "Protests and Political Opportunities," *Annual Review of Sociology* (30), 127.

[18] Zirakzadeh, *Social Movements in Politics*, p. 9.

institutional processes, and intra-elite struggles over power profoundly influence both decisions to join movements and the strategies and tactics that the movement employs.[19]

In general, during this phase, analysts looking at the processes of generating mobilization left out a lot of what is thought to comprise traditional politics, particularly the nature of the political context and activist grievances. Political opportunity theory[20] arose as a corrective to this in the second wave and was explicitly concerned with predicting variance in the periodicity, content, and outcomes of activist efforts over time across different institutional contexts (usually political institutions). The approach emphasized the interaction of activist efforts and more mainstream institutional politics.[21] Finally, the next section addresses another important determinant to help put into context our current digital age, which is the third "wave" in the social movement literature.

Zirakzadeh identifies the third wave of social movement inquiry as the "identity-formation" approach. In the identity-formation approach, Zirakzadeh notes two main subsets: scholars emphasizing popular culture[22] and the "autonomous movement-culture approach."[23] By the end of the 1970s historians, sociologists, political scientists, and anthropologists, drawing from different traditions of social theory, turned to the "cultural" dimension of social movements.[24] They argued that shared culture profoundly informs and shapes our political actions. Shared culture can be broadly defined as how people interpret social arrangements, how we see our places within those arrangements, and how we see our immediate opportunities, political power, and limitations. This focus shifts the

---

[19] Ibid.

[20] See Doug McAdam, Sidney Tarrow, and Charles Tilly, *Dynamics of Contention* (Cambridge, UK: Cambridge University Press, 2001); or Tilly and Tarrow, *Contentious Politics*.

[21] Meyer, "Protests and Political Opportunities," p. 127.

[22] Robin D. Kelly, *Race Rebels: Culture, Politics, and the Black Working Class* (New York: Free Press, 1994).

[23] Jan Kubik, *The Power of Symbols against the Symbol of Power: The Rise of Solidarity and the Fall of State Socialism in Poland* (University Park, PA: Pennsylvania State University Press, 1994).

[24] See Alberto Melucci, "Social Movements and the Democratization of Everyday Life," in J. Kean (ed.), *Civil Society and the State: New European Perspectives* (London: Verso, 1988), pp. 245–59; also, Alain Touraine, "An Introduction to the Study of Social Movements," *Social Research*, 52, 4 (1985), 749–87; Lawrence Goodwyn, *Breaking the Barrier: The Rise of Solidarity in Poland* (New York: Oxford University Press, 1991); and Ernesto Laclau, "New Social Movements and the Plurality of the Social," in D. Slater (ed.), *New Social Movements and the State in Latin America* (Amsterdam: CEDLA, 1985), pp. 27–42.

emphasis of the scholar more toward popular culture to analyze a social movement's activities, goals, and popular support. Under this approach, a social movement can hardly be portrayed as internally free of clashing ideas and corresponding fraction.

Now turning to social movements in the digital age (beginning around 1990) we see that NSM theory and the identity-formation approach both play an important role in theoretical understanding of modern movements, particularly the human rights movement. We can take from NSM that more specific social issues typically now lie at the heart of modern movements and that network politics is an appropriate explanation for the tools that ICTs offer. The identity formation approach exposes us to the importance of culture, and where individuals reside in it, as well as the importance of popular culture, clashing ideas in movements, and extent of political opportunities (or lack thereof) in shaping movements in the digital age. Lastly, the rise of the NSM and the identity formation approaches also corresponds to the accent of the human rights movement in the 1970s.

Enter ICTs: a new actor on the social movement scene

For twenty years, people have been calling this era of computers, the Internet, and telecommunications the "information age." But that's not what it is. What we're really in now is the empowerment age. If information is power, then this new technology – which is the first to evenly distribute information – is really distributing power.[25]

This quote from Howard Dean's 2004 Presidential campaign manager, Joe Trippi, who extensively utilized the Internet to help propel Dean to front-runner status in the race, illustrates an example of the view that through the Internet, with its publishing platform for all and ability to foster political empowerment, even mighty political power structures can be threatened by this new emergent actor. In fact, when reading about the Arab Spring, in both scholastic and journalistic publications, one could easily be struck by the notion that ICTs are a brand-new tool for political mobilization. However, they are not actually "new," as these tools were important in mobilization of protests in the cases of the Philippines in 2000, Ukraine's Orange Revolution in the winter of 2004 (and again in 2014), Moldova in 2009, and Iran's student protests of the Green

---

[25] Trippi, *The Revolution Will Not Be Televised*, p. 4.

Revolution in 2009. The use of ICTs in mobilizing massive protest movements appears as "new" only to the mainstream media and to rigorous academic analysis, as both have been surprisingly slow to analyze the mobilization capabilities of ICTs in the late 1990s and early 2000s. Noticeably absent is rigorous analysis of the transformative nature of mobile phones for mobilization in developing countries.

In the 1990s, there was excessive exuberance that ICTs, the Internet in particular, would radically change our political power structure. Joe Trippi is an example of a holdover of this view – also there were many enthusiastic reports that claimed that on their way to changing the power structure ICTs would also upend global poverty. However, by the early 2000s this exuberance waned because of the dot-com crash and the slow realization that development projects that employed the Internet were running into substantial difficulties across the developing world.[26] Also, the Internet did not seem to be threatening the entrenched political establishment in any meaningful way, as this was the case in both the developed and developing world. A manifestation of this failure was the initial lackluster response in developing countries to an English language–dominated Internet. In both governmental and foreign aid–sponsored technology rollouts in African countries such as Cameroon, Congo, Guinea, and Burundi, the Internet failed to transform poverty or anything else for that matter.[27] According to Charles Kenny, locals in these countries displayed little interest in a text-based Internet, which had little to offer them in their language (assuming that they were literate).[28]

However, beginning in the late 2000s and continuing today, enthusiasm began to shift back toward investigating the impact of ICTs on development and political empowerment. I argue this renewed vigor has been fueled by three dominant trends seen in the ever-evolving Internet: The first is the diffusion of technology, which is apparent in the explosions of penetration rates of the Internet in developing countries. According to Etal Solingen the "speed and reach of contemporary diffusion are unprecedented."[29] The concept of diffusion is a hot topic in international studies; and a lot of the attention generated is due to the rise of ICTs. Diffusion of ICTs also corresponds with the "democratization" or "flattening" in availability of these technologies.[30]

---

[26] Kenny, *Overselling the Web?*   [27] Ibid.   [28] Ibid.
[29] Etal Solingen, "Of Dominoes and Firewalls: The Domestic, Regional, and Global Politics of International Diffusion," *International Studies Quarterly*, 56 (2012), 631.
[30] Friedman, *The World Is Flat*.

In fact, the Internet and mobile phones have reached high penetration rates faster than any previous ICT technology.

The second dominant trend is the deepening of technology, seen in the spread of Web 2.0, defined as the increased technical and qualitative advances steadily progressing on the Internet since the early 2000s, and on mobile phones with Internet capability by the late 2000s. These Web 2.0 advances include video, audio, social networking, podcasting, and multimedia blogging. For Bertot, Jaeger, and Grimes, "Social media include but are not limited to blogs, wikis (e.g. Wikipedia), social networking sites (e.g. Facebook), micro-blogging services (e.g. Twitter), and multimedia sharing services (e.g. Flickr, YouTube). Social media are often associated with such concepts as user-generated content, crowd sourcing, and Web 2.0."[31] Put simply, much more multimedia is available on Web pages and increasingly available on the move via mobile devices. Social media has especially been getting a great deal of attention among Web 2.0 scholars for the power it has to connect people across geographic divides.

The third and final dominant trend purports that the Internet is a convergence technology, in that digital text, TV, radio, and various other audio technologies are now all being provided (at least in some form) on the dominant Internet data line. Furthermore, these capabilities are also increasingly available away from one's home via 3G and 4G cellular phone infrastructure on smartphones, on tablets, and across innovative operating systems such as Android, Linux, or Ubuntu that provide common functions on various types of devices. Some ICT scholars have dubbed the 2000s the "age of convergence."[32] In fact, among the few common threads in the communication literature is the predictions of "more convergence of information and communication technologies, blurring the lines between tasks and activities and between work and

---

[31] J. C. Bertot, P. T. Jaeger, and J. M. Grimes, "Using ICTs to Create a Culture of Transparency: E-Government and Social Media as Openness and Anti-Corruption Tools for Societies," *Government Information Quarterly*, 27 (2010), 266.

[32] Margherita Pagani, *Multimedia and Interactive Digital TV: Managing the Opportunities Created by Digital Convergence* (Hershey, PA: Idea Group, 2003); J. Pontin, "The Post-PC World: The New Era of Ubiquitous Computing," *Red Herring*, 61 (December 1998), 50–66; D. Shin, W. Kim, and D. Lee, "Convergence Technologies and the Layered Policy Model: Implication for Regulating Future Communications," paper presented at the annual meeting of the International Communication Association, Dresden International Congress Centre, Dresden, Germany Online (2006), http://citation.allacademic.com/meta/p91470_index.html; Henry Jenkins, *Convergence Culture* (New York: New York University Press, 2006).

play."[33] It appears that the Internet pipeline may be the only one that will matter in the near future. Thus, developing countries have an opportunity to invest in this potentially "leapfrog" technology, with early indications that it will – at a minimum – be a "convergence" technology. Despite widespread enthusiasm, its ability to be the *transformative* leapfrog technology that the developing world has been waiting for is far from certain.[34]

In fact, recent figures from Internet World Stats report that 39 percent of the world can now be considered Internet users and that there are rising rates of penetration in laggard developing regions such as Africa (21.3 percent), Asia (31.7 percent), and Latin America (49.3 percent). The United States is at 87 percent and the European Union is 76.5 percent, respectively.[35] Thus, there are substantial differences in penetration between rich and poor countries and also between rich and poor people within countries (i.e., the digital divide).

In reality, there is a much more complex relationship between social movements and Internet penetration rates that is not necessarily captured by national statistics on penetration. For example, I concur that any conceptualization of the digital divide – the disparity between people with access to ICTs and those without – as a binary distinction between the information "haves versus have-nots" is too simplistic and can be misleading. One of the most prominent scholars who initially made the anti-binary claim was Mark Warschauer, who posited that there are two problems with the conception of information as "haves and have-nots." The first is that it is too simple. Digital divide literature needs to consider complexities such as language, literacy, and physical and social resources in utilizing ICT effectively. The second is the digital divide's implication of a bipolar societal split (those with access and those without).[36]

Instead of falling into this rudimentary line of categorizing, other ICT scholars contend that there are gradations of access to ICT rather than a

---

[33] Christine Borgman, *From Gutenberg to the Global Information Infrastructure* (Cambridge, MA: MIT Press, 2000), p. 5.

[34] Also not to be forgotten is the surprisingly dynamic mobile phone, which is proving to be increasingly important in our daily lives and increasing in popularity around the world due to rapidly falling prices and their ability to provide relevant immediate information (e.g., market prices, political protests).

[35] Internet World Stats (2014), www.internetworldstats.com/stats7.htm. Accessed on May 1, 2014.

[36] Mark Warschauer, *Technology and Social Inclusion: Rethinking the Digital Divide* (Cambridge, MA: MIT Press, 2003).

binary split. I fully concur with the gradation scholars. Warschauer lucidly states: "The notion of the binary digital divide between haves and have-nots is thus inaccurate and can even be patronizing because it fails to value the social resources that diverse groups bring to the table."[37] On balance, one cannot equate penetration rates with social movement formation; the digital divide is too complex a phenomenon for that, and statistical analysis does not support a strong relationship. At this point, scholars cannot determine what penetration level would be considered a threshold level for social movement development. An illustration of the problem is the conundrum of why many richer countries in the Middle East, Asia, and Latin America have not developed strong social movements to counter their authoritarian regimes. Statistical answers to this question remain fleeting.

The impact of ICTs on social movements

Despite the lack of an easy statistical answer, there are strong relationships that can be teased out in analysis of the new digital age and social movements. The evidence supports Shirky: The Internet and mobile phones are helping social movements mobilize in various ways. Whether or not they are successful in achieving their goals is a different question, where the many political constraints facing movements across history would need to be taken into consideration (with variance across time and space). I argue in this section that social movements, as illustrated by the human rights movement, are influenced by ICTs in the following ways: (1) efficient sharing of information; (2) shrinking of distance; (3) enhancing the types of tactics employed by movements; (4) increasing social capital, civil society, and individual connections; and (5) organizing movements around flexible, dispersed, and horizontal networks. The human rights movement will be used to display how these factors are at work in the digital age.

Before making my argument a few caveats should be discussed. First and foremost, it should be mentioned that the focus in this chapter is not on what causes the "spark" that makes movements take off, which in the modern world still hail from the unexpected places they usually have throughout history and remain notoriously difficult to predict (the Arab Spring and Mohamed Bouazizi is just the latest example). Instead,

[37] Ibid., p. 7.

attention is devoted to whether or not ICTs help in the mobilization process, and whether they improve the salience of social movements, à la Shirky, or is their impact greatly overblown, as Gladwell purports? Second, new *agency*-oriented ICTs (e.g., Internet, mobile phones) need to be conceptualized as distinct from previous top-down communication advances. In social science generally, as well as in this chapter, *agency* refers to the capability of people to act individually and make their own free choices (especially from within an institutional top-down structure). It stands in opposition to structure in the "agency versus structure" debate where class, race, gender, religion, culture, and so forth limit individual choice. The agency-oriented nature of ICTs also clearly goes hand in hand with the human rights movement, where agency of the individual is key. I will assume that due to its ability to promote high levels of agency, the Internet is inherently different from other ICTs as well as previous "information delivery services" for social movements, and for human rights especially.

My first claim is that digital ICTs offer the technological capability to efficiently share information, thus reducing the information gap between citizens and governments, helping promote transparency, mitigating corruption, and improving human rights.[38] ICTs are therefore important channels for putting pressure on governments for credibility, transparency,[39] and accountability;[40] these are areas for reform that many social movements target. For example, the human rights movement is an illustration of how pressure for government reform is spurred on by ICTs, as is effectively described in many of the chapters in this book. ICTs achieve success through increasing speed of communication, higher penetration rates, and deepening of technology (e.g., Web 2.0 – similar to a printing press for all and an extensive, yet easy, process for sharing video around the world instantaneously).

This information sharing is vital for social movement development as well. I will end this section with a quote from the late Abid Hussain, former UN Special Rapporteur on the Right to Freedom of Opinion and Expression, which exposes some of the larger, more societal, difficulties

---

[38] Bertot, Jaeger, and Grimes, "Using ICTs to Create a Culture of Transparency"; Pippa Norris, *Digital Divide: Civic Engagement, Information Poverty, and the Internet Worldwide* (Cambridge, UK: Cambridge University Press, 2001).

[39] D. Cullier and S. J. Piotrowski, "Internet Information-Seeking and Its Relation to Support for Access to Government Records," *Government Information Quarterly*, 26 (2009), 441–49.

[40] Bertot, Jaeger, and Grimes, "Using ICTs to Create a Culture of Transparency."

that arise when information is denied and that social movements press back against:

> When individuals and communities are denied information, it becomes much easier to exploit and suppress them. . . . History has demonstrated that power lies in the hands of the informed. The uniformed, the illiterate and the uneducated – kept out of the mainstream of ideas and action – are generally regulated to the margins of society. . . . Today, information and knowledge when disseminated have the greatest power to generate change, not simply guns and bombs. And it is here that the Internet is playing an increasingly important role as a key disseminator of information.[41]

My second claim is that new ICTs shrink distance, allowing for easier social connection across international borders than in the past. In fact, connecting on the Internet may be the *only* way that citizens in far-flung geographical locations can find each other, forge networks, and keep abreast of news about social movements. Advocates of this perspective have emphasized the potential of ICTs to build social networks beyond the limits of space and time by providing a virtual meeting place through which people can maintain social relations they could not otherwise.[42] However, the notion of ICTs as full-fledged enablers of social inclusion is still disputed.[43]

Relatedly, ICTs can improve movement mobilization and salience through their ability to enhance linkages to international actors. ICTs provide a powerful "bridge" of communication and idea sharing between the developed and developing worlds (or between neighboring countries). This sharing has been prevalent since the beginnings of the human rights movement, with the promoting of human rights laws and norms through international treaties and UN declarations such as the Universal

---

[41] Steven Hick, Edward F. Halpin, and Eric Hoskins, *Human Rights and the Internet* (New York: St. Martin's Press, LLC, 2000), p. x.

[42] J. Cole, "Surveying the Digital Future," Center for Communication Policy University of California at Los Angeles (2000), http://ccp.ucla.edu/pages/internet-report.asp; K. N. Hampton and B. Wellman, "Netville Online and Offline: Observing and Surveying a Wired Suburb," *American Behavioral Scientist*, 43, 3 (1999), 475–92; Z. Papacharissi, "The Virtual Sphere: The Internet as a Public Sphere," *New Media Society*, 4, 1 (2002), 9–27; B. Wellman, J. Salaff, D. Dimitrova, L. Garton, M. Gulia, and C. Haythornthwaite, "Computer Networks as Social Networks: Collaborative Work, Tele-work, and Virtual Community," *Annual Review of Sociology*, 22 (1996), 213–38; B. Wellman, "Physical Place and Cyber Place: The Rise of Personal Networking," *International Journal of Urban and Regional Research*, 25, 2 (2001), 227–52.

[43] See Kenny, *Overselling the Web?*

Declaration of Human Rights (UDHR; 1948), the International Covenant on Civil and Political Rights (ICCPR), and the International Covenant on Economic, Social, and Cultural Rights (ICESCR; 1976), yet has gained significant velocity, power, and targeted intent through ICT-fueled sharing since. In fact, cementing its worldwide appeal in the 1990s the human rights movement was able to spread into most developing nations around the world, especially due to the political opening provided by the end of the Cold War and the information opening provided by the Internet.[44] There is little doubt that the Internet helped spread the ideas of human rights throughout the 1990s and continues to do so in the present time.

As a "bridge," ICTs foster new forms of development techniques for social movements often implemented by non-governmental organizations (NGOs) and allow for average citizens in developed countries to lend money, support, and political capital to citizens in the developing world.[45] Secondly, international actors can put demands on the government for reform; one example is the public "naming and shaming" of political regimes repressive of human rights by international human rights NGOs.[46] Keck and Sikkink argue that in the networked world there is a "boomerang effect" wherein activists on the ground in developing countries can turn to transnational advocacy networks – usually located in developed countries, where most of the influential NGOs are headquartered – to put pressure on the governments of developing countries for reform of their recognition and realization of human rights. Claiming that both technological capabilities and cultural change have contributed to the emergence of transnational advocacy networks, Keck

---

[44] A brief but prescient illustration of this opening is that the UDHR is one of the most translated documents in all of human history – in fact, there are many minority languages where a translated version of the UDHR online is one of the only webpages available in that language; see work cited in this chapter by Charles Kenny for a description of this phenomenon with the Igbo language in Nigeria.

[45] An example of political capital is citizens donating resources to international NGOs that engage in the politics of the developing country (e.g., Human Rights Watch, Amnesty International). An example in development (e.g., economic empowerment leading to political empowerment) is the Kiva model of development, which links "average" donors (donating $50 or less) to "average" recipients (e.g., donors have the choice of who receives their loan online); Kiva, www.kiva.org/. Also see Jack J. Barry, "Microfinance, the Market and Political Development in the Internet Age," *Third World Quarterly*, 33, 1 (2012), 125–41, for a detailed analysis of changes the microfinance industry is experiencing due to the Internet.

[46] Margaret Keck and Katheryn Sikkink, *Activists beyond Borders: Transnational Advocacy Networks in International Politics* (Ithaca, NY: Cornell University Press, 1998).

and Sikkink argue that faster, cheaper, and more reliable international ICTs and transportation technologies have helped to break government monopolies over information.[47] They also note how important the rise of ICTs has been for improving human rights realization around the world. As governments lose their monopolies over information, citizens have begun to demand that their human rights be respected in many authoritarian regimes – as quite evident in the Arab Spring, the Green Revolution in Iran, and the Color Revolutions in Eastern Europe.

Third, ICTs enhance tactics employed by social movements, including not only traditional tactics like protest mobilization but also many brand-new forms of tactics, ranging from political discourse/discussion on the World Wide Web to hacking government websites. For Van Laer and Van Aelst, most social movements, in general, have a "repertoire of collective action,"[48] a concept originally conceptualized by Charles Tilly.[49] The impact of the Internet and mobile phones on social movement mobilization has been strong and varied. Van Laer and Van Aelst state that two main ramifications of ICTs stem from the literature:

> [O]n the one hand, internet facilitates and supports (traditional) offline collective action in terms of organization, mobilization and transnationalization and, on the other hand, creates new modes of collective action. The internet has indeed not only supported traditional offline social movement actions such as the classical street demonstrations and made them more transnational, but is also used to set up new forms of online protest activities and to create online modes of existing offline protest actions. By doing so, the internet has expanded and complemented today's social movement "repertoire of collective action."[50,51]

The "new forms" that Van Laer and Van Aelst mention are very different from street protests yet can prove as effective, or perhaps even more so. For them, these "[v]irtual activities may range from online petitions and email bombings, virtual sit-ins to hacking the websites of large

---

[47] Ibid.

[48] Jeroen Van Laer and Peter Van Aelst, "Internet and Social Movement Action Repertoires: Opportunities and Limitations," *Information, Communication & Society*, 13, 8 (December 2010), 1174.

[49] Charles Tilly, "Social Movements and National Politics," in C. Bright and S. Harding (eds.), *Statemaking and Social Movements: Essays in History and Theory* (Ann Arbor, MI: University of Michigan Press, 1984), pp. 297–317.

[50] Ibid.

[51] Van Laer and Van Aelst, "Internet and Social Movement Action Repertoires," p. 1147.

companies, organizations or governments."[52] Furthermore, according to Campbell and Kwak the Internet now plays a vital role in political discourse and even moves participants from online political participation to offline:

> [W]ith the uptake of new media, scholars have begun to examine the links between political discourse online and its relationship to participation offline. This research reveals trends consistent with offline political talk, with positive direct relationships between discussion online and engagement offline[53] and findings that discussion online complements and is complemented by other sources of news and information.[54,55]

Evidence is now clear that the online political participation leads to more participation offline, particularly as the modern distinctions between online and offline communication has become increasingly blurred. For example, Van Laer and Van Aelst provide evidence of the extensive use of the Internet by social movements, which have translated into offline action:

> Via the internet, organizations provide detailed information on time, place and perhaps even a practical field guide for activists to "inform people on how to organize, on their rights and how to protect themselves from harm" as was the case during the FTAA protests in Quebec city, 2001. This lengthy document took activists by the hand and guided them

[52] Ibid., p. 1147.
[53] R. O. Wyatt, E. Katz, and J. Kim, "Bridging the Spheres: Political and Personal Conversation in Public and Private Spaces," *Journal of Communication*, 50, 1 (2000), 71–92; V. Price and J. H. Capella, "Online Deliberation and Its Influence: The Electronic Dialogue Project in Campaign 2000," *IT & Society*, 1, 1 (2002), 303–29, www.stanford.edu/group/siqss/itandsociety/v01i01/v01i01a20.pdf; T. J. Johnson and B. K. Kaye, "A Boost or Bust for Democracy? How the Web Influenced Political Attitudes and Behaviors in the 1996 and 2000 Presidential Elections," *The Harvard International Journal of Press/Politics*, 8, 3 (2003), 9–34; D. V. Shah, J. Cho, W. P. Eveland, Jr., and N. Kwak, "Information and Expression in a Digital Age: Modeling Internet Effects on Civic Participation," *Communication Research*, 32, 5 (2005), 531–65; B. W. Hardy and D. A. Scheufele, "Examining Differential Gains from Internet Use: Comparing the Moderating Role of Talk and Online Interactions," *Journal of Communication*, 55, 1 (2005), 71–84; B. W. Hardy and D. A. Scheufele, "New Media and Democratic Citizenship," in *Encyclopedia of Digital Government, III* (2006), pp. 1250–54.
[54] Shah, Cho, Eveland, Jr., and Kwak, "Information and Expression in a Digital Age"; B. W. Hardy and D. A. Scheufele, "Examining Differential Gains from Internet Use: Comparing the Moderating Role of Talk and Online Interactions," *Journal of Communication*, 55, 1 (2005), pp. 71–84.
[55] Scott W. Campbell and Nojin Kwak, "Political Involvement in 'Mobilized' Society: The Interactive Relationships among Mobile Communication, Network Characteristics, and Political Participation," *Journal of Communication*, 61 (2011), 1008.

through all the obstacles to effective participation.[56] During the Seattle WTO protests, a main rallying point was the StopWTORound distribution list, which enabled subscribers to receive detailed information on different aspects of the WTO.[57,58]

The enhanced organizational capacity the Internet allows was not only the case, rather ironically, during the antiglobalization-focused protests in Quebec City and Seattle. Van Laer and Van Aelst point out that a plethora of "rights" based movements, and many others, have been employing the Internet to expand their mobilization potential across national boundaries:

> A recent study among diverse types of demonstrations (like trade unions, anti-war, immigrant rights, but also right-wing mobilizations) showed how activists use the internet to cross movement and protest issue boundaries thereby significantly increasing their mobilization potential.[59] The processes of "brokerage" and "diffusion" these authors describe are important mechanisms that in cyberspace do not stop at national boundaries either, making every mobilization call in theory inherently transnational.[60]

Thus, the evidence is abundant that ICTs clearly help to coordinate global protests through improving message cohesion and logistics such as times, locations, and targets for protests. Although the global protests against the Iraq War in 2003 are quite different from other social movements, such as indigenous[61] or poor peoples' social movements,[62] it is worth mentioning how the antiwar protests in 2003 used a wide,

---

[56] P. Van Aelst, and S. Walgrave, "New Media, New Movements? The Role of the Internet in Shaping the 'Anti-Globalization' Movement," in W. van de Donk, B. D. Loader, P. G. Nixon, and D. Rucht (eds.), *Cyberprotest: New Media, Citizens and Social Movements* (London: Routledge, 2004), pp. 97–122.

[57] S. George, "Seattle, le tournant. Comment l'OMC fut mise en échec," *Le Monde Diplomatique*, 1 (2000), 4–5.

[58] Van Laer and Van Aelst, "Internet and Social Movement Action Repertoires," p. 1153.

[59] S. Walgrave, W. L. Bennett, J. Van Laer, and C. Breunig, "Multiple Engagements and Network Bridging in Contentious Politics: Digital Media Use of Protest Participants," *Mobilization: An International Journal* 16, 3 (2011), 325–49.

[60] Van Laer and Van Aelst, "Internet and Social Movement Action Repertoires," p. 1153.

[61] Donna Lee Van Cott, *The Friendly Liquidation of the Past: The Politics of Diversity in Latin America* (Pittsburgh, PA: University of Pittsburgh Press, 2000); Donna Lee Van Cott, *From Movements to Parties in Latin America* (New York: Cambridge University Press, 2005); Donna Lee Van Cott, "Indigenous Peoples' Politics in Latin America," *Annual Review of Political Science*, 13 (2010), 385–405.

[62] Francis Fox Piven and Richard A. Cloward, *Poor People's Movements: Why They Succeed, How They Fail* (New York: Random House, 1977).

inclusive political frame and employed the Internet effectively. In fact, the diverse protests against the Iraq War occurred in over 60 countries and 600 cities, simultaneously with estimates of between 10 and 15 million protestors taking to the streets.[63] The creation of this protest event, which some say was the largest coordinated protest in world history,[64] could not have occurred without the Internet.

Similar to many indigenous movements and other movements already in the dustbin of history, the Iraq War protests ultimately failed in achieving their goal (social movement success is another matter to be discussed below); however, by employing inclusive political frames – antiwar in this example, with many possible related movements invited to attend via the Internet – the protests were able to greatly expand their reach to hundreds of different antiwar movements around the world. The Internet clearly played an important role in spreading and fueling these protests; recent examples abound of ICTs stoking the fire of protest from Occupy Wall Street to the Arab Spring.

Finally, a bit more on the unconventional side, Barry Wellman, Zizi Papacharissi, and other optimistic scholars posit that one of the greatest merits of the Internet is that it goes beyond limits of space and time, providing a virtual meeting place through which people can maintain social relations, coordinate activities, and forge new networks with people that they could not have otherwise.[65] Furthermore, the Internet allows for social interactions beyond the limits of geography, which can improve social capital between people in different countries. For instance, the "Internet allows people to encounter mass audiences by extending the boundary of social networks in real life to virtual places, and therefore

---

[63] Van Laer and Van Aelst note: "Several authors have shown that this protest event would not likely have been as massive and diverse without the coordinating and mobilizing capacity of the internet . . . Van Laer (2009) contends that the internet was especially conducive in terms of 'mesomobilization,' which is the efforts of groups and organizations to coordinate and integrate other groups, organizations and networks for protest activities. . . . In a historical comparison of three eras of peace and anti-war mobilization, his research showed how several face-to-face international meetings each time served as the principal basis for coordination and collaboration, but that on the advent of the second war in Iraq in 2003, the internet was fundamental in 'spreading the fire,' bringing the call for a global day of action on an unprecedented worldwide scale, among hundreds of other national anti-war networks and social movement organizations, with a speed and efficiency that was not possible before." Van Laer and Van Aelst, "Internet and Social Movement Action Repertoires," p. 1154.

[64] Ishaan Tharoor, "Viewpoint: Why Was the Biggest Protest in World History Ignored?," *Time Magazine* (February 15, 2013).

[65] Papacharissi, "The Virtual Sphere," pp. 9–27.

fosters global interaction with people who have common interests."[66,67] Another related example is of political blogging, as recent studies have upended the prevailing notions of political participation and have shown that blogging has revolutionized civic engagement in a networked society.[68]

These new developments are related to my fourth claim: New digital ICTs, particularly Internet and mobile phones, have led to more connection between individuals and not less. In other words, ICTs enhance social capital, civil society, and individual connections, and this benefits social movements and human rights realization. This is in sharp contrast to the views of ICT and social connection skeptics, who posit that people are living more miserable, disconnected lives in front of their digital screens and not really connecting more with our fellow humans. Yet other scholars see a drastically different picture from the evidence. Lee and Lee report that optimistic scholars "argue that internet use improves relations between individuals with advanced technology and strengthens social networks.[69] They claim that society can benefit from the information distributed online and that the information makes society more effective and connected."[70]

Another proposition that is commonly put forth by the more optimistic scholars, is illustrated by de La Porta, Demchak, and De Jong's assertion that "[b]etter contact and information in turn will promote better accountability of public officials to citizens and produce fertile ground for reinvigorated civil society."[71] On balance, I concur with optimistic scholars who view ICTs as having on net a positive influence on social capital formation and thus social movements (later on in this chapter I will be making careful note of the limitations for this claim).

---

[66] Wellman, "Physical Place and Cyber Place," pp. 227–52.

[67] J. Lee and H. Lee, "The Computer-Mediated Communication Network: Exploring the Linkage between the Online Community and Social Capital," *New Media and Society*, 12 (2010), 714–15.

[68] Antoinette Pole, *Blogging the Political: Politics and Participation in a Networked Society* (New York: Routledge, 2010), p. 4.

[69] Wellman, Salaff, Dimitrova, Garton, Gulia, and Haythornthwaite, "Computer Networks as Social Networks," pp. 213–38; Hampton and Wellman, "Netville Online and Offline," pp. 475–92; Wellman, "Physical Place and Cyber Place," 227–52; J. Cole, "Surveying the Digital Future," Center for Communication Policy University of California at Los Angeles (2000), http://ccp.ucla.edu/pages/internet-report.asp; Zizi Papacharissi, "The Virtual Sphere," pp. 9–27.

[70] Lee and Lee, "The Computer-Mediated Communication Network," pp. 714–15.

[71] T. M. de La Porte, C. Demchak, and M. De Jong, "Democracy and Bureaucracy in the Age of the Web: Empirical Findings and Theoretical Speculations," *Administration and Society*, 34 (2002), 412.

However, I maintain that people's online behavior is likely to be similar to their offline: more politically engaged people offline will also be likely to be engaged online and vice versa. For instance, Lee and Lee posit from data on US college students that online social activity supplements offline, yet it does not create social capital from scratch:

> [O]nline community use neither decreases nor increases social capital. Rather, depending on the nature of the internet use, the online community may supplement the traditional community's accrual of social capital. This conclusion also implies that despite the evolution in people's relationships with the help of ICT, the online community by itself does not ratify the role of the traditional or local community, and face-to-face communication between community members is still required in order to fully benefit from communities.[72]

Therefore, due to strong evidence in newer studies, such as rigorous analysis mentioned above,[73] I conclude that ICT fosters social capital, and in turn, social movements and human rights realization. In fact, there is a large body of literature stemming from work by Robert Putnam[74] on the importance of social capital in spurring democratic consolidation, which tends to go hand in hand with civil and political human rights realization. Finally, harkening back to Gladwell, could the four young black men who started the Woolworth's protest in 1960 accomplish what they did without strong social capital? Would the civil rights movement have been successful without strong social capital? These questions and arguments deserve examination, yet clearly we can also imagine ICTs would have contributed to their social capital in many ways, and certainly not hurt it.

Lastly, today's prominent social movements, such as feminism, the environmentalism, and human rights, tend to be organized around flexible, dispersed, and horizontal networks as opposed to more top-down and rigid movements in the past.[75] ICTs have allowed this type of

---

[72] Lee and Lee, "The Computer-Mediated Communication Network," p. 721.

[73] De La Porte, Demchak, and De Jong, "Democracy and Bureaucracy in the Age of the Web"; Wellman, "Physical Place and Cyber Place," pp. 227–52; Lee and Lee, "The Computer-Mediated Communication Network"; Papacharissi, "The Virtual Sphere," pp. 9–27.

[74] Robert D. Putnam, *Making Democracy Work: Civic Traditions in Modern Italy* (Princeton, NJ: Princeton University Press, 1993); Robert D. Putman, *Bowling Alone: The Collapse and Revival of American Community* (New York: Simon & Schuster, 2000).

[75] See Jackie Smith et al., *Global Democracy and the World Social Forums* (Boulder, CO: Paradigm Publishers, 2008), pp. 28–29.

movement organization much easier than in the past. An example of how a movement can be flexible is Occupy Wall Street having online debate about what their specific demands actually were going to be (although certainly it might be particular to that unique movement at that time in its development). Perhaps the father figure of ICTs, popularizing the phrase "Network Society," is Manuel Castells, who in his classic three-volume tome, *Network Society*, argued that the speed with which more empowering opportunities emerge and grow exponentially is due to ICTs.[76] In Castells's later work, he turns more specifically to social movements in the age of the "Network Society."

In his 2012 book, Castells states that the development of autonomous networks of horizontal communications,[77] free from the control of those holding institutional power, has led to new forms of social change and political democracy: "The autonomy of communication . . . is the essence of social movements because it is what allows the movements to relate to society at large beyond the control of the power holders over communication power."[78] Castells goes on to claim: "the more interactive and self-configurable communication is, the less hierarchal is the organization and the more participatory is the movement . . . This is why the networked social movements of the digital age represent a new species of social movement."[79] I agree with Castells here, and the human rights movement's approach, and eventual success, in spreading its ideas across many authoritarian developing world countries in the 1990s[80] is a great example of Castells's claims in action. In concluding this chapter, my five statements purported above on the influence of ICTs may not be fully realized if the following limits of ICTs are not taken into consideration – in other words, there is nothing deterministic about the new digital technologies.

---

[76] Manuel Castells, *Networks of Outrage and Hope: Social Movements in the Internet Age* (Cambridge, UK: Polity Press, 2012).
[77] Ibid., p. 12.   [78] Ibid., p. 11.   [79] Ibid., p. 15.
[80] Wiktor Osiatynski, *Human Rights and Their Limits* (Cambridge, UK: Cambridge University Press, 2009); Samuel Moyn, "Why Anti-Colonialism Wasn't a Human Rights Movement," in *The Last Utopia: Human Rights in History* (Belknap, 2010), pp. 84–119; Filomena M. Critelli, "Women's Rights=Human Rights: Pakistani Women against Gender Violence," *Journal of Sociology and Social Welfare*, 37, 2 (2010), 135–60; and for a more critical view of the human rights movement's spread into the developing world and how it is influencing culture see Anne Griffiths, "Gendering Culture: Toward a Plural Perspective on Kwena Women's Rights," in Jane K. Cowan, Marie-Bénédicte Dembour, and Richard A. Wilson (eds.), *Culture and Rights: Anthropological Perspectives* (Cambridge, UK: Cambridge University Press, 2001), pp. 102–26.

The limits of the digital age: Big Brother
is watching you, Mr. Slacktivist

The argument presented in this chapter can be summarized as "guard-edly optimistic" about the impact of the Internet and mobile phones, as I believe they can, and already have, contributed to improving social movement development in many ways, in particular the human rights movement, but only when their limitations are addressed. Three major difficulties arise for social movements to effectively utilize all the tools ICTs offer: (1) compromised access for the populace to effectively use the technology; (2) Big Brother might be watching: the heavy hand of state control on information, privacy issues, and security; (3) slacktivism/clicktivism.

The first difficulty is the reality is that most people in the world still do not have access to the Internet; in fact, only 2.5 billion of 7 billion people have ever been online (data from 2014). Studies have shown that about 90 percent of the variation in access is due to high cost and poverty.[81] Further limiting the quality of access is the lack of education or when one speaks a minority language; the text-based Internet remains a difficult tool to navigate for many. For instance, many potentially useful websites for the poor are not translated into minority languages. In fact, over half of the world's poor (those living under $2 per day) speak a minority language, which are often conspicuously absent from the Web. It is certainly harder for the Internet to reach this segment of the population – that is also assuming the data infrastructure is in place anyway. Even in developed countries, language plays an important role in usage. Language is a "significant barrier to use, as is suggested by a study of users in Slovenia, which found that 75% of those who considered themselves fluent in English used the Internet, compared to 1% of non-English speakers."[82,83]

The second difficulty is that Big Brother is watching and taking action. As other sections of this book will display prominently, the government can also employ ICTs to spy on, gather information, squash protests, and

---

[81] Javier Corrales and Frank Westhoff, "Information Technology Adoption and Political Regimes," *International Studies Quarterly*, 50 (2006), pp. 911–33.

[82] Kenny, *Overselling the Web?*

[83] As estimated by Internet World Stats in 2014, English is the largest language in percentage terms on the Internet with 43.4% of users English speakers; Internet World Stats (2014), www.internetworldstats.com/stats7.htm. Accessed on May 1, 2014.

engage in more targeted prosecution, perhaps even more now than at any time in the past (e.g., China, Iran, and North Korea are particularly good at this, while the National Security Agency (NSA) in the United States is in hot water due to its spying on citizens). There are many instances where governments in the Middle East have used video footage shared online or have looked through Facebook and Twitter to determine who the ringleaders of a movement were and then proceeded to arrest them (e.g., Egypt, Libya, and most sadly, Syria). The extent of the chilling effect of government crackdown on dissident behavior is hard to determine scientifically yet remains an issue for social movements to navigate.

The third difficulty, returning one final time to our opening debate, perhaps Gladwell may be correct that "weak ties" online may not be as useful for "successful" movements, as Shirky and others assume they are. Is slacktivism, or maybe more appropriately in this case clicktivism, making up a large extent of movements today? At critical and difficult junctures, will these types of activists abandon their movement? To some extent when evaluating movement success it is worth thinking about these issues. Just because an incipient movement, often created online, seems to be followed by millions, at least evaluated by Internet traffic or other rather crude quantitative measures, does not mean that it is going to be a successful movement. It might be more analogous to a meme "liked" by millions on Facebook: not exactly revolutionary.

The difficulty with this critique is that since time immemorial the vast majority of social movements have fallen into the dustbin of history. Clearly, selecting the dependent variable of "successful" movements for ICT scholars is certainly a problem, but simply stating that ICTs generate only "weak ties" would also be false, as Shirky and others so clearly demonstrate. It should not be surprising that most social movements fail and will continue to do so in the digital age; however, as was displayed above, they have more tools, including some game-changing ones, at their disposal in the networked world.

Conclusion

A primary danger with technological determinism is that obsessing over the tools technology provides us with, which entails delegating more credit to ICTs than to the organizations, activists, and the support from the populace that a movement needs to survive, would be a mistake. Obviously, governments have been brought to their knees many times before the Internet was even a pipe dream and a "tweet" was only a birdcall. In fact, we are reminded of renowned media scholar Marshall McLuhan famously stating that the "medium is the message" to help illustrate his theory about the social unintended ramifications of the technology themselves.[84] Relatedly, when ICTs meet politics, protests, and social dissatisfaction with the status quo, this can create powerful and sustaining social movements, such as the human rights movement. Yet the "message" is likely to lie as much with the ideas of the social movement rather than with any change specific technologies may bring; put another way, movements thrive on strong ideas.

Countless social movements in the digital age have completely failed to gain popularity or any kind of strength offline through solely employing the Internet – in other words, their message did not resonate enough. However, just as in the offline world (i.e., the extensive historical record), ideas behind the movement need to be strong, pressing, and able to galvanize a large swath of the population. This will always remain a daunting task for movements – digitally savvy ones or not. On balance, despite the limitations of ICTs and the fact that most of the world is not yet online, the digital age remains bright for social movements, activists, and organizations as they employ the connective tools ICTs offer in new, always evolving ways.

Finally, it is clear that the human rights movement is well positioned to take advantage of the tools ICTs offer, as discussed above. First and foremost, the emancipatory power for human agency built into the ethos of the Internet goes hand in hand with the movement's emphasis on individual rights. In fact, there are now calls, from this author as well as the new UN Special Rapporteur on the Right to Freedom of Opinion and Expression, Frank La Rue, for access to the Internet to be considered a human right. Related to increasing agency, the Internet has also led to an expansion of political empowerment, which is vital to the promotion and sustenance of the human rights movement.

Secondly, the ideas behind human rights have already proven to be particularly popular in many areas around the world – and the Internet has already proven its power in spreading them. There is little doubt that the idea of human rights is gaining in strength, acceptance, and academic rigor but does seem to be reaching a saturation point. Lastly, the social networks that ICTs forge, as the "network politics" of

---

[84] Marshall McLuhan, *The Medium Is the Message: An Inventory of Effects* with Quentin Fiore, produced by Jerome Agel; 1st edn. (New York: Random House, 1967); reissued by Gingko Press, 2001.

NSMs displayed, are particularly useful for the human rights movement because of their ability to spread ideas quickly across borders/distance and also due to their contributions to the idea of a "cascade of rights" leading to progressive realization of human rights. In fact, the ability of ICTs to promote, explain, and transfer human rights across borders through diverse networks is a major explanation for the proliferation of human rights realization seen around the world since the early 1990s. Furthermore, the progress in human rights realization stems from what has been called a "cascade of rights," where the practical implementation of one kind of human right has led to others being realized in the same locale. ICTs help this cascading process by spreading information about realization from one realm of human rights to another. In sum, the diffusion of new digital technologies to societies around the world has led to positive changes in the sociopolitical environment for the spread of human rights norms and standards, helping the movement gain and sustain momentum. The emancipatory power of the Internet appears here to stay, a development the human rights movement can welcome with open arms.

3

What does human rights look like?

The visual culture of aid, advocacy, and activism

JOEL R. PRUCE

Introduction

Television viewers have all confronted at one time or another the searing gaze of an African child soliciting for donations to a humanitarian charity. The camera pans slowly across a sad landscape of red clay streets and makeshift homes until an older white man's voice can be heard describing the scene and asking for your assistance. This traditional fundraising strategy is common across the West and persists despite vocal criticisms that it demeans subjects, exoticizes poverty, and reinforces inequality. This mode of visual representation reflects humanitarian practice in an unflattering way and has deservedly received criticism, but it has also been repurposed to frame communications in other areas including human rights. As imagery becomes an increasingly prominent and a prior feature of global interventions, how nongovernment organizations (NGOs) utilize photography becomes ever more relevant, prompting critical questions.

Is there a motivating logic to the use of photographs in human rights and humanitarian campaigns? Do certain modes of imagery correlate with types of crisis and organizational objectives? What reactions do organizations hope to provoke among their audiences through the use of photography in marketing and communication outlets? What trends and shifts can be identified in this regard? What can we learn about human rights and humanitarianism as fields of practice through an analysis of the visual expressions of their work? These questions focus attention on the bounded space in which many diverse sectors overlap: NGOs, journalism and photography, war and disaster, state power and geopolitics, as well as marketing and public relations. In an environment of competing interests and complex emergencies, visual media become a lens through which to explore the representation of distant others as well as projections of self-image.

Given the rising prevalence of digital media in the twenty-first century, NGO communication expresses important qualities about areas of practice and provides a venue for critiquing NGO strategies. In an age when appearance and image are as politically relevant as action and impact, how human rights actors represent themselves visually matters tremendously. Human rights campaigns, for instance, demand more from the audience than charitable giving, which suggests that the gaze of the African child is misplaced. Human rights and humanitarianism may have similar orientations with respect to the protection of human dignity, yet cultivate distinct relationships with the public by virtue of the work they do. NGOs utilize visual media as a means to build constituencies of support for their issues, and, thus, campaign material and photo essays constitute a unique venue for investigating the basis for these relationships and reflecting on the nature of the organizations themselves.

However, visual media in the service of human dignity also becomes a focal site for power and contestation. Since imagery captures the likeness of individuals and articulates suffering and repression, there is an inherent risk that through its production and dissemination, vulnerability is reproduced as indignity. In the very process of seeking support, frailty may be communicated through stereotypes and motifs that exacerbate humiliation. A central tension running through this process is the non-reciprocal and unequal relationship of donor to recipient, north to south, and comfort to insecurity. Human rights and humanitarian campaigns attempt to forge bonds of compassion and solidarity across great expanses of space, as well as across provincial moral chasms. If we are to be made to care about strangers – so much so that we will give of our time, money, or political capital in their assistance – a message must be felt and believed that relies on a cosmopolitan sensibility that expands our current conception of inclusion and community. How the stranger is represented in the photograph shapes moral sentiment as well as public attitudes of favor or distrust for human rights and humanitarian efforts.

While television brought these questions to a critical mass audience, the broadsheet newspaper was the first platform that forged this connection between the audience, NGO, and distant sufferer. And in today's new media environment, complexity abounds. Imagery no longer only serves strategic objectives, political, financial, or other; images provide a venue for NGOs to represent their own identity. Facebook pages, Instagram accounts, and Twitter hashtags are the battlefields and trenches for massive media departments. Thirty years ago NGOs utilized fax machines to send out press releases and urgent actions. Social networks and digital technology have revolutionized NGO communications and raised the stakes significantly. An organization cannot be effective in its "real" work without a winning game plan for the placement, dissemination, and broadcast of the work. Media and information become both means to an end, as well as ends in themselves.

What does human rights look like? What does humanitarianism look like? Do the appearances of these fields accurately and appropriately reflect their foundational ideas, values, and norms? Aid, advocacy, and activism all have as their subject the dignity, respect, and concern for all human beings, but despite these common objectives, each field has a specific orientation with respect to the origins of vulnerability and the alleviation of suffering. Human rights emerge from social struggle and legal institutions that mobilize structural reform as a means of checking the arbitrary exercise of power. Human rights empower individuals and groups to assert autonomy and self-determination. Humanitarianism, on the other hand, is an urgent response to provide relief to innocent civilians during conflicts and disasters. Humanitarianism, in its traditional form, seeks to avoid questions of politics and power by pursuing a neutral agenda, absent self-interest and beyond corruption. Translating these abstract values into visual images is not a linear or obvious process.

This chapter examines these issues by theorizing the relationship between NGOs, the global audience, and the subjects of photography. First, I outline the world of NGO photography by investigating its purposes, political economy, intended audiences, and content. Second, I explore the practices associated with the fields of human rights and humanitarianism in order to lay a foundation for understanding the goals and orientation that drive forms of communication. Finally, I identify ideal-type motifs for human rights and humanitarian campaigns that outline trends in visual culture of these sectors. Media savvy, across platforms of traditional and new media, determines political penetration and organizational viability and, therefore, presents a ripe venue through which to understand human rights practice. I will conclude with some thoughts about the potential for imagery transmitted across digital networks to serve as a bridge for constituting relationships of solidarity.

NGO photography and visual culture

Dating back to Oxfam appeals for famine relief in Nigeria in the late 1960s, photojournalism has played a central role in communicating an ethical cause to a broad audience. At the time, journalists were flown into the secessionist region of Biafra by a European public relations firm on retainer by the rebels. In order to sway global public opinion to their plight against the government, images of starving Igbo people were disseminated in mass media.[1] These photos spread through the mainstream press because they were captivating as news stories, bringing the world to the West with visually arresting images. Foremost, photojournalism serves a purpose as a graphic conduit for news. Instead of relying on the "rational information relay" of text, photos demand the viewer use context clues, assumptions, associations, and memories to extract the story from the image.[2] Photographs of human suffering provoke visceral emotional responses that supplement the deeper investigation of text in communicating a complex storyline. Imagery of atrocity grabs the audience immediately and distills the details, history, and context of a story into a single frame.

In an important sense, this model developed a generation ago suited both NGOs and news outlets similarly. Humanitarian organizations then were essentially start-ups, struggling to conduct outreach and cultivate a donor base for their operations. Media outlets, then and now, balance the mission of publishing "all the news that's fit to print" with the commercial imperatives of selling ad space and moving units. Journalistic dictates tread carefully between "if it bleeds, it leads" and the "breakfast cereal test."[3] Reportage from wars, disasters, and famines generates atrocity photographs that posed a problem for publishers: the merit of the stories carried their own weight, but readers respond inconsistently to coverage of gruesome events. While graphic imagery of suffering may attract readership and boost sales, there are still ethical considerations to weigh regarding time and place appropriateness for certain kinds of news and images. Yet this linkage, and the symbiosis it permits, is being challenged by evolutions in both the media and NGO sectors.

As traditional print media and photojournalism face a changing environment of digital and citizen journalism, coupled with diminished budgets for foreign reporting, photographers have increasingly partnered

[1] Joel R. Pruce, "The Spectacle of Suffering and Humanitarian Intervention in Somalia," in Tristan Anne Borer (ed.), *Media, Mobilization and Human Rights: Mediating Suffering* (London: Zed Books, 2012).

[2] Barbie Zelizer, *About to Die: How News Images Move the Public*, 1st edn. (New York: Oxford University Press, 2010), p. 314.

[3] Ibid., p. 19.

with NGOs.[4] No longer are NGOs simply using the product of photo-journalism – now they have significant media departments of their own, retain their own staff photographers, and provide a worthy outlet for the work of freelance photographers. A strong current in photojournalism is the imperative of shedding light on untold stories of desperate plight and hidden abuse. In other words, photojournalism is endowed with a social purpose shared by human rights and humanitarian NGOs.[5] It is fair to say that their relationship is shifting yet remains synergistic in crucial ways; parasitic, but with roles reversed, still angled toward coaligned goals. This being the case, NGOs can exert more control over the process and the product. However, human rights and humanitarian NGOs have distinct needs for visual imagery based on their particular goals and orientation toward the public. Conceptualizing their divergent purposes advances the argument for unique motifs.

A primary rationale for utilizing visual imagery in NGO campaigns is to raise money to support operating expenses. This is the oldest and most persistent reason for an organization to communicate its message to a broad audience: "Look at what we do and who we help. You can help too." By grabbing the attention of a public preoccupied with daily life and other distractions, humanitarian NGOs focus on imagery that "tugs at the heartstrings" rather than challenges the intellect. Pictures on an aid appeal poster, direct mail piece, or television commercial need not explain the reasons behind the suffering or the causes, which meshes well with humanitarianism generally. All that matters in humanitarian aid is that some individual is suffering, regardless of why or where. From the perspective of the viewer/donor reacting to sadness and grief, coming into contact with desperate imagery and giving money to a cause is a humane moral gesture of participation in prevailing norms about assistance and inequality.

Human rights organizations, however, are confronted with a different set of considerations. On the one hand, human rights NGOs need money to operate too, though the relationship cultivated between human rights organizations and the public is not merely one of donor–recipient. Human rights NGOs require supporters to act on behalf of the organization, to legitimize their work, and to make it possible for advocacy to have political impact. Human rights advocates, at the behest of a trusted NGO, send urgent letters to elected officials, sign petitions, and attend

---

[4] James Estrin, "When Interest Creates a Conflict," *New York Times Lens Blog* (November 19, 2012), http://lens.blogs.nytimes.com/2012/11/19/when-interest-creates-a-conflict/.

[5] Ibid.

rallies in support of a cause. Creating a culture of action and engagement demands that NGOs motivate audiences in a different way because they expect a different sort of response. It may be sufficient to provoke empathy and compassion to solicit donations from viewers, but in order to mobilize a public to engage in action, the organization must marshal a different set of emotions and memories from its supporters.

Instead, human rights NGOs use images to make deeper, more rational appeals to (in)justice, hope, and resistance. To attract human rights advocates, organizations get the audience riled up, stirred, and inspired to action. Emphasizing fairness and dignity, NGOs project advocates as ordinary heroes who can save lives and right wrongs. Trafficking heavily in the moralizing language of good and evil, the advocate is the modern incarnation of social justice champion and social movement crusader. Coming of age in the 1970s and 1980s, the human rights movement is infused with the spirit of 1960s resistance and its culture of hope and change. Generationally, human rights advocates draw upon memories of activists and events that shaped their own moral and political outlooks: King and Gandhi, the defeat of apartheid, and fall of the Berlin Wall. However, as this chapter demonstrates, the visual culture of human rights has yet to arrive at an appropriate expression of its work, yet to articulate for itself what advocacy is in itself and how to represent the action visually.

Essentially, transnational advocacy exists at the intersection of human rights and humanitarianism: NGOs working *on behalf of* distant others while adopting the persona of a grassroots movement championing the rights of their own group. Human rights advocacy is not an insider practice, which is why it shares space with humanitarianism. However, it is also not purely outsider work for its appeal to universal concepts like "humanity" and "dignity." Human rights advocacy is neither in the aid business nor the social movement business. It is neither and both, but also a third thing in its own right – but that third thing does not have a unique visual identity.

Human rights advocacy is graphically discordant, failing to express a clear vision of itself to its multiple audiences: donors, states, supporters, and journalists. Failure to express a distinct visual identity and form is a symptom of deeper issues that need to be addressed. The concern at the heart of this critique is that human rights advocates project an image of themselves that is out of sync with who they really are. Busy borrowing from others, human rights organizations transmit a vision of themselves that is inaccurate and disingenuous, forging a false relationship with the audience and undercutting the salience of their message.

The proliferation of visual imagery in the digital realm and the preponderance of new media bring these questions to the fore. Human rights NGOs reach out to audiences across multiple platforms and rely largely on lucid graphic representation, rather than on lengthy texts, as was once the case. Web users are targeted through banner advertisements, email solicitation, and social media engagement. The first point of contact is visual. Before knowing anything about research methodology, country of origin, or mission statement, the audience's first association is what it sees, which means the impact of the NGO's initial impression is won or lost on optics. As instrumental as it may sound, appearance simply matters. Without an effective visual strategy, the most rigorous, most damning campaign work is in vain. The next section offers definitions and distinctions to differentiate from among the work of aid, advocacy, and activism, before delineating the distinct aesthetic motifs that emerge from these sectors.

Demystifying and disaggregating aid, advocacy, and activism

Humanitarian aid

Humanitarianism is a transnational pursuit focused on providing minimal support for vulnerable populations during moments of crisis. But humanitarianism is not practiced within one's own society. When serving or aiding the disadvantaged locally, we call that by another name: charity. An important sense of distance is built into humanitarianism that works to project compassion abroad. In this way, any form of humanitarianism is interventionist, as it necessarily travels across borders and involves individuals and organizations from one country in the affairs of a second country. Being from outside, these actors aim to be in-country for a relatively short period of time to address the problem at hand and return home. This quality can be construed either negatively or positively: either short-term emergency response is adequate and useful, or it can be perceived as insufficient, leaving reconstruction efforts up to weak states to handle alone. Humanitarians confront impossible scenarios and are forced into the unenviable task of making decisions and compromise: "These compromises are inevitable and are part of the price of doing business – even when that business is saving lives."[6]

---

[6] Michael Barnett, *Empire of Humanity: A History of Humanitarianism* (Ithaca, NY: Cornell University Press, 2011), pp. 6–34.

The occupation of saving lives can take many forms. Humanitarians are the world's social workers, placing bandages over wounds rather than curing infections.[7] They are not revolutionaries and in most cases are not reformers. These actors aim to provide only the most basic goods and services to those when all else is lost. Humanitarians respond to emergencies brought out by (largely) unpredictable events that civilians, especially poor ones, are not prepared to handle: violent conflict, natural disasters, epidemic disease, or a confluence known as complex humanitarian emergencies. This type of emergency arises when the outbreak of conflict disrupts life, systems, and markets. Institutions break down. Provisions become scarce. Normalcy is evasive. Insecurity thrives.

Humanitarians arrive on the scene of a complex emergency not to resurrect institutions or assist with market correction (sometimes having the effect of further disrupting both). Despite new trends in political advocacy, humanitarians are not preoccupied by the causes of suffering and therefore do not attempt to address them. Humanitarians deal mostly with the visible symptoms of subterranean problems, for better or for worse. Humanitarianism is a transcendent calling engaged in by individuals who sacrifice and risk a great deal to help others. Yet humanitarians are not gods and confront a concrete world of pragmatic considerations, resource limitations, and state power. In order to navigate the treacherous mundane world, humanitarians have identified certain limitations and established a set of guiding principles to inform their work and carve out space in which to operate.

Principle and purpose matter tremendously. Principle provides security and legitimacy to humanitarian actors even in the hyperpolitical context of war. Legitimacy and trust is crucial here because heads of state have good reason to be suspicious of foreign actors intervening during tenuous times. Sovereignty provides the basis for excluding any kind of actor from entry, but humanitarian principle is a free pass that endows the actor with leverage to work based on mission alone. If states derive their legitimacy from external recognition and domestic consent, nonstate actors must pursue legitimacy through alternate venues. Altruistic motivations and principled objectives provide cover and justification for nonstate actors, situating humanitarians as safe, apolitical partners in conflict mitigation and disaster relief.

---

[7] Ibid., p. 24.

Humanitarians must be seen as disinterested and noncorrupt from a political perspective; their involvement serves humanity, a universal imperative outside of power. "Neutrality" is the central tenet in the humanitarian lexicon and is most closely tied to the work of the International Committee of the Red Cross (ICRC). The first humanitarian NGO, ICRC was created along with the first Geneva Convention in 1864, tasked to monitor International Humanitarian Law and serves as neutral arbiter of humanitarian norms during war. Constructing humanitarianism and humanitarian space in this way creates "a space where ethics can operate in a world of politics."[8] During warfare, the claim of neutrality is more pronounced and more controversial, and refers specifically to the prohibition against taking sides; the alternative being to provide aid only to one side or the other. Neutral humanitarians assist wounded soldiers on both sides of the conflict, even if the battle is itself between unequal parties, one suffering more and one more egregiously violating humanitarian norms. Humanitarians pledge to serve all equally and have no opinion on the status of the conflict in progress. As an idea that declares what humanitarians *do*, neutrality also by default circumscribes what they *cannot do*.

Humanitarian principle attempts to locate humanitarian practice in a realm beyond politics where actors operate with full latitude, free from accusations of bias. If these principles work, it is because they present NGOs as "innocent by association."[9] However, there is marked dissent within the humanitarian community arguing that apolitical humanitarianism is an abrogation of the humanitarian imperative itself – a naïve and irresponsible way of approaching harm reduction and emergency relief. This debate has provoked splintering within the movement over the past fifty years and spawned organizations with different blends of politics and humanitarianism. Médecins sans Frontières (MSF) is most notable among them. Notions of testimony and witnessing are introduced to mold humanitarianism into a more aware and shrewd endeavor. As has been the case many times, if humanitarians are there to help and can be counted on for their silence, then all the more likely they are to be manipulated. The balance of neutrality and politics in humanitarian principle is a fragile, paradoxical blend, "part confidence trick and part self-delusion."[10] To the extent that neutrality, impartiality, and independence personify a "moral purity" that humanitarians strive

---

[8] Ibid., p. 34.   [9] Ibid., p. 34.   [10] Ibid., p. 34.

for, the very pursuit of nonpolitical engagement as a worthwhile, achievable end should be called into question.[11]

Human rights advocacy

Human rights advocacy is the practice of promoting the rights of others, guided by the internationally recognized system of norms designed to support and protect human dignity. In common parlance, to advocate is to support or recommend or to speak on behalf of an issue or a person. An advocate is the actor who performs this role (consider the work of a legal advocate in a courtroom). "Advocacy" refers to the practice itself, and the term captures a central programmatic and ordered quality essential to our comprehension of the subject. Advocacy occurs across the ideological spectrum and in wide-ranging issue areas including the environment, animal welfare, firearms, food, and innumerable others. Advocacy is not a random occurrence or stand-alone act, but an institutionalized, systematized, and habituated performance. On the global level, a well-developed and growing sector of actors participates in advocacy and shapes its work and the way it is perceived by the international community.

To understand advocacy as such, I believe, corresponds to the way the word is used in ordinary language, as well as the way it is used by both scholars and practitioners of human rights advocacy. Furthermore, and crucial to an honest representation, advocacy is practiced by advocates *on behalf of* others. In their seminal study of these issues, Margaret Keck and Kathryn Sikkink operate with this assumption but fail to problematize it all when they plainly write that "advocates plead the cause of others or defend a cause or a population."[12] The very constitution of transnational advocacy networks hinges on representation of one group by another.

We commonly speak of human rights advocates as those who advocate for the *cause* of human rights, but advocates are ultimately concerned with the human beings whose dignity composes "the cause." Excluding the human object of human rights advocacy ignores a key dimension that differentiates this act from that which addresses animal welfare or ecological threat. Advocates for human dignity are confronted by a distinct

[11] Didier Fassin, *Humanitarian Reason: A Moral History of the Present*, 1st edn. (Berkeley, CA: University of California Press, 2011), p. 224.

[12] Margaret Keck and Kathryn Sikkink, *Activists beyond Borders: Advocacy Networks in International Politics* (Ithaca, NY: Cornell University Press, 1998), p. 8.

set of ethical considerations that neither animals nor Earth present. Foregrounding the human object of human rights advocacy draws crucial attention to the ethical considerations that should guide the practice. Failing to do so abstracts away from the human dimension, creating opportunity for exploitation. This matters because issues pertaining to representation run through human rights strategies particularly due to the reliance on information and media.

As a core strategy of NGOs, the concept of information politics was designed to describe the activity of transnational advocacy networks. Processes such as framing, agenda-setting, labeling, categorizing, exposing, researching, reporting, monitoring, explaining, or persuading outline the terrain for the political use of information. Each of these verbs identifies a range of ways in which advocacy groups utilize information and knowledge to their advantage. By shaping discourse and narrative, advocates leverage publicity as a key political device. In a world of geopolitics dominated by material considerations, moral agents have normative tools at their disposal. While it is true that advocacy campaigns at times use divestment strategies or boycotts to assert their forcefulness, the coercive potency of information has proven to be the advocate's most effective weapon.

In practice, this weapon takes diverse shapes. Amnesty International (AI) is known for its strategy of "naming and shaming," which works precisely as it sounds. By exposing abusers and publicizing their wrongdoings, Amnesty invites embarrassment on the regime. Abusive states operate comfortably so long as their deeds go unknown. If a political prisoner is thrown in jail without due process and tortured, but his whereabouts remain a secret, those responsible are free to act with impunity. By calling violators by name on the global stage, Amnesty leverages this exposure, pressuring abusers to cease their practices. This works because no heads of state like to be called torturers or perpetrators of genocide.

Reason also suggests that this use of information may have a direct effect and perhaps a deterrent effect on future abuse, if regimes would prefer to avoid labels of this nature. Ultimately, questions of reputation may have material effects (perhaps being labeled a torturer makes a state a less preferable trade partner); and this is not unintentional. But the organization's use of information in this way is essentially the closest it can come to flexing power against a sovereign state. Amnesty's method has proven to be extremely effective in discrete circumstances in which their supporters can focus on singular cases or events. In more diffuse situations or more complex conflicts, naming and shaming has a variable rate of return,[13] which is why subsequent organizations have built on this approach.

Human Rights Watch (HRW), for instance, utilizes its own version of information politics with quick, reliable research and high-level deployment of its reports. Instead of AI's mass approach, HRW seeks the attention of major media outlets and policymakers, specifically in the United States. By casting themselves as an indispensable source of information, they in turn shape the debate, which influences decision-making and outcomes. Distinctly, MSF bears its own relationship to information politics manifested in the priority of "bearing witness." Similar to both AI and HRW, bearing witness refuses to permit secrecy and impunity and insists on such by being present in conflict zones. Health-care professionals, on behalf of MSF, who operate with a coherent system of ethics are uniquely positioned to bear witness and attest to crimes due to their neutral stance and humanitarian outlook.[14] MSF is distinct in its ability to straddle the fields of human rights and humanitarianism due to its political commitments to bear witness and testify. Also worth nothing, the financial independence of MSF avails the organization to pursue its agenda with full latitude, which has a positive impact on its potency and influence. In the final account, it is this seeming reliability that all human rights advocacy depends on for its fortitude: information politics embedded in unquestionable moral authority.

The category of moral authority constitutes the foundation of human rights advocacy and makes possible the very use of a politics of information. Stephen Hopgood suggests, "Crucial to being recognized as [a] legitimate [moral authority] is not what is said but the identity of who says it."[15] Power is derived from this authority, rather than from direct coercion. Separate from other forms of authority, in order to obtain and retain the moral position "it must claim a certain objectivity in speaking for the truth."[16] Knowing this, AI, HRW, MSF, and others work tirelessly to protect themselves against the accusation of corruption that might

---

[13] Emilie M. Hafner-Burton, "Sticks and Stones: Naming and Shaming the Human Rights Enforcement Problem," *International Organization*, 62, 4 (2008), 689–716.

[14] Joelle Tanguy and Fiona Terry, "Humanitarian Responsibility and Committed Action: Response to 'Principles, Politics, and Humanitarian Action,'" *Ethics & International Affairs*, 13, 1 (1999), 29–34.

[15] *Keepers of the Flame: Understanding Amnesty International* (Ithaca, NY: Cornell University Press, 2006), 5.

[16] Ibid., 4.

taint their moral authority. Corruption, partisanship, or ideological commitments would undercut the moral high ground imbued within the
language of universal human rights and, therefore, render impotent
advocacy campaigns from the outset.

Pragmatically, this requires an organization's leadership to be wary of
the origins of funding, to give fair treatment to all parties in a conflict,
and to be certain of the information on which they base their calls and
actions. Moral authority will certainly be challenged – by those very
targets of campaigns, the abusers, and the rogues – as having a Western
bias, being an arm of the American government, or the product of a
Zionist conspiracy. In this tense and fluid context, human rights
advocacy NGOs demonstrate a capacity to be effective when guided by
these basic tenets. These are not carved in stone, but merely evolved
through the experiences of central organizations and, therefore, are apt to
change over time. Thus far, this formula has been successful in elevating
human rights into the mainstream discourse of social justice claims on
the global level. It is crucial to account for the way in which global media
and digital networks provide invaluable conduits for the transmission of
human rights norms.

Lastly, human rights advocacy contains an inherent connection to
transnational action. The relationship between the Western advocate–
subject and non-Western victim–object is shaped by distance and fraught
with complex power differentials. That advocates opt to engage in human
rights issues in another country – often instead and at the expense of
local struggles – says a great deal about the politics of human rights.
Transnationality raises pervasive questions about what a truly global,
truly grassroots human rights movement would look like. By way of a
loose definition: When we talk about human rights advocacy, we talk
about a patterned practice, structured around professional NGOs, in
which masses of ordinary people support campaigns that seek to protect
and uphold the dignity of other people.[17] In this way, advocacy borrows
heavily from humanitarian action in the insistence on acting as surro-
gates for others. Therefore, when masses of ordinary people act as their

---

[17] The notion of "support," though, must also be unpacked because sometimes campaigns
are supported literally through letter-writing efforts and the like, but increasingly support
for advocacy is more loosely defined to capture the public reputation of an organization.
The notoriety of an NGO matters when it engages in elite-level lobbying, to leverage
broad, positive recognition and deploy it as political pressure.

own advocates we do not call it advocacy per se; instead, we generally employ a unique term with its own history and cultural associations.

Human rights activism

Activism is distinct from advocacy in that, as a practice, it articulates charges against an instrument of power directly by those affected, with-out proxy. The absence of an intermediary is an essential difference between advocacy and activism, for many of the reasons introduced in the process of defining humanitarianism above. Colonial histories and persistent inequalities inject suspicion into relationships constituted and justified by acting for the benefit of others. Good will and noble inten-tions do not go far enough to overcome the political obstacles presented by interlocutors in this sensitive area. Human rights advocates are con-scious of their vulnerability to accusation and, influenced by humanitar-ianism, assume an apolitical persona. Distancing themselves from politics, advocates defend their interventions as expressive of the univer-sal values that underwrite human rights norms. This articulation permits an opening for advocates to engage on "policy changes that cannot be easily linked to a rationalist understanding of their 'interests.'"[18] Activ-ism, on the other hand, sidesteps accusations of paternalism altogether as activists assert their own claims and pursue their own interests, often in the face of great risk to their physical security. Delineating among these practices provides a basis for theorizing about the role of subject and object in human rights advocacy.

Alex de Waal wrestles with these issues as well, suggesting a typology of activism that explains particular variations.[19] From a critical perspec-tive, de Waal's attempt seeks to "step outside the bounds of the human rights movement and loosen the shackles it has on our political and moral imagination"[20] and by doing so, determine how human rights in its organizational form (advocacy) relates to human rights in its social movement form (activism). De Waal models his "primary movement" after the American civil rights movement. A primary movement is "overwhelmingly a mass movement of individuals, mobilized in order to pursue their interest and claims."[21] Primary human rights movements

---

[18] Keck and Sikkink, *Activists beyond Borders*, 9.
[19] Alex de Waal, "Human Rights Organizations and the Political Imagination: How the West and Africa Have Diverged," *Journal of Human Rights*, 2, 4 (2003), 475–94.
[20] Ibid., p. 476.   [21] Ibid., p. 477.

are distinct from "second generation" and "third generation" movements that take place in professionalized organizations that cultivate relationships with powerful states, rather than oppose them. Primary movements are activist movements. Second- and third-generation movements are advocacy movements. These designations matter because they each carry with them unique politics that are too often conflated, obscuring important spaces of struggle and contestation.

Scholarly literature on transnational advocacy networks (TANs) reinforces the distinction between activism and advocacy. For Keck and Sikkink, TANs form out of the desire of indigenous activists to leap-frog their own state, utilize devices on the global level to bring pressure downward, and see their objectives realized. This is the essence of the "boomerang effect."[22] Domestic social movements working to change their own societies forge transnational networks as force multipliers in their struggles. The relationship between activists and advocates in this schema is one of mutual benefit at best and mutual exploitation at worst. Transnational NGOs have an interest in being seen as an essential component in domestic struggles, particularly in the global South, while local activist movements often lack resources that TANs can bring to bear. This is true among activist movements in the North as well as in the South. In the North, consider the American civil rights movement's engagement with the global human rights regime[23] as an example of a "primary movement" that sought transnational recognition. Charli Carpenter's research on issue emergence and NGO gatekeepers attests to this symbiotic relationship.[24]

Given the centrality of "moral authority" and "moral purity" in human rights and humanitarianism, the ethical dimensions of practice in these fields must be subjected to scrutiny. As powerful and visible as NGOs are, it is insufficient to simply project morality and assume that it is so. Organizations must be held accountable for their engagements: to donors, states, and the global public. Means and ends matter here. In order to meet reasonable standards of legitimacy, the methods NGOs use in their work must uphold the values they purport to serve. The exploration of visual imagery is one expression, one venue, in which means and

---

[22] Keck and Sikkink, *Activists beyond Borders.*

[23] Carol Anderson, *Eyes off the Prize: The United Nations and the African American Struggle for Human Rights, 1944–1955* (New York: Cambridge University Press, 2003).

[24] Charli Carpenter, "Studying Issue (Non)-Adoption in Transnational Advocacy Networks," *International Organization,* 61, 3 (2007), 643–67.

ends *should* coincide. If, through the use of imagery, NGOs impugn dignity rather than defend it, then the moral positions that they aspire to may be compromised. If images objectify their human subjects rather than empower and exalt them, then human rights and humanitarian actors have fallen prey to the very systems against which they struggle.

Power and competition shape the market for moral behavior, but these forces often go unnoticed.[25] Determining a "logic" for the deployment of NGO photography pins ethical consideration against rational, strategic objectives. However, it is my contention that human rights and humanitarian actors must resist instrumental trade-offs. It may be beneficial to traffic in pitiable images of poor children, for instance, because an emotional audience may be inclined to give money in greater amounts. But if this practice is deemed to be exploitative, then it undercuts a humanitarian's reason for being. Respect for the recipient–object of aid or advocacy appeal must be central to any media strategy. To address this directly, the final section seeks to identify visual motifs that NGO communication converges around and judge how these motifs accommodate the principles and practices of human rights.

Three motifs: desperation, determination, defiance

Based on this reading of the social practices of aid, advocacy, and activism, we would expect that capturing these distinct missions in photographs would produce divergent motifs.[26] For instance, advocacy organizations would want to personify strength, resistance, and solidarity, while humanitarian NGOs would desire a less antagonistic frame by evoking empathy and compassion. Drawing on emotional narratives of helplessness, the needy subject requires charitable assistance from affluent viewers. Human rights advocacy presents a different posture marked by a rougher edge and a confrontational attitude appealing directly to notions of (in)justice.

Depicting each of these areas visually, then, requires asking complicated questions: Should the subjects in frame be represented as suffering and pitiful or resilient and determined? Are these individuals shown faltering in desperate squalor or struggling forcefully against an abusive

---

[25] Clifford Bob, "Merchants of Morality," *Foreign Policy* (March 1, 2002), www.foreignpolicy.com/articles/2002/03/01/merchants_of_morality.

[26] I have collected representative examples of these motifs on a webpage, to supplement the text: www.joelpruce.com/threemotifs.

regime? Ultimately, the use of imagery provokes and circumscribes a range of possible responses while projecting a persona for the NGO at the center of the campaign. A survey of media products of human rights and humanitarian NGOs bears at least three prominent motifs that serve as identifiable articulations of the organizations that produce them: desperation, determination, and defiance.

NGOs have seized on photojournalistic accounts of crisis since Oxfam became active on the Biafran famine fifty years ago by literally reprinting images from the newspaper in their own appeal advertisements. The use of depictions of starving African children began in this moment due to the synergies between a humanitarian organization and the work of photojournalists. Both honed in on several particular qualities of these photos that make them iconic; blank, staring eyes; bodily damage; and the innocence of childhood. Making eye contact with a figure caught in frame draws in the viewer and personalizes the suffering. Witnessing knobby elbows and skin stretched tight across bones further humanizes suffering by locating it on a body that we all possess. Finally, the trope of childhood innocence adds an extra dimension of emotional personalization. Child vulnerability and helplessness is a circumstance that all viewers can relate to: not because of an experience with famine (presumably the viewer sits comfortably somewhere far from crisis), but because even outside of the context of famine, children depend on parents and communities for full support, and audiences latch onto that notion inherently.

However, while the photos of starving African children have proven useful in humanitarian campaigns to raise money and awareness, there is persistent sensitivity among observers that the icon has morphed into stereotype that informs bad policy and harmful interventions. This motif emerges out of the necessarily unequal and nonreciprocal nature of humanitarianism. The imagery used to communicate the values of humanitarianism gives comfort to postcolonial critiques about humanitarianism as imperial and disproportionately focuses on hopeless Africa, personifying the whole continent as child-like and disease-ridden. As the image below makes clear, while this motif originated in coverage of African crises, it holds true for circumstances throughout the developing world.

In fairness, this visual motif is increasingly being called into question among NGOs, and this critique primes the field for a shift in trends. It does, however, reflect many regressive principles that inform humanitarianism, which demonstrate an inertia and inability to evolve. The desperation motif relies certainly on the sense of urgency and emergency of humanitarianism, and the nonjudgmental care for those who truly are in desperate predicaments. Highlighting desperation in the photographed subject has the reflexive effect of focusing the viewer on her own status, affluent or otherwise. In doing so, the moral compulsion to give and to help is evoked, and humanitarian practice is set in motion. While limited in many significant ways, the desperation motif also has a role to play in the translation and cultivation of humanitarian sentiment to a mass audience.

The determination motif is an adaptation that, I suggest, forecasts new directions in NGO practice and use of imagery. Visually, these photographs utilize eye contact and personalization reminiscent of the early humanitarian appeals. Captured in frame are recipients, but they are not sickly and desperate. Instead, the recipient of aid is depicted as empowered, capable, and determined to overcome obstacles of crisis and underdevelopment. She is a partner in humanitarian aid, not merely a passive patient. There is a greater sensitivity to avoid old stereotypes about poor, riddled Southerners in need of help from rich, white saviors. Remaining is a focus on children and women, but not as helpless victims. This assertion confronts the persistent critiques of aid as "throwing good money after bad." Representing aid recipients as trustworthy partners in bringing about a remedy to global poverty and suffering combats donor fatigue. The determination motif correlates closely to transformative notions of political humanitarianism practiced by organizations utilizing a rights-based approach – one that conceptualizes vulnerability in political terms and seeks remedy through institutional change. This new turn in the visualization of humanitarianism aims to confront the troubled history and checkered track record of the aid sector, while also suggesting new approaches to practice.

Neither desperation nor determination adequately captures human rights principles and practices. It is insufficient for human rights NGOs to rely on dated tropes about sadness and grief associated with stereotypical humanitarian imagery. Human rights is inherently *not* about charity, not even "good" or "political" charity. Human rights imagery should reflect notions of strength, empowerment, and resilience that approximate the core values of the movement itself. But more so, human rights communication demands an articulation of essential notions of collective action and solidarity with others. Since the demands of human rights organizations are higher, individuals must be engaged in a different way. This is a marketing issue in one respect, but also one that should reflect the integrity of the movement and the moral authority that it seeks. How can average people be moved to care about and then act on behalf of individuals or groups on the other side of the world? It is one matter to ask for a meager donation, and it is quite another to ask for action.

To represent this, the defiance motif expresses the powerful potential for groups of people acting together to affect societal change. The images may appear angry or threatening, but not violent. Human rights advocacy situates itself alongside the civil disobedience tradition as indicated. Human rights action deploys information politics as a tool for masses of average people to use against decision makers; therefore the quantity of supporters pictured is important. Large public demonstrations symbolize awareness and mobilization. Marching, crying out, and holding banners, visual imagery of human rights advocacy focuses more on the actors than the recipients, so to speak (imagine an equivalent for humanitarianism in which the donor is pictured giving money). Human rights communications would be well served in fact to take as its object the audience itself, rather than the anonymous stranger whom the audience is asked to save. Finally, imagery of collective action in turn helps solve collective action problems. Communicating to the audience that there is already an engaged group of advocates may help the more reluctant viewer to overcome fear of the free rider problem.

Implications

Public relations efforts of human rights NGOs serve the purposes of recruitment, fundraising, mobilization, and general outreach. The way an organization presents itself impacts how its reporting and documentation efforts resonate with the audience and pressure elites and office holders. Human rights organizations in the twenty-first century are concerned with their image and identity for the way in which these seemingly superficial elements have consequences of the "real" work of advocacy. Brand management is as much an imperative for NGOs today as it is for multinational corporations, and, therefore, the ways organizations project themselves visually are central to their communications operations.

Against this backdrop, visual media converge on several distinctive motifs and the three above are not exhaustive, but they do present a typology of narratives that human rights and humanitarian actors create and traffic in. The motifs are expressions of how the organizations see themselves and want to be seen by the audience. Each reflects broader trends in global engagement and communication strategy, as well as slowly evolving NGO sectors. However, given this account of aid, advocacy, and activism, it is not clear that the motifs fit human rights practices well. Human rights advocacy in particular has not generated its own visual culture, as much as it has borrowed from cousins and neighbors.

Advocacy is not aid in that it is a practice that purports to stand in solidarity with the other, rather than in a charitable relationship of donor–recipient; the desperation motif is therefore not appropriate and miscasts advocacy efforts. Advocacy is also not activism – and I believe this distinction is crucial – because advocacy is a practice inherently based on external, often transnational, support for the other along human rights lines. Activism is undertaken by subjects claiming their own rights and recognition without proxy. The defiance motif co-opts the moral force and psychological persuasion of activism and transmits those feelings among the audience to draw them to advocacy projects. The human rights campaign contains two faces: home-grown movements struggling for their own futures and the transnational community based in the affluent West that wants to help. These are each distinct spheres of action and remain furthermore distinct from humanitarianism. Human rights advocacy occupies the space in between, balancing the ethical and political demands of self and other. This tension is present in the media products of advocacy organizations, which brings us back to conclude with a modified version of the question we asked at the outset: What should human rights look like?

In many instances, advocacy campaign materials attempt to sidestep pitfalls by eschewing images that contain individuals. For instance, consider the impact of a photograph of a bombed-out Syrian city block as it stands in for the human beings who once lived there, now dead or homeless. Inanimate objects, like a shelled concrete high-rise, refugee camp tents, or ashes from a razed village, all represent the human toll without exploiting the human beings at the center of such destruction. Infographics are another device NGOs use to represent their work through visualized statistics or documentation that communicate details about abuse while evading criticism about the use of atrocity photos. These mechanisms can be effective, but it is not reasonable to expect human rights actors only to utilize images devoid of human faces – human faces remain at the heart of human rights work and it is beholden on innovative thinking to conceptualize advocacy in a way that respects human subjects and effectively and accurately depicts the work of NGOs.

As mentioned at the outset, the transformative impact of digital technologies on the human rights sector magnifies the essential character of this debate over visual culture. The shift in scope and scale in terms of diffusion of graphic media is unprecedented and thrusts questions of appearance and optics to the fore of strategic thinking. "Real" human rights work is only as good as its resonance. And inasmuch as the new media environment presents new obstacles and pressures to engage across multiple platforms, there are also opportunities to deepen the penetration of human rights norms and strengthen the affiliations audiences have with the global human rights movement.

Solidarity as a concept has been particularly elusive, yet the emergence of global, digital social networks has provided new tools through which to cultivate relationships of equality and mutuality. It has been said that the technological capacity to witness distant suffering is one meaningful symptom of globalization that carries with it moral obligation on behalf of the suffering subject. Overcoming provincialism and nationalism, visual media possess the potential to contribute to a cosmopolitan foundation for the recognition of sameness and inclusion across traditional boundaries. NGOs should serve as conduits for borderless politics due to their position as key transnational civil society actors and for the way that such a perspective expresses what advocacy is and what it looks like in practice.

Furthermore, social networks provide a unique platform through which to forge relationships of solidarity. We could envision strategies that connect the experience of witnessing distant suffering to actions that express solidarity, for instance with the use of hashtags. When audiences can see the struggle of other groups in distant lands, NGOs can play a role in translating watching into acting. However, the same sorts of questions presented in the visual context carry over into other discursive outlets. Constructing communities of solidarity with hashtags risks accentuating power differentials present across networks. For instance, when the #BringBackOurGirls hashtag was started by Nigerian activists to raise awareness for a mass abduction, Western followers began weighing in and crowding out local voices.[27] Patterns of activity such as hashtag advocacy demand the same kinds of sensitivity and solidarity and must not simply be assumed into existence.

---

[27] Jumoke Balogun, "'Dear World, Your Hashtags Won't #BringBackOurGirls,'" *The Guardian* (May 9, 2014), www.theguardian.com/world/2014/may/09/nigeria-hashtags-wont-bring-back-our-girls-bringbackourgirls.

Finally, due to the fundamental role of information and media in human rights, the advent of digital technology only improves the tools available to advocates, and this is as true in the visual realm as in any other.[28] Partnerships and projects that utilize satellite imagery and surveillance equipment for human rights purposes have proliferated over the last decade, evidencing a trend certain to continue. NGOs including Amnesty International, Human Rights Watch, the Enough Project, WITNESS, and Videre each have sophisticated new programs that develop software and hardware to apply in the field. Devices and applications improve our ability to monitor and document abuse, revitalizing naming and shaming strategies.

Conclusion

I propose these questions at a moment when the global human rights community is undergoing a thorough self-assessment amid the shifting sands of American decline, rising powers, and miscellaneous instabilities. Envisioning a movement that acts more symbiotically with indigenous movements and organizations, rather than as gatekeeper and benefactor, requires a new approach to visual representation as well.[29] Prioritizing solidarity is key to this new vision. Visually, this requires featuring victim/survivor/stakeholder as equal partners. The determination motif begins to take proper steps in this direction but retains the residue of desperation tokenism, as if a communications officer took seriously critiques and merely did the opposite. Now photographs are happy instead of sad. But rather than merely reacting, the visual culture of human rights must be proactive to capture solidaristic political engagement in which actors stand shoulder to shoulder with recipient groups, in relationships of assistance and support. Photographs would represent advocates as humble and deferential to the communities they hope to help rather than as saviors and heroes.

In place of the defiance motif that triumphs advocates as liberators, I propose a fourth "D" motif: dissident. If human rights advocates are to

---

[28] Alexandra C. Budabin and Joel R. Pruce, "The Strategic Logic of Media Advocacy: New Modalities of Information Politics in Human Rights," Working Paper (2014).

[29] Cesar Rodriguez-Garavito, "The Future of Human Rights: From Gatekeeping to Symbiosis," *Sur: International Journal of Human Rights* 11, 20 (June 2014), http://conectas.org.br/en/actions/sur-journal/issue/20/1007380-the-future-of-human-rights-from-gatekeeping-to-symbiosis.

stand in true solidarity with the objects of their work, then advocates must consider themselves as dissidents. This posturing would truly take up the mantle of Mandela and King, who were scorned and imprisoned for their activism and targeted by the state for their views and for their actions. Assuming the role of radical, human rights advocacy would do well to reclaim the subversive position of human rights champions of the past in order to transcend the self–other divide that plagues twenty-first-century interventions. Advocacy as dissidence asserts the insurgent nature of the cosmopolitan claim that human dignity matters every-where. The presence of a global network of human rights defenders upends traditional assumptions of international affairs by challenging sovereign power and structural sources of abuse. An aesthetic transform-ation must accompany this new platform that communicates a sense of rebellion and threat. Rather than using tired narratives from charity or social movements, the visual culture of human rights should blaze new terrain because the politics of information in a digital age are not limited to words and slogans: pictures possess power as well.

4

Activism, the Internet, and the struggle for human rights

Youth movements in Tunisia and Egypt

MAHMOOD MONSHIPOURI, JONATHON WHOOLEY,
AND DINA A. IBRAHIM

The tendency of analysts to overstate the strength and the stability of authoritarian regimes and rulers has increasingly been called into question since the collapse of communism in the Soviet Union and Eastern Europe, the color revolutions in postcommunist Europe and Eurasia, and the 2011 Arab uprisings. Valerie Bunce has noted that scholars of authoritarian resilience have overlooked or at least minimized these regimes' limitations in managing their political environment. Authoritarian politics, Bunce explains, can be seen as the intersection between poorly informed publics and poorly informed leaders. Modern technologies have enabled the publics to overcome their information deficit by taking advantage of newly available resources to access information around the usual roadblocks erected by authoritarian regimes.[1]

A second factor is how the rise of prominent social actors has accompanied the development of digital technologies, especially online social networking. Together these have enhanced the level of public awareness and participation in cyberspace in a wide variety of ways, including access to information and participating in informal and formal groups. Marked by communication autonomy, these new technologies have become effective tools of organizing and instigating uprisings, making the search or the need for a centralized leadership arguably unnecessary and making mass mobilization and protest possible.[2]

---

[1] Valerie Bunce, "Rebellious Citizens and Resilient Authoritarians," in Fawaz A. Gerges (ed.), *The New Middle East: Protest and Revolution in the Arab World* (New York: Cambridge University Press, 2014), pp. 446–68; see pp. 467–68.

[2] Wael Ghonim, *Revolution 2.0: The Power of People Is Greater Than the People in Power: A Memoir* (Boston, MA: Houghton Mifflin Harcourt, 2012), p. 59.

These elements have enhanced young people's capacity to effectively engage and participate in mobilizing civic movements as well as advocate for human rights and social change. For millions of frustrated young people in the Arab world who were incapable of deploying the information they accessed and the knowledge they acquired, the 2011 uprisings provided a unique opportunity to demand a more open, transparent, and accountable government.[3] For the region's burgeoning youth population, especially women, Information and Communication Technologies (ICTs) and social networking technologies are tools of empowerment and agency. Evidence suggests that the region's women are especially active users of social networking, blogging, and other online activities, in part because the keyboard doesn't require them to cover their heads or be accompanied by a male guardian.[4] Online and social media activism among women in Egypt and Tunisia was a means toward achieving contained empowerment, as Newsom and Lengel argue.[5]

In line with this thinking, we argue that the basis for human rights has at many stages of history been a search, compelling or otherwise, for the concept of "interiority" – an idea that individuals have within them a relatable internal life that can be understood as being like another's life and different only in personal experiences. Lynn Hunt in her work *Inventing Human Rights* makes the case that this process has evolved within the narrative of human rights since such important human rights luminaries as Jean-Jacques Rousseau.[6] Hunt argues that Rousseau and other contemporary writers of his time such as Samuel Richardson created an inner world for their characters in works like *Julie* (1761) and *Pamela* (1740), whose wild success as novels allowed for their audiences in England and France to view the individuals at the heart of their stories as living, breathing creations.

---

[3] Lisa Anderson, "Authoritarian Legacies and Regime Change: Towards Understanding Political Transition in the Arab World," in Gerges (ed.), *The New Middle East*, pp. 41–59; see pp. 51–52.

[4] Bruce Feiler, *Generation Freedom: The Middle East Uprisings and the Remaking of the Modern World* (New York: HarperCollins Publishers, 2011), p. 117.

[5] Victoria A. Newsom and Lara Lengel, "Arab Women, Social Media, and the Arab Spring: Applying the Framework of Digital Reflexivity to Analyze Gender and Online Activism," *Journal of International Women's Studies*, 13, 5 (2012), pp. 31–45.

[6] Lynn Avery Hunt, *Inventing Human Rights: A History* (New York: W. W. Norton & Company, 2007), p. 48.

Hunt argues that this move, which was of course not entirely new, encouraged and provided a space for living through another's experience and seeing the world through another's eyes. This is important, she argues, because to care about another human being and thus their human rights requires by its nature an empathetic impulse possible only if you understand a human as like you and common to you. She states,

> [E]veryone learns empathy from an early age. Although biology provides an essential predisposition . . . [e]mpathy only develops through social interaction; therefore the forms of that interaction configure empathy in important ways. In the eighteenth century readers of novels learned to extend their purview of empathy.[7]

Thus, the epistolary novel created, in a sense, the empathy in eighteenth-century Europe that allowed individuals to empathize with others. Social media create this interiority as well; digital protest fundamentally personalizes the struggle of our contemporaries across the globe and through our computer screens. Like the novels of Rousseau and Richardson, Facebook and Twitter carried empathy across state borders, transcended regions, and created a larger community that human rights has become a part of. To achieve effective human rights advocacy, we must first empathize with and understand others, and digital media creates the ideational space for this to occur.

By prompting interactivity and participation, where one becomes not only consumer but also creator of online content, and where sharing ideas and exchanging feedback becomes the norm, these new digital technologies enable youth to redefine patterns of participation, civil involvement, and self-expression.[8] This globalized community, Forsythe argues, is as much a product of ideational influences as well as material ones.[9] The spread of globalized conceptions of human rights norms has created the space for individuals to embrace or resist based on a conceptual package of ideas that encourages dissent and the norms of peaceful protest.

From this premise, access to online and social media has transformed communications throughout the Middle East and North Africa (MENA) region, and, together with the prevalence of a vast array of satellite television channels with myriad viewpoints, citizens have more platforms

---

[7] Ibid., p. 40.
[8] *Council of Europe*, "Training Course: New Media in Youth Work," European Youth Center, Strasbrug, Budapest, July 5, 2011, DJS/TC Media (2011), p. 1.
[9] David P. Forsythe, *Human Rights in International Relations* (Cambridge, UK: Cambridge University Press, 2012), p. 45.

than ever to form public discourse around notions of accountability, justice, and freedom.[10] This has led to the emergence of a contemporary political culture informed by ideas, ideals, and values, which have spread largely through online activism – a phenomenon often known as "digital citizenship."[11] This form of citizenship emphasizes inclusive rights of an individual as "citizen" and of "social justice" as opposed to those of exclusive prerogatives such as sectarian and ethnic identities. Technology must therefore be seen not just as a set of neutral tools, but as *practice* – that is, a way that things are done.[12]

The Arab Spring indicated that, beneath a seemingly quiescent surface, the public's mood had turned against militants and autocrats. We contend this is a point Ken Booth explicitly addresses in his work on the three tyrannies embedded within the modern human rights discourse: presentism, culturism, and positivism. Dictators and autocrats use paltry excuses rooted in cultural norms (culturism) of particularity to justify their draconian policies.[13] Tunisia's "Jasmine Revolution" demonstrated new ways of expressing dissent and expanding the political space for protest found in norms just as profound and local as those in Tahrir; Ferguson, Missouri; or Baltimore, Maryland. Culture has nothing to do with protest, and norms in this sense can be found almost universally in most locations on the planet.[14]

It is worth noting that awareness alone does not lead to social change, but opening up a political space is essential to such a transformation. The changing methods of social media and engagement provide a way to connect people with real human rights problems. Ultimately, however, social media must be linked to grassroots organizations if such methods of communication are to not only mobilize collective action in the form of civil disobedience but also serve as a tool for assessing accountability.[15] This chapter examines the relationship between youth and revolt, and the

---

[10] Pamela Ann Smith and Peter Feuilherade, "Now, the Media Revolution," *The Middle East*, Issue 427, November 21, 2011, pp. 35–38; see p. 38.

[11] Engin Isin and Evelyn Ruppert, *Being Digital Citizens* (New York: Rowman & Littlefield, 2015).

[12] Quoted in Virginia Eubanks, *Digital Dead End: Fighting for Social Justice in the Information Age* (Cambridge, MA: The MIT Press, 2011), p. 31.

[13] Ken Booth, "Three Tyrannies," in Tim Dunne and Nicholas J. Wheeler (eds.), *Human Rights in Global Politics* (Cambridge: Cambridge University Press, 1999), p. 32.

[14] Ibid., p. 40.

[15] Johanna Herman, "Hashtags and Human Rights: Activism in the Age of Twitter," *Carnegie Council for Ethics in International Affairs* (November 12, 2014), www.carnegiecouncil.org/publications/ethics_online/0099. Accessed on January 20, 2015.

spread of modern modes of technology and democratization with a view toward demonstrating the impact of social media on the politics of protest.

The youth: opportunities and challenges

Five years after the Arab Spring, the people's hope for democratic reforms in the Arab world has been all but shattered. While the MENA region has changed, it is not clear where the broader trajectory of the region is going.[16] Young men and women, who spearheaded massive peaceful demonstrations in 2011, are generally not as eager to discuss political change and contest existing dynamics of power and domination. These activists, both digital and local, have grown up under repressive regimes and were told that they could or should trust no one. As experts have noted, "social media have allowed them to come together in meaningful ways," and the expansion of the digital landscape has crafted the rights and norms based in human rights that all regions and peoples share.[17]

As Jack Donnelly has noted, quoting the Universal Declaration of Human Rights, "All humans are born free and equal in dignity and rights. They are endowed with reason and conscience and should act toward one another in the spirit of brotherhood."[18] With this in mind, the youth generation is far more connected with their local, national, and international communities as a whole than any generation that preceded it, and it is expected to hold highly sanguine attitudes concerning what ordinary citizens can and should do to enjoy the same expansion of rights found in the West.[19]

With the exception of Tunisia, a reversion to the repressive tactics and heavy-handed policies enacted by the military-led Egyptian government,

---

[16] For more information on this, see Mahmood Monshipouri, "Tahrir's Legacy: Opportunities and Hazards for the Future of Youth Movements in the Middle East," *Georgetown Journal of International Affairs* (December 1, 2014), http://journal.georgetown.edu/tahrirs-legacy-opportunities-and-hazards-for-the-future-of-youth-movements-in-the-middle-east/.

[17] Michael Hoffman and Amaney Jamal, "Political Attitudes of Youth Cohorts," in Marc Lynch (ed.), *The Arab Uprisings Explained: New Contentious Politics in the Middle East* (New York: Columbia University Press, 2015), pp. 273–95; see p. 275.

[18] Jack Donnelly, *International Human Rights*, 4th edn. (Boulder, CO: Westview Press, 2013), p. 52.

[19] Ibid., p. 291.

coupled with the continuing political tensions in Yemen, Bahrain, Libya, and Syria, have all cast their dark shadows over the optimistic view that only recently engulfed the region. The phrase "demography is destiny" may be an old adage and somewhat overstated, but demographic realities cannot be ignored or even slighted. Today, in the MENA region, two-thirds of the population is under eighteen. This demographic is facing one of the highest unemployment rates in the world, as the region ranks among the worst for youth unemployment – approximately 30 percent – high population growth, and poor education.[20]

It would be far too facile to conclude, however, that the youth bulge caused the 2011 Arab upheavals, and we find clues to the roots of the mass rebellion both through contemporary examples and human rights theory. Arguably, a combination of bleak employment prospects, elitist power structures, and repression contributed to revolutionary upheavals.[21] This explains why youth demands during the Arab Spring were encapsulated in four concepts: change, bread, liberty, and social justice – aspirations largely based on secular motivations and universal claims made by many across the world and found within the Universal Declaration of Human Rights as well.

It is important to remember that these uprisings were driven just as equally by causes relating to economic justice and security as by the demands for liberty. Despite the fact that the prevailing mantra in Tahrir square was *heyya sawrit karma* (this is a revolution of honor and dignity), the underlying socioeconomic causes were decades in the making and led young protesters to take to the streets to express and demonstrate their anger and frustration. Dignity as a concept is at the core of all claims made about changes in reality relative to the aspirational nature of human rights. Ken Booth argues that the failure to imagine the world as something else is the sin of presentism. Dignity is a normative goal, and a largely positive one, and striving for this cardinal trait reveals the true nature of the Arab Spring revolts, not simply that citizens were young, but that citizens deprived of dignity will as a general rule eventually wrest it from authority.[22]

---

[20] Mahmood Monshipouri, *Democratic Uprisings in the New Middle East: Youth, Technology, Human Rights, and US Foreign Policy* (Boulder, CO: Paradigm Publishers, 2014), p. 27.

[21] Juan Cole, *The New Arabs: How the Millennial Generation Is Changing the Middle East* (New York: Simon & Schuster, 2014), p. 26.

[22] Booth, "Three Tyrannies," p. 46.

Just as the secular orientation of these demands called for a fresh need to scrutinize the failure of regimes in power, so did the all-too-familiar language of human rights and personal dignity that stood at the heart of newfound desires of the youth population. In Tunisia, Ben Ali was forced to flee the country as his youthful population staged huge demonstrations with new and old modes of communication to topple his regime. Likewise, in Egypt, the vibrant April 6 Youth Movement played a significant role in utilizing social media and the Internet to mobilize the opposition against Mubarak's rule. This group, however, was quickly sidelined by the military, which accused the Youth Movement's members of accepting American funding.[23]

In Iran, the youth movement, also known as the "Green Movement," emerged during the disputed 2009 presidential elections. It initially shook the foundation of the Islamic Republic but was subsequently squashed by the regime. One of the most dramatic aspects of the Green Movement was the split within the Islamic Republic. One observer aptly captured this development: "Iran suffered political fissures in 2009 precisely because the establishment (and almost anyone in the opposition could be considered a part of the establishment) has split so openly, not because dissidents had burst onto the scene."[24]

On balance, the prospects for youth empowerment are less than promising. Some youth movements attempted to form coalitions – or sought realignment – with nationalists and Islamists, an option that appeared to be more practical but ultimately ended up more detrimental. Others opted to stay out of the power structure and fight the regime externally; however, most of these youth movement members ended up in jail. In Egypt, they were accused in media discourse and public narrative of being *baltageyya*, or thugs, thus effectively marginalized.[25] Still others went underground while using violent means of fighting the regime, an eventuality that carried dire consequences for the country and the region at large. The appeal of Islamic State in Iraq and Syria (ISIS), especially its nihilistic brand of violent extremism when peaceful change has failed, is another alternative, one that seems to be gaining

---

[23] Marc Lynch, *The Arab Uprisings: The Unfinished Revolutions of the New Middle East* (New York: Pacific Affairs, 2012), p. 134.

[24] Hooman Majd, *The Ayatollahs' Democracy: An Iranian Challenge* (New York: W. W. Norton & Co., 2010), pp. 59–60.

[25] Hanan Sabea, "Still Waiting: Labor, Revolution and Social Justice in Egypt." *International Labor and Working-Class History*, 86 (2014), pp. 178–82.

momentum in inverse proportion to the failures of the Arab Spring to transition into sustainable change.

Finally, and no less important, is the fact that the combination of a suffocating political climate and rising unemployment rates in the aftermath of these uprisings has caused great concerns and disillusionment on the part of youth who see little or no hope for the future. In the wake of recent and rapidly unfolding economic pressures, massive brain drain is all but inevitable in the region. One study showed that an astounding 26 percent of young people aged 15 to 29 across the MENA region have expressed the desire to migrate and leave the Middle East in search of better educational and career opportunities. The region's high youth unemployment rates, coupled with poor economic conditions and local job prospects, discrimination, and insufficient investment in work-related skills, as well as exclusive access to tertiary education, have left many young people with profound dismay and distrust in their political systems' ability to grow.[26]

A key pressure point in the controversy over democratic reforms in the Middle East today is that many leaders still show an obstinate refusal to admit the necessity for socioeconomic change. The fact remains that political reforms are unlikely to be sustained over time if they are not shored up by socioeconomic development and foreign allies who support genuine reforms. This theory still holds and has yet to be discredited, which may explain why policies to tackle structural problems that cause inequality, exclusion, and disempowerment are absent; the future of democratic reforms remains problematic but not impossible.

The role of outside actors and foreign allies is vital to the sponsoring and promotion of human rights norms. The possibilities for the promotion of human rights norms, as David Forsythe notes, exist only when countries and the global community at large stand in support of those norms. Without the expansion of "soft law," human rights norms, and conventions, and the robust support of countries willing to not simply talk about human rights but implement them in practice, human rights theories are worth less than the paper they are inscribed upon. After all, what use are the norms included within human rights if offending

[26] Yara al-Wazir, "Brian Drain: Why a Quarter of Young Arabs Want to Leave Their Countries," *Al-Arabia News: Middle East* (April 25, 2014), http://english.alarabiya.net/en/views/news/middle-east/2014/04/25/Brain-Drain-why-a-quarter-of-young-Arabs-want-to-leave-their-countries.html. Accessed on November 7, 2014.

countries, especially powerful ones, can simply choose not to engage in the promotion of dignity and political redress?[27]

The unemployment rates throughout the MENA region are depressingly high. Youth unemployment rates for 2011 were noticeably high in Tunisia (42.3 percent), Palestine (35.7 percent), and Egypt (29.7 percent).[28] Even if they had won the right to free and fair elections, young people still did not have good prospects of earning a decent living or starting a family, perhaps the most important foundational elements of human dignity. They have become disillusioned with the Arab uprisings,[29] explaining why even in a country like Tunisia – where positive moves toward democracy have enabled young people to express their dissident views – uncertainty, mistrust, and the lack of job opportunities have led a disgruntled minority to embrace ISIS. According to one report, nearly 3,000 Tunisians have traveled to Syria and Iraq to join the group.[30]

The uprisings clearly showed the salience and interplay of both structure and agency. These young people were not (and are not) driven by religious beliefs, but instead were (and are) determined to confront societies that leave them with few opportunities. Unless the Arab world's leaders put in place effective economic policies addressing structural problems that their countries face, their bankrupt politics are certain to lead to more instability. The boiling Arab societies, which most recently exploded under economic insecurity and suffocating repression, were defused for a short time during the Arab Spring, but are flaring up again as the lack of real change has been made clear.

Demographics of revolt

Factors that contributed to Tunisian uprisings – such as high unemployment rates, high prices of food, and falling real wages – remain

[27] Forsythe, *Human Rights in International Relations*, p. 45.

[28] Marilena Stoenescu, "Youth Statistics – North Africa and Eastern Mediterranean," European Commission: *Eurostat* (October 2014), http://epp.eurostat.ec.europa.eu/statis tics_explained/index.php/Youth_statistics_-_North_Africa_and_Eastern_Mediterranean. Accessed on February 8, 2015.

[29] M. Chloe Mulderig, "An Uncertain Future: Youth Frustration and the Arab Spring," Boston University, The Papers/No. 16, April 2013, pp. 1–33; see p. 24, www.bu.edu/ pardee/files/2013/04/Pardee-Paper-16.pdf?PDF=pardee-papers-16-arab-spring. Accessed on February 9, 2015.

[30] David D. Kirkpatrick, "New Freedoms in Tunisia Drive Support for ISIS," *The New York Times* (October 22, 2014), pp. A1 and A8; see esp. p. A8.

widespread in the region, from oil-rich Libya to impoverished Yemen. The problem of youth bulge and unemployment has mounted enormous pressures to the region's education and health-care systems, natural resources, and labor markets. Tunisians, however, are better educated and more urbanized than their neighbors. With 7.2 percent of their GDP spent on education, Tunisians are steadily ranked among the most educated countries in the Middle East and North Africa. In contrast, Algeria spends 4.3 percent of its GDP on education, Egypt 3.8 percent, Libya 2.7 percent, Jordan 4.9 percent, and Yemen 5.2 percent.[31]

Ironically, but understandably, the question persists: Why did the revolt occur in Tunisia? Those who have traveled throughout the region, one expert reminds us, could see that Tunisia enjoyed a relatively high standard of living and quality of life. The country's per capita income is almost double that of Morocco and Egypt. It is higher than Algeria's, even though Algeria is an oil-rich nation and Tunisia lacks such national resources. Similarly, Tunisia scores high in poverty reduction programs, literacy, education, population control, and women's status. It is far from a rentier state in that it has built a middle-class society based on its human resources and investment rather than pumping oil from the ground. Tunisians export clothing, olive oil, and produce and are host to hundreds of thousands of European tourists each year.[32]

The fact remains that, like Iran, Tunisia has become a middle-class society imbued with rising expectations and demands for political freedoms. The façade of stability in these countries is misleading, and the preservation of the status quo ante is no longer sustainable as long as their citizens cannot freely express their economic and political grievances. A quick glance at the demographics behind the resurgence of Iran's Green Movement in 2009 explains why educated young women were at the forefront of this reformist movement. In the 1970s, toward the end of the Pahlavi monarchy, nearly 5 percent of college-age youth went to college. By 2009, the figure had reached 31 percent.[33] The girls

---

[31] Kristen Chick, "Why Tunisia? Why Now?," *The Christian Science Monitor*, January 31, 2011, pp. 8-10; see esp. p. 10.

[32] Eric Goldstein, "A Middle-Class Revolution," in Marc Lynch, Susan B. Glasser, and Blake Hounshell (eds.), *Revolution in the Arab World: Tunisia, Egypt, and the Unmaking of an Era* (Washington, DC: Foreign Policy, 2011), pp. 66–69; see esp. p. 66.

[33] Charles Kurzman, "Cultural Jiu-Jitsu and the Iranian Greens," in Nader Hashemi and Danny Postel (eds.), *The People Reloaded: The Green Movement and the Struggle for Iran's Future* (Brooklyn, NY: Melville House, 2010), pp. 7–17; see esp. p. 8.

outnumbered boys in secondary schools (1996), primary schools (1999), and higher education (2001).[34]

New technologies and struggle for freedom

Today's Internet-based media have become useful tools for nonviolent struggles and revolutionary youth on the Arab street, facilitating in some cases the downfall of several governments. This interiority, as Hunt might argue, allows for individuals to capture each other's hearts and minds as they attempt to universalize the struggle for rights and dignity. The internal and interior lives of each figure who stood in Tahrir Square, Tehran, or Tunis were magnified exponentially by spreading their feelings and sensibilities via Web 2.0.[35] All over the world, Web 2.0 has generated new types of social protests, creating new paths to collective action while challenging authoritarian governments' efforts to halt the flow of information and preclude mass movements.[36] The Internet and other mobilization technologies have been highly conducive to promoting extended discussion on freedoms and building autonomous public opinion in the MENA region. A combination of satellite television and the Internet has led to freer forums for interactive opinion, bypassing the ability of government to inspect and tamper. While private and state-owned satellite TV channels have reached audiences in their homes, the Web has targeted citizens individually and collectively all at once.[37]

Modern technologies have served as an important instrument not only in documenting human rights abuses, but also in mobilizing citizens to raise their dissenting voices. One prime example is the torture of Egyptian citizen Khalid Said. Shortly after Said's brutal death at the hands of police officers, a Facebook page called "We are all Khalid Said" was launched, and many videos were uploaded and circulated on YouTube that not only revealed graphic images of the abuse he suffered, but that also served to mobilize the Egyptian citizenry. Perhaps no single event, excepting the self-immolation of Mohamed Bouazizi, reveals the power of how an individual's internal struggle or interiority can be transmitted and transported into the households of citizens and partisans worldwide.

---

[34] Ibid., p. 8.   [35] Hunt, *Inventing Human Rights*, p. 78.
[36] Farhad Khosrokhavar, *The New Arab Revolutions That Shook the World* (Boulder, CO: Paradigm Publishers, 2012), pp. 158–59.
[37] Ibid., p. 161.

Likewise, the imagery campaign and platforms played a crucial role in mobilizing protests throughout the region. A demographic bulge of young people unable to find employment found in social media an avenue to air their grievances and a tool by which to organize opposition against their government. Accessibility to ICTs and social media has rendered any form of totalitarian control over information and political expression both implausible and obsolete. Thus, the role of the individual to create and produce real and substantial social change across borders is possible and desirable, given the current modern, human rights–infused political and technological reality.

While technology diffusion and democratization processes are significantly linked, the connection between the two is not necessarily causal. "No technology," as experts concur, "can ever take the place of social activities entirely."[38] The debate over whether the so-called weak ties generated by Internet relationships will promote contentious political action remains unsettled, even as there is widespread consensus that the Internet's transformative power lies in its ability to spread the seeds of future social norms and that public networking could potentially affect the logic of information cascades.[39]

In fact, a contrasting view holds that the Internet may prove to be an inadequate tool at building coherent social networks and sustainable trust at the heart of civil society. It could have a depoliticizing impact, as people operate within the privacy of their homes rather than getting out into the streets or doing the hard and riskier work of political organization.[40] Alternatively, it is argued that the impact of the Internet in the long term will be to "empower and transform the nature of the public sphere in authoritarian Arab societies."[41] That said, the successful transition to democracy in the MENA region rests on wide-ranging socioeconomic and political parameters, vibrant social movements, effective communication means, and independent media systems willing to resist perpetuating propaganda and challenge the status quo.[42] Additionally, sustainable democratic transitions require the presence of a

---

[38] Ibid., p. 162.

[39] Marc Lynch, "Media, Old and New," in Marc Lynch (ed.), *The Arab Uprisings Explained: New Contentious Politics in the Middle East* (New York: Columbia University Press, 2015), pp. 93–109; see p. 98.

[40] Ibid., p. 99.   [41] Ibid., p. 104.

[42] Rasha Abdullah, "Egypt's Media in the Midst of a Revolution," *Carnegie Middle East Center* (July 16, 2014), http://carnegie-mec.org/2014/07/16/egypt-s-media-in-midst-of-revolution#. Accessed on May 10, 2015.

normative bias toward expanding norms of personal dignity and human rights, ruling elites willing to accommodate popular demands for democratic change, and an international community willing to tolerate the chaos and instability that social change creates.

We make the case that a change in the international system is governed by legacies and stability. The crafting of the international community is as much about the promotion of equanimity and stability as it is about creating the space for human rights norms. The difference is in the case of human rights. We contend that the world is not created to be a simple construction; it is a contested, drastically unstable, chaotic contest for domestic and international rights. Ken Booth implores us to regard the present not as a concrete reality but rather as a challenge to be overcome and to move beyond. This is the nature not simply of protest, but of something more fundamental to governance; this is the question of dignity, and the lengths that some, including protesters and activists, government officials and policymakers, will go to preserve the existing order not because it is preferable, but indeed because through the pursuit of dignity, something better than the present state of diminished rights and norms in the international system is possible.[43]

Experts have noted that countries with strict forms of censorship and content filtering have experienced little regime change.[44] It is equally important to bear in mind that "in many Muslim countries, censorship is not simply about protecting political elites, it is about managing cultural production and consumption."[45] The rules of censorship of newspapers and broadcast media do not generally apply to digital content and tools, although countries such as Egypt, Saudi Arabia, and the United Arab Emirates regularly imprison bloggers and have imposed severe punishments for expressing antigovernment views on social media, particularly Twitter.[46] Attempts to completely cut off the entire country from Internet service during the Egyptian revolution backfired, and attempts by the Turkish government to ban Twitter have been desperate and ineffective

[43] Booth, "Three Tyrannies," p. 49.
[44] Philip N. Howard, *The Digital Origins of Dictatorship and Democracy: Information Technology and Political Islam* (New York: Oxford University Press, 2011), p. 179.
[45] Ibid.
[46] Bayly Philip Christopher Winder, "The Hashtag Generation: The Twitter Phenomenon in Saudi Society," *Journal of Georgetown University-Qatar Middle Eastern Studies Student Association*, 6 (2014), www.qscience.com/doi/abs/10.5339/messa.2014.6. Accessed on May 10, 2015.

attempts at censoring digital media.[47] That ruling elites and autocratic states relentlessly seek to manage information flow, gender politics, and identity formation suggests that digital media pose serious challenges to the traditional practices of cultural production, consumption, and management.[48]

In Egypt, economically and politically alienated young professionals from middle-class backgrounds led the revolt against Hosni Mubarak's regime while he was consumed by his own succession of power. Known as the Facebook generation, Egyptian young men and women went online, opting to remain anonymous and faceless for security reasons. Over the past thirty years, these young people have sought a confluence between the appeal of liberal ideals and the positive and dynamic energy that they can bring to the country's political, economic, and cultural scenes.[49] Caught between the military and Islamic movements, this generation of Egyptians, Tarek Osman writes, "is animated by a passion to escape the failure it feels it has inherited."[50] And now, they face new challenges of the postrevolutionary era.

Reclaiming the public space and democracy

In the aftermath of the 2011 uprisings, the question remains: How best to harness the momentum of defiance while simultaneously retaining the engagement of the newly mobilized public in the future tasks of registering, voting, and making one's voice heard through representation?[51] The leaders of the Arab youth movement have embraced the notion that democracy cannot be "imported, parachuted, imposed, or outsourced: its success will ultimately depend on their awareness, participation, and commitment to the public good."[52]

Equally important is the sober realization that Egyptians may in fact fall far short of experiencing a political revolution of the sort that could

---

[47] Saka Erkan, "The AK Party's Social Media Strategy: Controlling the Uncontrollable," *Turkish Review*, 4, 4 (July/August 2014), 418–23.

[48] Howard, *The Digital Origins of Dictatorship and Democracy*, p. 179.

[49] Tarek Osman, *Egypt on the Brink: From Nasser to Mubarak* (New Haven, CT: Yale University Press, 2010), p. 210.

[50] Ibid., p. 215.

[51] Charles Tripp, "The Politics of Resistance and the Arab Uprisings," in Gerges (ed.), *The New Middle East*, pp. 135–54; see p. 152.

[52] Marwan Bishara, *The Invisible Arab: The Promise and Peril of the Arab Revolution* (New York: Nation Books, 2012), pp. 228–29.

have deposed the ruling class. Some analysts have noted that the narrative of the Egyptian revolution is messy by design in large part because there are so many pivotal moments, many key actors, and many stories to be told. The battle to claim revolutionary legitimacy out of this perplexing and puzzling process has become a key political battlefield among a myriad of players involved.[53] Others have warned that the hopes for Tunisia and Egypt to make the transition to stable democracy with rapidity will most likely be disappointed. Revolutions, they assert, are just the beginning of a long and turbulent process. In cases where a civil war or a counterrevolution erupts, the reconstruction of the state takes still longer.[54]

The actions by protesters in Tahrir Square on January 25, 2011, have been credited for ending Hosni Mubarak's rule. In reality, what occurred was a transition borne of both expediency and a tendency toward stability by Western leaders. The Supreme Council of the Armed Forces (SCAF) allowed for the removal of Hosni Mubarak but retained a substantial amount of control within and without governance. As Yazid Sayigh argues, "At best, the mass protest movement thrust the role of midwife upon it; at worst the SCAF acted preemptively, removing the president to abort deeper revolutionary change and protect itself."[55]

On June 24, 2012, Mohammed Morsi, the candidate of the Muslim Brotherhood, was brought to power in a run-off election where he garnered 51.7 percent of the vote. Morsi ran on a package of reforms and economic proposals targeted at creating jobs, economic stimulation, and a revitalization of Egypt's youth population based on the creation of prosperity and a recommitment to the next generation of Islamic rule.[56] While some had hoped for a pro-Western or liberal candidate to accede to power based on the expectations of the perceived liberal tendencies and the capacity for toleration exhibited by the Tahrir protesters, it has been argued that while protests centered on Tahrir, in Cairo, Alexandria, and Port Said the broader expectations of the electorate were based on a more pragmatic read of Egypt's problems.

---

[53] Lynch, *The Arab Uprising*, p. 98.
[54] Council on Foreign Relations, *The New Arab Revolt: What Happened, What It Means, and What Comes Next* (New York: Council on Foreign Relations, 2011), p. 340.
[55] Yezid Sayigh, "Above the State: The Officer's Republic in Egypt," *Carnegie Endowment for International Peace* (2012).
[56] Yasmine El Rashidi, "Egypt: The Rule of the Brotherhood," *The New York Review of Books* (February 7, 2013).

The Muslim Brotherhood, banned from Egypt since the time of Gamal Abdul Nasser, who gained power in his famous Officer's Coup in 1952, retained power and relevance by existing as a nexus for patronage and community largesse for the majority of Egypt's population that existed outside of major cities and beyond the patronage circles of the Mubarak regime.[57] In other words, the Brotherhood responded to exile by effectively

> breaking the unwritten covenant agreed to with their subjects in the 1950s and 1960s in which the subjects relinquished their claims to basic human and civil rights in return for the state undertaking to provide them with education and health care, employment, and subsidies for such necessities as staples, cooking gas, and transportation.[58]

By providing basic goods and services to the population, the Muslim Brotherhood was able to adopt a level of nongovernmental economic populism entirely in line with the holistic vision of a complete Islamic society, in a sense existing as a pregovernmental ordering of society.[59] This is arguably the key to the electoral success of the Brotherhood that seemed to defy the expectations of Western and Eastern critics alike.

From Morsi's speech in Tahrir Square on June 29, 2012, the progress that he was envisioning still remained fairly vague. However, for a public that was arguably stifled by the Mubarak regime's lack of employment opportunities (ranging from 11 to 17 percent) it must have seemed like a breath of fresh air, even on such a sweltering day.[60] Morsi granted himself almost unlimited power without judicial oversight or public review. In reaction to what he perceived as the remnants of the old regime, Morsi centralized power and attempted to reform the constitution along the lines that he and his party argued were more broadly in line with Egyptian national priorities. Among them, as should be no surprise based on our earlier review of the principles of the Muslim

---

[57] Alexus G. Grynkewich. "Welfare as Warfare: How Violent Non-State Groups Use Social Services to Attack the State," *Studies in Conflict and Terrorism*, 31 (2008), pp. 350–70.

[58] Emmanuel Sivan, "Why Radical Muslims Aren't Taking over Governments," *Middle East Quarterly*, 4, 4 (December 1997), 3–9.

[59] Mohammad Ma'mun El-Hudaibi, "The Principles of the Muslim Brotherhood," *Ikwanweb*, www.ikhwanweb.com/article.php?id=813. Accessed on May 14, 2015.

[60] Yasmine El Rashidi, "Egypt: The Rule of the Brotherhood,"*The New York Review of Books*, 60, 2 (February 7, 2013), www.nybooks.com/articles/archives/2013/feb/07/egypt-rule-brotherhood/. Accessed on May 14, 2015.

Brotherhood, was the creation of *Shari'a* Islamic law as the basis for the new constitution.[61]

On July 3, 2013, following massive public protests against him, Morsi was removed from office by a coup engineered by the military and internal security forces, led by General Abdel Fatah el-Sisi – the coup was an event that upended the dawn of a new democratic era in Egypt. El-Sisi vindicated the coup by arguing that the military was fulfilling its "historic responsibility" to protect the country. The country's constitution was subsequently suspended, and a new caretaker government was installed. In the ensuing elections, held on May 26–28, 2014, less than 47.5 percent of Egypt's 53 million eligible voters participated. Former army chief Abdel Fattah el-Sisi won a landslide victory in the Egyptian presidential election by securing 93.3 percent of the votes cast.[62]

Former President Morsi was sentenced to twenty years in prison by an Egyptian court on April 21, 2015, the first verdict of the four major criminal charges against him since the military ousted him in 2013. The ruling illustrated the determination of President el-Sisi to crush the Muslim Brotherhood. This conviction, experts argue, would likely deepen the alienation of Mr. Morsi's supporters and render the chances of any reconciliation even more remote.[63] Following these events, many observers have argued that there is little evidence that Egypt is moving toward adopting a full-fledged socioeconomic revolution that will redistribute national wealth and power from the ruling elite to the underprivileged lower classes.

Although the transition to democracy in Egypt has been repressed, there is no denying that a civic uprising did occur, one in which diverse popular forces carved out public civic realms and proclaimed ownership of their own space and claims.[64] Citizens occupied public spaces, took charge of cyberspace, and maintained new channels of communication with global audiences. Irrespective of Sisi's successful counterrevolution, civic culture and spaces of public expression and dissent in Egypt have

---

[61] Ibid.

[62] *Al Jazeera*, "Sisi Elected Egypt President by Landslide" (May 30, 2014), www.aljazeera.com/news/middleeast/2014/05/sisi-wins-egypt-elections-landslide-2014529134910264238.html. Accessed on April 23, 2015.

[63] David D. Kirkpatrick and Merna Thomas, "Egyptian Leader Deposed by Army in '13 Gets a 20-Year Prison Term," *The New York Times* (April 22, 2015), p. A10.

[64] Sheila Carapico, "Egypt's Civic Revolution Turns 'Democracy Promotion' on Its Head," in Bahgat Korany and Rabab El-Mahdi (eds.), *Arab Spring in Egypt: Revolution and Beyond* (Cairo: The American University in Cairo Press, 2012), pp. 199–222; see p. 221.

been irrevocably informed by the exhilarating and unprecedented experience of becoming part of a *sha'ab* (people's movement) as never before.[65]

In the rest of the region, uncertainty reigns as the popular demands for
political opening and reform have stalled. After Muammar Qaddafi's
death, Libya's rebel militias have turned on each other. Confidence in
transitional leaders is eroding. Saudi Arabia's monarchy has preserved its
tight grip on society and is determined to stem the tide of democracy in
neighboring Bahrain. The latter's repressive state apparatus has effectively curbed mass protests, even as public disaffection remains. The
uprising against Syria's Bashar al-Assad has turned into an open war,
with the opposition increasingly resorting to violence. In Yemen, many
factions are jockeying for power in the post-Saleh period, as the country's
economy is suffering a sudden decline.[66]

Collapsing freedoms

Postrevolutionary societies face a myriad of new challenges and difficulties, none more obvious than undergoing a peaceful and steady
democratic transition by holding fair, free, and periodic elections. Much
of the debate over democratic transitions revolves around the timing,
procedures, and efficacy of elections. Elections, in fact, are a tool that
authoritarian regimes tend to use in various ways to try to maintain
their hold on power. Incumbents have often used elections to respond
to the crises that emerged in 2011. In some cases, electoral reforms were
part of a wider package of political reforms bent on alleviating opposition by showing their flexibility toward embracing further change, co-
opting opposition elites, and providing the mechanisms for allocating
patronage more broadly.[67] Whereas in both Tunisia and Egypt, electoral
institutions were well established, in Tunisia the *ancien régime* was
largely swept aside before new elections to the Constitution Assembly
were held. In Egypt, by contrast, the removal of the old regime
remained an incomplete task, undermining the viability of electoral
institutions. As such, the first elected parliament was disbanded, while
much of the power struggle over the country's future was undertaken

---

[65] Ibid., pp. 220–21.
[66] Dan Murphy, Nicholas Seeley, and Kristen Chick, "Arab Upheaval Begins to Settle,"
Christian Science Monitor (February 6, 2012), pp. 12–13.
[67] Ellen Lust, "Elections," in Lynch (ed.), *The Arab Uprisings Explained*, pp. 218–45; see
pp. 229–34.

through extra-electoral politics, including demonstrations, state-led violence, and public protest.[68]

And yet, this overemphasis on free elections tends to obscure the importance of strong institutions and constitutional guarantees of rights that are enshrined in other legal frameworks and protected by the courts.[69] For Egyptian women, who actively participated in the uprisings, civil society, and their own organizations, elections have failed to protect and promote gender equality, civil liberties, and inclusion. However, the aftermath of the Tunisian revolution and the ensuing election of Ennahda, followed by the reclamation of political power by a coalition of secular parties, maintained Tunisia's unique status in the MENA region toward respecting women's rights. Women's movement activism is a difficult and not easily generalized phenomenon. While on the one hand it has been equated with a type of democracy that aims at achieving economic parity and economic citizenship as well as participation in the polity, there are significant gains being made by women expressing their agency online and through social media in the most conservative countries such as Saudi Arabia.[70]

The Egyptian state has thus far failed to safeguard such rights of citizenship. Egypt's revolutionary narrative has become a deeply divisive issue, raising tough questions as to who owns and who speaks for the revolution. More critically, however, the December 29, 2011, Egyptian security forces' crackdown on the prodemocracy nongovernmental organizations (NGOs) on charges that they received millions of dollars annually in US government funding and that these NGOs sought to destabilize the country ratcheted up the pressure on Egyptian liberal and human rights groups who have often relied on external support and training.

The Egyptian court's inquiry into foreign funding of NGOs strained US–Egyptian relations and jeopardized – at least temporarily – US aid to the Egyptian military. Among forty-three employees of four democracy promotion organizations who were charged with illegally accepting foreign funds and operating without a license, nineteen Americans faced trial; most recognizable among them were Sam LaHood, head of the

---

[68] Ibid., p. 236.
[69] Valentine M. Moghadam, *Modernizing Women: Gender and Social Change in the Middle East* (Boulder, CO: Lynne Rienner Publishers, 2013), p. 218.
[70] Marlyn Tadros, "Stepping Out: Women Blogging Their Discontent," in Fatima Sidiqi (ed.), *Women and Knowledge in the Mediterranean* (New York: Routledge, 2013), pp. 232–49.

International Republican Institute and the son of President Obama's Transportation Secretary Ray LaHood, and Julie Hughes, who was the Egypt country director for the National Democratic Institute.[71] Egypt's ruling generals defused the crisis by lifting the travel ban on some NGO workers and dropping the prosecution. Subsequently, the US government authorized $1.3 billion annual military aid to Egypt. In September 2014, Nancy Okail was sentenced to five years in absentia and lives in the United States. All of her Egyptian colleagues are in jail.

Yet there can be no denying that Egypt under President Abdel Fatah el-Sisi has grown more repressive. On January 24, 2015, Ms. Shaimaa el-Sabbagh – an accomplished poet and an activist who in fact supported the military ouster of the Islamist President Mohamed Morsi – was mortally wounded in downtown Cairo, a powerful symbol of the lethal force the Egyptian authorities deployed to crush dissent and protest unleashed after Mubarak's overthrow. This brutal assault demonstrated how far the military-backed government was willing to go to coerce a return to the old authoritarian order. Photographers and videographers captured her death moment by moment. Rarely, if ever, has a gratuitous death by riot police of a nonviolent activist, who intended only to lay a wreath in Tahrir Square as a memorial, been so thoroughly and so movingly documented and shared.[72]

It is clear, Heba Morayef notes, that human rights activists and other prochange political forces in Egypt, who in 2011 thought they would have had ample time to reform state institutions and legislative structures, have grossly miscalculated their power. Arguably, one clear lesson learned was the need to institutionalize reform in the earlier period of the uprisings when public sentiment generated a unique momentum and when political determination within the regime to respond to protesters' demands was not in short supply. "Today," Morayef continues, "human rights groups find themselves with few allies and very limited access to subservient media."[73]

---

[71] Abigail Hauslohner, "Egypt's NGO Crisis: How Will US Aid Play in the Controversy?," *Time* (February 9, 2012), www.time.com/time/world/article/0,8599,2106420,00.html. Accessed on January 21, 2015.

[72] David D. Kirkpatrick, "Killed at Egypt Memorial, Activist Becomes Symbol," *The New York Times* (February 4, 2015), pp. A1 and A12.

[73] Heba Morayef, "Re-examining Human Rights Change in Egypt," *Middle East Research and Information Project* (April 17, 2015), www.merip.org/mer/mer274/reexamining-human-rights-change-egypt?ip_login_no_cache=30da42077c337905d9c01e95cfe0445e. Accessed on April 24, 2015.

In Tunisia, even before the Arab Spring, the Internet had greatly opened up space for Tunisian dissidents through blogs, discussion forums, and music. A young Tunisian rapper – known as El General, whose real name was Hamada Ben Amor – posted a song on his Facebook page and YouTube channel. The song was entitled "Raies lebled," meaning the president of the country. It expressed through music a youth culture of defiance and outrage against prevailing socioeconomic ills, including unemployment, poverty, and social injustice in Tunisia, placing the blame squarely on the Tunisian government. El General's video went viral after it was picked up by Al Jazeera and rapidly shared online and via social networks. The lyrics of this song quickly and forcefully resonated with many young people who lived under the repressive regime of Ben Ali for so long.

In 2011, the street demonstrations were captured on cell phone cameras and then uploaded as videos on various sites and blogs, such as A Tunisian Girl, Nawaat, and Les Révolutionaires de las Dignité, whose contents served as news feeds for satellite networks like Al Jazeera.[74] After Ennahda's electoral victory in October 2011, feminist organizations remained mobilized, insisting on broadening women's political participation and retaining the country's fairly egalitarian family law. In 2012, they successfully protested an attempted move on the part of the constituent assembly to replace the word "equality" with "complementarity" in the draft constitution.[75]

Social media

In Egypt, the roots of social media–driven uprisings can be traced back to the Kefaya movement (2004–5) that was in solidarity with textile workers who were planning a strike on April 6, 2008. Hence the origin of the name "April 6 Youth Movement," which referred to a loose coalition of many groups of activists, opposition parties, lawyers, professors, and student protesters. In 2008, workers at Al-Mahalla Textiles called a strike on April 6. Although no major protests ensued, two activist workers were killed and the city became, albeit briefly, a site of violent confrontation between workers and security forces.[76]

Ahmed Maher was 30 years old when he gained prominence in 2008 as one of the cofounders of this movement – a solidarity group

---

[74] Ibid., p. 229.   [75] Ibid., p. 231.   [76] Ghonim, *Revolution 2.0*, p. 36.

launched to support protests. Organizing mostly online, especially on Facebook, it was a decentralized network of activists who used the tools of social media to broadcast economic and political grievances against the Mubarak regime, mobilize support, evade the government's ubiquitous security forces, and, later, help bring down the Mubarak regime. Ahmed Maher and Ahmed Salah, young members of the Kefaya opposition group, branched off and helped launch a Facebook group to promote a protest planned for April 6, 2008.[77] The movement attracted 70,000 members on Facebook, making it the largest youth movement in Egypt at the time.[78]

Members of both the April 6 Youth Movement and Kefaya were behind the creation of another popular Facebook group, one supporting Mohamed ElBaradei, the former head of the International Atomic Energy Agency (IAEA), who returned to Egypt in 2010. In June 2010, activists, led by Wael Ghonim, a Google executive, created a Facebook page called *Kullena Khaled Said* ("We are all Khaled Said") in memory of a young man who was brutally beaten to death on June 6, 2010, by two secret police officers in Alexandria.

This page attracted more than one million supporters and became the focal point for a number of large protests against state abuses in the summer of 2010. Ghonim, AbdelRahman Mansour, and many of their colleagues brought the Khaled Said case into the public consciousness by organizing several Silent Stands on June 18 and 25 and July 9, 2010, mainly organized at the corniche in Cairo and Alexandria by online activists, while also posting on the *Kullena Khaled Said* Facebook page. These online activists, as well as many bloggers, brought out more than eight thousand people on June 25, 2010, when Dr. Mohamed ElBaradei, who at the time was running as a presidential candidate, took part. It was evident that the fear barrier was broken and virtual activism had been transferred into real-world action.[79]

Solidarity with the Khaled Said cause transcended national borders, as groups from Tunisia and Yemen began creating Facebook pages in support of Egyptian online activists. Khaled's Tunisian Facebook page

---

[77] David Wolman, "All Posts Tagged Ahmed Maher: Did Egypt Detain a Top Facebook Activist?," *Wired* (February 2, 2011), www.wired.com/dangerroom/tag/ahmed-maher/. Accessed on June 21, 2001.

[78] Dina Shebata, "The Fall of the Pharaoh: How Hosni Mubarak's Reign Came to an End," *Foreign Affairs*, 90, 3 (May/June 2011), 26–32; see esp. p. 28.

[79] Ghonim, *Revolution 2.0*, p. 85.

drew over 1,000 members within two days of its launch. The triggering event for the 2011 uprisings in Egypt happened some 1,300 miles away in Tunisia, when Mohamed Bouazizi – a street fruit vendor whose cart was confiscated by the police – set himself on fire on December 17, 2010. On January 4 he died, and shortly thereafter on January 14, Tunisian President Ben Ali fled to Saudi Arabia. What happened in Tunisia encouraged and enabled Egyptians to follow suit. Wael Ghonim took the Egyptians to task by posting on the Facebook page *Kullena Khaled Said* on January 14, 2011, the following message: "Today is the 14th . . . January 25 is Police Day and it's a national holiday . . . If 100,000 take to the streets, no one can stop us . . . I wonder if we can?"[80]

The interaction of organized groups, networks, and social media was crystallized in nonviolent anti-Mubarak protests that removed long-reigned autocrat from power on February 11, 2011. These protests, some experts contend, showed that Egyptian society, much like Western societies, has transformed away from traditional media – such as TV, radio, and newspapers – toward more loosely structured "networked societies" or "network individualism," whereby there is less group control and more individual autonomy. There is no denying that social media provided affordable access to social movements by curtailing the costs of mobilization and organization, while accelerating the dissemination of information. Young men and women in Egypt were able to use social networks, the Internet, and mobile phones to access large and diversified networks, reach beyond physical and social boundaries, and exploit more resources to attempt to bring about social change.

A contrasting view holds that Egyptians have paid a hefty price for their centuries-long tradition of authoritarian rule, while still seeing the army and its iron-clad rule as the only alternative to anarchy. The result has been an accumulation of political inexperience over a longer period of time (since 1952) in terms of challenging this notion. The Western media have exaggerated the extent to which new technologies, such as the Internet, Facebook, and YouTube, have circumvented government control of print and broadcasting mass media. With the meteoric rise of the support for the authoritarian regime of el-Sisi, Thanassis Cambanis observes, it has become clear that "The Internet age hasn't reconfigured the calculus of power."[81]

---

[80] Ghonim, *Revolution 2.0*, p. 134.
[81] Thanassis Cambanis, *Once upon a Revolution: An Egyptian Story* (New York: Simon & Shuster, 2015), p. 207.

Conclusion

Understanding the Arab uprisings requires a balanced analysis of structural and historical factors, on the one hand, and an examination of the role that the element of agency played in generating revolts against authoritarianism, on the other. Studies have shown that an overemphasis on structural factors alone fails to adequately explain how strategy and the dynamics of contention remold the political context in a way that it is more favorable to the protesters and challengers.[82] While conceding that not all nonviolent uprisings within the third wave of democratization have led to regime change, some experts have nevertheless underlined the fact that unarmed insurrections have indeed promoted elite-negotiated transitions to democracy, as in South Africa, and have toppled dictatorships disinclined to negotiate, as in the Philippines.[83]

We are at once on the threshold of greater inclusion and freedom in international society propelled by Web 2.0. Perhaps never before have the times in which we live been so marked by the growth and potential for new voices and forms of expression to be transmitted in real time around the world. The interior nature of human beings, described to us as interiority by Hunt, reveals that the first stage in representing human rights discourses relies upon the grounding of the inherently aspirational nature of our present moment.[84] Here and now lies the opportunity to gain a unique understanding that examines the interior lives of our peers and activists around the world.

While this chapter has particularly drawn attention to the role that agency has played in these uprisings, and while social media and new technologies have played a crucial role in mobilizing, organizing, and resonating across the large population of young men and women who took part in the uprisings, it is worth noting that these digital acts were not sufficient to bring about lasting, positive sociopolitical change in all the cases. As a result, the euphoria with which the Arab uprisings were greeted by experts has been dissipated to a large extent by counter-revolutionary movements and developments since 2011.

The reasons why these uprisings have thus far failed to promote democracy can to some extent be laid at the door of domestic politics and external influences, particularly in terms of irreconcilable interests

---

[82] Kurt Schock, *Unarmed Insurrections: People Power Movement in Non-democracies* (Minneapolis, MN: Minnesota University Press, 2005), p. 90.
[83] Ibid.   [84] Hunt, *Inventing Human Rights*.

involved in governing these nations. The Arab uprisings have not led to full-fledged democracies except perhaps in Tunisia, due in large part to the fact that transitions to democracy or turning elections into long-standing democratic gains have been infinitely complicated. These turbulent processes have demanded not only a necessary level of economic production, political stability, and good governance, but also conducive sociological context to the expansion of the public sphere and civil society.

A key element for social change is a profound shift in the attitude of Arabs toward confronting the dogmatic and arcane patterns of the ruling class. This has given meaning to a new politics in which civil sphere movements have brought to light the new capacity for building peaceful citizenship and a nonviolent moral agent in this part of the world.[85] Internet technology has undoubtedly broadened the awareness of an individual's power and has the potential to vigorously contribute to unprecedented gains already made in the pursuit of peaceful democratic change.

Citing Richard Rorty, who had devoted his career to elevating philosophy to contend with modern conceptual liberalism that values the role of the individual over the role of change, Booth argues that the worst possibility exists in privileging inaction while gross violations of human rights continues. Moving beyond liberal agonism, as Rorty asks us to do, and embracing a reduction in human suffering is a vital and needed benefit of our present era. Web 2.0 delivers to us the possibility of recognizing interior lives, and creating positive democratic change in the world, supported and assisted by active citizens and willing policy makers, we as observers must take up the cause of peaceful transition politics or risk betraying our role as passionate advocates for justice and empathy.[86]

The Arab Spring and the uprisings that rippled from the Middle East outward and throughout the world inspired many to reconsider their preconceptions in regard to the stability of authoritarian rule. Social media and Hunt's timely notion of interiority has helped outside observers and protesters within their cohort of opposition understand and empathize with social actors around the region and around the globe. Human rights as a concept is vital to understanding the role of social media and its impact upon actors seeking to make substantial changes in

---

[85] Khosrokhavar, *The New Arab Revolutions That Shook the World*, p. 300.
[86] Booth, "Three Tyrannies," p. 61.

their political and social lives. Human rights as a body of theory and practice also allow us substantial purchase to criticize normatively dele-terious practices that we observe in contemporary politics. Without human rights, we are left empirically unable to understand a world that we wish was more inclusive and transparent. In this chapter, we have highlighted the role of social media, while claiming that it is the most active element within the Arab Spring protests. In a world that is rapidly becoming smaller and more connected, it is very important to recognize the increasing humanity and empathy that is bubbling up through digital media, at once beckoning our attention and demanding political redress and reform.

PART II

Digital dissidence and grassroots politics

Grassroots sanctions

A new tool for domestic and transnational resistance for Palestine

SHANE WESBROCK, MAHMOOD MONSHIPOURI,
AND JESS GHANNAM

Introduction

The contentious history of economic sanctions has a way of speaking to us. The debate over the expected costs and efficacy of economic sanctions, as well as whether the use of such blunt instruments of economic statecraft are warranted, continues to invite controversy. There appears to be no consensus on the utility of such tools of foreign policy, as they represent a conundrum with no easy solutions. The legal or instrumental rationale behind the sanctions policy, as well as their implementation in an undifferentiated way, has been widely questioned by some observers who have raised ethical concerns over their harsh group punishments on target, and collateral, populations.[1] Others, while conceding that sanctions are costly, have argued that, in some cases, the threat of sanctions – not their implementation – has yielded significantly desirable results.[2] Still others have noted that the search should continue, particularly at the United Nations, for ways to render sanctions policies both more effective and less costly for innocent civilians.[3]

There are many fundamental questions concerning unacceptable consequences of these economic instruments, as well as conflicting aims among those states that push for sanctions. As cases of trade embargoes

---

[1] Kimberly Ann Elliott and Gary Clyde Hufbauer, "Ineffectiveness of Economic Sanctions: Same Song, Same Refrain? Economic Sanctions in the 1990s," *The American Economic Review*, 89, 2 (May 1999), 403–8.

[2] Daniel W. Drezner, "The Hidden Hand of Economic Coercion," *International Organization*, 57 (2003), 643–59.

[3] Peter Wallensteen and Carina Staibano (eds.), *International Sanctions: Between Words and Wars in the Global System* (New York: Frank Cass, 2005), p. 13.

and economic sanctions have persisted, their objectives often appear questionable at best and futile at worst. Nations such as Cuba, North Korea, and Iran have faced recent decades of economic sanctions, while changes in their respective internal political context have been negligible. Other nations, like South Africa, have seen massive international public backlash to their policies create a global atmosphere that insisted on change.

Much of the controversy over the sanctions policy today revolves around the issues of targeting, enforcement, and duration. What determines the long-term success of a sanction policy depends largely upon whether sanctions have been applied "broadly" or have "targeted" a specific group, as well as whether they have been applied unilaterally or multilaterally. There have been two methods to launch sanctions against a targeted nation: the first through the UN Security Council and the second at the national level by, for example, the US Department of State. The latter case points to the fact that state-inspired sanctions tend to be closely wedded to a state's specific political objectives, which their enforcement is designed to serve.

In recent years, however, with the rise of social media and the range of new digital communication technologies, communities around the globe can act in solidarity and effectively launch a sanctions movement regardless of their respective governments' policies. This grassroots sanction movement, also known as the Boycott, Divestment, and Sanctions (BDS) movement, underscores the importance of the personal initiative and power of individuals and communities. It is worth noting that social media invigorates new appearances of boycotts, highlights grievances, and mobilizes activists in a way that was previously impossible. Utilizing the new methods and broader extent of digital communication facilitated by the Internet to reach audiences that have been hitherto unreachable, social media has expanded "the participation of the audiences in ways that are not simply based on action and reaction, but rather collective action as interaction."[4]

This chapter seeks to explore the potency of social media and boycott applications through a comparative analysis, specifically comparing today's BDS movement targeting Israel with the traditional grassroots movements that challenged the government of South Africa during the apartheid era. Additionally, we gauge how technology has enhanced

---

[4] Toni Sant, "Art, Performance, and Social Media," in Jeremy Hunsinger and Theresa Senft (eds.), *The Social Media Handbook* (New York: Routledge, 2014), pp. 45–58; see p. 51.

international boycotts by comparing current efforts targeting Israel to those waged against South Africa a quarter century ago. We will measure the effect of grassroots sanctions using three metrics: (1) the degree to which social media enhances organization on the grassroots level; (2) the impact of grassroots sanctions on businesses, churches, and communities while examining their subsequent reactions; and (3) how targeted governments react to grassroots sanctions movements. In the sections that follow, we examine how grassroots sanctions have been enhanced through technology and what ultimate effect they have on societies where one group is elevated at the expense of another, using contemporary Israel and late twentieth-century South Africa as the primary case studies.

A paradigm shift in resistance strategy

With the failure of the Oslo Peace Process, deteriorating living conditions in Palestine, the continued expansion of Jewish settlements in the occupied territories, and Israel's ongoing domination over natural and other resources of the occupied territories, Palestinians have discovered the power within themselves to alter their own ideational and material conditions to achieve freedom, justice, and ultimately peace.[5] A collective paradigm shift has emerged with the transformation and resilience of the Palestinian struggle toward more sophisticated and nonviolent forms of resistance. Increasingly, Palestinian communities, scholars, practitioners, policymakers, journalists, and activists have turned to constructive and practical ways to attain social change, justice, human rights, and democracy. This viewpoint is informed by the theory of conflict transformation in power asymmetries that relies on nonviolent direct action and resistance by posing challenges to established methods of exercising social change and settling conflicts such as courts, legislature, lobbying, mediation, negotiation, or elections.[6] In addition, the collapse and failure of the Oslo Accords prompted Palestinian civil society groups to take ownership over their destiny and not rely on outside state actors, stakeholders, and interest groups. This represents a

[5] Mazin Qumsiyeh, "Evolution of Armed to Unarmed Resistance in Palestine," in Véronique Dudouet (ed.), *Civil Resistance and Conflict Transformation: Transitions from Armed to Nonviolent Struggle* (New York: Routledge, 2015), pp. 77–99.

[6] Véronique Dudouet, "Nonviolent Resistance and Conflict Transformation in Power Asymmetries," Berghof Research Center for Constructive Conflict Management (September 2008), http://edoc.vifapol.de/opus/volltexte/2011/2586/pdf/dudouet_handbook.pdf. Accessed on January 16, 2015, pp. 1–27; see p. 5.

dramatic shift in the locus of control for Palestinians, away from externally driven forces to a more internally driven engagement with their future.

The nonviolent resistance strategy, according to this perspective, fosters popular empowerment, ratchets up the pressure on opponents, and attracts the interest of powerful third parties, while providing a stronger position from which to negotiate. In most contexts of occupation and oppression, this strategy might be the only way to actively pursue justice and democracy in a peaceful and constructive way. Yet, it is equally important to realize that in highly polarized conflicts, such a transformation can unfold only through multiple forms of intervention, from negotiation, dialogue, external mediation to nonviolent activism and cross-border advocacy.[7]

Global awareness and interest in justice for Palestinians has increased in recent years as independent media, such as the film *Five Broken Cameras*, has focused attention on the brutal occupation of Palestine. The film, shot by the Palestinian farmer Emad Burnat in the West Bank village of Bil'in, documents the theft of Palestinian land by Jewish settlers. Jewish settlers lay claim and confiscate Palestinian-owned territory by simply putting containers or other structures on the land. Because the Israeli Defense Forces have a mandate to protect Jewish settlers and their property, the military defends the illegally placed containers with force, thus prohibiting Palestinians from accessing their own land. Once the military is in place, settlers then move to build permanent structures. Although the wholesale theft of land in this fashion is not legal under Israeli or international law, the military protection of the settlers amounts to *de facto* policy of land confiscation.

Five Broken Cameras also chronicles the peaceful protests of the people of Bil'in. One method these Palestinians use is to plant their own containers on their land, which the Israeli forces then promptly remove. The people of the villages regularly march to protest the Israeli separation wall and the loss of land to Israeli settlers. However, their peaceful efforts are often met with tear gas and bullets from the Israeli military. In the process of their activism, many members of the community in Bil'in are arrested, seriously wounded, or killed. This gives rise to the question as to whether tandem international activism in the

---

[7] Ibid., pp. 20–21.

form of boycotts – which lies outside the reach of the Jewish settlers and Israeli military – might be effective.

In the Israeli-Palestinian conflict, according to one expert, international activism complementary to the peaceful resistance seen in *Five Broken Cameras* was never previously utilized. Armed resistance during the first *intifada* failed to win over tangible forms of third-party support, and the ensuing mediated negotiation processes failed to guarantee the successes of the Palestinian uprising. The second *intifada*, by contrast, was marked by several cross-border solidarity activities, but the active nonviolent resistance of Palestinian villages, disrupted by the so-called security barrier, has been all but eclipsed by the armed strategies of the militant groups. This nonviolent strategy has yet to lead to any meaningful peacemaking or peacebuilding initiatives and processes.[8]

The BDS movement, which was started in 2005 by Palestinian civil society, is a systematic attempt to boycott Israeli products, divest from Israeli businesses and financial enterprises, and apply sanctions against Israel unless it complies with international law and Palestinian inalienable rights. From an organizational standpoint, the BDS movement has assumed two prevalent forms: maintaining direct engagement with elected officials through lobbying efforts and building and widening popular global support through education, information, and mobilization.[9]

The latter strategy has been given a major boost by social media. One of the most popular applications (or apps) is called "Buycott." With this application, users can scan universal barcodes on products with their smartphone cameras to determine whether actions of the product's producers are consistent with the consumer's politics. Use of the application is a growing phenomenon; for example, one boycott campaign called "Free Palestine" gained 403,246 users in only five months. With use of such applications, global political-economic prowess is being technologically diffused to the population.

Grassroots activist groups exist in a decentralized system with no hierarchical leadership with whom nation-states can develop dialogue and negotiations. Lack of centralization creates a scenario in which

---

[8] Ibid., p. 21.

[9] Brian Aboud, "Organizing and the Boycott, Divestment, Sanctions (BDS) Strategy: The Turn to BDS in Palestine Politics in Montreal," in Aziz Choudry, Jill Hanley, and Eric Shragge (eds.), *Organize! Building from the Local for Global Justice* (Oakland, CA: PM Press, 2012), pp. 202–15; see pp. 213–14.

leaders of targeted states will be beholden to their constituents and eventually forced to respond to global boycott actions. This chapter's central argument is that if individuals use social media and boycott-oriented smartphone applications to launch grassroots sanctions, then targeted nations will be forced to respond and be held accountable. Furthermore, the response will be dictated by the structure of the activism; with use of social media, individual activists functionally differentiate themselves from their respective state systems, engaging in a new form of transnational and/or international society that can practice economic statecraft.

Social media: consumer-generated information

Until recently, information was relatively localized by region. The information that was available was filtered through editors and management before being disseminated in a way that supported a narrow worldview, the perspective of the most powerful news agencies. Small groups of people determined content relevance and its ability to sell newspapers or cable television subscriptions. With an inequality of voices, information proliferated with an agenda other than informing the public.

Social media changes this power dynamic. Limitations of locality are negated because people can now pull from a large variety of sources and repost news articles better representing their views. Social media users take the role of editor, determining which articles and information are important. Users of social media, instead of seeing only a few headlines while passing newsstands, now see a broader and deeper aggregate of information from a variety of viewpoints, decentralizing media. Exposure to this larger and more varied flow of information and messaging is changing global perspectives and interest in international issues.

As social media spreads globally, we can observe the differences in international reactions to similar events. In 2008 and 2009, Israel launched a twenty-two-day attack in Gaza called Operation Cast Lead. During the offensive, approximately 1,400 Palestinians were killed, and 300 children were among the dead.[10] A little over five years later, in 2014, Israel launched Operation Protective Edge, a fifty-one-day attack that would leave 2,192 Palestinians dead, mostly civilians. Of the dead,

---

[10] "Israel/Gaza: Operation 'Cast Lead': 22 Days of Death and Destruction," Amnesty.org (2009), www.amnesty.org/ar/library/asset/MDE15/015/2009/en/8f299083-9a74-4853–860f-0563725e633a/mde150152009en.pdf.

519 were children. Approximately 18,000 homes were destroyed, and 108,000 residents of Gaza were left homeless.[11]

There have been countless complaints about the way the mainstream American media covers the conflict taking place between Israel and the Palestinians. Typically, major news organizations tend to be slanted toward the Israeli perspective. In 2014, however, the Palestinian perspective seems to have had a much farther reach than it did in 2008. This is evident by the international protests that took place in many major cities around the world. In Paris, London, San Francisco, and New York, people took to the streets en masse to show solidarity with the people of Gaza. The extent of the protests against Israeli actions was unprecedented. Along with civil protest, there was a notable acceleration in the BDS movement, which we will explain in the sections that follow.

The evolution in the reaction to the two Israeli military offensives mentioned above appears to coincide with increasing use of social media. In the beginning of 2008, approximately 30 percent of adult Internet users engaged with social media. Between 2008 and 2009, that number jumped to approximately 50 percent. As of January 2014, 74 percent of adult Internet users were using social media, as illustrated in Figure 5.1 below.[12] This increased Internet usage appears to correlate with international action taken in response to Israel's military adventures in Gaza.

Analysis of current data on the use of social media for political action shows significant trends. According to a report published in 2013, 72 percent of the adults using social media engaged in some sort of online political activity. In fact, social media users appear to be more engaged than people who are not using social media, as illustrated in Figure 5.2 below.[13] Greater availability of information via social media, in conjunction with increased civic engagement among social media users, may explain the different reactions to the two attacks on Gaza mentioned above.

One of the most striking aspects of the data that show a correlation between social media and Internet activism comes from Facebook. Facebook is the most widely used social media on the planet today. In 2008,

[11] "Families under the rubble: Israeli attacks on inhabited homes," Amnesty.org (2014), www.amnesty.org/en/library/asset/MDE15/032/2014/en/613926df-68c4-47bb-b587-00975f 014e4b/mde150322014en.pdf.

[12] Pew Research Internet Project, "Social Networking Fact Sheet," www.pewinternet.org/ fact-sheets/social-networking-fact-sheet/#. Accessed on November 22, 2014.

[13] Aaron Smith, "Civic Engagement in the Digital Age," *Pew Research Internet Project*, last modified April 25, 2013, www.pewinternet.org/2013/04/25/civic-engagement-in-the-digital-age/.

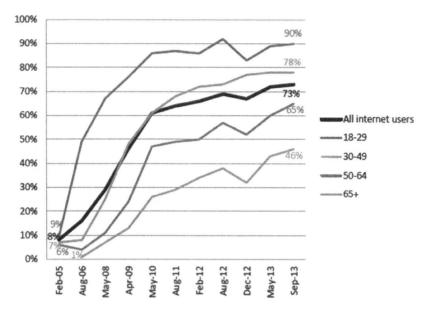

Figure 5.1   Social networking site use by age group, 2005–2013

Percent of internet users in each age who use social networking sites, over time.
Source: Latest data from Pew Research Center's Internet Project Library Survey,
July18–September 30, 2013. N=5,112 Internet users ages 18+. Interviews were conducted
in English and Spanish and on landline and cell phones. The margin of error for results
based on Internet users is +/− 1.6 percentage points.

during Operation Cast Lead, Facebook had only about 100 million users.
In 2014, this number has grown to an astonishing 1.35 billion active
users. Facebook members are connected across the continents, allowing
easy sharing of information around the globe. It is not uncommon for
someone in Copenhagen to post the same article as someone in Sri Lanka
or San Francisco. The use of Facebook allows individuals to differentiate
themselves from their respective traditional societal contexts along political lines, creating an international society of sorts. It could be that the
growth of Facebook alone between 2008 and 2014 is responsible for the
recent global reaction to Israel's attack on Gaza.[14]

---

[14] "Number of Monthly Active Facebook Users Worldwide from 3rd Quarter 2008 to 3rd
Quarter 2014 (in Millions)," *Statista.com*, www.statista.com/statistics/264810/number-of-
monthly-active-facebook-users-worldwide/. Accessed on November 22, 2014.

	% of SNS users who have done this	% of all adults who have done this
"Like" or promote material related to political/social issues that others have posted	38%	23%
Encourage other people to vote	35	21
Post your own thoughts/comments on political or social issues	34	20
Repost content related to political/social issues	33	19
Encourage others to take action on political/social issues that are important to you	31	19
Post links to political stories or articles for others to read	28	17
Belong to a group that is involved in political/social issues, or working to advance a cause	21	12
Follow elected officials, candidates for office or other public figures	20	12
Total who said yes to any of the activities listed above	66%	39%

Figure 5.2 **Political engagement on social networking sites.**
Sixty percent of American adults use social networking sites (SNS) such as Facebook or Twitter; these are some of the civic behaviors they have taken part in on these sites.

Buycott application

Online mobilization tools and activities related to the Israeli-Palestinian conflict were widely used well before the rise of social media. Grassroots Web campaigns reached their pinnacle since the outbreak of the second *intifada* in September 2000. Most of these campaigns have been led by international and local nongovernmental organizations (NGOs).[15] Prior to the rise of social networking sites such as Facebook and Twitter, the blogosphere was the key platform for online grassroots advocacy. With the rise of social media, however, Web campaigns became decentralized and adapted to the unique characteristics of each platform. Social media have since been used to mobilize opposition activities within Palestine and Israeli society.

[15] Anat Ben-David, "Israeli-Palestinian Conflict," in Kerric Harvey (ed.), *Encyclopedia of Social Media and Politics*, Vol. 2 (Los Angeles: Sage Publications, 2014), pp. 740–43; see p. 740.

The BDS movement has gained remarkable traction worldwide and has created a substantial network of activities that use social media to mobilize support for the recognition of statehood for the Palestinians and criticize the West Bank administration's approach to achieve this goal.[16] Omar Barghouti, a founding committee member of the Palestinian Campaign for the Academic and Cultural Boycott of Israel (PACBI), as well as a cofounder of the BDS movement, argues that the growing BDS movement provides the most moral, apt, and potent mechanism for conducting resistance against the Israeli occupation of Palestine. The BDS movement, Barghouti insists, represents a qualitatively "new stage" in the history of Palestinian resistance to colonization and occupation.[17]

The implications of social media's growth and its relationship to political activity are important to understanding the dynamics of grass-roots sanctions. This chapter investigates a specific aspect of social media activism and presents the growth and evolution from boycott to what is effectively a grassroots sanction. The new Buycott application allows users to avoid products that are not in line with their political ideology. The application is relevant to the conversation because it provides a user-friendly platform to those looking to engage in economic activism.

Buycott was developed by a twenty-six-year-old programmer to allow consumers to boycott businesses that they deemed unethical. It became available for use in 2013.[18] The application is downloaded from the Internet and allows shoppers to scan items with their smartphones. The various campaigns available on the application range from saving rain forests to avoiding genetically modified crops. With the Buycott application, campaigns are user-generated and the application itself is neutral, giving no advantage to any one particular perspective.

On April 13, 2014, a sixteen-year-old Briton named Luke Burgess created a campaign for the Buycott application called "Long Live Palestine Boycott Israel."[19] For almost three months, Burgess's application saw

---

[16] Ibid., p. 742.

[17] Omar Barghouti, *Boycott, Divestment, Sanctions: The Global Struggle for Palestinian Rights* (Chicago, IL: Haymarket Books, 2011), p. 61.

[18] Calire O'Connor, "New App Lets You Boycott Koch Brothers, Monsanto and More by Scanning Your Shopping Cart," *Forbes* (May 14, 2013), www.forbes.com/sites/clareocon nor/2013/05/14/new-app-lets-you-boycott-koch-brothers-monsanto-and-more-by-scan ning-your-shopping-cart/.

[19] Jonah Lowenfeld, "How One 16-Year-Old Brit Mobilized a Mobile App against Israel," *Jewish Journal* (July 29, 2014), www.jewishjournal.com/thenon-prophet/item/how_one_ 16_year_old_brit_mobilized_a_mobile_app_against_israel.

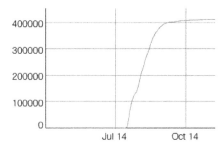

Figure 5.3 Growth in followers of the "Long Live Palestine Boycott Israel" campaign.

little activity. On July 8, the day that Israel began Operation Protective Edge, the campaign had only 470 followers.[20] By October 2014, the campaign, mostly publicized through social media, had grown to over 400,000 followers.

Figure 5.3 shows the growth in followers of the "Long Live Palestine Boycott Israel" campaign. We can see by this chart that the campaign rapidly gained membership as soon as Operation Protective Edge began. By the time the fighting stopped, on August 26, 2014, however, this graph begins to show a decline in growth, and finally levels off by October. This rapid growth and leveling-off trend suggests that this campaign can sustain growth only when Israel and the Palestinians are engaged in major conflict.

The Buycott application is a new tool in the BDS movement that has been established as an effective nonviolent strategy in the pursuit of justice and equality in Palestine. The BDS paradigm, according to some experts, has aimed to promote health rights and improvement in the health-related quality of life for Palestinians.[21] Others have regarded BDS action as a life-saving antidote to violence. Keen to advocate solidarity, partnership, and joint progress, BDS action has served the pursuit of peace, equality, and justice for the Palestinians under the occupation.[22]

---

[20] Patricia Sabga, "Campaign to Boycott Israel Gains Ground," *Al Jazeera* (August 13, 2014), http://america.aljazeera.com/watch/shows/real-money-with-alivelshi/articles/2014/8/13/campaign-to-boycottisraelgainsground.html.

[21] Jess Ghannam, "Health and Human Rights in Palestine: The Siege and Invasion of Gaza and the Role of the Boycoott, Divestment and Sanctions Movement," in Mahmood Monshipouri (ed.), *Human Rights in the Middle East: Frameworks, Goals, and Strategies* (New York: Palgrave Macmillan, 2011), pp. 245–61; see pp. 245–46.

[22] Udi Alonie, filmmaker and artist, quoted in "Boycotts, Divestments and Sanctions," in Mazin B. Qumsiyeh, *Popular Resistance in Palestine: A History of Hope and Empowerment* (London: Pluto Press, 2011), pp. 206–26; see p. 206.

A 2004 ruling by the International Court of Justice (ICJ) established the illegality of the Israeli apartheid wall or security barrier in 2004. Palestinian civil society has called for BDS actions against Israel until the latter complies with international law and the universal principles of human rights.[23] One core component of the BDS paradigm is an international grassroots movement referred to as the academic and cultural boycott of Israeli products made in settlements (ACBI).[24]

It should be noted, however, that the Buycott application's growth seems limited to periods of conflict. In global terms, the number of subscribers to the "Long Live Palestine Boycott Israel" campaign has little significance. At just over 400,000 followers the subscribers to this campaign are likely a fraction of the overall participants in the BDS movement. Nonetheless, this new tool of nonviolent political action may develop into an effective weapon in the BDS arsenal.

Technological advances from the 1980s to present

In the 1980s the world became better connected as technology advanced communication. Cable television allowed cultural influences to spread globally before the availability of the Internet. Although apartheid in South Africa had been in place since 1948, little international pressure had been applied to counter it. There existed a cultural disconnect between the seemingly remote nation of South Africa and the rest of the industrialized world. As people throughout the world felt more connected to the plight of black South Africans, individuals around the world moved to promote social freedoms through economic activism. One of the ways that antiapartheid messages were spread was through music, an industry with an increasingly global reach at the time.

Musician Peter Gabriel released "Biko," a song about martyred black South African activist Stephen Biko, in 1980. Gabriel's lyrics have the clear purpose of highlighting the human tragedy of apartheid. Some time later, actor and musician Steven "Little Stevie" Van Zandt was inspired by the song "Biko" and decided to create an antiapartheid collaboration called Artists United against Apartheid. The group released a single called "Sun City" in 1985. Sun City was the name of an elite resort in South Africa where many famous musicians played for wealthy white tourists. The single encouraged musicians to boycott the

---

[23] Ibid., p. 17.   [24] Ibid., p. 246.

Sun City venue by refusing to perform there. The project also served to shame other artists who did not honor the boycott. The album recorded by the group is now on *Rolling Stone*'s 100 Best Albums of the Eighties list.[25]

In the 1980s other artists followed suit and came out with their own antiapartheid songs. For example, British ska band The Special A.K.A. wrote a song called "Free Nelson Mandela" in 1984. Before the advent of social media, cable music television was a strong new medium for spreading the antiapartheid message. Although South African apartheid began in 1948, the technology to apply global pressure to the regime did not arrive until much later. As communication technology increased in the 1980s, people became aware of social issues abroad. Businesses were suddenly susceptible to a new paradigm requiring them to maintain a higher level of ethics in their transactions abroad. International boycotts spurred by musicians and activists led Coca-Cola, for example, to announce that they would cut ties with South Africa in 1986.[26]

Many artists have spoken out against Israel as well, at significant risk to their careers and reputations. Such actions are almost always met with accusations of anti-Semitism. In the summer of 2014, actors Javier Bardem and Penelope Cruz published an open letter that was critical of Israel. They later were forced to "clarify" a portion of their statement and revert to a softer stance.[27] In spite of the catch-22 of being labeled an anti-Semite for speaking out about human rights, one actor recently (although unintentionally) brought added attention to BDS.

The young movie star Scarlett Johansson unwittingly became the catalyst who bolstered the BDS movement in 2014. In January of that year Johansson accepted a position as spokesperson for SodaStream, an Israeli company that manufactures carbonated beverage home systems in a factory illegally located in the West Bank. Since 2007, Johansson had been serving as global ambassador for Oxfam, a British famine relief

---

[25] "100 Best Albums of the Eighties," *Rolling Stone,* www.rollingstone.com/music/lists/100-best-albums-of-the-eighties-20110418/artists-united-against-apartheid-sun-city-20110330. Accessed on November 24, 2014.

[26] Bill Sing, "Coca-Cola Acts to Cut All Ties with S. Africa," *New York Times* (September 18, 1986), http://articles.latimes.com/1986-09-18/news/mn-11241_1_south-africa.

[27] Loulla-Mae Eleftheriou-Smith, "Penelope Cruz and Javier Bardem Face 'Fury' of Hollywood Following 'Genocide' Letter Condemning Israel," *The Independent* (August 10, 2014), www.independent.co.uk/news/people/cruz-and-bardem-face-fury-of-hollywood-following-genocide-letter-condemning-israel-9659707.html.

organization.[28] The apparent hypocrisy of these two roles was well noticed by Facebook and Twitter users, leading to viral memes criticizing the actress. Whereas ten years ago, Johansson may have taken on both roles unnoticed, in the age of social media she found herself under a microscope and criticized for her apparent hypocrisy. As she stepped down from Oxfam, the issue of Israeli occupation exploded on social media and other news outlets.

The unwanted social media attention surrounding Johansson and SodaStream significantly damaged the company's profits. SodaStream faced massive divestment, and company shares fell 53 percent from the same period the previous year. Their third-quarter revenue fell by 13.5 percent. Although SodaStream offered a variety of reasons for the decline in their stocks, they omitted BDS as possible factor.[29] However, SodaStream's subsequent actions appear to confirm BDS as the primary element responsible for the lackluster sales and decline in stock price.

On October 30, 2014, the *New York Times* reported that SodaStream would be closing their factory in the West Bank, confirming suspicions that BDS was responsible for the decline in their stock prices.[30] In analyzing the chain of events regarding Scarlett Johansson and Soda-Stream between January and October of 2014, it appears social media was the primary agent of change, damaging the stock price and forcing closure of the West Bank factory. Furthermore, the evidence also suggests that the BDS movement makes the most notable headway when precipitated by a scandal or an Israeli military adventure. Noteworthy events that increase user-generated activity on social media lead to increased BDS activity and support.

Use of social media and events such as the Scarlett Johansson scandal allow for quick normalization of ideas in ways that were not possible during South African apartheid. The African National Congress, for example, called for boycotts in 1958; however, boycotts had no significant

[28] Vijay Prishad, "Scarlet Johansson Is Right – the Face of SodaStream Doesn't Fit with Oxfam," *The Guardian* (January, 30, 2014), www.theguardian.com/commentisfree/2014/jan/30/scarlett-johansson-sodastream-oxfam-israeli-settlement.

[29] Samantha Sharf, "SodaStream Shares Plunge to All-Time Low on 53% Income Decline," *Forbes* (October 7, 2014), www.forbes.com/sites/samanthasharf/2014/10/07/sodastream-shares-plunge-to-all-time-low-on-53-income-decline/.

[30] Jodi Rudorin, "Israeli Firm, Target of Boycott, to Shut West Bank Plant," *New York Times* (October 30, 2014), www.nytimes.com/2014/10/31/world/middleeast/sodastream-to-close-factory-in-west-bank.html?_r=0.

impact until the 1980s.[31] The call for change in South Africa finally resonated when values became more interconnected through pop culture and media. As the age of computer technology and user-generated media overtakes the cable television 24-hour news cycle, social values and actions can filter through international society at a much quicker pace than ever before. People around the world not only are more aware of social justice movements abroad, but are also endowed with an opportunity to act through economic activism.

Ripple effects

Boycotts, which are now being promoted on the Internet through social media, stopped consumers from purchasing many Israeli products, particularly by the beginning of Operation Protective Edge. Once consumers began to stray from Israeli goods in July 2014, merchants began canceling orders for Israeli products. By August 2014, Ireland's largest food distributor, SuperValu, announced that it was withdrawing Israeli-produced goods from the shelves of its 232 stores.[32] While it might be expected that some in a country like Ireland, with its own colonial history, might support the boycott of Israeli products, Israeli produce growers also suffered order cancellations from France, the UK, and Scandinavian countries.[33] As consumers take part in the grassroots sanctions, retailers are forced to respond to their demands.

One major online retailer has illustrated the ripple effects of BDS by choosing to no longer distribute products produced in the West Bank. The online shopping site Gilt, which has more than 6 million members, has removed Ahava Dead Sea cosmetics from its website. Ahava, a Jewish Israeli company, harvests minerals from Palestinian land on the Dead Sea for international sale in the form of beauty products. Although Gilt's elimination of Ahava from their product line was largely a result of correspondence with Code Pink, we can assume that increased BDS

---

[31] Adrian Guelke, *Rethinking the Rise and Fall of Apartheid* (New York: Palgrave Macmillan, 2005), pp. 195–96.

[32] Joyce Fegan, "SuperValu Boycotts Israeli Products," *Herald.ie* (August 5, 2014), www.herald.ie/news/supervalu-boycotts-israeli-products-30483160.html.

[33] Michael Deas, "Ireland's Biggest Food Retailer Drops Israeli Produce as European Boycotts Surge," *Electronic Intefada* (August 15, 2014), http://electronicintifada.net/blogs/michael-deas/irelands-biggest-food-retailer-drops-israeli-produce-european-boycotts-surge.

awareness was at least partially responsible for the action.[34] Gilt, after all, utilizes three social media platforms for its advertising.[35]

Grassroots sanction campaigns can filter up and infiltrate every area of life, as we can see with the United Methodist Church's divestment from Israel. The church's website defines apartheid and thoroughly explains how Israel fits the definition.[36] As a result, the church refuses to invest in firms that they deem to support apartheid in Israel or the West Bank in their business practices. This type of filtering up becomes economically dangerous to large corporations, effectively issuing an ultimatum to choose between Israel and the world.

One corporation that has responded to such an ultimatum is Africa Israel Investments. A subsidiary of the company, Danya Cebus, has been a major builder of illegal settlements in the West Bank and East Jerusalem for years. Between protests and divestments from the company over their practices, however, the company realized that it cannot be considered a legitimate business partner in the international community as long as it maintains its controversial practices. As of October 2014, the company announced that it would no longer be in the illegal settlement business.[37]

A major lightning rod in US–Israel relations is the ever-growing security industry. Many citizens find problematic elements in the security aspect of the relationship between the two states. In September 2014, an annual trade show took place in Oakland, California, called Urban Shield. This trade show, which promotes advanced weaponry for use on civilian populations, was met with a significant protest, spread largely via Facebook and Twitter. Although the protests were largely based out of concerns that the Oakland police were far too militarized and had violated human rights in the past, another of the most significant complaints was that part of the Israeli security apparatus was involved in the

---

[34] Adam Horowitz, "BDS Victories: Online Retailer Drops Ahava; Kuwait Boycotts Companies with Settlement Ties," *Mondoweiss* (October 29, 2014), http://mondoweiss.net/2014/10/victories-companies-settlement.

[35] Laura Stampler, "Gilt's Susan Lyne: Selling on Facebook 'Was Like Trying to Sell Something at a Bar,'" *Business Insider* (September 27, 2012), www.businessinsider.com/gilts-susan-lyne-on-social-media-2012-9.

[36] "Understanding United Methodist Divestment," *UnitedMethodistDivestment.com*, www.unitedmethodistdivestment.com/IsraelPractApartheid.html. Accessed on November 24, 2014.

[37] Haggai Matar, "Major Israeli Construction Company Pulls Out of Settlement Industry," *+972 Magazine* (October 27, 2014), http://972mag.com/major-israeli-construction-company-pulls-out-of-settlement-industry/98089/.

event. The protests were ultimately successful, and Mayor Jean Quan announced that Oakland would no longer host the event.[38]

BDS also filtered upward when the people of Durham, North Carolina, came together to exercise the power of their community, collectively rejecting a security company that perpetuated and profited from the oppression of Palestinians. G4S, a security contractor, has been doing business in Israel since 2007, providing both equipment and personnel. The company works in illegal settlements and impedes Palestinian freedom of movement at West Bank checkpoints. The people of Durham, in spite of the cozy US–Israel relationship, rejected a one-million-dollar contract with G4S to police civic buildings.[39] Based on the difference in the international reactions to Israeli attacks on Gaza in 2005 and 2014, Durham's action seems to demonstrate the global change in the flow of information via social media.

In the Internet era, the desires and political motivations of individuals can affect the way large corporations do business. Grassroots sanctions via social media not only can affect businesses, but also can have an expanding impact that grows horizontally and vertically. In the digital age, political boycotts can start as a seed in a church's membership and grow into church policy. They can grow organically in a community and become city or state policy. Boycotts cause businesses to reconsider their relationships with partners and vendors in order to maintain broader appeal to the consumer. Large businesses that are not consumer driven can be forced to change their activities in order to maintain credibility in the international business community.

Block the boat: enhanced outcomes in traditional protest

Until now, this chapter has primarily focused on economic action that can be taken via social media wherein people in one state divest or boycott a target state. In this section, we will discuss the use of social media to conduct direct action. Specifically, this section is about using social media to block commerce. Whereas the previous pages speak of relatively passive and risk-free actions, this section is

---

[38] "We Pushed Urban Shield out of Oakland, but the Struggle Continues!," *Facing Teargas*, http://facingteargas.org/stop-urban-shield-oakland. Accessed on November 26, 2014.

[39] "BDS Victory: Durham Drops $1 Million Contract with Israeli Occupation Profiteer," *Jewish Voice for Peace* (November 25, 2014), https://jewishvoiceforpeace.org/blog/bds-victory-durham-drops-1-million-contract-with-israeli-occupation-pr.

about actions taken by people who are less risk averse. In essence, this section seeks to show that media can enhance the outcomes of traditional protests.

The BDS movement has largely adopted methods used against South Africa in the 1980s. In 1984, longshoremen from the International Longshore and Warehouse Union (ILWU), Local 10 in San Francisco, refused to unload South African cargo from the Dutch vessel *Nedlloyd Kimberly*. For ten days local activists protested at Pier 80 in San Francisco while the South African cargo remained on the boat, untouched. Only after the federal government threatened an injunction was the cargo finally unloaded. One of the dynamics leading to success in this situation may have been the ethnic and racial makeup of the ILWU workers. About half of the union members were black, possibly indicating an awareness of the plight of other black people elsewhere in the world.[40]

Using this model, on August 16, 2014, several thousand activists marched to the Port of Oakland in an effort to keep the Israeli ship *Zim Piraeus* from unloading.[41] The Arab Resource and Organising Centre organized and promoted the action through social media. There were also handbills alerting individuals of the impending protest, which were handed out at weekly demonstrations taking place in San Francisco during Operation Protective Edge. Throughout the action, organizers made regular posts on Facebook and Twitter to alert individuals of any attempt the boat made to dock. They also used a text message alert system.

At the port, protestors picketed on the sidewalks and workers refused to pass the picket line. For four days, the boat remained unable to unload.[42] According to some sources, the *Zim Piraeus* was able to only partially unload.[43] In the months to come, similar actions took place in Los Angeles, Seattle, and Tacoma, but with limited success. On October 26, 2014, another ship, the *Zim Beijing*, was headed to Oakland, and protesters were ready to declare another victory. The *Beijing* eventually

---

[40] "Death of Nelson Mandela Recalls Decades of ILWU Support for Anti-Apartheid Struggle," *International Longshore and Warehouse Union*, www.ilwu.org/death-of-nelson-mandela-recalls-decades-of-ilwu-support-for-anti-apartheid-struggle/. Accessed on November 28, 2014.

[41] Numbers based on Shane Wesbrock estimations while witnessing the demonstration.

[42] Shane Wesbrock was present and able to witness these events firsthand.

[43] Ben Norton, "California Leads the Way in 'Block the Boat' Movement," *Mondoweiss*, October 17, 2014, http://mondoweiss.net/2014/10/california-block-movement.

diverted its course, never unloading in Oakland.[44] "The Block the Boat" movement was so successful that by October 28, 2014, the shipping company Zim had canceled future dockings at the ports of Oakland and Los Angeles.[45]

There has been substantial commentary regarding social justice actions and the role of social media. Typically, those involved with social justice movements have vested interests, and social media is indeed an intervening variable.[46] The protests against the Mubarak regime in Tahrir Square during the Arab Spring were made up of Egyptians seeking justice in Egypt; those involved in the "Green Movement" were Iranians seeking justice in Iran. In both Egypt and Iran, as in so many other places, local people did crucial work on the ground because they would ultimately be the ones affected by the outcome. Although the protests may have been aided by use of social media, they certainly were not a product of the new technology. Social media without human action is bereft of what it takes to promote a truly revolutionary change. Messages posted to social networking sites alone cannot effect formidable and sustainable change, unless they are followed up by action on the ground.[47]

Block the Boat was somewhat different because, although many of the organizers and participants were Palestinians, the action was largely comprised of local people working to affect the policies of a foreign state. Many involved did not have an obvious personal interest. This stands in stark contrast to the 1984 San Francisco action against South Africa, where many of those involved were of African descent and may have felt a sense of kinship toward black South Africans. Just as there is a gap between local actions and actions taken for an audience abroad, there is a gap between those with direct interest and those without.

In the world of social justice activism, specifically activism that seeks to boycott, divest, sanction, or otherwise interrupt commerce, social media

[44] Lena Dakessian, "Demonstrators Return to Port of Oakland to Protest Landing of Israeli Ship," *SFGate* (October 28, 2014), http://blog.sfgate.com/inoakland/2014/10/28/demon strators-return-to-port-of-oakland-to-protest-landing-of-israeli-ship/.

[45] Charlotte Solver, "Bay Area Activists Declare Victory after Israeli Carrier Cancels All Ships," *Electronic Intefada* (October 31, 2014), http://electronicintifada.net/blogs/char lotte-silver/bay-area-activists-declare-victory-after-israeli-carrier-cancels-all-ships.

[46] Mahmood Monshipouri, *Democratic Uprisings in the New Middle East: Youth, Technology, Human Rights, and US Foreign Policy* (Boulder, CO: Paradigm Publishers, 2014), p. 8.

[47] Ibid., p. 17.

can bridge this gap. Through social media, people who are not directly affected by a foreign government can passively boycott or actively participate in commerce interruption. When widely cast information appeals to moral sensibilities, even risk-averse people can divest. Those who are willing to take risks in solidarity with people abroad can be rallied with social media to participate in commerce disruption.

Increasingly, according to the *Economist*, social media and the Internet have made it possible for many Americans to see more reporting that is critical of Israel. When in late July 2014, NBC tried to reassign a reporter who had witnessed an Israeli bombardment that killed four children playing on a Gaza beach, he was reinstated after a fierce social media campaign.[48] Subsequently, an intense debate over whether Israel exaggerated Hamas's responsibility for the kidnapping and murder of three teenaged Israeli settlers has been spurred by tweets sent by reporters for the website Buzzfeed and for the BBC.[49]

Israel and grassroots sanctions: defy or comply?

The previous sections have examined the relationship between social media, individuals who participate in grassroots economic activism, and businesses associated with the target country. We already know that the South African apartheid government fell in 1994. We have also established a relationship between social media and increased BDS activity, particularly during Operation Protective Edge in 2014. The actions of the Israeli government from the end of Operation Protective Edge, at the end of August 2014, through December of that year are of particular relevance. The purpose of this section is to look at any possible correlation between the peak of the BDS movement at this time and the reaction of Israeli policy.

Days after the end of Operation Protective Edge, the Israeli government showed that it was in no mood for compromise. Although it was facing international condemnation for the thousands recently killed in the Israeli incursion in Gaza, the government immediately moved to confiscate more Palestinian land for Jewish settlement. In the largest land grab in thirty years, Israel announced that it would take four square

---

[48] The *Economist*, "Us and Them" (August, 2, 2014), www.economist.com/news/briefing/2161 0312-pummelling-gaza-has-cost-israel-sympathy-not-just-europe-also-among-americans. Accessed on January 12, 2015.

[49] Ibid.

kilometers of land in the West Bank for the expansion of the Gevaot settlement.[50] Given that Israel's West Bank settlements are already a violation of international law, the move appears to be a flippant response to global consensus, particularly after the tragedy of Gaza.

The reallocation of Palestinian-Arab land in the West Bank to the Jewish settlement was followed by an announcement in late October of 2014 by Prime Minister Benyamin Netanyahu that Israel will also build over 1,000 homes on Palestinian land in East Jerusalem. The area in question was annexed by Israel in 1967, but Israel's sovereignty over greater Jerusalem is not recognized under international law.[51] The move adds to existing housing pressures for Palestinians living in the West Bank and East Jerusalem, further degrading already intolerable living situations.

The impossibility of the housing situation in East Jerusalem and the West Bank further depletes any sense of emotional or physical security for the Palestinian people in the area. While the Israeli government often gives a green light to home building in Jewish neighborhoods and settlements, it is virtually unheard of for Arabs to acquire building permits. As Palestinian families expand, the only option is to build without permits. In response, Israel retaliates by demolishing Palestinian homes. In fact, since 1967, Israel has destroyed 27,000 Palestinian buildings.[52] In late 2014, the Israeli government stepped up demolitions of Palestinian homes as a form of collective punishment for violence committed in Jerusalem. Although the demolitions often target the homes of suspected attackers, they often leave tens of people homeless and destitute.[53] This form of collective punishment is a flagrant violation of international law.

Israel often leaves Palestinians with very little choice, maintaining an ethno-racial system that deprives them of basic human rights, privileging Jewish people, often immigrants, above them. Few legitimate channels exist for the rectification of the Palestinian grievances. The result can be

---

[50] "Israel to Take over West Bank Land," *BBC News* (September 1, 2014), www.bbc.com/news/world-middle-east-29008045.

[51] Isabel Kershner and Jodi Rudoren, "Netanyahu Expedites Plan for More Than 1,000 New Apartments in East Jerusalem," *New York Times* (October 27, 2014), www.nytimes.com/2014/10/28/world/middleeast/benjamin-netanyahu-east-jerusalem.html?_r=0.

[52] "The Facts," *The Israeli Committee against Housing Demolitions,* www.icahd.org/the-facts. Accessed on November 29, 2014.

[53] "Israel: Stop Punitive Housing Demolitions," *Human Rights Watch* (November 22, 2014), www.hrw.org/news/2014/11/21/israel-stop-punitive-home-demolitions.

uprisings, which often include rock throwing. In an effort to mitigate Israeli concerns over rock throwing, Israel has passed a draconian law that would allow sentencing Palestinians to twenty years in prison for throwing stones.[54] Jewish settlers in the West Bank often throw stones at Palestinians, but are not subject to the same harsh military laws.[55]

While taking more land, demolishing Palestinian homes, and passing laws that further discriminate against and harm Palestinians, the Israeli government is also engaging in post-ceasefire attacks on Gaza. According to one NGO, there was at least one attack per day on Gaza in September of 2014.[56] In November of 2014, the Israeli navy fired upon and injured three fishermen from Gaza.[57] Another man was murdered in November by Israeli forces in Gaza while searching for songbirds.[58] Under the circumstances, it does not appear that BDS has yet curbed Israel's belligerence toward Palestinians.

The increasingly harsh approach toward Palestinians appears to be accompanied by a rise in nationalist attitudes within the Israeli government. In November of 2014, the Israeli cabinet passed nationality legislation, which encodes the Jewish identity of the state of Israel into law.[59] While it is uncertain what the end result of this legislation may be, it appears threatening to the non-Jewish minorities who would essentially be denied national identity. History has shown that when nations begin passing laws to define national identity and exclude minorities, atrocities often follow.

Further indicating this trend toward nationalism, on November 28, 2014, Israeli foreign minister Avigdor Lieberman proposed paying Arab

---

[54] "Israeli Ministers Pass Bill Jailing Stone Throwers for 20 Years," *Russia Today,* last modified November 4, 2014, http://rt.com/news/201695-israel-stone-throwing-law/.

[55] Jamee Hadad, "In the West Bank, Israeli and Palestinian Kids Who Throw Stones Face Unequal Justice," *PRI's The World* (April 22, 2014), www.pri.org/stories/2014-04-22/west-bank-israeli-and-palestinian-kids-who-throw-stones-face-unequal-justice.

[56] Ben White, "NGO: More Than One Israeli Attack on Gaza per Day in September," *Middle East Monitor* (October 24, 2014), www.middleeastmonitor.com/blogs/politics/14842-ngo-more-than-one-israeli-attack-on-gaza-per-day-in-september.

[57] "Israeli Forces Open Fire at Gaza Fishermen, Injure 3," *Ma'an News Agency* (November 10, 2014).

[58] "Israeli Forces Shoot Dead Palestinian Man in Gaza Strip," *The Guardian* (November 23, 2014), www.theguardian.com/world/2014/nov/23/israeli-forces-shoot-dead-palestinian-man-gaza-strip.

[59] Gregg Carlstrom, "Israel Set to Make Arabs Second Class Citizens," *The Australian* (November 24, 2014), www.theaustralian.com.au/news/world/israel-set-to-make-arabs-second-class-citizens/story-fnb64oi6-1227133224679?nk=b4b52d9a24977049c97f5ed984ecc8f7.

citizens to abandon their Israeli citizenship and leave the state of Israel.[60] However, Lieberman also still maintains the revisionist ideology of Greater Israel, that Israel should acquire all Palestinian lands in the West Bank and Gaza.[61] Paying Arabs to leave would be a mere stepping stone in the process of creating an expanded Jewish state with a guaranteed Jewish majority; in the meantime it is an avenue to push more Palestinians into fragmented Bantustans. Moreover, the proposed policy solidifies a radically separatist ideology, working against any peace process and strongly countering the goals of the BDS campaign.

Extreme nationalism, particularly when unchecked, can lead to rifts within right-wing parties. In 1969, the National Party in South Africa purged members from its ranks who did not vote along party lines on specific issues.[62] Similarly, Netanyahu fired two ministers for not falling into an extreme right-wing Zionist line.[63] It appears that far-right nationalism may be a catalyst for dysfunction in governments that push policies of discrimination. If, as some scholars suggest, sanctions lead to increased nationalism – and extreme nationalism is inherently unstable – then heightened nationalism is actually a step toward the objective of the sanctions.

It is impossible to know what the future holds for Israel in the coming years. However, it is evident that during the latter part of 2014, as BDS activity has increased globally, Israel is defiant and its policymakers' actions are stubbornly resistant to any effects of the grassroots economic activism. Furthermore, at the time of this writing, Israeli actions appear to confirm the assertion that "an authoritarian government tends to become even more repressive"[64] when sanctions are imposed. However, this repression may cause internal conflict. Although we can see the

---

[60] "Offer Israeli Arabs Money to Move to Palestinian State: Lieberman," *Reuters* (November 28, 2014), www.reuters.com/article/2014/11/28/us-mideast-israel-lieberman-idUSKCN0 JC12Q20141128.

[61] Avaneesh Pandey, "Israel's Foreign Minister Urges Government to Encourage Departure of Arabs to Future Palestinian State," *International Business Times* (November 29, 2014), www.ibtimes.com/israels-foreign-minister-urges-government-encourage-departure-arabs-future-1730716.

[62] Adrian Guelke, *Rethinking the Rise and Fall of Apartheid* (New York: Palgrave Macmillan, 2005), p. 121.

[63] Peter Beaumont, "Israel Set for Elections as Netanyahu Fires Two Ministers," *The Guardian* (December 2, 2014), www.theguardian.com/world/2014/dec/02/israel-set-for-elections-netanyahu-fires-ministers.

[64] Ernest H. Preeg, *Feeling Good or Doing Good with Sanctions* (Washington, DC: CSIS Press, 1999), pp. 7–9.

profound effect that economic activism has on individual businesses, so far there appears to be no positive change in Israeli policy. The hardliners are clinging to oppression while stifling more moderate voices.

Looking ahead

The advantages and limits of grassroots sanctions advocated by Palestinians are worth addressing not only through such broad historical analysis of nonviolent resistance as a strategy to redress structural and power asymmetries, but also through examining security policies and practices pursued by Palestinian leaders in their drive for statehood. The priority for Palestinians today is an internationalization of their collective rights to achieve freedom and self-determination wherever they may be.[65] Grassroots sanctions have provided the Palestinians with the necessary, enduring, and flexible tools to achieve this goal. Additionally, modern technology has significantly transformed the manner and method with which nonviolent resistance can be exercised, allowing much more decentralized, dispersed, fluid, and community-based resistance. With the use of social media and new boycott-oriented applications, activists can now engage in economic statecraft. As greater access to information and the utility of technology increases, boycotts will likely be further utilized as grassroots sanctions.

Targeted states could eventually be forced to react due to the decentralized nature of grassroots sanctions. Social media can enhance direct action against a target country's freight lines. Although in 1984 protesters and dockworkers temporarily kept South African cargo from being unloaded for several days in San Francisco, Block the Boat, which relied heavily on social media, was more successful in disrupting commerce. Moreover, Block the Boat showed that social media can rally supporters to come out and physically engage in a cause even when they lack a personally vested interest.

We can also gauge how activism is enhanced by social media when we compare the boycotts against SodaStream in 2014 with those against Coca-Cola in the 1980s. The SodaStream case is particularly interesting, with all the intrigue of a gossip magazine and the geopolitical implications typically reserved for political or economic publications. Aside from having a further reach than the boycott of Coca-Cola, the manner in

---

[65] Michael Jansen, "Cairo's Smart Strategy," *Panorama: Gulf Today* (January 16–22, 2015), pp. 40–41; see p. 41.

which the SodaStream boycott spread transcended traditional media formats and filled a unique Internet niche.

Against the positive trends in grassroots sanctions captured in this chapter and the hopes that such broader trends have spawned, there are many challenges to such trajectories. Although social media appears to turn boycotts into grassroots sanctions, and while there is great potential for boycott applications, it is doubtful whether such boycotts will have significant impact on policies adopted in Israel. The effect of these grassroots sanctions on Israeli policy is less clear. If anything, it appears that BDS has encouraged the Israeli government's belligerence. Grassroots sanctions certainly do not seem to hinder the current right-wing Israeli government from attacking those who disagree with its policies. This appears to support the pervasive view in the literature that sanctions have limited application, even when they are grassroots sanctions. Grassroots sanctions may become a growing force within the aggregate of forces pushing for policy change in Israel, but this will require future analysis.

As we have seen, economic and social impact of the BDS movement – especially when supported by social media – is deep, direct, and palpable. It is also important to remember that unless digital activism, involving collaborative displays of collective knowledge, is complemented by many offline strategies that invoke collective action, the impact of such grassroots sanctions will be limited. This suggests that BDS and grassroots campaigns would not be enough to pressure Israel; rather, international pressure would still be needed. Grassroots sanctions may prove more valuable if related activists can capture the popular imagination. A grassroots sanction scheme may prove successful where there is complementary opposition within the target state. As Palestinians resist Israeli oppression on the ground, popular culture may influence state policy to isolate Israel. This is of particular importance in regard to US foreign policy, due to the massive foreign aid provided to Israel – roughly $3.6 billion in 2013.[66]

Going forward, pro-Palestinian activists should continue to pursue BDS efforts and work with IT professionals in order to further develop an Internet-based presence and distribute information using social media. Interested parties should promote the "Buycott" application and its "Long Live Palestine Boycott Israel" campaign. Individuals and groups

---

[66] Philip Weiss, "House Committee Votes to Give Israel Another 1/2 Billion in Aid," *Mondoweiss* (June 10, 2013), http://mondoweiss.net/2013/06/committee-another-billion.

should look for hypocrisies among businesses and public figures and seize upon opportunities to spread provocative Internet memes. Also, because Israel utilizes paid Internet propagandists (usually college students with multiple false accounts), activists should organize means to overcome their voices with the counter narrative.[67]

---

[67] "Israel to Pay Students to Defend It Online," *USA Today* (August 14, 2013), www.usatoday.com/story/news/world/2013/08/14/israel-students-social-media/2651715/.

6

Social media, Kyiv's Euromaidan, and demands for sovereignty in Eastern Ukraine

BRYON J. MORASKI

One of the most intractable problems confronting democracy's advocates involves the question of what constitutes a people deserving of an independent unit.[1] The move toward greater integration in Europe under the auspices of the European Union, for example, has done little to silence, and may have even increased, calls for independence on the continent. Elsewhere, questions about the democratic credentials of a regime may fuel separatist demands, particularly when the mobilizing forces of the Internet give greater visibility to public concerns, mass dissatisfaction, and political dissent. Thus, although democracy promoters may view new media as a welcomed addition to the toolbox of political empowerment, such optimism may be less warranted where democracy's roots are shallow, corruption is rampant, and popular trust is low.

In such cases, internal and external actors may, theoretically, use social media to foment national division and – when political and social divisions assume a geographic component – separatist conflict. This chapter considers these dynamics by focusing on demands for sovereignty in eastern Ukraine following President Viktor Yanukovych's removal from office in February 2014.

The chapter begins by highlighting the ambiguity of the implications of mobilization via the Internet and social media, drawing particular attention to the question of localized empowerment within the literature on communication technology and democratization. With this foundation laid, the work discusses the 2013–14 events leading to the deposing of Ukraine's president

The author thanks the Fulbright Program, the National University of Kyiv-Mohyla Academy in Kyiv, Ukraine, and the University of Florida for supporting fieldwork that contributed to this chapter. The work benefited from research assistance by Jung Hoon Park and Jessie-Leigh Thomas. The opinions expressed in the chapter do not reflect the positions of these institutions or individuals; the author is solely responsible for all interpretations or errors.

[1] Robert A. Dahl, *Polyarchy: Participation and Opposition* (New Haven, CT: Yale University Press, 1973), p. 193.

and considers how regional distrust and heightened levels of uncertainty combined with social media as parts of eastern Ukraine advanced demands for greater sovereignty. In general, the events preceding the removal from office of Ukraine's President, Viktor Yanukovych, nicely parallel the arguments of those who see social media as a powerful democratic tool. Yet the events that followed Yanukovych's departure suggest that social media can exacerbate the uncertainty that inherently accompanies dramatic regime change while also further politicizing existing societal divisions. Thanks in part to intervention by a meddling authoritarian neighbor, these developments quickly degenerated into demands for secession and civil war.

The uncertain effects of the Internet and social media

The potential for the Internet to complement if not contribute to separatist demands undergirds, if implicitly, the positions of both advocates of social media as a democratizing force as well as its detractors. In *Networks of Outrage and Hope*, Castells identifies networked social movements as new forms of democratic movements. By his account, networked social movements have been mobilized for a host of causes, from battling dictatorship in the Arab world to a perceived mishandling of economic crises in Europe and the United States.[2] Castells contends that the interaction between the Internet and local communities has allowed networked social movements to reconstruct the public sphere and experiment with assembly-based decision making that is autonomous from the confines of existing systems.[3] On one hand, the Internet and social media facilitate this development by permitting what Castells calls "mass self-communication."[4] On the other hand, Castells reminds the reader that social movements – even networked ones – emerge when elites (political and economic) lose the trust of the masses. Castells's point that trust is the fabric of the social contract between rulers and the ruled is one worth emphasizing, especially where societal divisions follow, if weakly, geographic lines and the regime itself is in transition.

By allowing individuals to communicate unencumbered by governmental interference, the Internet and social media, in some instances at least, may become what Diamond labels, "liberation technology":[5]

---

[2] Manuel Castells, *Networks of Outrage and Hope: Social Movements in the Internet Age* (Cambridge, UK: Polity Press, 2012), pp. 2–3.

[3] Ibid., p. 246.   [4] Ibid., p. 6.

[5] Larry Diamond, "Liberation Technology," *Journal of Democracy*, 21, 3 (2010), 69–83. Specifically, Diamond labels as liberation technology any form of information and

They allow citizens the chance "to report news, expose wrongdoing, express opinions, mobilize protest, monitor elections, scrutinize government, deepen participation, and expand the horizons of freedom."[6] Selnow takes a more poetic stance, asserting that the opportunity for feedback and interactivity on the Internet "cultivate the soul of democracy."[7] How this occurs for Selnow is particularly noteworthy: "It provides a sense of control, and its user-driven choices reinforce this medium as a metaphor for *self-determination*."[8] Thus, Selnow's work in the Balkans appears to have bred an appreciation for the Internet's potential to facilitate democratic self-rule.

While the Balkans' location in the heart of Europe may have advanced democracy's cause by linking people across borders,[9] in locales with authoritarian neighbors, especially ones that might be perceived as external homelands,[10] such cross-border ties are less likely to represent democratizing forces. In the former Soviet space, for example, a primary concern driving Russian foreign policy is the protection of Russians and Russian speakers in its "near abroad," even if those populations do not necessarily view Russia as an external homeland.[11] This dynamic has grown in salience under Russian President Vladimir Putin, as evidenced by the August 2008 war with Georgia and the current conflict in Ukraine. In some cases, then, new communication technology and social media not only may permit antidemocratic sentiments to flow across borders but also may serve those who want to divert or manipulate information on ongoing events.[12]

Similarly, Diamond tempers any unwarranted enthusiasm for the potential of "liberation technology" by noting that, like the printing press and telegraph before it, new media are merely tools, and tools that can be

---

communication technology (ICT) that can expand political, social, and economic freedom. This technology, therefore, includes computers, the Internet, mobile phones, and the innovative applications that accompany them, like new social media platforms (e.g., Facebook and Twitter); see p. 70.

[6] Ibid., p. 70.

[7] Gary W. Selnow, "The Information Age Is Fostering the Spread of Freedom and Democracy," in James D. Torr (ed.), *The Information Age* (Farmington Hills, MI: Greenhaven Press, 2003), p. 33.

[8] Ibid., p. 33; emphasis added.   [9] Ibid., p. 32.

[10] Rogers Brubaker, "National Minorities, Nationalizing States, and External Homelands in the New Europe," *Daedalus*, 124 (1995), 107–32.

[11] Lowell W. Barrington, Erik S. Herron, and Brian D. Silver, "Research Note: The Motherland Is Calling: Views of Homeland among Russians in the Near Abroad," *World Politics*, 55, 2 (2003), 290–313.

[12] Ian Bremmer, "Democracy in Cyberspace: What Information Technology Can and Cannot Do," *Foreign Affairs* (November/December, 2010), www.foreignaffairs.com/articles/66803/ian-bremmer/democracy-in-cyberspace. Accessed on November 20, 2014.

used for "both noble and nefarious purposes."[13] For present purposes, social media then may allow individuals of similar minds to aggregate and, like other information technologies before them, assist in the creation of imagined communities.[14] Just as new media can grant people opportunities to share outrage and hope, its use also can reinforce fears and fuel resentment among local communities. In turn, these local communities may either express little interest in democracy, in general, or little interest in democracy as it operates (or is expected to operate) within the state in which these communities currently reside.

The potential for social media to nurture local demands for sovereignty complements the prevailing view that the Internet's openness and nonproprietary status can undermine existing hierarchies.[15] According to Diamond, for example, one of the most direct threats to authoritarian regimes in recent years has been the ability of communication technology, starting with cell phones and SMS text messaging, to facilitate large-scale mobilization,[16] or what Rheingold calls "smart mobs."[17] Diamond's position largely reflects the role of technology in the overthrow of authoritarian rulers – though not their replacement with democratic regimes. Scholars had been quite pessimistic about the prospects for democratization in the Middle East and North Africa until the role of social media during the Arab Spring of 2010–11 captured the imagination of democracy promoters. Thanks to the proliferation of mobile devices, particularly cell phones, Internet access has expanded across the Arab world. As a result, blogs, news websites, Twitter feeds, and political Listservs emerged as the "best and perhaps the only place" where critics could reach a wide audience, where women could debate policy with men, and "where regime secrets could be exposed."[18]

One lesson of the Arab Spring, then, is that social media were instrumental in airing grievances, spreading opposition, organizing and

---

[13] Diamond, "Liberation Technology," p. 71.

[14] Benedict Anderson, *Imagined Communities: Reflections on the Origin and Spread of Nationalism* (Verso Books, 2006 [1983]).

[15] Andrew Shapiro, "The Information Age May Not Foster Democracy," in Torr (ed.), *The Information Age*, p. 52.

[16] Diamond, "Liberation Technology."

[17] Howard Rheingold, *Smart Mobs: The Next Social Revolution* (New York: Basic Books, 2003).

[18] Philip N. Howard and Muzammil M. Hussain, "The Role of Digital Media," in Larry Diamond and Marc F. Plattner (eds.), *Democratization and Authoritarianism in the Arab World* (Baltimore, MD: Johns Hopkins University Press, 2014), p. 42.

coordinating protests, and driving coverage by mainstream media. These dynamics may prove amenable to separatism as easily as the overthrow of an authoritarian regime. Of course, social media alone cannot bring down regimes, and one should not expect them to be the primary explanation for state dissolution. For cyber activism to succeed in the dismantling of the status quo, it needs action by people on the ground.[19] That is, while digital media can help "turn individualized, localized, and community-specific dissent into a structured movement with a collective consciousness,"[20] a collective consciousness alone is not enough. Successful protest requires a physical presence. Only with the sight of thousands of people in the streets opposing the regime will international actors, for example, take notice or lend support.[21]

Large-scale protests also may generate an interaction effect between social media and traditional news outlets. According to Bunt, Iran's 2009 "Green Revolution" became a template for social network activism by demonstrating how relatively small protests can gain momentum and size as events that circulate on social media garner local, national, and international media coverage.[22] The fact that domestic and satellite television relied on clips captured by cell phones and additional information disseminated via online posts testifies to this "symbiosis" in the Iranian case.[23] Lotan et al.'s work also points to a symbiotic relationship between mainstream media outlets and new media, Twitter in particular. By tracing information flows during the 2011 Tunisian and Egyptian revolutions, Lotan et al. find that interactions between activists

---

[19] In Egypt, ironically, one reason why so many Egyptian protesters went to Tahrir Square was the Mubarak regime's decision to clamp down on Internet access, thus depriving much of Egypt's urban youth of an online outlet. See Michael S. Doran, "The Impact of New Media: The Revolution Will Be Tweeted," in Kenneth M. Pollack et al., *The Arab Awakening: America and the Transformation of the Middle East* (Washington, DC: Brookings Institution Press, 2011), p. 44.

[20] Howard and Hussain, "The Role of Digital Media," p. 41.

[21] See Doran, "The Impact of New Media," p. 44. At the same time, such protests may benefit from their egalitarian nature. Since the organization of such "smart mobs" tends to be leaderless (see Rheingold, *Smart Mobs*), authoritarian regimes struggle to contain them using conventional tactics. According to Doran, Tunisia's secret police were busy trying to hunt down a subversive organization and failed to realize that "the most dangerous opposition network actually had no leader and no organization" (ibid., p. 42).

[22] Gary R. Bunt, "Mediterranean Islamic Expression: Web 2.0," in Cesare Merlini and Olivier Roy (eds.), *Arab Society in Revolt: The West's Mediterranean Challenge* (Washington, DC: Brookings Institution Press, 2012), p. 85.

[23] Ibid.

and journalists generated more retweets than other interactions.[24] For these authors, the results support the argument that news on Twitter is mutually constructed by bloggers and activists alongside journalists.[25]

Not all causes, of course, turn "slacktivists" – those Internet users content with simply liking a cause on Facebook[26] – into street protesters. A medium can function as a mobilizing agent only if the message disseminated resonates with its audience, and this requires a message that maps onto existing grievances. In the case of Egypt's 2011 revolution, Carapico contends that the metaphor of a digital or Twitter revolution confuses the medium with the message.[27] While Carapico does not deny the critical role of Internet users and how forums like the "We Are All Khalid Said" Facebook page allowed them to reach wider audiences around the country and abroad, she gives more credit to the message of Khalid Said's mother, Umm Khalid, in a YouTube video. In that video, Umm Khalid implored her countrymen and women to show solidarity against police brutality on Police Day. For Carapico, it was a mother's plea that galvanized moral outrage, not the electronic medium that delivered the message.[28] In Tunisia, meanwhile, the lavish lifestyle of President Zine al-Ábidine Ben Ali, which had been documented and publicized for years by a Tunisian blogger known as Astrubal, took on new salience when Ben Ali visited the bedside of the self-immolated fruit vendor, Mohammed Bouazizi, in December 2010.[29] For Castells, such outrages and juxtapositions capture a common desire among networked social movements to find dignity amid suffering and humiliation.[30] Additionally, one might argue that the public display of another's actions can serve as a catalyst, one that mobilizes those people whose utility preferences had been on the cusp. Given the right ordering of individual utility preferences in society, then, the action by one individual may result in a cascade effect that brings throngs of people to the streets. While Kuran offered this explanation to understand the

---

[24] Glad Lotan, Erhardt Graeff, Mike Ananny, Devin Gaffney, Ian Pearce, and Danah Boyd, "The Revolutions Were Tweeted: Information Flows during the 2011 Tunisian and Egyptian Revolutions," *International Journal of Communication*, 5 (2011), 1375–1405.

[25] Ibid., pp. 1399–400.   [26] Doran, "The Impact of New Media," p. 41.

[27] Sheila Carapico,"Egypt's Civic Revolution Turns 'Democracy Promotion' on Its Head," in Bahgat Korany and Rabab El-Mahdi (eds.), *Arab Spring in Egypt: Revolution and Beyond* (Cairo: The American University in Cairo Press, 2012), p. 212.

[28] Ibid., pp. 212–13.   [29] Doran, "The Impact of New Media," p. 42.

[30] Castells, *Networks of Outrage and Hope*, p. 3.

unexpected nature of the 1989 revolutions against communism,[31] the logic fits other settings well and suggests that social media may allow more signals of discontent to be sent more often and received by a wider audience.

Still, most scholars assess the role that social media plays in revolutionary events with caution. Howard and Hussain, for example, emphasize that although journalists tend to focus on the visible use of technology, social scientists generally identify additional factors to explain the upheavals and are even more reticent to conclude that revolutionary events will lead to a consolidated democracy.[32] Bunt, meanwhile, notes that longstanding issues like regional economic and social deprivation, dissatisfaction with the government, the lack of political accountability, and human rights abuses helped spur the Arab Spring.[33] Doran not only concurs, but also submits that victorious protests do not end the battle between freedom and oppression: "Dictators have the capacity to learn, and the clever ones find ways to exploit the Internet to their advantage."[34]

Authoritarian regimes have developed the ability to filter and control the Internet as well as identify and punish their opponents.[35] Many states also deploy a wide range of legal strategies to control information technology and its users. These strategies include expanding laws that regulate traditional press, mandating the registration of online journalists and bloggers or requiring them to join state-controlled associations, intensively prosecuting for defamation, criminalizing traditional forms of protest, passing special laws that prohibit communication with foreign countries during potentially volatile periods, and banning or sanctioning information sharing with countries identified as enemy states.[36]

While dictators may initially be skeptical of the Internet, many have recognized its power. In Venezuela, for example, President Hugo Chavez

---

[31] Timur Kuran, "Now Out of Never: The Element of Surprise in the East European Revolution of 1989," *World Politics*, 44 (1991), 7–48.

[32] Howard and Hussain, "The Role of Digital Media," p. 40.

[33] Bunt, "Mediterranean Islamic Expression," p. 85.

[34] Doran, "The Impact of New Media," p. 40.

[35] In Iran, for example, chat rooms in its closed online network permit only two people at a time to communicate; see Shapiro, "The Information Age May Not Foster Democracy," p. 48.

[36] Giovanni Ziccardi, *Resistance, Liberation Technology, and Human Rights in the Digital Age* (New York: Springer, 2013), pp. 14–15.

responded to the opposition's use of Twitter in April 2010 by opening an account of his own.[37] Within months, Chavez boasted that he received nearly 288,000 requests for help from citizens, and, more importantly, he promised that 200 staffers with access to public funds would help him win "the Twitter war."[38] In Russia, the Kremlin has cultivated close relations with leading lights of the country's Internet culture.[39] In 2009, a think tank called The Kremlin's School of Bloggers held a series of public talks and workshops designed to counter Western-backed threats to Russian sovereignty.[40] At the same time, the Kremlin has actively pursued those who use the Internet to oppose the regime. The most prominent case involves the anticorruption blogger and regime critic Aleksei Navalny, who helped lead demonstrations against the results of Russia's 2011–12 election cycle. Navalny quickly found himself charged with criminal fraud. After almost a year of house arrest, he was convicted on December 30, 2014, and given a suspended sentence while his brother, Oleg, received three and a half years in prison.[41] As these examples suggest, agents of democracy are not the only users of the Internet and social media. Authoritarian actors, including state representatives, are there too, promoting their own interests and, if possible, controlling what users can see and do.[42]

---

[37] Evgeny Morozov, *The Net Delusion* (New York: Public Affairs, 2011), pp. 113–14.

[38] Ibid., p. 115.

[39] They include Yevgeny Kaspesky, who founded the popular antivirus software Kasperky Lab, and Konstantin Rykov, whom Morozov (ibid., p. 124) identifies as "an undisputed godfather of the Russian Internet." One of Rykov's best-known works of pro-Kremlin propaganda is his company's documentary, *War 08.08.08: The War of Treason*, which examines the 2008 Georgian-Russian war from a highly ideological, pro-Russian perspective. Rykov also served as a deputy in Russia's lower chamber while "moonlighting as the Kremlin's unofficial ambassador to 'all things Internet'" (ibid., p. 125).

[40] The project emerged as a direct response to the Glasnost Foundation's The School of Bloggers. Since that foundation was partially funded by the US National Endowment for Democracy, the notion that the American government was backing schools of bloggers with the intent of launching a "color revolution" in Russia set the Russian blogosphere abuzz with conspiracy theories and suggestions for countering this virtual threat. The mastermind behind The Kremlin School of Bloggers, Alexey Chadayev, went on to become a top ideological functionary within Russia's ruling party, United Russia (Morozov, ibid., pp. 128–29).

[41] See David M. Herszenhorn, "Alekski Navalny, Putin Critic, Is Spared Prison in a Fraud Case, but His Brother Is Jailed," *New York Times* (December 30, 2014), www .nytimes.com/2014/12/31/world/europe/aleksei-navalny-convicted.html. Accessed on January 14, 2015

[42] Bremmer, "Democracy in Cyberspace."

Ukraine's Euromaidan

On November 21, 2013, a few hundred protesters took to the streets of Kyiv, Ukraine, in response to then-President Viktor Yanukovych's volte-face on the country's plans to sign an association agreement with the European Union prior to an EU summit scheduled for November 28–29 in Vilnius, Lithuania. While the government stated that the policy reversal was based on the need to protect the country's "national security," both the EU's commissioner on enlargement, Stefan Fuele, and Sweden's Foreign Minister, Carl Bildt, laid blame for the decision at the feet of the Kremlin.[43] In July and August 2013, Russia instigated what was perceived to be a trade war with Ukraine as a way to demonstrate Ukraine's economic reliance on Russia and force Ukraine to reject the association agreement in favor of the Russian-sponsored Eurasian Customs Union.[44] The Russian side, meanwhile, emphasized the European Union's failure to adequately consider the economic costs of Ukraine's European pivot to Ukraine, let alone to Russia.[45]

President Yanukovych's reversal surprised not only the Ukrainian public, but also members of Yanukovych's own staff who had been preparing the president's speech in Vilnius.[46] On the day of the announcement, disappointment was quickly voiced on social media.[47] Among those disappointed was Ukrainian journalist Mustafa Nayem, who is credited with using social media to draw people to the streets of Kyiv. Apparently fearing the danger of "slacktivism," Nayem's Facebook

---

[43] "Ukraine Suspends Preparations for EU Trade Agreement," *BBC News* (November 21, 2013), www.bbc.com/news/world-europe-25032275. Accessed on January 6, 2015.

[44] See, for example, "Trading Insults: A Trade War Sputters as the Tussle over Ukraine's Future Intensifies," *The Economist* (August 24, 2013), www.economist.com/news/europe/21583998-trade-war-sputters-tussle-over-ukraines-future-intensifies-trading-insults. Accessed on January 6, 2015.

[45] See "To Deal or Not to Deal? Ukraine's EU-Russia Crossroads in Facts and Numbers," *RT News* (November 29, 2013), http://rt.com/business/eu-trade-deal-vilnius-449/. Accessed on January 15, 2015.

[46] Serhii Tereshko, Senior Expert at the Department for European Integration of the Presidential Administration, made this point during a conversation with the author in Kyiv on February 11, 2014.

[47] According to Portnov and Portnova, demonstrators were not angered so much by the decision as by the way it was communicated to society: without public explanation or justification even though governmental representatives had just the day before confirmed that they would be signing the Association Agreement in Vilnius. See Andriy Portnov and Tetiana Portnova, "The Dynamics of the Ukrainian Eurorevolution," *Religion & Society in East and West*, 42 (2014), 9–12.

post stated: "Come on guys, let's be serious. If you really want to do something, don't just 'like' this post. Write that you are ready, and we can try to start something."[48] On Twitter, Nayem called on people to meet in Kyiv's Independence Square – or Maidan Nezalezhnosti – encouraging attendees to "dress warmly and bring umbrellas, tea, coffee, and friends."[49] The initial protests in Ukraine, then, developed from the ground up. While their numbers would rise to tens of thousands of people as early as November 23, not a single political leader had reacted to Yanukovych's decision by calling for mass demonstrations.[50]

Although Ukraine's Euromaidan, as it came to be called,[51] began with Ukrainian demonstrations promoting European – rather than Russian – economic integration, the cause quickly changed from a disagreement over policy direction to questions about the regime's legitimacy. In the early hours of Saturday, November 30, Ukraine's riot police, or *berkut*, entered the Maidan on "the pretext of safeguarding the erection of the New Year's tree."[52] After entering, the *berkut* violently broke up a pro-Europe rally, injuring hundreds of demonstrators in the process. By Saturday night, an estimated 10,000 protesters gathered outside Kyiv's Mikhailovsky Cathedral, which had given sanctuary to those hurt in the early morning's violence.[53] While President Yanukovych subsequently condemned the use of force against the protesters, the opposition had a new, more powerful message, one about the regime's legitimacy rather than simply a policy decision. Not surprisingly, the opposition used the incident to call for early elections.[54] Demonstrators, meanwhile, erected

---

[48] Tom Balmforth, "From the Streets to the Rada: Euromaidan Activists Enter Politics," *Radio Free Europe/Radio Liberty* (October 23, 2014), www.rferl.mobi/a/ukraine-euromai dan-activists-parliament-elections/26651905.html. Accessed on January 12, 2015.

[49] Luke Johnson, "Eight Tweets That Show How the Maidan Is Being Remembered Differently," *Radio Free Europe/Radio Liberty* (November 21, 2014), www.rferl.org/content/ukraine-russia-remembering-the-maidan-differently/26704172.html. Accessed on January 14, 2015.

[50] Portnov and Portnova, "The Dynamics of the Ukrainian Eurorevolution," p. 9.

[51] On Twitter, one could follow @euromaidan and track additional activity using the appropriate hashtags in Ukrainian, Russian, and English (#Євромайдан, #Евромайдан, #Euromaidan).

[52] Portnov and Portnova, "The Dynamics of the Ukrainian Eurorevolution," p. 9.

[53] According to Portnov and Portnova (ibid.), "up to a million" citizens gathered in Kyiv on Sunday, December 1.

[54] "Ukrainian Opposition Urges Early Elections amid Mass Protests," *Deutsche Welle* (November 30, 2013), www.dw.de/ukrainian-opposition-urges-early-elections-amid-mass-protests/a-17263842. Accessed on January 7, 2015.

tents and barricades in the heart of Ukraine's capital with social media continuing to serve as an important organizational and mobilizing tool.

The Social Media and Political Participation lab at New York University closely monitored social media activity related to the protests in the three months between the onset of Euromaidan and Yanukovych's removal from office.[55] Barberá and Metzger found significant spikes in the number of tweets per day during critical events on Maidan. This includes January 16, 2014, when the Ukrainian parliament, the Verkhovna Rada, voted in favor of a state budget that conformed to a December 2013 agreement negotiated by President Yanukovych with Russian President Vladimir Putin.[56] In the same session, the majority of legislators voted (by a show of hands) in favor of a series of repressive laws resembling Russian legislation.[57]

Barberá and Metzger's data reveal that Twitter activity remained high in the days and weeks that followed, including on Sunday, January 19, when tens of thousands of people once again swelled the Maidan in response to the new laws. That evening, demonstrators marched on the Rada and clashed with riot police, turning Hrushevskii Street, which joins Independence Square and European Square (located along the path to the Rada) into a battlefield. Molotov cocktails and stun grenades left a scene of burnt-out buses while newly erected barricades formed a new frontline in the fight for Ukraine's future.[58] Over the course of February 18, the start of the last wave of clashes between demonstrators and riot police, Barberá and Metzger found that the number of tweets originating from protesters using the hashtag #Euromaidan (as well as its Ukrainian and Russian equivalents) increased significantly as the conflict grew more

---

[55] Pablo Barberá and Megan Metzger, "Tweeting the Revolution: Social Media Use and the #Euromaidan Protests," *Huffington Post* (February 2, 2014), www.huffingtonpost.com/pablo-barbera/tweeting-the-revolution-s_b_4831104.html. Accessed on January 12, 2015.

[56] Portnov and Portnova, "The Dynamics of the Ukrainian Eurorevolution," p. 11.

[57] In Kyiv at the time, these laws were referred to as the "dictatorship laws," and some darkly joked that Yanukovych had done in five minutes what Putin had taken five years to do. It was also rumored that the presidential administration had threatened deputies of the ruling Party of Regions with physical harm if they violated party discipline (personal communication with Ukrainian activists at the Fulbright-Ukraine office in Kyiv).

[58] On January 22, Ukraine experienced its first deaths from the conflict when snipers shot protesters on Hrushevskii Street. As the president and opposition leaders, including Arsenii Yasteniuk and Vitalii Klitschko, negotiated a ceasefire, demonstrators in Ukraine's western city of Ternopil stormed and occupied the regional administrative headquarters. The act was soon emulated in other western regions. See Portnov and Portnova, "The Dynamics of the Ukrainian Eurorevolution," p. 11.

violent. Notably, the proportion of tweets in English jumped relative to previous days, possibly as Ukrainians used English-language tweets to directly engage the international community. On Facebook, meanwhile, Barberá and Metzger found pages dedicated to logistical issues such as sharing information on how to handle emergencies and where to take those in need of medical care.[59] With snipers killing approximately eighty people in the heart of Kyiv on February 20,[60] these pages sadly proved to be valuable resources at the time.

As the preceding discussion suggests, Ukraine's Euromaidan illustrates how social media can facilitate mass mobilization and empower those who oppose an existing political hierarchy. Indeed, the tendency to label the events as "The Revolution of Dignity"[61] echoes Castells's point that networked social movements share a common goal of finding dignity amid despair.[62] Yet, like their counterparts studying the Arab Spring, scholars seeking to understand the events in Ukraine have placed them in a larger context, whether temporally or comparatively, by emphasizing the systemic causes underlying the events. For example, Shveda identifies low levels of public confidence in governmental institutions, low GDP per capita with Ukraine behind post-communist counterparts like Albania and Turkmenistan, and an economic and social situation "complicated by total corruption" with Ukraine ranking 144th alongside Nigeria, Papua New Guinea, Iran, Cameroon, and the Central African Republic on Transparency International's Corruption Perception Index.[63] Indeed, the democratic gains associated with the 2004 Orange Revolution were widely seen as having slipped away even before the laws of January 16, 2014.[64] For Shveda, then, the "Revolution of Dignity" constitutes a

---

[59] Barberá and Metzger, "Tweeting the Revolution."

[60] The individuals are collectively referred to as the "Heavenly Hundred."

[61] Yuriy Shveda,"The Revolution of Dignity in the Context of Social Theory of Revolutions," *Religion & Society in East and West*, 42 (2014), 20–22.

[62] Castells, *Networks of Outrage and Hope*, p. 3.

[63] Shveda, "The Revolution of Dignity," pp. 20–21.

[64] For example, Motyl notes that while Yanukovych had presented himself as a moderate democrat seeking to heal past divisions during his 2010 election campaign, upon assuming office he undermined Ukrainian democracy, neglected the country's broken economy, and began realigning the country with Russia. See Alexander J. Motyl, "Ukrainian Blues: Yanukovych's Rise, Democracy's Fall," *Foreign Affairs*, 89 (2010), 126. Indeed, Motyl (ibid., p. 136) predicted that the most likely outcome of Yanukovych's election would be an "ineffective and embattled" president destabilizing the country. Freedom House, meanwhile, downgraded Ukraine's democracy rating in 2011 from "free" (with a score of 2.5 on its scale of 1 "most free" to 7 "least free") to "partly free" (3). See Freedom

continuation of the Orange Revolution, one that was successful but incomplete.[65]

Stepanenko also sees the Euromaidan as possessing longer historical roots.[66] Specifically, he sees the Maidan protests as attempts to deinstitutionalize key elements of post-Soviet politics, specifically the mechanisms and logic of centralized decision making, which are heavily burdened by the institutional memory of "state-bureaucratic and single-party machinery."[67] To the extent that President Yanukovych himself embodied this system, it is notable that demonstrators celebrated his removal from office by descending on his personal residence and using social media to share with the world the extravagant lifestyle of their former leader.[68]

For Riabchuk and Lushnycky, Ukraine's post-Soviet system increasingly contradicted the growing Western values of Ukrainian citizens.[69] They assert that trends from the 1995, 2000, and 2006 rounds of the World Values Survey disprove pessimistic assertions that a post-Soviet mentality would continue to define Ukrainian values for the foreseeable future. Instead, more Western-oriented attitudes on value-charged issues from democracy versus a "strong hand" to lamenting or not lamenting the demise of the Soviet Union can be found among Ukraine's younger, more educated, and ethnically Ukrainian population.[70] From this perspective, then, one should not be surprised that those with increasingly Western values would go to the streets to oppose a regime that not only sought closer relations with Russia, but also made this shift after having openly committed to a European trajectory.

House, *Freedom in the World Report: Ukraine* (2011), https://freedomhouse.org/report/freedom-world/2011/ukraine#.VLgsBVobtUQ. Accessed on January 15, 2015. In 2012, Ukraine would fall another half point overall (to 3.5) as Freedom House added one point to its Political Rights scores due to efforts to "crush the opposition" that included the politicization of courts, crackdowns on free media, and forceful dispersals of demonstrators. See Freedom House, *Freedom in the World Report: Ukraine* (2012), https://freedomhouse.org/report/freedom-world/2012/ukraine-0#.VLgsGVobtUQ. Accessed on January 15, 2015.

[65] Shveda, "The Revolution of Dignity," 22.

[66] V. Stepanenko,"Ukraine's Farewell to Post-Soviet Politics," *Religion & Society in East and West*, 42 (2014), 26–28.

[67] Ibid., p. 26.

[68] Espreso TV illustrates the symbiosis between social media and traditional media outlets in Ukraine during the Euromaidan. The Kyiv-based station streamed events from the Maidan live on the Internet.

[69] Mykola Riabchuk and Andrej N. Lushnyky, "Ukraine's Third Attempt," *Religion & Society in East and West*, 42, (2014), 29–31.

[70] Ibid., p. 30.

From celebration to separation

Although Riabchuk and Lushnycky observe changing values among Ukrainians, they also acknowledge that ethnic Russians and Russian speakers living in Ukraine are more likely to exhibit Soviet values since these individuals could more easily internalize Soviet ideology as their own as opposed to Ukrainians and Ukrainian speakers who sought to preserve their cultural identity.[71] Mapped onto this linguistic and cultural divide in Ukraine is a geographic one. As Wilson and Birch note, where a person lives in Ukraine is an important predictor of the language he or she speaks, with rural residents and those living in central and western Ukraine much more likely to speak Ukrainian than those living in southeast Ukraine and in large cities, where Russian predominates.[72]

From a comparative perspective, such reinforcing identities are often associated with culturally segmented societies,[73] and, in such cases, major political, economic, or social changes can destabilize an otherwise balanced system. According to Enloe, for example, ethnic identity may be grasped more tenaciously in a climate of turbulence and uncertainty as a familiar and reassuring anchor.[74] And while ethnic grievances alone are unlikely to become sufficient causes for revolution,[75] conditions that deprive authorities and institutions of their legitimacy can become catalysts for popular action.[76] From this vantage point, then, the rise of secessionist and irredentist demands in Ukraine, particularly in the aftermath of regime change, makes sense.

Yet divisions in Ukrainian society are more nuanced and complicated than most talk of an East-West divide would suggest. Wolczuk submits

---

[71] Ibid.

[72] Andrew Wilson and Sarah Birch, "Voting Stability, Political Gridlock: Ukraine's 1998 Parliamentary Elections," *Europe-Asia Studies*, 51, 6 (1999), 1039–68.

[73] See J. S. Furnivall, *Colonial Policy and Practice* (Cambridge: University Press, 1948), and M. G. Smith, *The Plural Society in the British West Indies* (Berkeley: University of California Press, 1965).

[74] Cynthia Enloe, *Ethnic Conflict and Political Development* (Boston: Little, Brown and Co., 1973), p. 15.

[75] Ibid., p. 224.

[76] Ibid., p. 232. It is precisely because regime transitions may alienate important segments of society, from the military and key economic actors to different sides of a communitarian divide, that O'Donnell and Schmitter promote pacts as important steps in a process that can increase the prospects of a country seeking viable democracy. See Guillermo O'Donnell and Philippe Schmitter, *Transitions from Authoritarian Rule: Tentative Conclusions about Uncertain Democracies* (Baltimore, MD: Johns Hopkins University Press, 1986), pp. 37–47.

that Ukrainian regional identities differ along three dimensions: "1) How to interpret nationalism (and the role of Russia) in Ukrainian history; 2) the position of Russian language and culture; and 3) relations with Moscow, especially regarding Russia-led integration projects."[77] Moreover, she argues that these differences have become manifest when political and economic elites from Ukraine's eastern regions seek to exploit them for political gain. While such behavior has characterized Ukrainian politics since independence, a more recent demonization of Ukrainian nationalism, including the notion that fascists or neo-Nazis dominated the Euromaidan agenda, was used to justify eastern demands for sovereignty.[78]

Although Riabchuk and Lushnycky note that Ukrainians remain divided about the country's geopolitical orientation, they also point out that 94 percent of western residents and 70 percent in the southeast supported Yanukovych's ousting, while 91 percent of western residents and 70 percent of eastern residents condemned Russia's invasion of Crimea.[79] Likewise, based on interviews and focus group discussions with protests and activists, Onuch emphasizes that some of the most radical Euromaidan protesters were Russian speakers from the east.[80] Similarly, Fisun and Avksentiev observe that Euromaidan movements in southeastern Ukraine grew significantly after the November 30th dispersal of demonstrators in Kyiv – that is, when the issue became less about Europe and more about how the state treated its citizens.[81] While the growth in these regions was from only a handful of people to hundreds of participants, the authors depict these efforts as "no less heroic" due to the

[77] Kataryna Wolczuk, "Ukraine's 'Regionalism' of Convenience,'" *Washington Post* (May 6, 2014), www.washingtonpost.com/blogs/monkey-cage/wp/2014/05/06/ukraines-regionalism-of-convenience/. Accessed on January 7, 2015.

[78] Wolczuk notes that the question of separatism and federalism in eastern Ukraine was also raised after then-President Leonid Kuchma's anointed successor, Viktor Yanukovych, faced accusations of electoral fraud during presidential elections of 2004 that led to the Orange Revolution. However, while elites advanced a vaguely defined notion of "separatism," no signs of mass support for separatism emerged in the east (ibid.).

[79] Riabchuk and Lushnycky, "Ukraine's Third Attempt," p. 30.

[80] Olga Onuch, "What Have We Learned in the Year since Ukraine's EuroMaidan?," *Washington Post* (November 26, 2014), www.washingtonpost.com/blogs/monkey-cage/wp/2014/11/26/what-have-we-learned-in-the-year-since-ukraines-euromaidan/. Accessed on January 15, 2015.

[81] Oleksandr Fisun and Anton Avksentiev, "Euromaidan in South-Eastern Ukraine," *Religion & Society in East and West*, 42 (2014), 23–25.

local authorities' counter-measures and the negative reporting on regional "Euromaidans" in local media.[82]

On the other hand, Haran and Bukovskiy argue that while Ukraine's traditional divisions were declining in the years prior to Ukraine's Euromaidan movement,[83] significant regional variation still marked the country including when it came to popular support for the Euromaidan movement. For example, although the Euromaidan protests enjoyed the support of 50 percent of Ukraine's population in December 2013, the distribution varied dramatically across Ukraine's macroregions. In the regions of western Ukraine, support reached 80 percent, while it was 63 percent in the central regions. In Ukraine's eastern regions, however, support for the Euromaidan dropped to 30 percent. In the south, which included Crimea, it was only 20 percent. A February 2014 survey, meanwhile, revealed that 57 percent of respondents in the east and 44 percent in the south believed that Western influence was fueling the protests, and 45 percent of respondents in the east and 35 percent in the south feared that nationalistic sentiments among the active participants were inspiring the demonstrations.[84]

Regardless of what level of aggregation is the most appropriate for assessing popular attitudes,[85] such variation is important for present purposes because it illustrates the presence of potentially fertile ground

---

[82] Ibid., p. 24.

[83] Olexiy Haran and Petro Bukovskiy, "Before and after Euromaidan: European Values vs. Pro-Russian Attitudes," *Religion & Society in East and West*, 42 (2014), 13–16. Haran and Bukovskiy (ibid., p. 13) note that while everyone seemed to accept an "East-West" divide in politics as predetermined with the inhabitants of different regions seeing the struggle between pro-Western and pro-Russian forces as a zero-sum game, the 2012 parliamentary elections actually signaled change. In that election, pro-European and pro-Western parties won new levels of support in several key eastern and southern industrial regions, while pro-Russian forces lost ground thanks to public disappointment with the rule of the Party of Regions and President Yanukovych, widespread corruption, and the impunity of officials who committed crimes against ordinary people.

[84] Ibid., p. 15.

[85] Clem emphasizes that focusing on larger swathes of territory in Ukraine, as opposed to finer-grained analysis, exaggerates Ukraine's "Russia problem." For a discussion of how the level of aggregation determines the results that one draws from such surveys, see Ralph S. Clem, "Location, Location, Location: Measuring Public Opinion in Ukraine's Regions," *Washington Post* (May 22, 2014), www.washingtonpost.com/blogs/monkey-cage/wp/2014/05/22/location-location-location-measuring-public-opinion-in-ukraines-regions/. Accessed on January 15, 2015. Also see Ralph S. Clem, "Two Important Facts about Ukraine," *Washington Post* (August 15, 2014), www.washingtonpost.com/blogs/monkey-cage/wp/2014/08/15/two-important-facts-about-ukraine/. Accessed on January 14, 2015.

for agents interested in exacerbating the uncertainties and tensions that accompanied President Yanukovych's removal from power. In fact, attitudes in the east and south echoed the interpretation of events broadcasted by domestic pro-presidential media as well as Russian media, the latter of which enjoy particular influence in Crimea and Ukrainian regions adjacent to Russia. These broadcasts depicted protesters as fascists, terrorists, and outlaws and the Euromaidan itself as resulting from Western pressure. Unfortunately, the presence of radical right-wing elements on the Maidan as well as visits by high-profile Western politicians, like US Senators John McCain and Chris Murphy, complemented these narratives, making them difficult to dismiss out of hand. Yet while pro-Yanukovych agents throughout the country promulgated the contention that radical nationalists and western agents were organizing the protests and fomenting violence in Kyiv, it was in the *eastern and southern* regions where the messages led to the establishment of paramilitary organizations. As Haran and Bukovskiy note, pro-regime media and misinformation out of Russia stoked division by consistently focusing on far-right elements within the protest movement.[86] At the same time, these outlets concealed facts that pointed to the demonstrations' broad support base, including participation among activists from the Jewish community, the Russian and Ukrainian Orthodox churches, and war veterans.[87]

While pro-Yanukovych paramilitary organizations disbanded after the president's fall,[88] "hacktivists" quickly filled the gap. On Sunday, March 16, 2014, hackers crashed several public NATO websites in what observers interpreted as an escalation of tensions over Crimea and the city of Sevastopol, the former of which houses Russia's Black Sea Fleet. A group called "CyberBerkut" claimed responsibility for the attacks, saying that it was upset with the alliance's interference in Ukraine. At the time, computer security experts noted that the attacks on NATO were only the latest in a series by groups calling themselves "CyberBerkut" with

---

[86] See Haran and Bukovskiy, "Before and after Euromaidan." In 2014, viewers of Russia's three main state television channels could hear fabricated stories about how Ukrainian soldiers had crucified a three-year-old boy in Ukraine's eastern city of Slovyansk, how Nazi-style concentration camps had been established to detain Ukraine's Russian-speakers, or even how the country's new government was conspiring with Satanist lamb torturers. See Glenn Kates, "Russia's Media Machine Looks West," *Radio Free Europe/ Radio Liberty* (December 29, 2014), www.rferl.mobi/a/russia-media-machine-looks-west/ 26767603.html. Accessed on January 7, 2015.

[87] Haran and Bukovskiy, "Before and after Euromaidan," p. 16.   [88] Ibid.

Ukrainian websites serving as previous targets.[89] Like so-called hacktivists elsewhere,[90] these actors operated neither in a vacuum nor without a cause in mind. Even if the majority of Russian speakers in the east may have wished to see a united Ukraine preserved, many residents in the region still had grievances against the central state, which was universally recognized as mismanaged.

Alongside these general concerns was a distrust of the new interim government and a fear that the victors of the Euromaidan revolution would use their new positions in Kyiv to benefit their supporters in the west at the expense of citizens residing in the east. The perceived gravity of this prospective injustice was compounded further by a belief among eastern residents that the fate of the national economy depended on the east, particularly the mining industry,[91] as well as a system where local tax revenue goes to the central government before any is channeled back home.[92]

The new government in Kyiv also did little to placate easterners' fears. Not only was the opposition slow to react to allegations of anti-Semitism and radical nationalism upon assuming office, but the newly invigorated parliament voted, on February 23, 2014, to cancel the status of Russian as the country's second official language. It did not help matters that the far-right faction, Svoboda, advocated in favor of the bill as a way to stop the "Russification" of Ukraine.[93] Moreover, the public had yet to prove that far-right politicians lacked widespread popular support, as the May 25 presidential elections made evident. So, while acting president Oleksandr Turchynov refused to sign off on the change in the status of the Russian language, the damage was done: Protecting the status of the Russian language in Ukraine became a major rallying point for a pro-Russian separatist agenda.[94] With these developments in mind, one can understand why many of Ukraine's eastern residents would doubt the

---

[89] Adrian Croft and Peter Apps, "NATO Websites Hit in Cyber Attack Linked to Crimea Tension," *Reuters* (March 16, 2014), www.reuters.com/article/2014/03/16/us-ukraine-nato-idUSBREA2E0T320140316. Accessed on January 7, 2015.

[90] Ziccardi, *Resistance, Liberation Technology, and Human Rights in the Digital Age.*

[91] Although the mining industry is heavily subsidized today, this perception lingers due to the region's position as an industrial powerhouse during the Soviet era.

[92] "What Are Eastern Ukraine's (Legitimate) Grievances with Kyiv?," *Radio Free Europe/ Radio Liberty* (May 29, 2014), www.rferl.mobi/a/ukraine-explainer-eastern-greievances/ 25402922.html. Accessed on January 6, 2015.

[93] Haran and Bukovskiy, "Before and after Euromaidan," p. 16.

[94] "What Are Eastern Ukraine's (Legitimate) Grievances?,"

assertion that life for them would be better under the new regime than it was for them under the old regime.

Equally important, of course, was the presence of a neighboring "black knight,"[95] Russia, with an interest in reacquiring at least part of Ukraine, Crimea, and Sevastopol and a desire to stir up enough trouble to complicate any attempt by the new Ukrainian government to pursue its desired European pivot. In pursuit of these goals, the Kremlin has consistently advanced the message that Yanukovych's removal from power resulted from an anti-constitutional, neo-fascist coup, muddied any counterclaims using disinformation, and even placed actors on the ground in Ukraine to make sure that the Russian interpretation of events was adequately received and acted upon.

According to Pomerantsev and Weiss, the crisis in Ukraine illustrates how the line between fact and fiction has been thoroughly distorted in Russian media and public discourse.[96] One such claim, particularly sensitive among Western audiences, was the Russian contention of rising anti-Semitism in Ukraine following Yanukovych's fall. Ukraine's Jewish community has rejected this assertion, even placing a full-page advertisement to this effect in *The New York Times* in March 2014.[97] Still, the appeal of the anti-Semitic message (thanks to the presence of neo-Nazi groups in Ukraine and on the Maidan) led John Pilger, a prominent journalist for Britain's *The Guardian*, to report an unnamed doctor's account of the May 2014 violence in the port city of Odesa. In his commentary, Pilger quoted the alleged doctor's Facebook description of how, on his way to help the injured, pro-Ukrainian neo-Nazis stopped him and threatened him and "other Jews of Odesa." Yet, as it turns out, the Odesa doctor did not exist. Not only did the page soon disappear, but the person who posted the story used a picture of a dentist from the Russian republic of Karachai-Cherkessia.[98]

---

[95] Steven Levitsky and Lucan A. Way, *Competitive Authoritarianism: Hybrid Regimes after the Cold War* (Cambridge, UK: Cambridge University Press, 2010), p. 41.

[96] Peter Pomerantsev and Michael Weiss, "The Menace of Unreality: How the Kremlin Weaponizes Information, Culture and Money," *The Interpreter* (2014), p. 10, www.interpretermag.com/wp-content/uploads/2014/11/The_Menace_of_Unreality_Final .pdf. Accessed January 16, 2015.

[97] See "Ukrainian Jews Slam Putin in Full-Page Ad in New York Times," *Jewish Telegraphic Agency* (March 27, 2014), www.jta.org/2014/03/27/news-opinion/world/ukrainian-jews-slam-putin-in-full-page-ad-in-new-york-times. Accessed on January 14, 2015.

[98] Luke Johnson, "'Guardian' Op-Ed Quotes Cryptic Odesa 'Doctor' Seen as Hoax," *Radio Free Europe/Radio Liberty* (May 14, 2014), www.rferl.org/content/guardian-op-ed-quo

The Russian propaganda machine has not gone wholly unchecked. On March 2, 2014, Yevhen Fedchenko, the director of Kyiv's Mohyla School of Journalism, founded StopFake.org, a self-described fact-checking website that publishes in English, Russian, and Ukrainian.[99] In December 2014, StopFake.org published a video listing the Top 75 "lies and untruths" about the crisis in Ukraine.[100] In addition, the new Ukrainian government moved to establish a Ministry of Information following new parliamentary elections in October 2014, although this move also prompted demonstrations from journalists and activists concerned about increased governmental control over Ukraine's media.[101] The information war also has witnessed the emergence of pro-Ukrainian hackers like the Ukrainian Cyber Troops led by Yevhen Dokunin, which has used distributed denial-of-service (DDoS) attacks against rebel websites. Dokunin also claims to have hacked two Russian interior ministry servers and to have hijacked networked printers in eastern Ukraine and Crimea to print pro-Ukrainian messages.[102]

Still, the violence in eastern Ukraine that followed the Russian annexation of Crimea in March 2014 has turned the Internet into an inaccessible luxury for many living in eastern Ukraine. As a result, those still residing in places like Luhansk have been left primarily with information from Russian, Crimean, or Belarussian television.[103] Moreover, Pomerantsev and Weiss submit that the goal of Russian propaganda is not to convince or persuade but to keep viewers hooked, distracted, passive, and paranoid.[104] In their view, the Kremlin has used tactics like

tes-cryptic-odesa-doctor-seen-as-hoax/25385076.html. Accessed on January 12, 2015.

[99] See Kates, "Russia's Media Machine Looks West," and "About Us," *StopFake.org*, www.stopfake.org/en/about-us/. Accessed on January 15, 2015.

[100] "The Kremlin's Top 75 Lies about the Ukraine Crisis," *Radio Free Europe/Radio Liberty* (December 12, 2014), www.rferl.mobi/a/russia-ukraine-lies-stopfake-kremlin-propaganda/26739439.html. Accessed on January 12, 2015.

[101] Charles Recknagel, "'No Big Brother!' Ukrainian Journalists Oppose Kyiv's New Ministry of Information," *Radio Free Europe/Radio Liberty* (December 3, 2014), www.rferl.mobi/a/ukraine-ministry-information-journalists-protest/26723352.html. Accessed on January 14, 2015.

[102] Vitaly Shevchenko, "Ukraine Conflict: Hackers Take Sides in Virtual War," *BBC News* (December 19, 2014), www.bbc.com/news/world-europe-30453069. Accessed on January 15, 2015.

[103] "Letters from Donbas," *Radio Free Europe/Radio Liberty* (December 11, 2014), www.rferl.mobi/a/ukraine-personal-stories-conflict/26737914.html. Accessed January 13, 2015.

[104] Pomerantsev and Weiss, "The Menace of Unreality," p. 11. The day before Ukraine's October 26, 2014. parliament elections, hackers used electronic billboards to broadcast

denial of service attacks, threatening journalists with libel, and confusing the West with mixed messages to demoralize their enemy, shatter communications, and take out command structures.[105]

Since attempts to control information depend on well-positioned advocates of the preferred message, it is notable that when separatist sentiment in eastern and southern Ukraine appeared to be on the wane,[106] reports of Russian provocateurs within Ukraine began to wax. In the case of Russia's annexation of Crimea and Sevastopol, these activists came in the form of what Ukrainians labeled "little green men," a description that captures both their uniforms without insignia and their alien (i.e., Russian) origin. In Sevastopol and other eastern cities, pro-Russian groups used Maidan-style tactics against the new regime, holding mass rallies and storming local governmental offices. Then, on February 27, 2014, armed men seized the parliament building of Crimea and raised the Russian flag.

The following night men in military uniforms without insignia took over the airport in Simferopol, while representatives of local "self-defense" forces took control of government buildings there. Later, on Thursday, April 17, 2014, President Putin would admit that Russian military servicemen were, as suspected but previously denied, on the ground in Crimea prior to the referendum that preceded the region's annexation by Russia.[107] Similarly, Russian officials initially denied the presence of Russian troops in Ukraine's eastern regions of Donetsk and Luhansk only to later state that they could not stop Russian citizens from going to fight in Ukraine as "volunteers."[108]

images of alleged civilian carnage at the hands of Ukrainian forces fighting in the east. Yet at least one image, showing a Russian soldier near mass graves, actually came from Russia's first Chechen war. See Carl Schreck, "Ukraine Unspun: Chechnya War Pic Passed Off as Ukraine Atrocity by Hackers, Russian TV," *Radio Free Europe/Radio Liberty* (October 27, 2014), www.rferl.org/content/russian-media-propaganda-ukraine-conflict-chechnya/26660126.html. Accessed on January 14, 2015.

[105] Pomerantsev and Weiss, "The Menace of Unreality," p. 14.

[106] Haran and Burkovskiy, "Before and after Euromaidan," p. 16.

[107] The acknowledgment was widely reported, including by RT News, a stridently pro-Kremlin, international-oriented news outlet. See "Putin Acknowledges Russian Servicemen Were in Crimea," *RT News* (April 17, 2014), http://rt.com/news/crimea-defense-russian-soldiers-108/. Accessed on January 15, 2015.

[108] In October, a Russian action film star, Mikhail Porechenkov, was caught by the rebels' Novorossia TV channel firing a machine gun toward Ukrainian lines alongside pro-Russian rebels near the Donetsk airport. See Christopher Miller, "Russian Action Star Caught Firing a Machine Gun toward Ukraine," *Mashable* (October 31, 2014), http://mashable.com/2014/10/31/russian-action-star-ukraine/. Accessed on January 15, 2015. In December 2014, the head of the Russian-based Sverdlovsk Fund of Spetsnaz

Perhaps the best-known Russian "volunteer" in Ukraine is Igor Girkin, a Russian citizen and former colonel in Russia's Federal Security Service (FSB), who arrived in the eastern town of Slovyansk in April 2014. Girkin, who goes by the *nom de guerre* Strelkov (Russian for "shooter"), boasted on the Russian social media site *VKontakte* of shooting down a Ukrainian warplane just before reports surfaced that the civilian Malaysian flight MH17 from Amsterdam to Kuala Lumpur had crashed in eastern Ukraine on July 17, 2014.[109]

After returning to Moscow, Girkin not only admitted to fighting in eastern Ukraine but also suggested that the protests in eastern Ukraine would have fizzled out without his effort to escalate the situation there.[110] Less known, perhaps, is the story of a Russian soldier, Alexander Sotkin, who in July posted "selfies" on Instagram using a phone or tablet that geotagged his locations: the rebel-controlled villages of Krasna Talycha and Krasny Derkul.[111] Both cases illustrate how the increasing ubiquity of the Internet and social media can undermine official governmental positions. More difficult, however, is the task of filtering through the cacophony of information disseminated to determine which contentions are credible. According to Pomerantsev and Weiss, the Russian position has been not only to embrace this uncertainty but to add to it so that all arguments appear equally plausible and none wholly defensible.[112]

(i.e., Special Forces) Veterans outlined in previously unprecedented detail how Russians are participating in the violent conflict in eastern Ukraine. See James Rupert, "How Russians Are Sent to Fight in Ukraine," *Newsweek* (January 6, 2015), www.newsweek.com/how-russians-are-sent-fight-ukraine-296937. Accessed on January 7, 2015.

[109] See "Ukraine Separatist Social Media Site Claims Plane Downing," *Radio Free Europe/Radio Liberty* (July 17, 2014), www.rferl.org/content/ukraine-separatist-leader-boasts-downing-plane/25460930.html. Accessed on January 15, 2015. Of course, social media has been rife with debates about who is actually to blame for the downing of MH17. See, for example, "US Dismisses Russian MH17 Pictures That Blame Ukraine for Disaster," *The Guardian* (November 15, 2014), www.theguardian.com/world/2014/nov/15/ukraine-fighter-shot-mh17-claims-russian-tv-photo-fake. Accessed on January 15, 2015.

[110] Corey Flintoff, "The Russian Who Claims Credit for Fanning the Flames in Ukraine," *National Public Radio* (January 6, 2015), www.npr.org/blogs/parallels/2015/01/06/372872870/the-russian-who-claims-credit-for-fanning-the-flames-in-ukraine. Accessed on January 6, 2015.

[111] Paul Szoldra, "Without Realizing It, Russian Soldiers Are Proving Vladimir Putin Is Lying about Eastern Ukraine," *Business Insider* (July 31, 2014), www.businessinsider.com/russian-soldiers-social-ukraine-2014-7. Last accessed on January 6, 2015.

[112] Pomerantsev and Weiss, "The Menace of Unreality."

Conclusion

Advances in information technology, and increased popular access to these advances, have permitted opponents of existing hierarchies to reach wider audiences. However, as the literature examining social media's impact on regime change and democratization emphasizes, the ability to tangibly undermine the status quo requires a message capable of moving one's audience out from behind the computer desk and onto the streets. Events in Ukraine over the course of 2013 and 2014, which led to the ouster of President Yanukovych, seem to illustrate many of the arguments that previous scholars have made about the democratizing potential of information technology and social media. These media served as critical tools that the regime's opponents employed to initiate protests as well as sustain them. Moreover, when clashes between the government and protesters turned violent, Facebook pages and Twitter feeds became resources for those wishing to track developments, disseminate information to a larger national and international audience, and even treat the injured.

Yet the case of Ukraine also reveals that the overthrow of an existing regime may create a power vacuum where uncertainty can combine with prior grievances to fuel regional tensions. While Ukrainians across the country recognized that President Yanukovych had political warts, he won an election in 2010 that was widely recognized as relatively free and fair. At the same time, Yanukovych's removal from office was predicated on the Rada's interpretation of his fleeing Kyiv, first for the eastern city of Kharkiv and then for Russia, as a decision to vacate office, something that Yanukovych would subsequently deny. These developments, then, exacerbated the existing atmosphere of mutual distrust among incumbent legislators, between protesters and politicians, and even among residents of eastern and western regions of the country. Regardless of the breadth or depth of these feelings, social media provided a forum for some to celebrate and others to mourn the change. For the latter, concerns focused on both the composition and the motives of the incoming regime, concerns that were raised by traditional media outlets that had backed the former president as well as those in Russia. Moreover, uncertainty about the new government combined with the precedent that locally organized street protests could change not just the direction of government but the system itself. For some opponents of the new regime, then, the system to be challenged was centralized rule from Kyiv.

Despite these dynamics, however, domestic actors alone have not determined the direction of events in Ukraine. Russian intervention, both via an information war and with boots on the ground in Ukraine, has undermined the ability of the new government to peacefully establish its authority. At a minimum, Russia's annexation of Crimea and Sevastopol raised the stakes of the conflict between the new government and the regional strongholds of the former regime. This action shifted the conversation away from questions about how greater regional sovereignty might protect local interests to a precedent in which regional politicians, unhappy with the direction of Ukraine's national government, could employ the trappings of democracy, though not the substance – referenda supervised by armed representatives of another country – to not only break away from Ukraine but possibly join the Russian Federation. As a result, the resolution of Ukraine's political crisis tilted away from a discussion of democratic principles and a prospective reallocation of political power toward an escalation of violence with pro-Russian separatists benefiting from Russian manpower and weaponry.

7

Networks of protest in Latin America

JUANITA DARLING

Latin America was the place where, two decades ago, social movements discovered the potential of the Internet. The protosocial media of List-servs turned an indigenous uprising in southern Mexico into an international protest against the Washington Consensus form of globalization. Within six years of the Zapatista rebellion, a seventy-year regime famously described as "the perfect dictatorship" fell. Democracy, aided by new media, triumphed. Yet at this writing, the triumph seems less than decisive: Social media on three continents are sharing news of protests against the disappearance of forty-three Mexican students followed by the discovery of sixty-two unrelated bodies in unmarked graves.[1] The once-defeated regime is back in power, despite a student social media campaign that ranged from animated satire to reasoned statements to coverage of street protests.[2] While Mexico, as a precursor, may be the most dramatic case, the nation is hardly alone in the ambivalent results of using social media as a tool for human rights. Throughout Latin America, there are examples of both the promise and limitations of digital media. The region presents the opportunity to examine the varying ways that established and emerging social movement networks are attempting to incorporate digital media into a repertoire of protest in support of human rights.

This chapter posits that communication technology has become a site of struggle in the region, indicating its relevance to the allocation of power. Thus, much of the struggle over media is part of a struggle over

---

[1] Harry M. Cleaver Jr., "The Zapatista Effect: The Internet and the Rise of an Alternative Political Fabric," *Journal of International Affairs*, 51, 2 (1998); Rolando Aguilar, "Sicario Ordenó La Matanza en Iguala; CNDH Pide a Gobierno de Guerrero No Frenar Justicia," *Excelsior* (October 6, 2014); "Todos Somos Ayotzinapa," *Regeneación*, #AccionGlobalpor-Ayotzinapa, http://regeneracion.mx.

[2] Francisco Javier Gómez Carpinteiro, "The Subject's Tracks: The Other Campaign, Self-Knowledge, and Subjectivity in the Liberal Democratic Cycle," *Latin American Perspectives*, 40, 5 (2013), 150.

norms, values, and beliefs as formerly oppressed and repressed groups become empowered, challenging control of media. Previously, freedom of the press was a right that could be exercised only by those who owned a press, which did not inspire support for free expression among the general citizenry. In the current context, interest groups are struggling over ownership of presses (and television stations) at the same time digital media are being used to protest and exercise civil disobedience, alternately challenging and reinforcing older technologies. This chapter argues that by facilitating the reach across borders, social media have strengthened and transformed the transnational advocacy networks that have been key components of change in the area since the 1970s. This horizontal communication has challenged the vertical and hierarchical Latin American political traditions, leading authorities to respond, often successfully, with corporatist strategies that also are ingrained in the region's culture. Authorities are not the only obstacle. In the twenty-first century, the strongest challenges to the use of media to promote human rights have come from violent nonstate actors.

Government media activism

In Latin America, the relationship between empowerment and norms and values is especially complex. Electoral democracies have emerged over the past three decades in the context of a political culture that has not been amenable to universal empowerment.[3] The resulting struggle over access to communication has become most evident in countries such as Venezuela, Argentina, and Ecuador, where groups previously excluded from power have gained political office through electoral majorities. After elections, mass media initially remained under the ownership of families linked to the traditional rulers, therefore, opponents of the new regimes.[4] As Kitzberger has noted, the influence of traditional elites has prompted the new leaders to view media as examples of the social and economic inequities that they have pledged

---

[3] *See* Guillermo O'Donnell, "On the State, Democratization and Some Conceptual Problems," Kellogg Institute Working Paper, 192 (1993); Daniel M. Brinks, Marcelo Leiras, and Scott Mainwaring, *Reflections on Uneven Democracies: The Legacy of Guillermo O'Donnell* (Baltimore, MD: Johns Hopkins University Press, 2014).

[4] Pascal Lupien, "The Media in Venezuela and Bolivia: Attacking the 'Bad Left' from Below," *Latin American Perspectives*, 40, 3 (2013), 227; Graciela Mochkofsky, *Pecado Original: Clarín, los Kirchner y la Lucha por el Poder*, Espejo de la Argentina (Buenos Aires: Planeta, 2011), p. 201.

to redress, leading to "media activism on the part of leftist governments in Latin America."[5] Waisbord has noted that activism is manifested in limitations on media influence through revocation of broadcast licenses, strengthening of state-controlled media, and increased media regulation, measures that are not completely alien to Latin America's long tradition of government intrusion on media.[6] Given that history, the question that arises is whether the activism is aimed at freeing the media from the control of institutional power or merely changing who is in control. Either way, while traditional media groups have attempted to expand into newer media, the government has tried to curtail their activities and the influence of the media they already own.

Levitsky and Way have found that media access can be curtailed through state monopolies or near monopolies on electronic media or links between the government and private media owners through proxy ownership, patronage, and cronyism. They noted that "Perhaps the most widespread form of 'legal' repression is the use of libel or defamation laws. In numerous countries, governments routinely used libel and defamation laws to arrest journalists and editors and/or suspend and even close down media outlets.... In some cases, the government's repeated use of costly lawsuits led to the disappearance of many independent media outlets."[7] They found significant disparities in controls on radio and television, compared with print media, "with a diversity of independent newspapers and magazines circulating freely, [because] these papers were often confined to a small urban elite.... only a tiny fraction of the population read newspapers."[8] They did not address where new media fell on this spectrum of control or how they have responded to controls on other media. That response, including efforts to elude control, is an intriguing development.

Venezuelan government media policy, by demonstrating how such controls function, has drawn criticism from both ends of the political spectrum. That Radio Caracas Television (RCTV) owners opposed the loss of their license in 2007 is hardly surprising. What provides more pause for reflection is anarchist Rafael Uzcategui's accusation that the

[5] Philip Kitzberger, "The Media Politics of Latin America's Leftist Governments," *Journal of Politics in Latin America*, 4, 3 (2012), 124–25.

[6] Silvio Waisbord, "Between Support and Confrontation: Civic Society, Media Reform, and Populism in Latin America," *Communication, Culture & Critique*, 4, 1 (2011), 98, 101–2.

[7] Steven Levitsky and Lucan Way, *Competitive Authoritarianism: Hybrid Regimes after the Cold War* (New York: Cambridge University Press, 2010), pp. 12, 14.

[8] Ibid., pp. 12, 14.

government forged alliances with other media owned by the oligarchy to silence opposition voices.[9]

At the turn of the century, Venezuelan media was a typical example of elite domination of media.[10] Four newspapers with links to the oligarchy accounted for 86 percent of circulation, and conglomerates with mining and manufacturing interests controlled the electronic media.[11] Following Hugo Chavez's election in 1998, the dominant media reported critically on his administration, even supporting the failed 2002 coup d'état.[12] Since then, the Chavez and (following his death) Maduro regimes have followed the tactics that Waisbord, Levitsky, and Way outlined.

Increased regulation: Two years after the failed coup, a New Law of Social Responsibility in Radio and Television took effect.[13] Legal scholar Angel Luis Soto has found that the law "is characterized by its vague language, overbroad regulation of content of expression, and

---

[9] Rafael Uzcátegui, *Venezuela, la Revolución como Espectáculo: Una Crítica Anarquista al Gobierno Bolivariano*, trans. Chaz Bufe (Tucson: See Sharp Press, 2010), pp. 6, 122–23.

[10] Elite media domination has been an issue in Latin America at least since the zenith of the New World Information and Communication Order (NWICO) in the 1970s, when movement adherents argued that despite a seeming variety of media, powerful private financial and economic interests dominate the message because the most influential media are owned by different members of the same power structure, creating a form of private censorship that silences the voice of the majority. See Seán Ó Siochrú and Bruce Girard, *Communicating in the Information Society* (Geneva: United Nations Research Institute for International Development, November 1, 2003); Luis Ramiro Beltran, "A Farewell to Aristotle: 'Horizontal' Communication," in Alfonso Gumucio Dagron and Thomas Tufte (eds.), *Communication for Social Change Anthology: Historical and Contemporary Reading* (South Orange, NJ: Communication for Social Change Consortium, 2006).

[11] Lupien, "The Media in Venezuela and Bolivia," p. 228; Uzcátegui, *Venezuela, la Revolución como Espectáculo*, pp. 121–23.

[12] After months of labor union strikes and a fatal confrontation between Chavez supporters and opponents, military officers arrested the president and held him in custody at a remote military base for three days, until loyal officers rescued him in a counter-coup. Media coverage led Venezuelans to believe, incorrectly, that the president had resigned. Alez Bellos, "Chavez Rises from Very Peculiar Coup," *The Guardian* (April 15, 2002); Nerliny Caruci, "Ustedes Debieron Callarse la Boca. Asi Chavez Nunca Hubiera Regresado," *Venezuela de Verdad* (2012), www.venezueladeverdad.gob.ve/content/%E2%80%9Custedes-debieron-callarse-la-boca-as%C3%AD-ch%C3%A1vez-nunca-habr%C3%ADa-regresado%E2%80%9D; Angel Luis Olivera Soto, "Prior Restraints in Venezuela's Social Responsibility on Radio and Television Act: Are They Justified?," *The George Washington International Law Review*, 40, 2 (2008), 404.

[13] European Union Observation Mission, *Final Report: Presidential Elections: Venezuela 2006* (Caracas: European Union, 2006), p. 28.

excessive sanctions for noncompliance." He further noted that the regulation

> states that its purpose is to guarantee freedom of speech without any restraints as per the Constitution and human rights treaties ratified by Venezuela, and to promote the effective exercise and respect for human rights. Nevertheless, its provisions suggest that the real objective behind this legislation is to strictly regulate the content of all messages transmitted by radio and television, which in conjunction with its vague language and excessive sanctions, results in the establishment of prior restraints and self-censorship.

Still, he concluded that the law was justified by the role that media had played in the political unrest that led to the attempted overthrow of an elected president.[14]

State-controlled media: While media directly owned by the government has not been successful in attracting a wide audience, "Venezuela has become a leader in the creation of state media."[15] Those media, in an apparent revival of NWICO solutions, include TeleSur, a twenty-four-hour news channel that acts as a compiler, sharing news broadcasts from across the region.

Revocation of licenses: For decades, rivals RCTV and Venevision had dominated the Venezuelan airwaves with just over one-third each of the viewing audience. Both of their licenses were up for renewal in 2007. Venevision's license was renewed; RCTV's was revoked. Five months later, Venevision was drawing just over half of Venezuela's viewers. Both stations had supported the failed 2002 coup, but four years later, Venevision changed course.[16] While RCTV devoted 69 percent of its coverage to the opposition and more than half the coverage Chavez received was negative, on Venevision, the coalition of parties supporting Chavez received 84 percent of coverage, little of it critical, according to the final report of European Union observers.[17] Within a year, RCTV no longer existed and Venevision had half the country's television audience. Venezuelans turned to neighboring Colombia for news until the Venezuelan government blocked their access.[18] Contrary to what Levitsky and Way

---

[14] Soto, "Prior Restrainsts in Venezuela's Social Responsibility," p. 420.

[15] Lupien, "The Media in Venezuela and Bolivia," p. 238.

[16] Uzcátegui, *Venezuela, la Revolución como Espectáculo*, pp. 122–23.

[17] European Union Observation Mission, *Final Report: Presidential Elections: Venezuela 2006*, pp. 31–32.

[18] Ana Cristina Nuñez, "State-Censorship of the Press and of Dissenting Voices in 'Competitive Authoritarian' Regimes: A Case Study of Venezuela (1999–2014)," in *CLAS Lecture Series* (Stanford University, Palo Alto, CA: November 14, 2014).

would have predicted, the government has more recently reverted to a traditional Latin American tool, similar to licensing, against newspapers: using the government monopoly on newsprint to restrict paper available to opposition newspapers.[19]

Proxy ownership, patronage, and cronyism: After setting the example of RCTV, the heavy-handed use of licensing power was not always necessary, leaving space for more subtle tactics, Ana Cristina Nuñez has found, in examining three other cases. The owners of Globovision, a twenty-four-hour news channel, and two major newspapers, *Ultimas Noticias* and *El Universal,* decided to sell to government supporters to avert bankruptcy.[20] While newspapers are not subject to licensing, they do depend on newsprint and advertising. Besides its own substantial advertising budget, the government can also pressure business owners eager to remain on good terms with the administration. All three media have shifted from the opposition to support for the government.[21]

While Venezuela's media have been subsidiaries of conglomerates, Argentina's media are dominated by vertically integrated corporations that produce content across a variety of platforms. That can magnify their influence, but also increase their vulnerability as they find themselves in conflict with the government on several fronts. Friction between media and the populist government has reached the point of causing concern about the quality of Argentine democracy. Carlos Gervasoni lists "official harassment of the independent and critical media; the blatant use of many supposedly public media outlets for the private ends of the rulers; the 'soft' punishment of journalists, business people, union leaders, intellectuals and artists who express criticisms of the government" as among the factors that are undermining democracy from within Argentina.[22]

---

[19] Paola Nalvarte, "Government Censorship in Venezuela Increased by 87% Compared to 2012, Organizations Say," *Journalism in the Americas* (November 7, 2013), https:// knightcenter.utexas.edu/blog/00–14727-government-censorship-venezuela-increased-87-compared-2012-organizations-say.

[20] While Nuñez found that *Ultimas Noticias* has been sold, although she was not sure to whom, Uzcátegui wrote that only the editorial line, not the ownership, had changed. The murkiness of the ownership issue perpetuates alternative versions of truth that support different hypotheses. What is not contested is that the newspaper's editorial line has changed from opposition to support, resulting in increased advertising. Uzcátegui, *Venezuela, la Revolución como Espectáculo,* p. 21.

[21] Nuñez, "State-Censorship of the Press."

[22] Carlos Gervasoni, "Argentina's Democracy Four Years after Modernization and Bureaucratic-Authoritarianism," in Brinks, Leiras, and Mainwaring (eds.), *Reflections on Uneven Democracies: The Legacy of Guillermo O'Donnell,* pp. 53–54.

The most notorious example is the Kirchner-Fernandez administration's open war with the Clarin Group using tactics that have included questioning the human rights record of the media group's major shareholder, Ernestina Herrera de Noble. Cristina Fernandez de Kirchner has escalated the conflict with the media group that began during the presidency of her late husband, Nestor Kirchner. The conflict with the government has undermined the group's finances to such an extent that when Kirchner died of a heart attack in 2009, Clarin's shares jumped 49 percent. The state-controlled television station has led the attack, with the nightly political discussion show 6, 7, 8 serving as a point of encounter for government officials and sympathetic journalists, reinforcing Waisbord's factor of state media with that of cronyism. Patronage is reflected in the loss of government advertising. Using traditional tactics against the group's efforts to expand into newer media, the government canceled the license of Clarin's Internet service provider subsidiary, which had more than a million subscribers and was the corporation's most profitable affiliate.[23] In 2009, the government passed a new communications law that would require the Clarin Group to divest assets that created monopolies, such as owning a newspaper and a television station in the same city. Clarin has resisted by filing lawsuits, which are still pending.[24]

While most developments have followed the expected route, the Argentine government's use of the courts against the Clarin Group has been exceptional and tailored to that nation's particular history. The thousands of people who "disappeared" before and during the 1976–83 military dictatorship included hundreds of pregnant women. Human rights groups have fought for legal institutions, which have found 115 of the children born to kidnapped mothers and illegally adopted.[25] The government turned that apparatus on Herrera de Noble, who had adopted two babies in 1976. Fifteen years of legal action failed to prove that the children, now adults, were the offspring of disappeared women, but they have raised questions about the publisher's character and conduct.[26] The case also illustrates how citizens who were once

---

[23] Mochkofsky, *Pecado Original*, pp. 208–12.   [24] Ibid., pp. 190–91.
[25] Comision Nacional por el Derecho a la Identidad, "Avances y Logros Producidos Como Consecuencia de la Búsqueda," www.conadi.jus.gov.ar/home_fl.html; "Historia de Abuelas," Abuelas de la Plaza de Mayo, www.abuelas.org.ar/institucional.php?institucional=historia.htm&der1=der1_hist.php&der2=der2_inst.php.
[26] Mochkofsky, *Pecado Original*, pp. 218, 390.

oppressed, such as the human rights groups formed around the issue of the disappeared, have been empowered by the change to a populist government. That government views the media, such as the Clarin Group, that were allied with the dictatorship as part of the mechanism of oppression whose destruction is vital to building a different society. Using the institutions created to find the children of the disappeared against the publisher served the double purpose of demonstrating that there is no longer impunity and of discrediting a perceived crony of the traditional elites.

Ecuador's President Rafael Correa has used courts in a more traditional way, punishing journalists under insult laws and seditious libel laws that have long traditions but are no longer common.[27] His treatment of domestic media seems at odds with the asylum he extended WikiLeaks founder Julian Assange in his country's London embassy.[28] However, the incongruity lessens when viewed from a NWICO perspective: The issue is who controls the media and whose secrets the media – whether traditional or newer – is making public. In defending his actions to the World Leaders Forum at Columbia University in 2011, Correa reasoned:

> The focus of the debate is not freedom of speech ... but the ethical and technical contradiction of private, for-profit businesses and political groups interests that supply this indispensable good for society: information... At least in Latin America, the media have always been against progressive governments.... They define themselves as a counter power, that is, as political actors. However, they do not tolerate a political response. If the media defame, misinform, or slander our governments, it is called freedom of speech. If a president dares to answer back, it is an attack against freedom of speech.[29]

Answering back, whether through the courts or other methods that the theorists indicated, is the essence of how populist governments view their

---

[27] Brian Ellsworth and Alexandra Valencia, "Ecuador Backing for Snowden Spurs Criticism of Correa Media Law," *Reuters* (June 27, 2013), www.reuters.com/article/2013/06/27/usa-security-ecuador-idUSL2N0F213820130627. Accessed on September 20, 2013; David Corn, "Ecuador's Edward Snowden Problem," *Mother Jones* (June 24, 2013), www.motherjones.com/politics/2013/06/edward-snowden-ecuador-rafael-correa. Accessed on September 20, 2013.

[28] Juan Forero, "Ecuador's Strange Journey from Embracing Snowden to Turning Him Away," *The Washington Post* (July 2, 2013); Rory Carroll, "Ecuador Says It Blundered over Snowden Travel Document," *The Guardian* (July 2, 2013).

[29] Rafael Correa, "Vulnerable Societies: Media and Democracy in Latin America," in World Leaders Forum, Columbia University, New York, September 25, 2011.

media activism. In that view, the media reproduce a system of values based on exclusion and privilege that the governments are challenging. To change the system, they must change the media.

As the conflict between governmental media activism and the right to free expression has moved to new media, governments have found traditional strategies less effective. In Venezuela, journalists who have quit or lost jobs have developed Web pages and opened Twitter accounts.[30] Television stations ignored the arrest of opposition leader Leopoldo Lopez on February 18, 2014, leaving Twitter as the only source of reporting on a detention that is widely regarded as a human rights violation.[31] In turn, the government has nationalized the Internet provider and blocked selected Twitter photos. Chavez in 2010 famously threatened, "You messed with me little bird."[32] The newly launched satirical blog *El Chigüire Bipolar* responded with a mix of the president's words set to cumbia rhythms and intercut with improvisations on the Twitter logo.[33] Chavez then opened his own Twitter account, which provided further fodder for *El Chigüire Bipolar.*[34] Still, Twitter remains an elite medium in Venezuela, with an estimated 14 percent penetration, which is still three percentage points higher than the United States, indicating that Twitter may be slightly more influential there, although still used by a small portion of the population.[35]

Run from a US-based service provider, *El Chigüire Bipolar,* named for a large rodent, is emblematic of new media's potential and limitations for defending the right of free expression. The blog is similar to *The Onion,* combining inside political jokes with sometimes crude humor. Significantly, one of the blog's three founders is the son of a Globovision cofounder, whom shareholders forced to resign as managing director in

[30] Associated Press, "Venezuela's Hugo Chavez Takes to Twitter," *USA Today* (April 29, 2010); Nuñez, "State-Censorship of the Press."

[31] Samantha Badgen, "New Online Project Seeks to Leverage Social Media in Coverage of Venezuelan Crisis," *Journalism in the Americas* (April 24, 2014); "Leopoldo Lopez, Arrestado en Caracas," *infobae* (February 18, 2014). Significantly, *infobae* is an online publication based in Buenos Aires.

[32] Nuñez, "State-Censorship of the Press."

[33] *El Chigüire Bipolar*, "Te Metiste Conmigo Pajarito," http://vimeo.com/9048083; Anahi Aradas, "Isla Presidencial, la Version Venezolana de South Park," *BBC Mundo*, www.bbc .co.uk/mundo/cultura_sociedad/2010/03/100330_venezuela_serie_animada_isla_presiden cial_internet_jrg.shtml?print=1.

[34] Associated Press, "Venezuela's Hugo Chavez Takes to Twitter."

[35] Nico Schoonderwoerd, "4 Ways Twitter Can Keep Growing," *Peerreach* (November 7, 2014), http://blog.peerreach.com/2013/11/4-ways-how-twitter-can-keep-growing/.

2010.[36] The Twitter mix was the precursor of the blog's popular animated video series *Isla Presidencial*, now in its third season. The conceit of the series is that Ibero-American presidents gathered for a summit set off together on a cruise that ends in a shipwreck, not unlike the vintage television series *Gilligan's Island*. None of the presidents or Spain's King Juan Carlos is spared the pillory of politically incorrect humor.[37] The series defies both insult laws and the image of Ibero-American unity presented by TeleSur.

However, the reach of the blog is limited. Visitor's Worth pegs average daily visitors at 7,141, and 83 percent of those visits come from inside Venezuela. Further, advertising revenue is estimated at $1,144 a month, which may indicate a model that relies on other revenue sources.[38] *Isla Presidencial* has 86,177 subscribers. The first episode has logged more than 5 million views and more recent episodes have half a million views, although it was not possible to obtain the number of unique viewers.[39] More than 2.2 million Venezuelans are Internet subscribers and 55 percent of the population of 30 million has Internet access, according to World Bank figures.[40] Those numbers indicate that only a fraction of those who can view the blog do so, leaving *El Chigüire Bipolar* and *Isla Presidencial* with a minuscule audience, compared with Venevision or Globovision. While government attempts to regulate new media have met with little success, that could be because they are considered low priority, a more recent form of elite media, and are thus treated with the tolerance traditionally accorded print media. Thus, their defense of free expression becomes nominal and nearly symbolic.

New media sites also face competition from a plethora of voices, which combined with the censorship and self-censorship in traditional media has created the opportunity for an innovative media vocation: curator. During their year as Knight Fellows at Stanford University in 2014, a group of mainly Latin American journalists developed the website *Venezuela Decoded*, as a clearing house for Twitter feeds. Key players are

---

[36] Aradas, "Isla Presidencial, la Version Venezolana de South Park."

[37] *El Chigüire Bipolar, Isla Presidencial*, YouTube, January 6, 2010.

[38] Visitors Worth, "El Chigüire Bipolar," http://visitorsworth.com/getinfo/?q=elchiguirebipolar.com+&updateButton=Check.

[39] *El Chigüire Bipolar, Isla Presidencial*.

[40] World Bank, "Fixed Broadband Internet Subscribers," in *World Development Indicators* (Washington, DC: World Bank, 2014); "Internet Users (per 100 People)" in *World Development Indicators*.

identified with short biographies that include their Twitter activity, and tweets feed into a classification of government, opposition, Spanish, or English. However, during a recent viewing, English-language tweets appeared on the Spanish feed and vice versa. The site's timeline of events was updated through October 2014, and a message to the site was not answered.[41] These indications that the site is not being updated frequently may indicate problems of continuity.

That the curators were based in Northern California and *El Chigüire Bipolar*'s service provider is in Southern California is indicative of the transnational nature that makes media part of what Levitsky and Way have termed

> the growing transnational infrastructure of organizations and networks... committed to the promotion of human rights and democracy. Strengthened by cheaper air travel and new information technologies such as the internet, transnational human rights and democracy networks drew international attention to human rights abuses, lobbied Western governments to take action against abusive governments, and helped to protect and empower domestic opposition groups.[42]

Transnational advocacy networks

The social media tools that transnational advocacy networks (TANs) are employing to update their strategies are transforming the networks themselves, while demonstrating both their potential and limitations for human rights advocacy. Social media are conducive to both the "boomerang" and "signal-flare" strategies that TANs used in the 1980s to support human rights issues. First identified by Keck and Sikkink, a boomerang strategy is used by activists whose government is unresponsive to domestic calls for an end to human rights abuses. They form alliances across borders and through information persuade allies in powerful countries to pressure their governments to influence the offender to respect human rights.[43]

---

[41] "Venezuela Decoded," http://venezueladecoded.com/lists.html.

[42] Levitsky and Way, *Competitive Authoritarianism*, p. 18.

[43] Margaret E. Keck and Kathryn Sikkink, *Activists beyond Borders: Advocacy Networks in International Politics* (Ithaca, NY: Cornell University Press, 1998), p. 16.

A signal flare more directly pressures a donor government to withdraw funding from governments accused of human rights violations. Hector Perla Jr. defines a signal flare strategy as

> a transnational political strategy where materially weak actors adversely affected by the policies or actions of a foreign entity rely on information . . . to: (i) draw the attention of potential allies to their plight in the transgressing entity's own country, (ii) highlight the culpability of the transgressing international entity's policy or actions in creating their suffering and (iii) attract or mobilize (material, financial, political) aid for the aggrieved population from within the transgressing country.[44]

TANs used both strategies to fight for human rights in Latin America in the twentieth century. Three recent cases demonstrate how these strategies have adapted to social media, resulting changes in the movements, as well as the potential and limitations of the movements, even when fortified with social media.

Former Guatemalan President Efrain Rios Montt's conviction for genocide in 2013, although later vacated, exemplified the potential of sustained media use in a transnational human rights campaign and also how media can transform networks. Social media were used to raise funds, to attract volunteers to protect witnesses, and to raise awareness of the trial as it progressed or sometimes failed to progress. Traditional media provided key evidence at the trial. Filmmaker Pamela Yates documented the pretrial process in *Granito: How to Nail a Dictator*, which played in theaters and online before the trial.[45] International viewers could watch trial updates in online footage that was reedited into the film series *Dictator in the Dock,* including an educational release with interactive features, such as a forum.[46]

Yates and her team also created an interactive digital archive that links official documents of the genocide to the work of forensic anthropologists and the memories of survivors. To record the memories, youths interview elders, creating a conversation across generations about the genocide. "All of my films have been about human rights and the quest for justice," Yates explained. "Now we have all of this evidence of the genocide and I thought that there could be a way across digital platforms

---

[44] Héctor Perla Jr., "Central American Counterpublic Mobilization: Transnational Social Movement Opposition to Reagan's Foreign Policy toward Central America," *Latino Studies*, 11, 2 (2013), 169.

[45] Pamela Yates, *Granito: How to Nail a Dictator* (Skylight Pictures, January 25, 2011).

[46] *Dictator in the Dock* (Skylight Pictures, 2013).

to make this documentation accessible."[47] Significantly, the documentation will be accessible not only to the TANs that are partners in the project, but also to the people who participated in producing it. Yates pointed out that people in the Guatemalan highlands are accustomed to being the subjects of photographs, documentaries, and news stories that producers then take away. This interactive project brings the product back to them, allowing them to be audience members also. Partners range from nongovernmental organizations (NGOs) with a long history of advocacy in Guatemala, such as NISGUA, to organizations with a broader mandate, such as the Corporation for Public Broadcasting and the Ford Foundation. A "team report" directs the project with one staff in Guatemala and one in the United States, serving as a bridge between partners in the two countries.[48] In addition, the work of the forensics team has become the subject of a TED talk that is now available via the Internet.[49]

New media amplified the work of established TANs and traditional media. Information became available more widely, more quickly. Guatemala's justice system was exposed to an international audience on a daily basis for the two months that the trial lasted. Just as significantly, the relationship between the members of the TAN shifted because of the potential that new media offered. The relationship among subject, producer, and audience has blurred, adding an additional nuance to Mark Poster's observations about the changes in roles that new media produce.[50] The change is also reminiscent of Garcia Canclini's description of traditional tourism and craft production that transforms indigenous customs into a show for outsiders.[51]

Similarly, in traditional strategies, the experiences and memories of those affected by human rights abuses were the evidence that TANs used to draw the attention of supporters in transgressor countries. Through new media, experiences and memories are making their way back to the

---

[47] Skylight Pictures, *Granito: Every Memory Matters* (Vimeo, November 30, 2011); *Granito: Cada Memoria Cuenta* (November 30, 2011).

[48] Skylight Pictures, *Granito: Every Memory Matters*; *Granito: Cada Memoria Cuenta*.

[49] Fredy Peccerelli, "A Forensic Anthropologist Who Brings Closure for the 'Disappeared,'" in TEDYouth 2014, Brooklyn, NY, November 15, 2014.

[50] Mark Poster, *The Mode of Information: Poststructuralism and Social Context* (Chicago, IL: University of Chicago Press, 1990), p. 128.

[51] Néstor García Canclini, *Arte Popular y Sociedad en América Latina: Teorías Estéticas y Ensayos de Transformación*, 1st edn., Teoría y Praxis (México: Editorial Grijalbo, 1977), p. 69.

communities that produced them, encouraging dialogue between generations. The network becomes more horizontal, with communication flowing both from the affected communities and into them. What changed less was the Guatemalan justice system. Ten days after the trial court convicted Rios Montt of genocide on May 10, 2013, the Constitutional Court overturned the conviction and ordered a new trial, which has been repeatedly suspended as the defense raises legal issues, most recently in January 2016.[52] Media were an instrument that could be successfully used to create the pressure to bring a trial and the evidence to secure a conviction. However, the upper levels of the justice system could not be moved to uphold the conviction.

In another recent case, scholar activists contacted US colleagues via email, asking for their signatures on a letter to President Obama, demanding that he cut off military and police aid to Mexico until the government can prove that its agents are not implicated in human rights violations. For ease in collecting and tracking signatures, the organizers circulated the letter in the form of a petition through Change.org, an online petitioning site.[53] The purpose of the letter is to point out US culpability in promoting drug interdiction policies that have resulted in heightened violence, culminating in evidence that the mayor and local police instigated the disappearance and murder of forty-three college students in Iguala, Guerrero, in September 2014. The campaign is directed at US academics, calls attention to the US role, and asks the recipients to take political action by signing the letter. The letter recalls previous demands for certification of respect for human rights that ultimately resulted in withdrawal of aid for the Nicaraguan counterrevolutionaries and Guatemalan government as well as modifications in Salvadoran policies. The human rights requirements have since become US law under the Leahy Amendment to the Foreign Assistance Act.

The letter was linked to the campaign for a National Day of Action for Peace, identified by an English-language Twitter hashtag

---

[52] Technically, only the final portion of the trial is being repeated. Elizabeth Malkin, "Former Leader of Guatemala Is Guilty of Genocide against Mayan Group," *The New York Times* (May 10, 2013); "Guatemala Overturns Historic Genocide Conviction," *Amnesty International*, www.amnesty.org/en/news/guatemala-overtuns-historic-geno cide-conviction-2013-05-21; Sofia Menchu, "Genocide trial for Guatemala ex-dictator Rios Montt suspended," Reuters, January 11, 2016, www.reuters.com/article/us-guate mala-trial-idUSKCN0UP21F20160111.

[53] Hector Perla Jr., email, Central American Studies–Latin American Studies Listserv (November 25, 2014).

#USTired2 (a translation of a Spanish-language hashtag that began in Mexico) and supported by an online video produced in English and localized Facebook pages as well as a national page.[54] Media networks, in this case Listservs, petition-gathering applications, Twitter, and online video, facilitate an established process for exerting pressure to promote human rights, which included traditional demonstrations on December 3, 2014, that drew on memes familiar to the audience.

At the San Francisco demonstration outside the Federal Building, about fifty protestors gathered to listen to speakers and a guitar-playing singer-songwriter. Organizers handed out posters, each with the photograph and name of a disappeared student, reminiscent of the posters of the disappeared in the weekly silent marches of the Mothers of the Plaza de Mayo in Argentina. Several participants recorded the parts of the event on cell phones, and one woman was particularly assiduous in recording the entire event on a tablet. One of those recording was Michelle White, a reporter from Mexico City with Spanish-language Radio KIQI in San Francisco. "I am planning to send these out on media networks because the mass media are not covering this movement," she said. She planned to post on Facebook and Twitter as well as sending information directly to colleagues in Mexico.[55]

The following day, video and photos from the demonstrations had been posted to several localized Facebook pages.[56] The national page consolidated information posted to the local pages, strengthening the sense of community. Linking the social media together through a hub-and-spoke design of pages created a sense of community across the United States and between the US focus cities and Mexico. The New York City page reposted web coverage, while the national page showed front-page media coverage of the event in leading Mexican newspapers, indicating a boomerang effect. The national page also noted a statement from Senator Patrick Leahy (author of the Leahy Amendment) and a White House statement the day after the event, demanding an

---

[54] #USTired2, "USTired2 We're Tired of the Drug War Too" (November 29, 2014); "USTired2sanfrancisco," www.facebook.com/USTired2SanFranciscoCA.

[55] Michelle White, interview with author (December 3, 2014).

[56] "USTired2sanfrancisco"; "Dallas for Ayotzinapa Coalition," www.facebook.com/Dallas ForAyotzinapa; Sonia Cuellar, "#USTired2 San Jose Event for 12/3 National Day of Action!," www.facebook.com/events/328756933974101/; Dulce Maria, "USTired2 Sonoma County with Ayotzinapa," www.facebook.com/events/503668576441660/.

investigation, with the comment, "Coincidence?"[57] That encouraged the perception that the boomerang strategy was succeeding.

Activists utilized an event linked to the oldest mass medium, books, to draw global attention to the disappearances. A flash mob laid on the floor in the middle of Guadalajara's International Book Fair, which bills itself as the world's top Spanish-language publishing event, until someone blew a sea shell, a method of summoning from the indigenous past. Demonstrators stood, waving placards, each with a photo of a disappeared student, and counted to forty-three. Organizers filmed the event and posted it to YouTube. Then, activists in the United States circulated the video on Facebook and other social media, reaching 542,426 views in two days.[58] Choosing an international event was calculated to draw global attention, which was amplified through the use of social media as part of a boomerang strategy to pressure the Mexican government into action.

Established TANs, such as the Committee in Solidarity with the People of El Salvador (CISPES) have integrated social media into their campaigns for human rights, but such media are less central to their strategies. CISPES followed a classic signal flare strategy in pressuring the US government not to intervene in the 2014 Salvadoran presidential elections. The group sponsored a US speaking tour of teacher union leaders to raise awareness of the importance of the election, then lobbied US Congressional representatives to pressure the State Department to issue a neutrality statement. Taking 100 delegates to monitor the elections, CISPES also put observers on the streets to discourage right-wing violence at demonstrations. Social media were used to facilitate these processes, but became central only during the final phase of the strategy, when CISPES "affirmed the integrity of the electoral process in the face of right-wing destabilization attempts through our blog, social media, radio & TV interviews in Salvadoran media." Even at that point, traditional mass media remained an integral part of the strategy, as CISPES representatives spoke to international news media.

A second round of Congressional lobbying to (successfully) pressure the State Department to officially recognize the election followed. CISPES

---

[57] USTired2 NYC Student Coalition with Ayotzinapa, "USTired2 Nyc Student Coalition with Ayotzinapa," www.facebook.com/USTired2NYCStudentCoalition; "USTired2," www.facebook.com/USTired2.

[58] ContrasentidoMX, "Flashmob por Ayoztinapa en Fil 2014" (YouTube, December 6, 2014); Salvador Caro, "Flashmob por Ayoztinapa in Fil 2014," Lisa Geduldig, www.facebook.com/hashtag/ayoztinapa?source=feed_text&story_id=10204414749723210.

reached its goal of holding the US government to a position of neutrality in the close election.[59] Social media appeared to change this veteran TAN far less than they did networks that sprang from media, such as the *Granito* cluster or #USTired2. This indicates a need to distinguish between TANs created around specific issues and ongoing organizations, such as CISPES, founded in a pre-Internet era, thirty-four years ago. While such TANs clearly work together, they appear to prioritize social media differently.

The TANs employed social media as both an organizing tool and a method for transmitting coverage of more traditional protests. Social media have been integrated into a repertoire of protest that includes tools used in labor protests during the Great Depression and against twentieth-century military dictatorships. Activists used social media to provide coverage that mainstream media denied their movement, to elicit that coverage, and to convince their audience that the movement was succeeding. They also fortified the sense of community that TANs foster as integral to their strategies. While social media proved useful to all three TANs, the organizations' level of adaptation to the media varied.

Challenges of traditional political culture

The ready availability of newer media promotes what Beltran termed "horizontal" access, which directly challenges the vertical structures that typify Latin America's authoritarian, hierarchical, and elitist political traditions.[60] Ruling groups have utilized another tradition, corporatism, to draw the most visible participants of such horizontal organizations back into vertical structures.

In Mexico, student protests over the presidential candidacy of a politician accused of ordering an attack on protesting peasants when he was governor led to a movement that became known as "I am 132." Appropriately, the movement announced itself in a video: To refute mainstream media reports that 131 outside agitators had organized the protest at a conservative private university where the candidate, Enrique

---

[59] Committee in Solidarity with the People of El Salvador, "Annual Report," 2014, pp. 3, 5. A former guerrilla commander, Salvador Sanchez Ceren, won the presidency, but his victory was not the stated goal of CISPES.

[60] Howard J. Wiarda and Harvey F. Kline, *Latin American Politics and Development*, 7th edn. (Boulder, CO: Westview Press, 2011), p. 12; Beltran, "A Farewell to Aristotle."

Peña Nieto, was speaking, students wearing T-shirts that proclaimed, "I am 132," explained their inconformity.[61] This was the first of numerous videos (a YouTube search of "yo soy 132" produced 7.7 million hits) that movement supporters posted. Using social media to organize protests across the country, the movement complemented attacks on the candidate with accusations of collusion against the country's television duopoly, Televisa and Azteca TV. Free speech overshadowed the original issue of Peña Nieto's role in the repression six years before.

Five weeks later, Peña Nieto was elected president in a three-candidate race with 38 percent of the vote. Three months later, Antonio Attolini, an outspoken member of the movement, announced that he would appear on a weekly political talk show on Televisa. Calling the program "a poor intent to legitimize the nation's media monopoly through the cooptation of Antonio," the movement rejected the characterization of him as a leader.[62] Televisa has portrayed the show, which was still on the air in December 2014, as a space for students to air their ideas without censorship.[63] Nevertheless, by drawing dissidents back into the fold of mainstream media – giving their spokesmen a voice likely to attract viewers with similar ideas – the show is functioning in the tradition of corporatism. The talking heads and the viewers are now part of the Televisa family, sitting around a table talking late Sunday night, and not posting their disrespectful videos or shouting in the streets. Passing over the question of Peña Nieto's human rights record also missed a point that became more salient with the disappearance of the forty-three students in Iguala in September 2014.

A Chilean student group grounded in more traditional organizing appears to have been more resistant to the corporatist pull. Chile's students began protesting for education reform shortly after socialist President Michelle Bachelet was elected in 2006. After initial attempts at repression, Bachelet invited six students and six professors to form an advisory panel, but did not implement their advice. When a center-right administration replaced her, protests escalated during what became known as the "Chilean winter" in 2011–13. Four former student leaders

[61] #yo soy 132, "Yosoy132" (January 9, 2012).

[62] Comisión de comunicación y prensa, "Comunicado del #Yosoy132-ITAM con Respecto a Antonio Attolini y el Programa 'Sin Filtros'" (Mexico City: #Yosoy132-ITAM, October 25, 2012). For more on the corporatist role of television in Mexico, see William A. Orme, *A Culture of Collusion: An Inside Look at the Mexican Press* (Coral Gables, FL: North-South Center Press, 1997).

[63] FOROtv, "Sin Flitro, Conducido por Genro Lozano," Noticieros Televisa, http://noticieros.televisa.com/foro-tv-sin-filtro/.

successfully ran for Congress in the elections that swept Bachelet back into power in 2013 on a platform that included education reform. Disappointed that what the president has proposed now that she is in office falls far short of the fundamental change they demand, the students were marching again in 2014 and began 2015 with threatening more demonstrations.[64]

Significantly, while the students have criticized coverage of the protests, filing at least one successful complaint with the Journalists Association, media has not been as central to the Chilean movement as its Mexican counterpart, either as an object of complaint or as an organizing tool.[65] With access to mainstream media, students have found newer media less important, although they have posted videos. Further, the older form of organization has proven more resilient in the face of corporatist overtures, whether advisory appointments or elected office. It has survived leadership changes, which could be anticipated in a student organization, whether former leaders became politicians or simply graduated. The Chilean student movement has remained constant to its goals by relying more on proven organizing methods than on new media.

The fragility of movements based on digital media is not isolated to student groups. Brazil's "barbecue protests" proved equally transitory. Organized by invitations on Facebook, the protests were mainly aimed at local issues. Despite Facebook's tremendous popularity – Brazil is second only to the United States in members – the protests attracted large crowds but produced few results. When that pattern continued in gatherings that questioned government spending on the 2014 World Cup games, dissidents turned to more traditional demonstrations, such as marches, which, ultimately, were equally ineffective.[66]

The Latin American experience thus tends to support Hopgood's concerns about "slacktivism." Despite the deep identification, reflected

---

[64] Eilis O'Neill, "Is the Chilean Student Movement Being Co-Opted by Its Government?," *The Nation* (June 16 2014); "Universitarios Amenazan con Movilizaciones: Dicen Sentirse Poco Escuchados en Discusión de Reforma Educacional," *Cambio 21* (January 11, 2015). The crux of the argument is whether education is a commodity for purchase or a fundamental right, reflected in the student demand to replace the voucher system instituted during the Pinochet dictatorship with direct subsidies to public schools and universities.

[65] Pilar Gonzalez, "Directorio de TVN Reconoce Error Frente a Utilizacion de Imagen de Encapuchado para Gratificar las Movilizaciones Estudiantiles," *Cambio 21* May 15, 2011.

[66] Samantha Pearson, "Brazil's BBQ Protesters Turn up the Heat," *Financial Times* (June 19, 2013).

in "I am" statements, that supports Poster's observation about the intimacy of cyber media, movements centered on social media ultimately appeared fragile. While more traditional movements showed more resistance to traditional pressures, the possibility of producing fundamental change – whether through elections, social media, or traditional organizing – remained limited. The mere existence of social media does not assure their success against well-rehearsed responses to social movements. Organizations must find ways to utilize the strong identification that cyber media generate to effectively adapt and implement change.

Threats from nonstate actors

Governments are not alone in their efforts to undermine digital media. Nongovernmental actors have tried to use the transnational character of such media against them. An early example is the libel suit that the Mexican bank Banamex brought in New York in 2001 against *The Narco News Bulletin*, an online publication based in Mexico. The bank had already lost three suits against the publication in Mexico, which is known for far more strict libel laws than the United States. Ultimately, the New York court ruled that it did not have jurisdiction and that the defendants had not committed libel in any case. However, the defendants contended that the purpose of the suit was never to win, rather to drive them out of business through costly legal maneuvering in a distant venue.[67] Thus, the suit was a transnational version of the sort of legal harassment that the Levitsky and Way had characterized.

More recent attempts of nonstate actors to silence media, especially on issues related to human rights, have become more violent. Violence against journalists is hardly a new phenomenon in Latin America.[68] What is new is the scope and barbarity of the wave of antimedia violence intertwined with reporting of human rights violations in Mexico's drug war. From 1992 to 2014, the Committee to Protect Journalists has confirmed that thirty-one Mexican journalists have been killed as a direct result of reporting, twenty since 2004 and all but three of them

[67] Juanita Darling, "Forum Shopping and the Cyber Pamphleteer: Banamex v. Rodriguez," *Communication Law and Policy*, 8 (Summer 2003).

[68] See Jacobo Timerman, *Preso sin Nombre, Celda sin Número*, The Americas (Madison: University of Wisconsin Press, 2000); Héctor Aguilar Camín, *Los Días de Manuel Buendía: Testimonios*, 1st edn. (México, DF: Océano: Fundación Manuel Buendía, 1984); Bernardo Ruiz, *Reportero* (Quiet Pictures, 2011).

murdered.[69] Two-thirds of the victims were covering crime and the remaining one-third were covering human rights. The increase in murders of journalists coincided with rising narcotics violence and former president Felipe Calderon's declaration of all-out war on drug cartels in 2006, peaking in 2010, when seven journalists were killed.[70] Using different criteria, Human Rights Watch reported that thirty-five journalists were killed from 2007 to 2010 and eight were missing and feared dead, "generating a climate of impunity and self-censorship."[71]

Cowed, national media sharply reduced coverage of the violence. Bloggers filled the void. However, drug traffickers proved more tech savvy than anticipated and tracked down the Internet informers. In 2011, the bodies of two young bloggers were hung from a pedestrian bridge across the US–Mexico border along with a banner that read: "This is what will happen to Internet troublemakers, look out, I am watching you. Sincerely, Z," an apparent reference to the notorious Los Zetas drug cartel.[72] The same year, a Mexican branch of the "hacktivist" network Anonymous threatened to reveal the names and addresses of the police, politicians, journalists, and taxi drivers who collaborated with Los Zetas. The cartel kidnapped a member, returning him only in exchange for silence and with a warning that ten family members would be killed for every name revealed. "We cannot avoid threats to civilians who have nothing to do with our actions," the masked speaker explained. The customary sign off – "We are Anonymous; we are legion; we do not forgive; we do not forget; wait" – sounded hollow.[73] Digital media have proven as vulnerable as traditional media to violent censorship.

---

[69] The number of journalists killed is higher, but the organization reports only deaths that can be proven as the direct result of coverage.

[70] Committee to Protect Journalists, "31 Journalists Killed in Mexico since 1992/Motive Confirmed," www.cpj.org/killed/americas/mexico/.

[71] Human Rights Watch, *World Report 2011*, (Washington, DC: Human Rights Watch, 2011). During the same period, the organization reported a total of 35,000 deaths related to the drug war.

[72] "Matan y Cuelgan de un Puente en México a Dos Jovenes por Denunciar por Internet a Criminales," *apocalipticus* (2011), http://apocalipticus.over-blog.es/article-matan-y-cuelgan-de-un-puente-en-mexico-a-dos-jovenes-por-denunciar-por-internet-a-criminales-84324198.html; José Antonio Fúster, "El Miedo a los Sicarios: El Blog del Narco Ya No Se Actualiza en México," *Periodista Latino* (2013), www.periodistadigital.com/inmigrantes/negocios/2013/04/28/el-miedo-a-los-sicarios-el-blog-del-narco-ya-no-se-actualiza-en-mexico.shtml.

[73] Anonymous X, "Anonymous Informa Sobre Miembro Liberado" (YouTube, 2011).

Transnational advocacy groups for journalists have responded with digital media sites. Since 2012, two US-based NGOs, Freedom House and the International Center for Journalists, have hosted the website *Periodistas en Riesgo* (Journalists at Risk), tracking attacks on journalists across Mexico on an interactive map and providing resources to journalists under threat. The site defines journalists broadly to include "bloggers, citizen reporters and users of social networks who use digital and mobile tools to report crimes, corruption and abuses of human rights." That definition, combined with an invitation to citizen participation by reporting attacks on journalists as part of a larger effort to unite journalists and citizens in fighting crime and corruption, indicates adherence to a model of horizontal communication.[74] In late 2014, the Brazil office of Article 19, a UK-based NGO named for the article in the International Declaration of Human Rights relating to free expression, launched an interactive map of attacks on free speech in Brazil.[75] The choice of the term "free speech" is more inclusive than the words journalist or press, also indicating a more horizontal understanding of communication.

Digital media have proven just as vulnerable as traditional media to attacks from nonstate actors. Their transnational nature can expose them to additional forms of legal persecution. The anonymity of the Web is a thin veil that does not fully hide media activists from violence in the physical world. What digital media have changed is the response to those threats. Freedom of the press has evolved into free expression, a right to be exercised and protected by all citizens, using digital tools.

Conclusion

Digital media have coincided with the emergence of democracy in Latin America, contributing to the region's redefinition of centuries-old norms and values. In that scenario, early adapters have included the economic and traditional media elite clinging to power in populist regimes as well as the more predictable college students and youths. Social media have become useful organizing tools, drawing crowds to marches and informing activists about the results of demonstrations in other places. However, they have not been especially successful in transforming

[74] Freedom House and Centro Internacional de Periodistas, "Periodistas en Riesgo: Un Registro de la Violencia contra los Periodistas en Mexico," www.periodistasenriesgo.com/.

[75] Article 19 – South America, "Violações à Liberdade de Expressão," http://violacoes .artigo19.org/.

society. What they have transformed are the advocacy networks that in turn have a longer record of transforming society. Whether their aim is the prosecution of a dictator or the protection of journalists, those networks have become more horizontal, inviting participation and encouraging exchange of information. As a result, through the use of social media the networks have come to better reflect the democratic, inclusive values that they advocate. Latin America's protest networks thus illustrate both the promise and the limitations of digital media in asserting human rights. Social media can call attention to abuses, but cannot single-handedly prevent them. In addition, new technologies can be effective when they take the state by surprise, but with time, the state learns how to mitigate their effects. This is particularly true in Latin America, where a deep digital divide marks the boundaries of access and corporatist states adeptly co-opt leaders of dissident movements. Nevertheless, social media have provided a meaningful way for citizens to become advocates. More than T-shirts that proclaim "I am . . . ," such participation demonstrates deep affinity with the human rights movement and commitment to its goals. That deep identification with advocacy networks, which is the purview of digital media, may be their most valuable contribution to the struggle for human rights in Latin America.

PART III

Network politics and social change

Iran's Green Movement, social media, and the exposure of human rights violations

ELHAM GHEYTANCHI

The new social media such as mobile phones, Persian social networking sites, and satellite TV that broadcasted citizen journalism enabled – or better yet, mobilized – the youth movement in Iran to make their presence felt not only in Iran but also in the region during and after the disputed 2009 presidential election. The new social media allowed a higher rate of political participation and protest while documenting human rights abuses. The new social media, along with satellite TV by exiles, proved to be a great platform to call for demonstrations on a specific day. The loose online network affiliations lowered the cost of mobilization and membership in a progressive social movement. Though social media can widen the grassroots base of social movements, it is also used by the authorities as a means to arrest and suppress social movements such as the Green Movement. Arguably, lack of central authority and a clear strategy in the Green Movement led to its defeat. But activists' effective use of social media has proved that a new wave of social movements is in the making in Iran in which human rights violations, arrests, and political repression will not go unnoticed in the international community.

The tenth presidential election in Iran was supposed to show the democratic face of the Iranian political system. Instead, the events following the presidential election on June 12, 2009, inspired Iranians, and later many people in the Middle East, to rise up against their nondemocratic governments. The Iranian government's suppression of dissent was largely ineffective due to people's determination and creativity as well as their access to social media, the Internet, and mobile phones. This chapter demonstrates that while the Iranian government has consistently continued its censorship efforts, the Green Movement's activists succeeded in using the Internet and social media to their advantage. The human rights violations by the authorities were shown to the world via the people's videos posted on the Internet, further exposing the repressive measures that the Islamic Republic has relentlessly applied since the 1979 Revolution.

In their most recent book, *Access Contested*, Ron Diebert and Rafal Rohozinski describe three generations of censorship techniques used by governments to crush dissent.[1] The first generation of techniques focuses on "Chinese Style" Internet filtering and Internet café surveillance. Second-generation techniques attempt to construct a legal environment that legitimizes the control of information. Authorities make informal requests to companies for the removal of information and technical shutdowns of websites, and computer attacks are commonplace. Third-generation techniques consist of warrantless surveillance, the creation of "national cyberspaces," state-sponsored information campaigns, and direct physical action to silence dissidents.[2] In the aftermath of the presidential election, the Iranian government utilized third-generation techniques in its attempt to censor the Internet.

Authoritarian political systems, like those of China and Iran, monitor their Internet to control the flow of news and information. As MacKinnon explains, "when an authoritarian regime embraces and adjusts to the inevitable changes brought by digital communications technologies the result is 'networked authoritarianism.'"[3] In this networked authoritarianism, the ruling elite tend to use the Internet for their own purposes while suppressing dissent through the same channels. While it is increasingly hard to sustain an oppositional movement in the face of networked authoritarianism, Iranians and Chinese have maintained a vibrant blogosphere.[4] Such efforts have continued despite persistent government controls, arrests, and intimidation of bloggers.[5] The presence of exiled activists also allows activists in Iran to stay connected across the borders.

The Persian blogosphere helped create the discourse for democracy, pluralism, and tolerance in the years prior to the election. Furthermore,

---

[1] Ronald Deibert, J. Palfrey, R. Rohozinski, and J. Zittrain, *Access Contested: Security, Identity, and Resistance in Asian Cyberspace* (Cambridge, MA: MIT Press, 2011).

[2] Ronald Deibert and Rafal Rohozinski, "Beyond Denial: Introducing Next Generation Information Access Controls," in Deibert, Palfrey, Rohozinski, and Zittrain (eds.), *Access Contested*, p. 6.

[3] Rebecca MacKinnon, "China's Networked Authoritarianism," *Journal of Democracy*, 22, 2 (April 2011), 33.

[4] Nasrin Alavai, *We Are Iran* (New York: Soft Skull Press, 2006).

[5] G. Yang, *The Power of the Internet in China: Citizen Activism Online* (New York: Columbia University Press, 2009); John Kelly and Bruce Etling, "Mapping Iran's Online Public: Politics and Culture in the Persian Blogsphere," Berkman Center for Internet and Society (April 2008), http://cyber.law.harvard.edu/sites.

reformist presidential candidates Mir Hossein Mossavi and Mehdi Karoubi and their supporters used the Internet and social media throughout their campaigns. These campaigns took place on blogs, political websites, Balatarin (a Persian social news aggregator and networking site), microblogging sites like Twitter, and other social networking sites such as Facebook. There were real discussion and exchange of ideas during the campaigns that gave Iranians a taste of democratic political process.

In the months following the election, the Iranian government banned foreign journalists from reporting in Iran, arrested and jailed many Iranian journalists, and slowly enforced the monitoring of citizens' online activism. However, just as the government forced foreign journalists to exit the country, people, including human rights activists, resorted to using social media to report the news quickly and anonymously. Thus, citizen journalism via social media made it possible for news to flow from Iran despite governmental censorship of the Internet and bans on foreign media coverage.

Blogs changed the political culture in Iran by allowing views that oppose the ruling party to appear online. This is important because, as Philip Howard has shown in his study of information and communication technologies (ICTs) in Muslim countries, "the route to democratization is a digital one."[6] In repressed societies the online discussion of social, political, and cultural issues appears crucial for social movements and transitions to democracy. "For democratic transitions," Howard goes on to assert, "having a comparatively active online civil society is the most important ingredient of both necessary and sufficient solutions."[7] Through social media sites such as Balatarin, the Iranian online community can engage in debates, discuss sociopolitical issues, and plan strategies for the accommodation of government supporters willing to compromise. The children of Sepahis (IRGC, or the Revolutionary Guards) as well as the Basijis also want more social freedoms in their families as well as in their society.

Historical background

Using the Internet as a safe haven for discussion is not a new tactic in Iran. After the Iranian government cracked down on the Iranian press in 2000,

---

[6] Philip Howard, *The Digital Origins of Dictatorship and Democracy: Information, Technology and Political Islam* (Oxford and New York: Oxford University Press, 2010), p. 201.

[7] Ibid., p. 183.

many Iranian journalists and activists found refuge on the Internet. Many Iranian activists living in Iran or abroad started blogging soon after that. In 2006, blogs in Persian ranked tenth for the number of blogs posted in any language worldwide.[8] Journalists and activists brought discussions during the relative freedom of the press era initiated by Mohammad Khatami's presidency.[9] The journalist and civil society activists' discussions were about building a civil society, reform, and rule of law to the Web.

The Internet provided a forum where many new ideas and thoughts were openly shared and discussed. The dominant discussions on the Web revolved around freedom of speech, freedom of assembly, and political reform. These discussions began to receive more notoriety. More political figures in the government and the official newspapers referred to blogs than they had in the past decade.[10]

During the first term of Ahmadinejad's presidency (2005–9), political dissent continued on the Web. The Iranian government quickly moved to limit freedom of speech on the Internet. However, as censorship increased, dissent became more widespread on the Internet.[11] The Iranian government began using the Internet to counter this dissent as well as for its own purposes, such as domestic and international propaganda and internal governmental affairs.

The presidential election in June 2009 created an opportunity for the government to demonstrate the degree to which it can tolerate opposing views. The unblocking of Facebook and Twitter in January 2009 surprised many Iranian Internet users. A large number of Iranians signed up for these services in a short period of time. In less than a month, Facebook became the fifteenth most visited website in Iran.[12] Facebook soon became a popular destination among reformists and social activists

---

[8] "Technocrati: Persian among the Top Ten Languages in Blogsphere," *BBC News*, www.bbc.co.uk/blogs/persian/2006/11/post_132.html.

[9] Babak Rahimi, "Cyberdissent: The Internet in Revolutionary Iran," *Middle East Review of International Affairs*, 7, 3 (September 2003), http://meria.idc.ac.il/JOURNAL/2003/issue3/rahimi.pdf.

[10] Aiden Duffy and Philip N. Howard, "Iran's Political Parties Link to Persian Blogosphere More Than News Sources," Project on Information Technology and Political Islam, Research Memo (2010), University of Washington, Seattle.

[11] Elham Gheytanchi and B. Rahimi, "Iran's Reformists and Activists: Internet Exploiters," *Middle East Policy*, 15, 1 (Spring 2008), 45–59.

[12] "Facebook among the Top 15 Most Visited Websites from Iran," http://mhmazidi2 .wordpress.com/2009/02/26/fa-to-15/.

who were engaged in nonviolent social movements for teachers, women, and students, to name just a few.

The first political activism of the pro-reform camp in Iran started on a website called *Mowj Sevvom* (The Third Wave). In their campaign, they called on former president Mohammad Khatami to run against Ahmadinejad. The *Mowj Sevvom* site collected more than 450,000 signatures calling on Khatami to run.[13] Khatami signed up for the presidential election and acknowledged the role of The Third Wave campaign in his decision to do so.[14] Khatami later left the race as Mir Hossein Mousavi announced his candidacy. Mousavi maintained an active campaign website called *Ghalam News* that was censored by the government on June 21, 2009, after it posted images of a defiant Mousavi among the cheerful and nonviolent demonstrators in Tehran the previous day. Not surprisingly, the government-backed TV and radio managed to censor the news of the demonstration.

Likewise, the other reformist candidate, Mehdi Karoubi, was active online. His party's newspaper, Etemad-e Melli, was regularly updated online. His campaign manager, Gholamhossein Karbaschi, created and maintained an active Twitter account. According to an adviser to one of the candidates, the two reformers even discussed who had enough seniority points on Balatarin.com and should be allowed to create the daily headline news for their campaign.[15] Thus, the campaigns, protests, civil disobedience, and mass demonstrations following the controversial presidential election in 2009 were planned, reported, and widely discussed online through an already established social media network.[16]

Crisis of legitimacy for the government

On Election Day, the Internet and social media provided "Accountability Technology," which, as Larry Diamond explains, "enables citizens to report news, expose wrongdoings, express opinions, mobilize protest, monitor elections, scrutinize government, deepen participation, and

---

[13] The *Mowj* website petition list, www.mowj.ir/PetitionList.php.
[14] Khatami talking to Mowj reporter, YouTube.com, www.youtube.com/watch?v= DiTq5Tjng8Y.
[15] Phone interview (May 2009).
[16] Mehdi Yahyanejad and Elham Gheytanchi, "Social Media, Dissent, and Iran's Green Movement," in Larry Diamond and Marc F. Plattner (eds.), *Liberation Technology: Social Media and the Struggle for Democracy* (Baltimore, MD: Johns Hopkins University Press, 2012), pp. 139–53.

expand the horizons of freedom."[17] Just as Ushahidi, a free and open-source mapping software, allowed election accountability in Egypt and Sudan, the Internet, social media, and mobile phones allowed Iranians to remain vigilant about widespread election fraud in their country.[18]

The speed of events on June 12, 2009, was unprecedented. Although fraud has always been a part of elections in Iran, it was evident that this time was different. The Iranian government disabled text messaging (SMS) across Iran. This damaged the efforts of political activists to monitor the election. Mousavi's camp had more than 20,000 observers in different polling locations. The observers were supposed to report back the results and/or any voting or polling station irregularities via SMS to Mousavi's campaign headquarters. Later, the Mousavi campaign announced the interruption of SMS services as one of the primary pieces of evidence for fraud in the presidential election. The government, on the other hand, claimed that SMS service was interrupted in order to prevent illegal campaigning by different candidates on Election Day.

Then the paramilitary forces attacked one of the main campaign headquarters of Mousavi in Tehran. The Mousavi campaign had set up a room on the fifth floor of the Qeytarieh campaign headquarters for Web broadcasting of interviews with politicians and celebrities who encouraged people to vote for Mousavi. The hostile militia attacked the building to disrupt this broadcast. VahidOnline, an Iranian Internet celebrity who remained anonymous until that day, was present in the building. He had witnessed the attack and posted his account of it on Twitter and his blog.[19] Meanwhile the attackers made it to the fifth floor of the campaign headquarters and broke the broadcasting equipment. People in the building called the police, fought back, and were able to arrest four of the militia. The video of the attack on the Mousavi headquarters was later shown on BBC Persian's evening news. It provided important evidence of the government's concerted effort to violently suppress the reformist candidates and their supporters. Videos, such as the one by VahidOnline, persuaded the public that a coup was underway. VahidOnline went into hiding and later escaped Iran. He posted an emotional statement on his

[17] Larry Diamond, "Liberation Technology," *Journal of Democracy*, 21, 3 (July 2010), 70.

[18] Patrick Meier, Mary Joyce, and Anahi Ayala Iacucci, "Is Ushahidi a Liberation Technology?," paper presented at Stanford University's Center for Democracy Development and Rule of Law Conference on Liberation Technologies in Authoritarian States, October 11–12, 2011.

[19] Exclusive phone interview with VahidOnline (unpublished), January 2010.

blog, entitled "The Crime of Being Online," before crossing the border with the help of smugglers.[20]

As the events of the day unfolded, the perception of a coup by government-backed militia strengthened. At 6:30 p.m., several hours before the polling stations closed, Fars News Agency, a website close to the IRGC, predicted that Ahmadinejad would win with 60 percent of the votes. There was general disbelief that this could be true among the Iranian online community. The announcement from Fars News was posted to Balatarin with the altered title of "Is this believable: Mousavi 28 percent!! Ahmadinejad 69 percent? The biggest fraud of the century has begun." This link was posted on Balatarin at 12:09 p.m., only three hours after the polling stations closed.[21] This posting marked the establishment of Balatarin as the hub of what was later called the Green Movement.

The case of Neda's video: exposing human rights violations

Government-backed militia killed a young woman, Neda Agha Soltan, at 7:20 p.m. on June 20, 2009. The person who took the video sent it to a contact outside of Iran who posted it on Facebook at 8:53 p.m. The video was subsequently posted to YouTube at 10:19 p.m. In less than three hours, the video of Neda's death was broadcasted to thousands of viewers worldwide. Neda's horrific death has been referred to numerous times in President Obama's speeches as "heartbreaking."[22] This video has come to represent the Iranian government's violent repression of its citizens' nonviolent movement.[23]

Due to widespread use of social media, mobile phones, and the advent of citizen journalism, violations of human rights on the streets by Iranian officials were no longer kept in the dark. A women's rights activist told the author that "in 1988, thousands of Iranians were killed in mass executions inside the Iranian prisons within a short period of time and to this day the prison massacre has received very little publicity. In 2009 atrocities have been documented and the Iranian government is

[20] "The Crime of Being Online," http://vahid-online.net/1388/05/20/be-online/.
[21] http://balatarin.com/permlink/2009/6/12/1617273.
[22] "Obama Calls Neda Video Heartbreaking," *Reuters,* http://blogs.reuters.com/talesfromthe trail/2009/06/23/obama-calls-neda-video-heartbreaking-2/.
[23] Metter Mortensen, "When Citizen Photojournalism Sets the News Agenda: Neda Agha Soltan as a Web 2.0 Icon of Post-Election Unrest in Iran," *Global Media and Communication Journal,* 7 (April 21, 2011), 14–16.

forced to come up with explanations for them."[24] Frequently these explanations are lies. For example, during a massive nonviolent demonstration in Tehran on December 26, 2009, a police truck drove over a protestor several times.[25] The video was immediately posted on YouTube, Balatarin, and Facebook and was broadcasted in Iran through satellite TV. The Iranian government had to provide three different explanations for the scene.[26] Similarly, the Iranian government changed its story regarding Neda's fate many times.[27] At first, the government claimed Neda had not died and that the video showed fake blood. Later, government officials made a documentary that was broadcast on national TV. It showed that Neda was assassinated by a woman who ran from the scene.

Neda became an instant icon, the symbol of innocence in the face of crude brutality of the state response to the crisis that followed the presidential election in Iran. To mark the fortieth day after the bloody death of Neda Agha Soltan, Sohrab Arabi, and other young Iranians killed by gunshots fired on the streets of Tehran, a newly formed committee of Mourning Mothers of Iran gathered at Neda's graveside, chanting, "*Nirooyeh Entezami, Sohrab baradaret koo? Neda Khaharet koo? Nedaye ma namordeh, in jomhouri ast ke mordeh.*" "Security forces, Where is Sohrab, your brother? Where is Neda, your sister? Our Neda [*neda* also means *voice*] has not died, it is the Republic that has died."[28]

Neda has figured into international politics regarding Iran. President Obama referred to Neda in his speech to accept the Nobel peace prize (October 9, 2009), and the Yemeni government named a street in the capital for Neda to show their discontent with alleged Iranian involvement in their internal affairs.[29] The Iranian state TV has responded with a

---

[24] MR, an Iranian women's rights activist, told the author of this comparison.

[25] "A Protester Is Run over by an Armored Truck," YouTube.com, www.youtube.com/watch?v=J2d3M203aAg&feature=related.

[26] "Tehran Police Chief Doesn't Admit That the Truck Belonged to Security Forces," YouTube.com, www.youtube.com/watch?v=YZbDU8KBE98&feature=related.

[27] "Iran Ambassador Suggests CIA Could Have Killed Neda Agha-Soltan," *LA Times*, http://latimesblogs.latimes.com/washington/2009/06/neda-cia-cnn-killing.html; "Zarghami Claims That Neda's Death Is Fake," *Khabar Online*, http://khabaronline.ir/news-11915.aspx; "Press TV Documentary of Neda's Death," YouTube.com, www.youtube.com/watch?v=Shp7HE2YA_c&skipcontrinter=1.

[28] Elham Gheytanchi, "Symbols, Signs, and Slogans of the Demonstrations in Iran in 2009," in Yahya Kamalipour (ed.), *Media, Power and Politics in the Digital Age: The 2009 Presidential Election Uprising in Iran* (Lanham, MD: Rowman & Littlefield, 2010), pp. 251–65.

[29] Ian Black, "Iran and Yemen in Tit-for-Tat Battle for Street Cred," *The Guardian* (November 27, 2009), www.guardian.co.uk/world/2009/nov/27/iran-yemen-street-cred-rename.

theatrical show displaying their version of the killing of Neda, namely, a conspiracy plot performed by the British journalists who were in Iran and were trying to stage a velvet revolution with the help of traitors such as Arash Hejazi, the Iranian doctor who tried, in vain, to save Neda's life. In addition, the hardliners staged a demonstration in front of the British embassy demanding the extradition of Dr. Hejazi to Iran. Neda's story shows the power of information flow through the medium of the Internet and social media in countries where the government heavily censors news.

Protest, Dissent, and Opposition via Social Media

In Iran, national TV, radio, and major newspapers are under the direct supervision of the Supreme Leader. Iranian press and TV experienced short periods of relative freedom of expression during the revolutionary days in 1979 and again during the first term of Khatami's presidency. Prior to the presidential election of 2009, satellite broadcasts by BBC Persian and VOA enjoyed a wide reach among the general public, but there is currently no such thing as free TV, radio, or press in Iran. Most of the newspapers in Iran are state-owned or belong to pro-government politicians.

Students, journalists, and activists use Persian language websites as their main source of alternative news. However, due to Internet censorship, Iranian government-owned websites, such as Mehr and Fars News, still receive numerous visitors. For example, Fars News Agency has more visitors than Radio Farda, which is the Persian broadcast of Radio Free Europe funded by the US government, or Gooya News, JARAS, a Green Movement news website, or Balatarin, which are independent websites based outside of Iran.

Information from social media and citizen journalism flowed despite the government's repeated jamming and censorship. News from these independent sources managed to impact mainstream media. News networks such as CNN started broadcasting YouTube videos from Iran. BBC Persian and VOA also began using uploaded videos from YouTube in their reporting. It became difficult for these networks to prevent their airtime from becoming a platform for social action because many of their journalists were supporting the movement.

Nonviolent mass demonstrations on the Quds Day demonstrated the interaction of satellite TV programming with new social media in Iran. The last Friday in the month of Ramadan is called the Quds (Jerusalem) Day and is used by the Iranian government for state-supported anti-Israel demonstrations. In the summer of 2009, after the violent government crackdowns on protests, the Iranian government believed that the demonstrations had died out. It was wrong. Online activists called for Green Movement supporters to show up at the Quds Day demonstrations in order to protest the crackdown.

This mobilization started several weeks before and initially did not have any support among the opposition figures in Iran. Many of them were hesitant to use the demonstrations against Israel to protest against the Iranian government. Only in the days close to the Quds Day did Mehdi Karoubi, one of the opposition leaders, respond to the calls of online activists.[30] Mousavi waited until the last day to announce his participation. The Quds Day's demonstration, therefore, was born on the Internet.

There were no YouTube videos of the demonstrations for several hours after the demonstrations because the Iranian government disrupted Internet services on the Quds Day. This led BBC News to publish an erroneous article that stated, "Reformist opponents of the controversially re-elected President Ahmadinejad seem to have been massively outnumbered by system loyalists eager to demonstrate their support for the president and his patron, the Supreme Leader, Ayatollah Ali Khamenei."[31]

Online activists quickly posted links to pictures and new videos on YouTube to show the large demonstrations by Green Movement supporters.[32] The BBC website updated the article without even acknowledging the correction: "Thousands of opposition supporters have clashed with security forces during a government-sponsored rally in Tehran."[33] Thus, social media forced the BBC, a major international news outlet, to correct a story based on reporting by viewers.

Far from having given up, the Green Movement protesters were present in large numbers and subverted the official demonstration.[34] In

---

[30] "Karoubi: You Will See the Power of People on the Quds Day," www.radiofarda.com/content/f3_karoubi_protest_Iran_Quds_rally_green_movement_postelection/1810580.html.

[31] This was deleted from the website the following day.

[32] "Despite Warning, Thousands Rally in Iran," *New York Times*, www.nytimes.com/2009/09/19/world/middleeast/19iran.html.

[33] "Clashes Erupt at Iran Mass Rally," *BBC News*, http://news.bbc.co.uk/1/hi/world/middle_east/8262273.stm.

[34] "Iran Protests on Quds Day," *The Guardian*, www.guardian.co.uk/news/blog/2009/sep/17/iran-protests-quds-day.

a way, the Quds Day protest transformed the Green Movement into a longer-lasting movement. Mousavi was well aware of the significance of the demonstration. He called it a turning point for the movement.[35] He also acknowledged the role of social media in a speech after the demonstration:

> Today, there has been a network created in the virtual space acting very efficiently when there isn't any other type of [independent] media available. The social groups acting within this virtual space are less venerable. Members of these groups have given dynamism to the movement which has made us much more hopeful. There hasn't been any official call [by the leaders of the movement] for demonstration on the Quds Day, but we witnessed this great demonstration. This was at a time where there had been many, many threats in the past three months and many of the families were preventing their children from going [to the demonstrations]. This could have not have been achieved without this [virtual] network.[36]

Similar to the Quds Day, the mass protest over the death of reformist Ayatollah Montazeri demonstrated how activists used social media, satellite TV, SMS, and word of mouth to successfully mobilize. The idea for a mass protest originated on a blog and was publicized through Balatarin. An anonymous blogger posted a link on Balatarin that suggested protesters gather in Mohseni Square in Tehran for a public mourning for Ayatollah Montazeri. In less than nine hours, people circulated the announcements and about 3,000 people gathered.[37] It is important to note that the blogger in this case acted alone and grassroots groups implemented the idea without prior coordination with reformist leaders Karoubi or Mousavi.[38]

New social media became so pervasive that they were able to utilize Iranian national TV as an unwilling platform. Take, for example, the symbolic "green" voting during the most watched program on the Iranian state-run TV, the sports program called *90*. During this program, people are asked a question and invited to vote for one of several answers via SMS. Early in January 2010, online activists asked people to send an

---

[35] "Mousavi Calls the Quds Demonstration a Turning Point," *BBC News*, www.bbc.co.uk/persian/iran/2009/09/090928_si_mousavi_Qudsday.shtml.

[36] "Mosavi's Speech after the Quds Day," www.parlemannews.ir/?n=4128.

[37] Video of the gathering after the death of the dissident Ayatollah Montazeri, YouTube.com, www.youtube.com/watch?v=KLNteL_V6QY.

[38] "The Call for Gathering to Commemorate the Dissident Ayatollah's Death," Balatarin.com, http://balatarin.com/topic/2009/12/20/1003993.

SMS to the next program of *90* and choose the green option regardless of what the question was.[39] The idea for this nonviolent tactic spread quickly through SMS in Iran. The last choice was chosen because it was usually shown in green. During this live program, the host changed the last option from green to yellow, but people still voted for the last option. More than 1.8 million people voted and 75 percent of them chose the third option (which was not the right answer). This simple and fairly low-risk action proved to the people who were watching the program that at least one million Iranians were ready to show their dislike of the government by following the campaign of the Green Movement.[40]

Another effective protest that was entirely conducted online concerned a political prisoner. Majid Tavakoli, a student activist in Iran, was arrested after a speech in which he criticized Iran's leaders. Fars News Agency claimed that Tavakoli was arrested when he tried to escape wearing women's clothing. It was evident this had been published to discredit Tavakoli.[41] Masih Alinejad, a journalist and blogger, posted an article asking men to wear headscarves in solidarity with Majid and to protest the forced Islamic dress code for women in Iran.[42] This was posted on Balatarin, became the most voted item of the day, and quickly spread to Facebook and other social networks.[43] More than 450 men took pictures of themselves with headscarves and posted them on Facebook in support of Tavakoli.[44]

While many platforms had a significant impact on the Green Movement, some are ascribed a greater influence than they deserve. Many people using the phrase "Twitter Revolution" imagined activists running in the streets of Tehran, coordinating demonstrations, and tweeting about their future plans. That never happened. As mentioned before, there were not that many Twitter users in Iran, and the Iranian government disabled the SMS system during critical times of protest. Social media, on the other hand, was used in a number of ways to call for

---

[39] "The Idea of Sending One Million Green SMS to the Program *90*," Balatarin.com, https://balatarin.com/permlink/2009/9/21/1766073.

[40] "The Result of the SMSs Sent to the Sport Program," YouTube.com, www.youtube.com/watch?v=LrfigqKfuD0&feature=player_embedded.

[41] "Iran Regime Depicts Male Student in Chador as Shaming Tactic," *The Guardian*, www.guardian.co.uk/world/2009/dec/11/iran-regime-male-student-chador.

[42] "The Story of Majid Tavakoli Is the Story of Humilation of the Women in My Country," Masihalinejad.com, http://masihalinejad.com/?p=953.

[43] The Green Movement Wear Headscarf in a Symbolic Gesture," Balatarin.com, http://balatarin.com/permlink/2009/12/9/1867237.

[44] "Iran's Veil Campaign," *Fox News*, http://liveshots.blogs.foxnews.com/2009/12/11/veil-campaign/.

action, but it was not always successful. The role of Twitter was overhyped since most of the tweeting occurred outside of Iran.[45]

Although the use of Twitter by outsiders shows how new social movements can be instantly connected, it also shows it might be harder to decipher the source of news and strategies within a social movement in the digital age. It also reflects the nature of reporting social protest in repressive countries where Western reporters' access to sources is limited. The repressive governments such as the one in Iran are also able to track down the protesters using Twitter and/or Facebook and arrest them. This is especially true of Iran where the government bans Twitter for its own population, while the Supreme Leader uses it to spread the message of the Iranian revolution beyond its borders.

When the large demonstrations on the eve of the Shia religious cere-mony of Ashura (December 27) were over, the Green Movement activists started discussing ideas for a similar mass demonstration on the anniver-sary of the 1979 revolution. The annual demonstration, organized by the state, starts from the main street in central Tehran and leads to the large Azadi (Freedom) Square. Ebrahim Nabavi, a well-known Iranian satirist and blogger, suggested that the protestors hide their green signs until they reach Azadi Square. Once there, Nabavi suggested they would be able to take over the square and disrupt Ahmadinejad's speech. Nabavi posted his idea on *Jaras*. The idea was debated online and most commentators agreed with the plan. Many of the Green Movement activists compared it to the day in which Ceaușescu, the Romanian dictator, was overthrown.

When the day of action arrived, the Iranian government showed that it had been preparing for this event. Security forces controlled the streets of Tehran and people were scared to leave their houses. Support-ers of the government were bused into the main street leading to Azadi Square. Supporters of the Green Movement who made it to the rally were too spread out and were not able to recognize each other to form groups of protesters. Iranian security forces blocked all routes leading to the Azadi Square. Only a preselected group was allowed to enter and was placed in the front row near Ahmadinejad's podium.

A satellite picture taken by Geo Eye during the rally showed exactly what had happened.[46] Azadi Square had been kept mainly empty. A large

---

[45] This point is scientifically shown in Zicong Zhou et al., "Information Resonance on Twitter: Watching Iran" (2010), http://snap.stanford.edu/soma2010/papers/soma2010_17.pdf.

[46] Satellite picture of the progovernment rally, www.geoeye.com/CorpSite/gallery/detail .aspx?iid=294&gid=20.

number of buses could be identified in the picture that had brought the supporters of the Iranian government to the main street leading to Azadi Square. The Trojan horse strategy had obviously failed. The Iranian government knew the intentions of the Green Movement supporters well in advance and prepared for them. In hindsight, many people realized it was not practical and the plan required greater attention to logistical details, such as an effective strategy to counter blocked roads and the government's reaction. This failed demonstration was the last major attempt by the Green Movement to protest in the streets.

Social and political activism by women

During the uprising in 2009 over the widely assumed fraudulent results of the presidential elections, women's rights activists used Facebook to create a group of mothers – one that is still active – called "Mothers of Park Laleh" (originally called The Mourning Mothers of Iran). These women's rights activists consisted of activists (men included as well) in Iran, Europe, and the United States[47] who were (and still are) communicating in Persian via email Listservs that have long been created and maintained by grassroots, transparent, and socially connected networks of activists.

The main purpose of this newly found group activity was to find the best, most efficient, and culturally sensitive strategy to mobilize mothers whose sons and/or daughters had disappeared or been imprisoned, tortured, or forced to appear in state-run TV shows to "confess to their crimes, namely endangering national security." Many have since fled Iran and live as refugees in Turkey, Germany, France, and the United States. They demanded that the Iranian authorities identify and prosecute those responsible for the loss, execution, or imprisonment of their sons and daughters. Members of the group in Iran were harassed by the authorities, but the transnational ties they had made via Facebook and email lists allowed the group to withstand the pressure and publicize the arrests.

The mourning mothers first started gathering in Park Laleh in Tehran and later other parks in major cities on Saturdays at 4:00 p.m. to commemorate the loss, disappearance, or execution of their adult children who had joined the public demonstrations by supporters of the Green Movement in the aftermath of the presidential election.[48] The

---

[47] The author was an active participant in this group since its inception.

[48] Here is the author's short call to action on Iranian.com (run by Diaspora Iranian activists): http://iranian.com/main/blog/elham-gheytanchi/join-us-saturdays-park.html.

Iranian security apparatus did not tolerate the mourning mothers' peaceful gatherings as the mothers started reaching out to international entities such as the UN.[49] Despite pressures to shut down their activities on the ground, activists used Facebook pages to stay connected and publicize their cause. The supporters on Facebook were varied; some had never been involved in any political campaign and many would not have known about them if it were not for Facebook.

When this group was formed in the immediate aftermath of the 2009 elections, many like-minded Iranian-American feminists championed their cause and collaborated via active email lists with their counterparts in Iran. They were inspired by the "Mothers of the Plaza de Mayo" in Argentina,[50] mothers in black in Israel, and transnational feminist movements that emphasize peaceful conflict resolution without the involvement of military and state apparatus over the injustices done to their politically dissenting

[49] Here is the text of what a number of activists drafted in Los Angeles on September 20, 2009: "Petition to: UN Secretary General, Mr. Ban Ki Moon: We, the supporters of 'The Committee of Mourning Mothers of Iran,' call upon the UN secretary General, Mr. Ban Ki-Moon to immediately send a delegate to Iran in order to investigate, identify, and prosecute those responsible for imprisonment and tortures of our children during and after June 2009 presidential election. The mournful mothers of Iran have no access to international authorities to plea for justice. Hereby, we call upon the UN secretary general, Mr. Ban Ki-Moon to take action addressing the violation of human rights in Iran.

[50] The supporters of Mourning mothers in Los Angeles wrote this letter on February 11, 2012:
   "Warmest Regards to the Mothers of Plaza de Mayo whose courage during the past thirty years has been an inspiration to all activists engaged in non-violent struggles. We, the supporters of the Mourning Mothers of Iran have received your statement in support of your counterparts in Iran. We are grateful for your acknowledgement and continued support.
   "The Mourning Mothers of Iran have shown incredible resilience in the face of violent suppression, threats and continuing arrests. Mourning the loss of their children in the aftermath of fraudulent presidential election on June 12 2009, all mothers who have mourn the loss of their children involved in non-violent struggles have gathered to champion for human rights in Iran. These mothers have risen up to the state authorities and have rightfully demanded a permanent halt to execution of political prisoners as well as identification and persecution of those responsible for killings.
   "We, the supporters of the Mourning Mothers of Iran feel obliged to support them in their plight and echo their voices. Under the current situation in Iran where no dissent is tolerated and the authorities lie about gross human rights violations in the country, your support is heartening and indeed vital.
   "May we have a peaceful and just world,
   "The Supporters of Mourning Mothers of Iran in Los Angeles, San Francisco and Sacramento."

sons and daughters.[51] Like mothers in Uruguay and their expatriate counterparts around the world,[52] the exiled mothers (those who fled Iran
after or at the time of 1979 revolution) showed their solidarity with mothers
in Iran and joined the campaign. Many of these exiled mothers later formed
their own branch of Laleh Park Mothers in various cities in which they
have taken refuge since the revolution. The supporters of "Laleh Park
Mothers"/Valley-LA   created   websites   (www.parklaleh.blogspot.com,
www.facebook.com/mourningmothersofIran?fref=ts, and www.facebook
.com/LalehMothersValley), while their counterparts in Iran formed the
online group "Laleh Park Mothers"/Iran (www.mpliran.org).[53] In contrast
to the first group of bloggers and Facebook participants, the mothers of
Park Laleh (initially called The Mourning Mothers of Iran) are politically
and explicitly vocal and publicly voice their opposition to the status quo
in Iran.

The post-2009 era

Hassan Rouhani's victory in Iran's 2013 elections was a clear protest
vote against Iran's disputed 2009 elections, repressive measures adopted
toward the Green Movement's leaders, and perhaps most notably,
Rouhani's predecessor's management of Iran's relations with the
Western world. Rouhani, who was widely regarded as a man of prag-
matism and unique ability to align himself with the center of
power in Iran's complicated political structure, emerged as the compromise candidate of reformists, democrats, women, and even many
conservatives who were wary of the country's political isolation and
economic crisis.[54]

Although Rouhani's support for broader social freedoms, as well as his
advocacy for women's rights, made him a favorite candidate for change,

---

[51] Elahe Amani, "Mourning Mothers Iran Stand with Activist Mothers Worldwide," Women-
NewsNetwork.net,   http://womennewsnetwork.net/2009/10/08/mourning-mothers-iran-
stand-with-activist-mothers-worldwide/.

[52] Gabriela Fried-Amilivia, "Remembering Trauma in Society: Forced Disappearance after
Uruguay's Era of State Terror (1973–2001)," in Noel Packard (ed.), *Sociology of Memory:
Papers from the Spectrum* (Newcastle upon Tyne: Cambridge Scholars Publishers, 2009),
pp. 135–58.

[53] Here is the latest plight of Mothers of Park Laleh reflected in Amnesty International:
www.amnesty.org/en/library/info/MDE13/031/2013/en.

[54] Abbas Milani, "Iran's Democratic Movements," in Abbas Milani and Larry Diamond
(eds.), *Politics and Culture in Contemporary Iran: Challenging the Status Quo* (Boulder,
CO: Lynne Rienner Publishers, 2015), pp. 217–58; see p. 250.

his campaign pledge to resolve Iran's nuclear dispute with the West with an eye to lifting economic sanction proved to be a key factor in his victory. This demonstrated the prevalence of a much broader sense of economic insecurity caused by the imposition of economic sanctions by the Western world in reaction to Iran's nuclear program. Whether the election of yet another reformist generates false promise remains to be seen. We have to wait and see if Rouhani's administration can provide the perspective necessary for breaking away from Iran's futile approach of the past.

Rouhani's victory demonstrated that the Green Movement's demands had not faded away. Rather, they were still vibrant and relevant today. Despite the pessimistic outlook and the multitude of constraints that opposition has faced and continues to face today, Mehrangiz Kar argues that "the Green Movement has had fundamentally important results, one of which is the deepened internal divisions with the regime itself."[55] Kar goes on to argue that President Rouhani vowed to unblock social media outlets such as Facebook and Twitter – a telling testimony about the opportunity of turning the youth bulge into a constructive and cooperative force. This approach epitomizes the central challenge encountered by the Rouhani administration, as his government faces a myriad of battles with the judiciary, Majles, and IRGC over the Internet censorship. The Green Movement brought out internal divisions and growing mistrust that have undermined the foundation of the regime as never before.

While Rouhani has succeeded in his foreign policy, his promises regarding free Internet freedom have not yet surfaced. The Arab Spring and the continuing political change that is taking place in the Middle East might have hindered Rouhani's plans for Internet freedom. Nevertheless, Rouhani's presidency is a window of opportunity. According to some observers, "Rouhani not only has a popular mandate to become the agent of change he promised to be during his campaign, he also enjoys the conditional blessing of power brokers at the highest levels to restore the credibility of the regime."[56] In order for Iran to continue its influence in the Middle East, Rouhani has to open

---

[55] Mehrangiz Kar, "Democracy after the Green Movement," in Milani and Diamond (eds.), *Politics and Culture in Contemporary Iran: Challenging the Status Quo* pp. 69–90; see p. 88.

[56] Mahmood Monshipouri and Manochehr Dorraj, "Iran's Foreign Policy: A Shifting Strategic Landscape," *Middle East Policy* (2013), 133–47.

up the Internet and maintain an image of a moderate Iran where civil society activists are not suppressed.

Conclusion

The impact of modern modes of communication, such as social media, on politics in repressive political systems is evident in Iran, as discussed in this chapter, and in the Arab world and other parts of the world, as elaborated in the other case studies in this book. The repressive measures adopted by the Islamic Republic compelled activists, human rights lawyers, journalists, and reform-minded politicians to retreat, but their demands did resurface in Rouhani's election. It is important not to glorify the role of the Internet and the new digital communication modes and remember that oppressive political apparatus also use ICTs for their own political gains.

There are also more opportunities for repressive governments to manufacture their own versions of protests. But the human rights violations will be known to the world because the citizen journalism that has taken place is irreversible. Whereas Iranian authorities were able to hide human rights violations during the first decade of the revolution as the result of their supremacy over mass media and their hold on the flow of information from and to Iran, the existence of the Green Movement and the Mourning Mothers of Iran clearly show that it is no longer possible to cover up.

The new social media, such as mobile phones, Persian social networking sites, and satellite TV that broadcasted citizen journalism enabled or, better yet, mobilized the youth movement in Iran to make their presence felt not only in Iran but also throughout the region during and after the disputed 2009 presidential election in Iran. The new social media allowed for a higher rate of political participation and protest while documenting human rights abuses. It also proved to be the only place to call for demonstrations on a specific day.

The loose online network affiliations lowered the cost of mobilization and membership in a progressive social movement. Though social media can widen the grassroots base of social movements, it is also used by the authorities as a means to arrest and suppress social movements such as the Green Movement. Lack of central authority as well as a robust strategy in the Green Movement led to its defeat. But activists' effective use of social media further proves that a new wave of social movements are in the making in Iran in which human rights violations, arrests, and political repression will not go unnoticed in the international community.

The new social movements in the digital era have to rethink their political strategies and operational frameworks. While the Internet and social networking sites offer an emancipatory potential as the most potent and decentralized mobilization tool the world has yet encountered, as Jack Barry notes in Chapter 2, the lack of strategies and the proper political framework can lead movements that capitalize on the Internet to defeat, as in the case of the Green Movement. Demanding the free flow of information, relying on the growing phenomenon of cyber activism, especially in the political blogosphere, as well as staging demonstrations and protests in an attempt to expose and ultimately stop human rights abuses and official wrongdoing, are not enough to change political systems. These factors have to be ingrained in the political culture in every context and have to make the necessary links to world politics at the same time.

9

The politics of protest and repression in the digital age

Turkey during and after the Gezi Park protests

IHSAN DAGI

When Turkish police dispersed Gezi Park protesters in Istanbul's Taksim Square on May 31, 2013, using water cannons and tear gas, Turkish actor Mehmet Ali Alabora sent a Twitter message calling on the people to join the demonstrators. He tweeted: "It is not just Gezi Park, mate. Have you not understood yet? Come along." This was one of 15 million tweets sent throughout the day of unrest. Turkey's Prime Minister Recep Tayyip Erdoğan picked on this particular tweet. During a party rally broadcast live on all of Turkey's news channels, Erdoğan publicly targeted Alabora: "You see, he's confessed that it's not about Gezi Park. What is your problem then? To bring down the AK Party government. If this country is ruled by law, you will be held accountable for this."[1] Within days the police started an investigation into his activities during the protests, and the public prosecutor accused him of "inciting an armed rebellion against the government."[2] Facing threats to his life, he first asked the police for "close protection," and then moved to the UK. He now lives in London and does not want to talk about the Gezi protests.[3] Despite having over 2 million followers, he is no longer an active user of Twitter.

The prime minister's public intimidation of Alabora reflected the disproportionate power relationship between the government and social protests in Turkey. Yet it was also an admission of the power of social media as a space for individual freedom and social opposition.

---

[1] "Başbakan Erdoğan'dan Önemli Açıklamalar," *Hurriyet* (June 15, 2013), www.hurriyet.com.tr/gundem/23513523.asp.

[2] "Mehmet Ali Alabora Hakkında Gezi Felzekesi," *Aksam* (November 12, 2014), www.aksam.com.tr/guncel/mehmet-ali-alabora-hakkinda-gezi-fezlekesi/haber-353329.

[3] Muge Akgun, "Mehmet Ali Alabora Gezi'yi Konuşmak Istemiyor," *Radikal* (November 2, 2014), www.radikal.com.tr/yazarlar/muge_akgun/mehmet_ali_alabora_geziyi_konusmak_istemiyor-1222703.

Social media has indeed proved to be an effective new form and outpost of protest, influencing political changes as played out during the Arab Spring. With its individualized yet massive interconnectivity that escapes conventional control mechanisms of a state, social media networks deeply disturb authoritarian regimes.

In Turkey, acts of protest via social media and government attempts to control it in response have intensified since the Gezi Park protests that erupted in the summer of 2013. "Social media is the worst menace to society," Turkish Prime Minister Erdoğan said, reflecting the unease of authoritarian regimes with unconventional challenges posed by social media, and he even resorted to block it several times along with YouTube, Facebook, and Google. Moreover, new regulations have been introduced on Internet use, limiting individual access, expanding government surveillance of users, and prosecuting social media activists. The government has gone so far as to declare social media a threat to national security, and added it among the top threats to Turkish security alongside terrorist organizations like ISIS and PKK.

The government's description of social media as a menace and its clampdown on social media did not happen in a vacuum. Massive opposition waged against the government in Turkey with the Gezi protests woke the government up to the "dangers" of social media.[4] But it was not social media per se that triggered the Gezi Park protests. The suppression of individual rights and liberties by an authoritarian government paved the way, and accumulated resentment that found a channel to express itself via social media resulted in a massive protest movement. Though social media played a magnifying effect, the protests grew out of an increasing discontent over the way in which the ruling party had governed the country and over the attitude of its leaders, including their aggressive and exclusionary policies.

In a country where freedom of expression is limited, conventional media are largely brought under government control, and freedom of association and demonstration is curbed, social media have emerged as a space with relative freedom to advocate and exercise human rights that, in turn, create clashes between protest movements and the repressive government. This chapter aims to explore this new battleground between an increasingly authoritarian government and social and political dissidents who found a refuge in social media, and discuss the power of social

---

[4] Z. Tufekci, "Social Movements and Governments in the Digital Age: Evaluating a Complex Landscape," *Journal of International Affairs*, 68, 1 (2014), 1–18.

media to induce political change and endure governmental pressure in relation to the Gezi protests.

Gezi protests as social opposition

What led the Turkish government to view social media as a "menace" was the Gezi protests that shook the country in the summer of 2013. At the end of May, a handful of protesters came together in Gezi Park, a small green area near Istanbul's Taksim Square, to stop the construction of a shopping center and the replica of a military barracks demolished sixty years prior as a residential block. The first confrontation took place on May 27 when the police encountered dozens of protesters in Gezi Park trying to stop bulldozers from demolishing the trees in the park.

This early encounter resulted in an increasing awareness, especially among the young and environmentalists, who started a sit-in protest within the park, turning it into a communal space with various activities such as a library, broadcasts from the park, music concerts, yoga exercises, and so forth. Yet this concern for the environment, blended with an urban challenge to government-sponsored gentrification, took a different form when the police intervened violently against the demonstrators on the morning of May 31, 2013, dispersing the crowd by force, burning down their tents, and cordoning off the park. The crowd regrouped in nearby Taksim Square with new participants, who were informed about the crackdown through Twitter, Facebook, and other social media outlets.

The police used tear gas and water cannons. Tear gas canisters were shot at close range and directly aimed at demonstrators, leaving many injured. Disproportional use of police force against the protesters that was instantly recorded and disseminated via social media escalated the events. Even more people took to the streets in Istanbul and the rest of the country in support of the Gezi protesters, who were beaten up, tear gassed, and soaked with water from water cannons, denouncing the police violence and protesting the government. Within the first three weeks of the protests, around 3.6 million people took part in demonstrations all over Turkey, according to the Ministry of Internal Affairs. A total of 5,532 protests took place in eighty of Turkey's provinces. During the protests, seven protesters and one police officer died, 4,329 people were wounded, and 5,513 demonstrators were detained.[5]

---

[5] Tolga Sardan, "Gezi'den Kalanlar ve Farklı Bir Analiz," *Milliyet* (November 25, 2013), www.milliyet.com.tr/gezi-den-kalanlar-ve-farkli-bir/gundem/ydetay/1797280/default.htm.

Prime Minister Erdoğan's uncompromising and provocative statements played an important role in the escalation of the events. Statements like "Whatever you do, we have made our decision and we will implement it" right at the beginning closed the debate, dialogue, and deliberation expected by the protesters.[6] Furthermore, Prime Minister Erdoğan's insulting remarks in which he termed the protesters *"çapulcu"* (thugs) caused resentment and a reaction. From that point on, the Gezi protests evolved from a case of concern for the environment into nationwide and violent demonstrations in response to an increasingly authoritarian and paternalistic government and its uncompromising leader.

Meanwhile, the lack of interest of the mainstream media in covering the events led social media and citizen journalists to report on the events, demonstrate police brutality, and display public discontent with a government that not only appeared adamant but even provocative in demonizing the demonstrators and downgrading their demands. At the peak of the event, Turkey's major "independent" news channel, CNN Türk, was broadcasting a documentary about the lives of penguins. The silence of the mainstream media meant more than silence; it was plain proof of government control and even censorship over the media. Thus, it amplified the sense of repression felt by the protesters and the power of a ruling party that appeared capable of denying the people access to the news.

The failure of the mainstream media created a vacuum for information about the developments on the ground that was filled by social media. By disseminating pictures of police violence, the protesters generated public outrage against the government, and by calling for solidarity they mobilized the masses to take part in demonstrations throughout Turkey. Not only did this tactic prove successful, the effective use of social media also created international solidarity and visibility. Demonstrations were organized in numerous cities around the world in support of the Gezi protests. Ironically, while CNN Türk opted to broadcast documentaries the night the demonstrations reached their apex on May 31, CNN International offered hours of live coverage of the later stages of the protests.

The Gezi protests were a multifaceted phenomenon. They were both an environmental concern to protect a park in the midst of Istanbul and an urban movement to reclaim the "right to the city" resisting the

---

[6] "Gezi Parkı İçin Karar Verdik," *Hürriyet* (May 29, 2013), www.hurriyet.com.tr/gundem/23390657.asp.

practice of urban development of the past ten years.[7] Yet, in the process, it evolved into a protest movement against the increasingly paternalistic, patronizing, and authoritarian government that saw no limit to its interference in social life and individual choices.

Like the Arab Spring demonstrations that took place in an area stretching from Tunisia to Egypt, the Gezi protests were not led by any leader or an organized political group. They were spontaneous and organic.[8] They did not have a political program but only specific demands such as a stop to the gentrification project, an end to police violence, and the release of those detained during the protests. Most participants in the demonstrations did not have formal political links to any association. They were mainly nonactivists connected to each other not through any formal association but through social media. For 44 percent of the protesters, the Gezi protests were their first political demonstration.[9]

The protesters were socially, ethnically, and politically heterogeneous, coming from diverse backgrounds with different demands and motivations. There were liberals, secularists, Kurds, Alevis, nationalists, socialists, and even some conservatives out in the crowd. Environmentalists, football fans of rival teams, feminists, and members of the LGBT community were on the streets protesting. As such, the Gezi protests went beyond a uniform political movement and reflected the diversity of a social protest bringing together unlikely allies.

Kurds were present alongside Turkish nationalists. There was no tension or quarrel between these ardent opponents during the protests. On the contrary, they appeared to have reached a "modus vivendi" in the face of challenges they faced. Neither separatist slogans were uttered nor ultranationalist aggression was committed. All sides were present with their flags and symbols but showed a case for coexistence despite their differing political preferences and priorities. One iconic photo of the

---

[7] N. Göle, "The Gezi Occupation: For a Democracy and Public Spaces," *Open Democracy* (June 11, 2013), www.opendemocracy.net/nilufer-gole/gezi-occupation-for-democracy-of-public-spaces.

[8] Ayşe Buğra, "Turkey: What Lies behind the Nationwide Protests?," *Open Democracy* (August 6, 2013), www.opendemocracy.net/5050/ayse-bugra/turkey-what-lies-behind-nationwide-protests.

[9] "Gezi Raporu: Toplumun 'Gezi Parkı Olayları' Algısı," *Konda* (June 5, 2014), www.konda.com.tr/tr/raporlar/KONDA_GeziRaporu2014.pdf, p. 18; "Gezi Parkı Direniş-çilerinin Yarısı Polis Şiddeti Olduğu İçin Eyleme Katıldı!" *T24* (June 12, 2013), http://t24.com.tr/haber/konda-gezi-parki-anketi-cikardi,231889.

protest in Taksim showed a Turkish nationalist holding a Turkish flag and escaping from tear-gas and water cannons together with a Kurdish nationalist holding up a flag with the national colors of the Kurdish movement. A deeper grievance was there, bringing people with dissimilar ideas and identities together.

Similarly, there were occasions in which a will for peaceful coexistence was demonstrated between the secularists and some devout Muslims who took part in the Gezi protests. The Anti-Capitalist Muslims, a Muslim group that took part in the protests, organized a Ramadan breaking of the fast in the streets of Istanbul where both devout Muslims and utterly secular Gezi protesters came together in solidarity and in opposition to the ruling Justice and Development Party (AKP)'s gentrification projects and authoritarian policies. Such a display of peaceful coexistence of pluralities – despite the polarizing political language employed by government representatives who depicted the protesters as immoral and anti-Islam – generated hope known as the "Gezi spirit." As such, Gezi showed the possibility that differences can be temporarily deactivated for a common cause.

Nevertheless, the Gezi movement was predominantly secular, though some conservatives and anticapitalist Muslims took part, especially in its initial stage and particularly in Istanbul. But the secularism of the Gezi protests differed from the old, exclusive, authoritarian mode of secularism that excluded Islamic elements from the public sphere. On the contrary, the Gezi protesters called for respect for diversity and showed they could coexist with conservative and Islamic elements while protesting the ruling party's authoritarian intrusion into their private lives. Rejecting the politics of polarization and stigmatization along secular-Islamic axes, the Gezi movement attempted to reunite people across old divides and asked those in power to abstain from intrusions motivated by their understanding of morality as well as to stop the police violence.

Before the police violence began, a festive mood dominated the group that had occupied Gezi Park. Public buildings were decorated, graffiti was colorfully displayed, stairs in the streets were colored, and flags and posters were put up, going hand-in-hand with the diversity of the crowd. Humor was another characteristic of the Gezi protests. Creative slogans and the out-of-the-box thinking of the Gezi protesters led to humoristic criticism that they were using "disproportional intelligence" vis-à-vis a brutal police force and discursive violence of the government. From the beginning, people who took to the streets reflected their political humor in their graffiti, Twitter messages, posters, and so forth. It was ironic that a movement that used creative humor as its weapon encountered a brutal police reprisal using tear-gas and water cannons, and which aimed tear-gas canisters at the crowd.

Gezi was also mainly a youth movement. According to a survey conducted in Gezi Park in the early days of the protests, the average age of a protester was 28. Forty percent of the participants in Istanbul were aged between 19 and 25, and 24 percent were aged between 26 and 30.[10] The people who came out to defend Gezi Park and took part in protests in other cities had mainly been considered "apolitical youth." Yet it turned out that they were concerned about environmental issues, sensitive to their freedom in public spaces, and angry with an increasingly paternalistic and authoritarian government. The initiators of the Gezi protests can be described as Generation Y graduates and professionals who knew how to use social media, were conscientious of their rights and liberties, and were anxious to draw a line against the interference of the government in their lifestyles and choices.

Demonstrations were not violent, especially in the first couple of days. People of diverse backgrounds and views occupied Gezi Park, put up tents, played music, danced, practiced yoga, and even built a library. Once the Gezi occupiers were forcefully dispersed by the police force, people took to the streets in the thousands and displayed solidarity with those who were subjected to police violence. Only then did they start to build barricades to stop the police, and some marginal groups attacked several official buildings, burning down public transportation vehicles and police cars. However, even then the main body of the crowd did not approve or take part in the violent resistance against the police, and constant calls were issued pleading nonviolent means even against the violent police.

The roots of Gezi: politics as protest

The Gezi protest meant more than protecting a park. It was an explosion of social discontent directed at a government that appeared increasingly authoritarian, self-righteous, and paternalistic.[11] Up until the protests, it

---

[10] "Gezi Raporu: Toplumun 'Gezi Parkı Olayları' Algısı," *Konda* (June 5, 2014), www.konda.com.tr/tr/raporlar/KONDA_GeziRaporu2014.pdf, pp. 6–7.

[11] A public opinion survey conducted by Metropoll polling company during the Gezi Park protests verified that 50 percent of people regarded the ruling party "increasingly going authoritarian," while 36 percent disagreed; see www.metropoll.com.tr/arastirmalar/siyasi-arastirma-9/1731.

had been widely observed that the ruling party had adopted a majoritarian notion of democracy, reducing democracy to the ballot box, and assumed that the mandate acquired in elections would give the government the right to do whatever it chose to do, and whatever it chose to do was right and should be accepted as such by all without question. The "national will," it believed, would not be bound by any other force or value, including the rights and liberties of those who opposed the ruling party. Those who are elected and thus hold the "mandate" to rule are believed to have the power and legitimacy to do as they please.[12]

Since his party came to power in 2002, Prime Minister Erdoğan had managed to repeatedly defeat his political opponents, eliminate secularist forces within the military and the judiciary that opposed his government, and establish total control within his own party. This resulted in the monopolization of power at the hands of Erdoğan without any effective checks and balances within the system. It was neither the party nor the parliamentary group of the ruling party but Erdoğan who decided on any one issue, big or small, local or national. For instance, Gezi Park was under the administrative authority of the Istanbul Metropolitan Municipality, but it was Erdoğan who made the decision and defended it without the presence of the mayor of Istanbul. The personalization of power left no room for consulting the people who would be affected by the decisions or letting the Istanbul Metropolitan Municipality decide about Gezi Park.[13] Thus, when his decision to turn the park into a shopping center and residence block was challenged, Erdoğan took the issue very "personally" and sought to reclaim his "unquestionable right to rule" and the people's obligation to obey and be grateful.

Erdoğan had been seduced by an amalgam of the power of the state apparatus he controlled and the popular votes he generated. The result was a belief that he could do as he wished because he enjoyed democratic legitimacy generated through elections, controlled the state apparatus which has historically had the capability to repress the masses, and utilized Islamic values and symbols that are capable of mobilizing the

---

[12] E. Özbudun, "AKP at the Crossroad: Erdoğan's Majoritarian Drift," *South European Society and Politics*, 19, 2 (2014), 155–67.

[13] N. Göle, "The Gezi Occupation: For a Democracy and Public Spaces," *Open Democracy* (June 11, 2013), www.opendemocracy.net/nilufer-gole/gezi-occupation-for-democracy-of-public-spaces; N. Göle, "Gezi: Anatomy of a Public Space Square Movement," *Insight Turkey*, 15, 3 (2013), 1–7.

conservative masses. Thus, before the Gezi protests the leadership of the ruling party came to regard itself as invincible at the ballot box. This mindset and style of governance were displayed in a variety of ways and forms up until the Gezi protests.

The prime minister, while introducing an educational reform that incorporated the teaching of the Qur'an and the Prophet Muhammad's life to the school curriculum, publicly and proudly announced that he wished to "raise a religious generation." This amounted to an attempt at "social engineering" using the coercive apparatus of the state and tax-payer funds to construct a "new conservative society." The leader of the ruling party declared that religious people would be more honest and better citizens in comparison to the secular. He defended the expansion of Imam Hatip religious vocational schools, arguing that these schools would breed neither terrorists nor anarchists, implying that "terrorists" are graduates of secular schools.[14]

The prime minister constantly reiterated that women are first and foremost mothers, according to "our values," and that they should give birth to at least three children. He also told women how to give birth – natural birth, not cesarean – angering women's rights groups and sparking an intense debate. Moreover, women should not have an abortion: "I consider abortion murder. No one should have the right to allow this to happen," he said.[15] In a reference to babies born as a result of rape, his health minister said the state would look after the babies if "the mother [had] been through something bad."[16] Faced with a solid and widespread reaction, the government backed down from reducing the period in which an abortion can legally be obtained from ten weeks to the first four weeks of pregnancy. These forms of intervention in women's life and attempts to guide them were resented by many secular, educated women, and they reacted to such a paternalistic perspective that pre-vailed at the top of the government.

New legislation was passed introducing strict control over the sale and consumption of alcohol.[17] Prime Minister Erdoğan depicted all

[14] "Erdoğan: Terörist Yetişmediği İçin Mi Imam Hatipleri Kapattınız?," *BloombergHT* (September 17, 2012), www.bloomberght.com/haberler/haber/1213423-erdogan-teror ist-yetismedigi-icin-mi-imam-hatipleri-kapattiniz.

[15] A. Ahmadi, "Turkey PM Erdogan Sparks Row over Abortion," *BBC News* (June 1, 2012), www.bbc.com/news/world-europe-18297760.

[16] Ibid.

[17] "Turkey Alcohol Laws Could Pull the Plug on Istanbul Nightlife," *The Guardian* (May 31, 2013), www.theguardian.com/world/2013/may/31/turkey-alcohol-laws-istanbul-nightlife.

consumers of alcohol as alcoholics.[18] The government appeared to be interfering in the personal lives of its citizens in line with its conservative views and enforcing its norms throughout the society.

The demand for "morality" turned into grounds for unlimited interference in not only the lives of people in the real world but also the lives of fictional characters. It went so far as to compel two characters of a TV show who lived together without being married to get married after being criticized for promoting unmarried relationships.[19] On several occasions the prime minister harshly criticized a popular TV show, *Muhteşem Yüzyıl* (The Magnificent Century), whose central character is Süleyman the Magnificent, the famous sultan of the Ottoman Empire. Erdoğan condemned the TV series and threatened the producers and the owner of the TV channel that broadcast the soap: "I publicly condemn the directors of those shows and the owners of the television station. We have warned the authorities on this matter and are awaiting a decision by the judiciary. We cannot have this sort of an understanding; the people need to, within the confines of the law, teach the appropriate lesson to those who play with the people's values."[20]

After criticism that Süleyman the Magnificent was not a sultan running after women in his harem, but instead spent his life in the fight against infidels, the TV producers sent the sultan off to fight against his enemies for several episodes. Such cases portray a "benevolent ruler" who wishes to protect his subjects, who are incapable of making the right decisions themselves.

It seems Turkey's rulers believed they were entitled to interfere in the lives and choices of the people to shape their minds, attitudes, and appearance. The mandate to rule was taken as a blank check to transform the identities and lifestyles of the people in order to construct a conservative society via the state apparatus.[21] With all these and others, the AKP

---

[18] "Bir Anne Baba Kızının Birini Kucağında Oturmasını Ister Mi?," *t24* (June 2, 2013), http://t24.com.tr/haber/basbakan-fatih-altaylinin-sorularini-yanitliyor,231158.

[19] "Bir Erkek Bir Kadın Sonunda Nikah Masasında," *Beyazperde.com* (May 30, 2012), www.beyazperde.com/haberler/diziler/haberler-52649/.

[20] Ihsan Dagi, "TV Soaps: People's Choices vs. State's Choice," *Today's Zaman* (December 2, 2012), www.todayszaman.com/columnist/ihsan-dagi/tv-soaps-peoples-choices-vs-states-choice_299996.html.

[21] According to a public opinion survey by Metropoll, conducted right after the Gezi Park events, 54 percent of people said the government had been interfering in their lifestyles and choices, while 40 percent disagreed; see www.metropoll.com.tr/arastirmalar/siyasi-arastirma-9/1731.

government and its leader Erdoğan appeared to be not only micromanaging government affairs but also wishing to do the same with the lives of all citizens.

Thus, the underlying cause for the spread of the Gezi Park protests was the public perception that viewed the ruling party as increasingly arrogant, authoritarian, and paternalistic. People from different political inclinations protested a government that in recent years had acted along these lines. The protesters knew how unlikely it was that they could force the government to step down through street protests or beat it at the ballot box. In fact, this simple realization kept the protests unwavering and widespread; they did not try to change the government, only to remind it that it had a limit it should not cross while governing. The Gezi protesters did not care who was in power, but whoever was should not interfere in their choices. It was, therefore, not about "who should govern" but "how." Right from the beginning the protests in Istanbul were driven by the quest to show the government that the people were dissenting from the views, the style, and the projects of Turkey's "one man," Tayyip Erdoğan. Those who "occupied" the park used their right to dissent in a passive, peaceful way with humor reflected in their slogans and social media messages. People protesting in Gezi Park and other cities were simply saying, "Do not interfere in my life and choices."

Prior to the Gezi protests, the ruling party had appeared to be engaging in a social engineering project seeking to generate a conservative society in which the secular would be treated as anomalies to be corrected. The protests thus emerged as a reaction to the state-supported attempt of the conservative mind and lifestyle to dominate the social space and exclude the secular from politics. As such, the protests did not remain as only opposition to the gentrification of the Gezi Park area but involved the opposition to the imposition of Islamic conservative values and lifestyle on the rest. As Ayşe Buğra puts it, the protests were, among other things, against a "form of governance that included the imposition of a centrally defined form of Islamic culture on society."[22] Based on the restrictions on the freedom of expression and the crackdown on the opposition, Nilüfer Göle describes preprotest Turkey as a country in which "the public sphere has been suffocating for some time."[23] Intrusion into the choices

---

[22] Ayse Buğra, "Turkey: What Lies behind the Nationwide Protests?," *Open Democracy* (August 6, 2013), www.opendemocracy.net/5050/ayse-bugra/turkey-what-lies-behind-nationwide-protests.

[23] Göle, "The Gezi Occupation: For a Democracy of Public Spaces."

and lifestyles of people worried especially young, educated, and professional urban elements. The language used by Erdoğan, who referred to his opponents as thugs, marginal, drunks, traitors, and collaborators, offended and angered many.

These were reflected in a public opinion survey conducted during the Gezi Park protests in Istanbul among the protesters in which the protesters said their primary motivation to take to the streets was the prime minister's authoritarianism (92 percent), violations of democratic rights (91 percent), police violence (91 percent), the attitude of the media (84 percent), and the cutting down of trees (56 percent).[24]

Governmental response: social movements as conspiracy

The government took a confrontational stance against the Gezi protesters right from the beginning despite some softer voices, including those of Deputy Prime Minister Bülent Arınç and President Abdullah Gül. Deputy PM Arınç struck a conciliatory tone by accusing the police of using excessive force that led the event to get out of hand and apologizing to those who were subjected to police violence.[25] Then President Gül remained moderate in his approach, saying the demonstrators' "message has been received," implying that their demand would be considered.[26] But the prime minister congratulated and rewarded the police forces for their bravery after weeks of violence against the protesters. Speaking at the graduation ceremony of the Police Academy, he said, "Our police acted legendarily in Taksim."[27] Obviously the ultimate decision maker was Prime Minister Erdoğan, who oversaw the whole process. He turned the issue into a test case. For his opponents he tested the repressive efficiency of his government apparatus, while for his supporters he tested their loyalty.

---

[24] "İste Gezi Parkı Olayları Anket . . . Eylemciler Neden Sokakta?," *Aksam* (June 5, 2013), www.aksam.com.tr/guncel/iste-gezi-parki-olaylari-anket-eylemciler-neden-sokakta/haber-212795.

[25] "Çevre Duyarlığı Sonucu Şiddet Görenlerden Özür Diliyorum," *Haberturk* (June 3, 2013), www.haberturk.com/gundem/haber/849747-cevre-duyarliligi-sonucu-siddet-gorenlerden-ozur-diliyorum.

[26] "A. Gül: Mesaj Alınmıştır," *Bugun* (June 3, 2013), www.bugun.com.tr/gundem/mesaj-alindi-haberi/650217.

[27] "Polis Destan Yazdı," *Milliyet* (June 24, 2013), www.milliyet.com.tr/polis-destan-yazdi/siyaset/detay/1727367/default.htm.

Erdoğan called the demonstrators *"çapulcu"* (thugs) in an attempt to downgrade and strip them of political context and legitimacy, reducing the whole event to one of law and order. For him, the protesters were not exercising a democratic right but attempting to topple his democratically elected government, and therefore had to be confronted. So, according to Erdoğan, the Gezi protests were a coup attempt of the looters, who sought to topple a government that represented the nation. The way in which the leaders of the ruling party viewed the Gezi events was an outcome of their self-image, the role they assigned to themselves, and their view of the "others."

The AKP and its leader considered "themselves" the embodiment of the nation and the national will. Erdoğan's will and wishes were equated to the will and wishes of the nation. It was believed that the good was represented by the nation and must be upheld by Erdoğan, who receives the nation's mandate through elections. Thus the AKP leadership viewed itself as the sole representative of the nation and the national will. Any attempt against the ruling conservative majority was by definition against the will of the nation, and thus the Gezi protest was a coup attempt initiated, encouraged, and manipulated by foreign powers and their local collaborators who did not want Turkey to succeed. Therefore, those who betrayed the nation and did not respect its government deserve to be considered not part of the nation but looters who would pay a price for their treason.[28]

What alarmed the AKP more was that it interpreted the Gezi protests as a challenge to the AKP's claim to hegemony in the social realm, not an objection to an urban development plan.[29] The AKP had been comfortable in the formal political realm of opposition political parties without any real challenger as it continued to win elections by increasing its share of the vote over the years. But the Gezi Park protests demonstrated that the AKP's imagined conservative society was far from being constructed in the social space. On the contrary, the non-AKP diversities in the social space served as a reminder that the political hegemony had been incomplete despite more than ten years of AKP rule. The problem it saw was that without a strong and entrenched social presence in urban areas and

---

[28] "Erdoğan: Türk Baharı 2002'de Oldu," *Aktif Haber* (June 9, 2013), www.aktifhaber.com/erdogan-turk-bahari-2002de-oldu-802085h.htm.

[29] N. Moudouros, "Rethinking Islamic Hegemony in Turkey through Gezi Park," *Journal of Balkan and Near Eastern Studies*, 16, 2 (2014), 181–95.

social space, the AKP's political hegemony would not be sustainable in the long run, and hence it chose not to compromise but to confront.

It was in this context that Erdoğan provocatively said they had made their decision about the Gezi project and that nothing would change, adding that the "nation is behind him," that if he wanted he could bring out millions into the streets, and that he was having "difficulties in holding 50 percent of the people (who voted for the AKP) in their homes," implying that if he wanted he would let his supporters confront the demonstrators in the streets.[30] A few took to the streets indeed. In some cities, civilians with long sticks were photographed patrolling the streets and attacking protesters. In Istanbul, a shopkeeper took to the street attacking demonstrators with a long knife used to slice Turkish döner kebab.[31]

To discredit the protesters, the government resorted to an old political tool, declaring them agents, lackeys, and tools of foreigners who masterminded the Gezi protests in order to stop the rise of Turkey to regional and global prominence and topple the government that was behind Turkey's recent successes. Prime Minister Erdoğan said, "Turkey's economic performance has been disturbing the enemies of Turkey, who attempted to sabotage the rise of Turkey."[32] Government media outlets were quick to fabricate news that foreign agents, Otpor, the "interest rate lobby," and so on had led the movement and manipulated the masses.[33] Germany, and more specifically Lufthansa, disturbed by Turkey's success and its decision to build a third bridge over the Bosporus and a third airport in Istanbul, were behind the "Gezi conspiracy."[34] Such conspiracy theories put forward by the AKP leadership and

---

[30] "Basbakan: Yüzde Elliyi Evinde zor Tutuyorum," *Hurriyet* (June 4, 2013), www.hurriyet.com.tr/gundem/23429709.asp.

[31] "Gezi Gösterisinde Pala Dehşeti," *Vatan Gazetesi* (July 7, 2013), www.gazetevatan.com/gezi-gosterisinde-pala-dehseti–551892-gundem/.

[32] "Türkiye'yi Allah'tan Başka Hiçbir Güç Engelleyemez," *Anadolu Ajansı* (June 7, 2013), www.aa.com.tr/tr/manset/190639–bu-milletin-alin-terini-faiz-lobisine-yedirtmeyecegiz; "Şeytan Üçgeni," *Yeni Şafak* (June 9, 2013), www.yenisafak.com.tr/dunya/seytan-ucgeni-10.06.2013–530641.

[33] "Gezi'nin dış Bağlantıları Çözülüyor," *Türkiye* (June 6, 2013), www.turkiyegazetesi.com.tr/gundem/43282.aspx; "Gezi'nin Provası ODTU'de," *Yeni Şafak* (June 15, 2013), www.yenisafak.com.tr/gundem/gezinin-provasi-odtude-532836.

[34] "Erdoğan: Faiz Lobisi Dedim Hoplamaya Başladılar," *Sabah* (July 20, 2013), www.sabah.com.tr/ekonomi/2013/07/20/faiz-lobisi-dedim-hopladilar; www.patronlardunyasi.com/haber/Erdogan-Faiz-Lobisi-dedim-hoplamaya-basladilar/146535.

its allies in the media somehow appeared convincing to the AKP grassroots.

Instead of recognizing the events as a social phenomenon and a political problem to tackle, the government resorted to conspiracy theories by which it effectively denied agency to the people, who were portrayed as incapable of acting on their own as opposed to being mere lackeys of foreign agents.[35] While the government claimed to be the embodiment of the nation, the protesters, by aligning themselves with foreign agents who wanted to stop Turkey's rise, ceased to be part of the nation. Resorting to such conspiracy theories reflects the mindset of the AKP leadership; namely, that it has a special, "historical mission" to revive Turkey after years of being a peripheral power to the status of a global power just as in the past during the glorious age of the Ottoman Empire. So by taking to the streets and occupying Gezi Park, the protesters played – deliberately or not – into the hands of Turkey's enemies, who were trying to stop the rise of the new and great Turkey.

This mindset resulted in numerous and absurd varieties of conspiracy theories during and after the Gezi protests in an attempt to define reality in a way to acquire moral superiority and mobilize the conservative masses. Among them was a rumor that a young headscarved woman with a baby was assaulted in Kabataş by dozens of male protesters who wore leather jackets. They allegedly beat the woman up and urinated on her. Such an unbelievable scene was described by the prime minister, who said, "They attacked my sister in hijab."[36] The prime minister also claimed that he had seen a video documenting the abuse. Yet no criminal charges were filed. Later, a video was released showing no such abuse at the location on the date in question, but the video did show a headscarved woman moving through the crowd near a tram station with her baby in a baby carriage, without any disturbances taking place.

Another case of attempting to construct a false reality and mobilize Islamic masses against the Gezi protests was a claim put forward by Erdoğan himself in which he said demonstrators had occupied the Dolmabahçe Mosque in Beyoğlu one evening and consumed alcohol inside, disrespecting the holy site. This amounted to a serious indictment

---

[35] S. Özel, "A Moment of Elation: The Gezi Protests/Resistance and the Fading of the AKP Project," in U. Özkırımlı (ed.), *The Making of a Protest Movement in Turkey: #occupygezi* (Basingstoke: Palgrave Macmillan, 2014), pp. 7–24.

[36] "Benim Turbanlı Bacıma Saldırdılar," *T24* (June 9, 2013), http://t24.com.tr/haber/erdogan-capulcunun-sozluk-anlamina-baksinlar-dogru-soyledigimi-anlayacaklar,231618.

in Turkey, as it meant a violation of the sacred. The prime minister throughout the summer of the Gezi protests repeatedly made this claim. But from the beginning the imam of the mosque, who was there when the protesters took refuge in the mosque, denied that such a thing took place. He was questioned for hours by the police about the issue but vehemently denied the statement of the prime minister and reports in progovernment media. Instead, he said the wounded protesters were treated by volunteer medical doctors in the mosque. A few weeks later the imam was reassigned to another mosque.

Then an old issue resurfaced on the agenda. The prime minister declared that his government would build a mosque in Taksim Square, an issue that in the late 1990s was the most ambitious project of the Islamists but was put off after public fury.[37] In response to the Gezi protests and criticism over the gentrification project in Taksim, resorting to the old idea of building a mosque reflected the difficulties of justifying the government's Gezi Park project and the need to utilize religious symbols in order to mobilize the conservative and Islamic AKP grassroots.

Social media in Gezi protests and repressive backlash

Especially since the Arab Spring it has widely been observed that social media play a significant role in the politics of protest and opposition. From Tunisia and Egypt to Brazil and Turkey, social media networks have contributed to participation in and organization of antigovernment demonstrations. Social media facilitate a flow of information, help the mobilization of like-minded people, enable organization of the masses, and legitimize their cause.[38] Social media also set the agenda in an interactive manner, one that satisfies the demand for democratic deliberation among the people. Thus, social media have brought a new vitality to social opposition in the face of authoritarian governments.

Turkey is active in the use of social media networks such as Facebook and Twitter. It ranks fourth largest in the global use of Facebook and

---

[37] Ihsan Dagi, "Last Resort: Building Mosque in Taksim," *Today's Zaman* (June 2, 2013), www.todayszaman.com/columnist/ihsan-dagi/last-resort-building-mosque-in-taksim_317225.html.

[38] O. Z. Gokce et al., "Twitter and Politics: Identifying Turkish Opinion Leaders in New Social Media," *Turkish Studies*, 15, 4 (2014), 672, 674, 675.

eighth in Twitter.[39] When the Gezi protests started, there were 1.8 million Twitter users in Turkey. Within the first ten days of the Gezi protests, the number skyrocketed to 9.5 million.[40] Its usage also peaked during the protests. The day the police raided Gezi Park, 15,077,500 tweets were sent from Turkey, a significant increase from an average of 9 million a day.[41] Even after midnight that particular day, 3,000 tweets were posted in a minute despite the fact that 3G networks were down in the main areas of protest in Istanbul. The following day the number of tweets posted reached 18,835,909, and the third day of the uprising saw 16,720,801.[42] These demonstrate the intensity of Twitter usage with hashtags such as #direngezi, #geziparki, #occupygezi, and #resistancegezi. On May 31, fifteen out of the twenty most retweeted posts were related to the Gezi protests.

The objective for the use of social media varied. News was disseminated, calls for mass protests announced, proof of police violence documented, and information about the need for medical and legal support for the injured and detained was shared. Thousands made audio and visual recordings with their cell phones, and shared them instantly via social media. Websites were established on which such information was posted, including Instanbuldaneleroluyor.com, Whatishappeninginistanbul.com, Everywheretaksim.net, and Delilimvar.tumblr.com. Some shops and hotels in the Taksim area opened their Wi-Fi networks to allow Internet access in the area out of solidarity with the people on the ground.[43] This rapid and unprecedented explosion in the usage of Twitter and other social media platforms shows how, during the Gezi protests, they functioned as a vehicle of information, mobilization, justification, and solidarity.

---

[39] Dorian Jones, "Turkey Embraces Social Media," *VOA News* (April 26, 2012), www.voanews.com/content/turkey-embraces-social-media-149236475/370184.html.

[40] S. Kuzuloglu, "Gezi Parkı Eylemlerinin Soyal Medya Karnesi," *Radikal* (June 19, 2013), www.radikal.com.tr/yazarlar/m_serdar_kuzuloglu/gezi_parki_eylemlerinin_sosyal_medya_ karnesi-1138146; B. Arda, "The Medium of the Gezi Movement in Turkey: Viral Pictures as a Tool of Resistance," APSA 2014 Annual Meeting Paper, http://papers.ssrn.com/sol3/ papers.cfm?abstract_id=2453044, p. 3.

[41] K. Varnali and V. Gorgulu, "A Social Influence Perspective on Expressive Political Participation in Twitter: The Case of #occupygezi," *Information, Communication and Society*, 18, 1 (2015), 2.

[42] Kuzuloglu, "Gezi Parki Eylemlerinin Soyal Medya Karnesi."

[43] P. Barbera, M. Metzger, and J. Tucker, "A Breakout Role for Twitter in the Taksim Square Protests?," *Al Jazeera*, www.aljazeera.com/indepth/opinion/2013/06/201361212350593971 .html.

Though Facebook and Twitter emerged as the primary social platforms during the Gezi protests, livestreamed channels, Tumblr pages, websites, blogs, Instagram, and YouTube were also used to upload, download, and attach Gezi-related data, images, videos, and comments.[44] Videos shared on social media with its horizontal and nonhierarchical structure reached a broad segment of society, disregarding political preferences and social backgrounds.[45] As trust in mainstream media was low, the alternative social media, with its egalitarian and participatory components, helped the formation of ideas and more effectively mobilized the masses in favor of the demonstrators.

The Internet, Facebook, and Twitter became channels to circumvent the government's attempt to control the traditional media, which, fearful of government reprisal, chose not to broadcast news of resistance and police brutality. Moreover, the emergence of social media as an effective medium deprived the mainstream media of the ability to define an event a "non-event" by not covering it. Broadcasting a documentary about the lives of penguins did not mean that the Gezi protests did not exist or attract public attention. Thus, social media gained the role of defining the event, displaying the content, and legitimizing the cause. Such a powerful tool of information, mobilization, and organization did not escape the authorities' attention. Social media was immediately targeted by the government when the Gezi Park protests started. The Turkish prime minister blamed social media for the protests. He declared, "Twitter is the worst menace to society."[46] Such was an attempt to demonize and discredit social media, as it did not serve the government's agenda; on the contrary, it challenged its authority and hegemony with its status as autonomous from the government.

Yet the ruling party could not ignore the importance of Twitter for public opinion formation. After Gezi Park, the AKP organized its own Twitter network. A deputy chairman of the party was assigned to the job of training a group of volunteers within the party's branches throughout

---

[44] Kuzuloglu, "Gezi Parkı Eylemlerinin Soyal Medya Karnesi."
[45] Arda, "The Medium of the Gezi Movement in Turkey: Viral Pictures as a Tool of Resistance," p. 3.
[46] "Erdoğan: Baş Belası Twitter," *Milliyet* (June 2, 2013), www.milliyet.com.tr/erdogan-bas-belasi-twitter/siyaset/detay/1717630/default.htm; Constanze Letsch, "Social Media and Opposition to Blame for Protests, Says Turkish PM," *The Guardian* (June 3, 2013), www.theguardian.com/world/2013/jun/02/turkish-protesters-control-istanbul-square.

Turkey about Twitter and asking them to set the agenda, counter government critics, and mobilize AKP sympathizers on social media. Their number was reported to be around 6,000, and they later came to be known as AKtrolls. Through such a project, the government tried to address its weakness in social media, which became apparent during and after the Gezi protests. What marked this effort is its lack of authenticity; it was carried out from top down to increase the visibility of AKP fans on social media, as if a "social presence" can be produced like building roads, bridges, and urban social space through the "intervention" of the state. Thus, social media emerged as a new area in which the party tried to implement its "social engineering" schema.

An assault was also launched on the dissidents in social media. In June 2013, the police detained and indicted thirty people amid the protests for "spreading untrue information" on social media and provoking protests.[47] Evidence described in the indictment included tweets that merely relayed information about the Gezi protests or called for emergency services or other medical aid to help the protesters. A Twitter user with less than 200 followers who sent the tweet "We are resisting under the rain, come on Izmir to Gundogdu #resistizmir #resistgezipark #gezi-parkinizmir," which was retweeted 100 times, was among those prosecuted. This was an attempt not only to intimidate Twitter users but also to dissuade society at large from participating in the demonstrations.[48]

Meanwhile the government sought to control opposing views and individuals using social media by engaging with the providers of the services. Arguing that Twitter avoids paying taxes on its income from Turkey, the government insisted Twitter have a corporate presence. Given that this had not bothered the government up until the Gezi protests, this argument was bogus. The more plausible motivation of the government was that with a corporate presence in Turkey, Twitter would be more cooperative with government authorities when it comes to providing information about users, taking down content, and removing accounts.[49] The corporation turned down the request but maintained

---

[47] https://freedomhouse.org/report/freedom-net/2014/turkey; www.hrw.org/news/2014/09/02/turkey-internet-freedom-rights-sharp-decline.

[48] K. Collier, "Turkey Takes 29 Dissidents to Trial for Protest Tweets," *The Daily Dot* (April 17, 2014), www.dailydot.com/politics/turkey-29-twitter-trial/.

[49] O. Ozbilgin and J. Burch, "Turkey Seeks to Tighten Grip on Twitter after Protests," *Reuters* (June 26, 2013), http://uk.reuters.com/article/2013/06/26/uk-turkey-protests-twitter-idUKBRE95P0X620130626.

some degree of cooperation with the Turkish government in addressing its requests for removal of accounts and withholding tweets. According to Twitter's transparency reports, Turkey leads the world with removal of content requests. The Turkish government filed 663 removal requests with Twitter in 2014; the total requests from all countries combined stood at 1,228, meaning that Turkey on its own provided half of the removal requests worldwide. With this move, the Turkish government wanted the removal of 2,948 accounts. In response, Twitter withheld 79 accounts and 2,003 tweets in 2014.[50]

Turkey's censorship record on Facebook is also high. It is the country with the second-highest level of censorship on Facebook, blocking nearly 2,000 "pieces of content" in the first half of 2014.[51] Censorship and a tight control of the Internet are displayed in the number of websites blocked by the Turkish Telecommunications Authority (TIB). According to Engelliweb.com, 65,672 websites were blocked in Turkey at the beginning of January 2015. The latest "Freedom of the Net" report published by Freedom House describes the Turkish Internet as "partially free" and notes its score deteriorated significantly in recent years.[52]

A new wave of social media restrictions started when corruption was disclosed on December 17, 2013. Several Cabinet members and their close relatives were allegedly involved in massive corruption. Later, dozens of recordings of wiretapped conversations between top government officials, including Prime Minister Erdoğan, businessmen, and their relatives, were posted on YouTube and disseminated through Twitter and Facebook.

The government desperately sought to bring social media under control as nationwide local elections and a presidential election were approaching amid spreading claims of corruption. Access to the website of SoundCloud was blocked as a user uploaded recorded phone calls between politicians, businessmen, and their relatives suggesting corruption. YouTube was also blocked on national security grounds when an illegally recorded conversation of government officials was uploaded to the site.[53]

---

[50] https://transparency.twitter.com/removal-requests/2014/jan-jun; https://transparency.twitter.com/removal-requests/2014/jul-dec.

[51] https://govtrequests.facebook.com/country/Turkey/2014-H1/; "Turkey Has Second-Highest Level of Facebook Censorship," *Today's Zaman* (February 9, 2015), www.todayszaman.com/anasayfa_turkey-has-second-highest-level-of-facebook-censorship_372200.html.

[52] "Freedom on the Net 2014," *Freedom House*, https://freedomhouse.org/report/freedom-net/freedom-net-2014#.VOL1Nnau0b8.

[53] C. Letsch and D. Rushe, "Turkey Blocks YouTube amid 'National Security' Concerns," *The Guardian* (March 28, 2014), www.theguardian.com/world/2014/mar/27/google-you

Facing this new challenge, the government's determination to bring social media under control took a different form. On February 5, 2014, the Turkish Parliament adopted a new Internet law that introduced new mechanisms of control and surveillance. With the new law, TIB was empowered to block any website without first seeking a court order. According to Human Rights Watch, "The grounds for blocking are so broadly and vaguely defined that they allow discretion for abusive application and interpretation."[54] Moreover, the law required Internet providers to store all data on Web users' activities for two years and make it available to the authorities, including Turkey's intelligence agency, upon request.[55] This meant that the government was now able to gather communications data about all Internet users without any legal limits or restrictions. The surveillance capacity of the government on the Internet activities of opponents moved up to be limitless under the protection of law.[56] Furthermore, in April 2014, a law was passed that expanded the powers of the National Intelligence Organization (MIT) and allowed intelligence agents to gain unrestrained access to any data, including that passing through Internet activities, without a court order.[57] The new legislation was a response to the independence of social media as a source of information, dissemination, and organization of dissent as proved

tube-ban-turkey-erdogan. In response to individual petitions the Constitutional Court ruled that the bans violated the freedom of expression of all users; the blocking orders were subsequently overturned, and access to YouTube was restored on June 3, 2013.

[54] www.hrw.org/news/2014/09/02/turkey-internet-freedom-rights-sharp-decline.

[55] "Bill to Ban Websites without Court Order Passes Parliamentary Commission," *Today's Zaman*, www.todayszaman.com/national_bill-to-ban-websites-without-court-order-passes-parliamentary-commission_371835.html.

[56] Eight months after the application of the opposition party the Constitutional Court repealed the articles in the new Internet law concerning blocking of websites without a court order and gathering of information to be shared with government authorities; see "Anayasa Mahkemesinden 4 Iptal, Iki Yürütmeyi Durdurma Kararı," *Hurriyet* (October 3, 2014, www.hurriyet.com.tr/gundem/27317474.asp. But the government has not given up. A new law was drafted and passed by the parliamentary commission enabling, this time, the prime minister or minister to order Turkey's telecommunication authority (TIB) to close down the website and block the content without court order. "Yeni Internet Yasası Komisyondan Geçti," *Medyatava* (February 12, 2015), www.medyatava.com/haber/yeni-internet-yasasi-komisyondan-gecti_119777.

[57] The new law also included a provision that anyone in conventional or social media who publishes leaks on MIT activities may be imprisoned for three to nine years; see www.hrw.org/news/2014/09/02/turkey-internet-freedom-rights-sharp-decline.

during the Gezi protests. The law made censorship and surveillance legal in Turkey.[58]

It is against this background that the Turkish prime minister declared in a party meeting in March 2014: "We'll eradicate Twitter. I don't care what the international community says. Everyone will witness the power of the Turkish Republic."[59] He was obviously concerned about damaging allegations of corruption in his inner circle put forward and disseminated through social media while the mainstream media under severe government control kept silent just before national elections. The free circulation of information and the formation of opinion through social media were deemed threatening to the ruling party. Following such an assault by Prime Minister Erdoğan, TIB decided to block Twitter on March 20, 2014, to prevent the posting of content likely to damage the ruling party in the upcoming elections. The ban was publicized via the hashtag #TurkeybannedTwitter, tweeted by millions, including, ironically, by users in Turkey who were able to gain access to Twitter by using proxy servers or by changing their DNS server settings.[60]

The AKP government's attempt at controlling social opposition and social media went so far as enlisting them as "threats to national security." The National Security Policy Document authored by the National Security Council headed by the president of Turkey, Erdoğan, assessing Turkey's threat perception for the next five years, described social media and civil disobedience as among the main threats to Turkey's domestic security, alongside terror groups such as ISIS and the Kurdistan Workers' Party.[61] Out of a sense of insecurity vis-à-vis social opposition that was kept alive and mounting by social media, the AKP rule resorted to mobilize all state apparatus to silence and suppress them both.

---

[58] "Turkey Pushes through New Raft of 'Draconian' Internet Restrictions," *The Guardian* (February 6, 2014), www.theguardian.com/world/2014/feb/06/turkey-internet-law-cen sorship-democracy-threat-opposition.

[59] "Turkey Blocks Twitter, after Erdogan Vowed 'Eradication,'" *Hurriyet Daily News* (March 20, 2014), www.hurriyetdailynews.com/turkey-blocks-twitter-after-erdogan-vowed-eradication.aspx?PageID=238&NID=63884&NewsCatID=338.

[60] Twitter was unblocked on April 3, 2014, after the AKP emerged victorious in the March 30 local elections.

[61] "Sivil Itaatsizlik ve Kaosa Teşvik Kırmızı Kitap'ta," *Haberturk* (April 7, 2015), www.haberturk.com/gundem/haber/1062804-sivil-itaatsizlik-ve-kaosa-tesvik-kirmizi-kitapta.

In short, the events that unfolded with the Gezi protests resulted in the revival of heavy-handed regulations by the state aimed at suppressing any dissent movement in the streets and on social media. Yet the elections of June 2015 in which the ruling AKP lost its parliamentary majority have raised expectations that political and social opposition may now have a breathing space and the AKP's undemocratic policies may be reversed. However, given the fact that President Erdoğan, the architect of the new authoritarian structure, will continue to serve until 2019 and the AKP as the largest political party will dominate any coalition government, it is unlikely that legal and institutional order set up to suppress social and political opposition will soon disappear. In the meantime, social media remain a significant arena of social opposition and thus the target of governmental assaults, in large part because formal political opposition once more has proven to be unable to lead to radical change in Turkey.

Conclusion: success and limits of the Gezi protests

To stop a government-funded gentrification project in a public space was the most concrete objective of the protests. So far this has been achieved; the park is there, still intact. But, as Göle asserts, "at the heart of this movement lies the desire for the restoration of public space in democracies."[62] The call for deliberation, dialogue, and democracy has strongly been uttered, but whether Turkey has moved into this direction as a result of the Gezi protests remains uncertain at best.

What is clear, however, is that Turkey after the Gezi Park protests has become ever more authoritarian as the Internet came under greater government control and surveillance; the police and intelligence agency acquired new powers; and the separation of powers was weakened by the reordering of the judiciary by the government. The Gezi protesters continued to be tried in courts; freedom of expression and assembly were ever more curtailed; and the uncompromising and authoritarian leader of the ruling party was elected president in August 2014. In the short run, so it seems, the state apparatus has effectively suppressed the type of social opposition that had found such a comfortable refugee in social media.

---

[62] Göle, "The Gezi Occupation: For a Democracy of Public Spaces."

Nevertheless, the Gezi movement has had a great impact on the mind and psyche of the people, including those in power. The protesters, by claiming their public space untouched by the authorities, acquired a quality of active citizenship, realizing the need to reach more inclusionary, participatory, and deliberative forms of democracy as opposed to the majoritarianism of the ruling party.[63] People claimed their right to the city, and they attained it to some degree. Following the Gezi protests, numerous neighborhood forums were established in small parks in the cities where people gathered and debated issues of importance to the neighborhood and demonstrated solidarity with one another.

The process gave birth to a new term: "the Gezi spirit," meaning the willingness and ability of the citizens to resist the authoritarian allocation of public space by the government as part of political and economic patronage.[64] This spirit rises in solidarity after each incident in which public authorities fail in their responsibility or exceed their mandate, such as mining accidents, the murders of women, and the prosecution of journalists and social media activists for their activities, as well as bans on freedom of expression and assembly.

In response, the ruling party, under a constant sense of insecurity accelerated by the Gezi protests, has resorted to ever more authoritarian measures to counter any opposition, including on social media, which turned out to be an effective platform to oppose and mock Erdoğan's way in a virtual space. Erdoğan demonstrated his inability to counter social opposition since the Gezi protests, apart from resorting to police suppression or attempting to silence Twitter, Facebook, and YouTube. Social media are the territory of social opposition that hits his public standing and damages his image as an all-powerful leader. It mocks his charisma, demystifies his power, and challenges the perception that he is in control. Moreover, it may be the only platform that is beyond his reach and control. Thus, the fight for control over social media has become a matter of asserting the government's claim to total hegemony, which seems an exercise in futility.

The Gezi protests asserted the "abolition of the monopoly of the 'new' by the AKP government" and ended its discursive supremacy that had

[63] Ilay Romain Örs, "Genie in the Bottle: Gezi Park, Taksim Square, and the Realignment of Democracy and Space in Turkey," *Philosophy and Social Criticism*, 40, 4–5 (2014), 496.

[64] O. Bakıner, "Can the 'Spirit of Gezi' Transform Progressive Politics in Turkey?," in Özkırımlı (ed.), *The Making of a Protest Movement in Turkey: #occupygezi*, p. 65.

dominated Turkish politics for a decade.[65] With Gezi, the AKP no longer appears to represent the new but instead the status quo. It is no longer a political party of change but rather the oppressive defender of the status quo that it has built. It is the Gezi movement that now challenges the status quo and holds the asset of the new, denouncing both Kemalist and Islamic authoritarianism while representing social and cultural diversity.

---

[65] N. Moudouros, "Rethinking Islamic Hegemony in Turkey through Gezi Park," *Journal of Balkan and Near Eastern Studies*, 16, 2 (2014), 193.

10

Social media and the transformation of Indian politics in the 2014 elections

SANJOY BANERJEE

The 2014 Indian elections and social media

The 2014 Indian elections witnessed the inversion of some important patterns in politics that had held firm for decades. It saw the ranks of the poor, by a certain definition, reduced to a fifth of the electorate from a majority position in preceding decades. It also saw voter turnout rates among the non-poor surpass that among the poor, in contrast with the established pattern. By 2014, cell phones and text messaging were available to nearly all adults including the poor, and Internet social media became accessible to the wealthiest one-fifth of the population. In short the 2014 elections saw an electorate that was in economic ascent and those who had ascended becoming politically active. Even the remaining poor showed stronger aspirations for class mobility than before.

The election provided the medium in which two variants of Indian national identity could compete, given voice by the Congress Party and the Bharatiya Janata Party (BJP), and given pathways by social media, mass media, and the old fashioned politics of rallies and face-to-face communication. The Congress Party propagated a national identity that visualized Indian society mainly as the confluence of the Hindu and Muslim communities and that combined populist and developmentalist views of popular economic needs. The BJP projected an identity of national homogeneity with a more developmentalist construction of popular economic needs. These identity variants contained and implicated different conceptions of human rights. The Congress Party variant recognized tacitly community-level rights and extended the language of rights to the economic needs of individuals. The BJP recognized more uniform rights of people regardless of their religion and with a more utilitarian approach to economic needs.

The result of the election was a resounding victory for the BJP, which had promoted as its leader Narendra Modi, who had led the state of

Gujarat through double-digit economic growth for the preceding decade. The other major party was Congress, which had led India through a decade of the fastest and most widely beneficial economic growth in its history, even with a slowing in the last three years. Despite its achievements in power, Congress was decisively rejected by the electorate. The Congress prime minister in this decade was the aging Manmohan Singh, who was not projected by the party as its prime ministerial candidate.

While Congress did not name a prime ministerial candidate prior to the elections, the presumptive candidate was Rahul Gandhi, heir of the Nehru–Gandhi dynasty. Rahul Gandhi had never attained mass popularity and contributed only modestly to state and national election campaigns. In 2004, Sonia Gandhi, the Italian-born matriarch of the dynasty and leader of the party, chose to sacrifice her own opportunity to be prime minister and put forward the former Finance Minister Manmohan Singh once her coalition gained a parliamentary majority. That decision was widely admired. In 2014, Congress abandoned those leaders who delivered the economic boom and retreated instead back to the dynasty. Further, Congress rhetoric in the campaign was distinctly more populist and less developmentalist than the rhetoric of the Manmohan Singh government has been. Perhaps ironically, the Congress Party abandoned the social classes whose rise its government had enabled, and appealed instead to a would-be downtrodden class, most of whose members it had already liberated.

It was the BJP that was more in touch with the new class. First, the BJP changed its leadership in 2013, elevating Narendra Modi. Most other parties in India, including Congress, were effectively under the private ownership of an individual leader or family and could not change leadership. The BJP also generated a larger narrative that unified a rhetoric of national homogeneity with weak recognition of religious minorities and with a rhetoric of aggressive economic development. These adaptations gave the BJP an overwhelming advantage in the polity that its rival had created. The weak recognition of minorities meant that the BJP projected the population as relatively homogenous. This did entail acknowledgment of uniform human rights for all persons. What this formulation derecognized were collective rights of minorities transcending the individual rights of their members.

This chapter argues that social media played a secondary but distinctive role in the BJP's victory and in the larger transformation of the Indian polity. Despite its economic growth, India remained one of the poorer countries in the world, and within Asia itself. Only a fifth of Indians had

Internet access in 2014, and Facebook users, at a hundred million, were about 8 percent of the population.[1] Twitter users were about half the number on Facebook, but most Twitter users are likely to be on Facebook as well.

The political impact of social media in India was different from that in authoritarian states. In the authoritarian setting in which the Arab Spring occurred, social media played a key role in enabling networks of communication and political organization that were otherwise difficult or impossible. India was already an institutionalized democracy with fairly efficient intermediation between politicians and voters through mass media with diverse political biases. Social media's impact was on the propagation of political class consciousness among the upper middle class. Further, a political party that could utilize social media with the imagination to connect with the upper middle class would gain a major competitive advantage within this class.

In the Indian political context of many parties contesting each parliamentary seat and the one with the most votes winning the seat, the advantage of a few percentage points in the popular vote can lead to decisive swings in seats. In fact, in 2014 the winning coalition led by the BJP won 62 percent of parliamentary seats with only 39 percent of popular votes.[2] Since there are several significant parties contesting each seat, the winner can often prevail with far less than half the total votes. This typically leads to a situation where a small advantage in votes yields a big advantage in seats. In the 2014 elections, the BJP-led coalition received just under double the number of votes as the Congress-led coalition, but won five and a half times the number of seats.[3] Thus even if social media worked to add a few percentage points of votes to the BJP-led coalition, it would have a large impact on parliamentary outcome.

Competitive political discourse in India

The explanation of the 2014 elections in India offered here ties together contending national identity narratives, different social groups undergoing transformations, and new media by which the narratives disseminate

---

[1] Shrikant Yelegaonkar, "Media Effects on Political Elections," *Indian Streams Research Journal* 8, 4 (2014), 1–5.

[2] Election Commission of India (ECI), "Archive of General Election 2014," Delhi (2014), http://eci.nic.in/eci_main1/statistical_reportge2014.aspx.

[3] Ibid,

to the social groups. I shall argue that the main political message of a political party is its distinctive variant of the national identity narrative. The national identity variants of different parties comport unevenly with the internal discourses of different social groups. These narratives are communicated on a mass scale to different social groups through mass media such as newspapers, radio, and television, as well as through social media on the Internet like Twitter and Facebook. These media and the messages conveyed through them have levels of credibility to the various social groups.

Political parties in democratic states face the challenge of persuading voters. They must build their arguments and slogans from premises a wide range of voters find credible. Within a society differentiated socially, economically, and politically, a single party must convey multiple messages to multiple audiences, while their rivals highlight contradictions among the party's different messages. At the same time, the party must persuade its diverse supporters that they should sacrifice on behalf of each other, reconcile their differences, and share a common destiny.

In developing countries like India experiencing moderate to rapid growth, the challenge to political parties takes on distinctive features. Life expectancy and income growth have risen to a point where the average person can expect a four-fold rise or more in income over her lifetime. There are few examples of developing countries experiencing aggregate economic growth for decades and declining welfare for the majority over the same decades. Rising inequality is far more common. Under these conditions, traditional or classic Marxian conceptions of class struggle lose credibility. At the same time, class differences persist and even intensify, and distinct discourses arise in different social classes. In a growing capitalist developing economy, the educated middle class gains demographic ascendancy. It becomes the fastest growing among the classes, and within a few decades arises as the largest. The middle class presents itself, with credibility, as the future of society. Any successful political party must gain a strong foothold in the rising middle class. The poor see significant improvements in their welfare and see substantial numbers among their ranks climb into the lower middle class. At the same time, the poor observe persistent inequality. Political argumentation must address this range of experiences to build a coalition spanning social classes.

Within this setting of rapid economic growth, declining poverty, but continuing and even intensifying inequalities, the developing nation must be imagined in common and a national identity must be maintained so that there is adequate loyalty to the state within society. Benedict Anderson finds that nations exist not by virtue of any common features of its members but by a shared imagination of the nation.[4] He finds that the embrace of one-way historical time and the abandonment of cyclical historical time, as well as the emergence of daily newspapers updating common knowledge, plays key roles in the emergence of nationalism.

Banerjee argues that national identity narratives are autobiographies of the nation with a particular plot structure. These narrative plots designate a national *heritage* selectively condensing a vast history, a *destiny* for the nation as well as a *danger* to be averted, and *vanguard* social classes and institutions whose vision and skill is leading the nation toward that destiny as well as *laggard* groups diverting or obstructing the nation.[5] Widely shared national identities are hegemonic ideologies for the powerful social groups emplotted as vanguards. The rest of the nation acquiesces in the vanguard's economic and political ascendancy in the expectation of receiving an eventual reward. Billig shows that national identities are propagated not only on dramatic occasions but in banal form in public spaces and the media, though the reiteration of national perspective in language grammar and in physical symbols.[6] Mihelj demonstrates that even in globalized media systems, nationalist messages, with fine-grained ordering of subgroups of the citizenry and of cultural themes, proliferate.[7]

I shall argue that democratic national politics has to be a contest of variants of the national identity. Those political leaders who can persuade the most people of their variant of national identity win elections. While individual leaders play a creative role in revising and rearticulating their identity variant, there is also a sense in which the impersonal identity variants compete with each other for mass allegiance through the politicians who advocate them. The identity variants win through superior credibility among the mass audience. That means these narratives must be composed of categories, causal beliefs, and allegorical norms the masses take seriously at the time. National identity narratives also

---

[4] Benedict Anderson, *Imagined Communities* (Ithaca, NY: Cornell University Press, 1983).

[5] Sanjoy Banerjee, "The Cultural Logic of National Identity Formation: Contending Discourses in Late Colonial India," in Valerie Hudson (ed.), *Culture and Foreign Policy* (Boulder, CO: Lynne Reinner, 1997), pp. 27–44.

[6] Michael Billig, *Banal Nationalism* (London: Sage, 1995).

[7] Sabina Mihelj, *Media Nations: Communicating Belonging and Exclusion in the Modern World* (London: Palgrave Macmillan, 2011).

implicate human rights norms. Insofar as the narratives recognize social groups as integral to the nation or marginalize them, their coequal rights are implicated. Different national identity variants will construct human rights differently.

National identity narratives are known to large segments of nations and electorates, at least in a sketchy form. Typically, the vast majority of people are also familiar with the partisan variants of national narratives and can recognize the variants when articulated. However, national identity narratives are never articulated in full on a single occasion. Instead, only fragments of these narratives are articulated and propagated, and the audience members must assimilate these fragments and reassemble the larger narratives in their own minds.

National identity narratives and their variants are shared in an internally differentiated nation. There are major segments of society where each possesses its own politicized common knowledge. Persuasive communication must connect with these clusters of common knowledge. Within India the urban middle class formed such a segment. It had taken to social media with enthusiasm in the years preceding the 2014 election. For this segment, both mass media and social media provide credible messages. For the rural poor, credible knowledge of conditions in distant parts of India comes from migrant workers. As Gujarat, under Modi's leadership, attracted migrant workers from Uttar Pradesh and other states, the credibility of Modi's model of governance was enhanced among this class.[8]

There have been two principal lines of rhetoric about economic policy on the Indian political scene: populist and developmentalist. Different variants of national identity incorporate these lines of rhetoric in particular ways. Populist rhetoric has been based on the premise that economic development is either impossible or of little benefit to ordinary people and that redistribution from the rich to the masses is the only reliable option to benefit the people. Populist rhetoric draws a sharp distinction between the elites and the people. It holds that the people should not be asked to sacrifice for future economic growth and should receive subsidies instead. Populist rhetoric puts great stock in direct and visible government action to benefit the people and does not believe in the working of market forces over time.

[8] *DNA India*,"Narendra Modi's Star Rising in Eastern Uttar Pradesh, but Is That Enough to Win State?" (March 11, 2014); *Times of India*, "How Migrant Laborers Worked in Narendra Modi's Favor" (May 18, 2014).

Populist rhetoric does not offer or mention the prospect of growth in employment but focuses instead on the preservation of existing jobs of those who have them and the property rights of farmers and other small proprietors. Populist rhetoric presents a relatively simple narrative of conflict between a devious and powerful elite, virtuous masses, and heroic politicians coming to the rescue of the masses through subsidies and other protections. Further, populist rhetoric in India does not highlight education or health. Populism projects a static vision of society and offers incremental gains in the consumption of the poor.

Developmentalist rhetoric, by contrast, relies on the logic of market forces and promises increased employment and improved infrastructure and services, such as education and health, in exchange for market discipline. It pays secondary attention to distributive issues. The developmentalist narrative lacks a prominent villain, except possibly populist politicians.

The implications of populist and developmentalist approaches to economic management for social and economic human rights depend on the conceptualization of those rights. Insofar as one conceptualizes these rights as purely distributive, populist action does offer modest equalization and thus rights gains. Under such a conception of human rights, overall development is foregone and poverty persists, but no human rights are violated. According to developmentalist rhetoric, in a favorable scenario poverty declines, education and health improves, and overall wealth increases. Developmentalist rhetoric offers the impoverished masses the prospect of empowerment through employment and wage increases, eventually. But this is not assured in any particular decade.

The 1990s in India were a decade of developmentalist reforms, but agriculture stagnated with declining food availability for the rural poor.[9] A likely outcome under contemporary developmentalist strategy is that even if poverty declines, the rich gain proportionately more and income inequality increases. China, the most successful developmentalist state, has seen this scenario unfold.[10] The outcome for social and economic rights depends on whether their conceptualization prioritizes poverty reduction or equality. In the global postcolonial experience, there has

[9] Ramesh Chand, *India's National Agricultural Policy: A Critique*, Working Paper No. 85, Institute of Economic Growth, Delhi (2004).
[10] Pranab Bardhan, *Awakening Giants, Feet of Clay: Assessing the Economic Rise of China and India* (Princeton, NJ: Princeton University Press, 2010), pp. 90–103.

been no development strategy that has consistently yielded both rapid aggregate economic growth and relative equal or even equalizing income distribution. The debate between populists and capitalist developmentalists has taken place against this frustrating reality.

In the Indian political scene, the same parties, especially the BJP and Congress, switch between developmentalist and populist rhetoric on different occasions. As we shall see, the credibility of subsidies as a source of benefit was on the decline among voters, while that of infrastructure building was on the ascent. The Congress Party entered the 2009 elections with a predominantly developmentalist rhetoric under the leadership of Prime Minister Manmohan Singh and won a resounding victory. However, immediately afterward Singh was denied his choice of finance minister by the Congress Party, and over the next few years a more populist rhetoric took hold. No substantial capitalist reforms were enacted after 2009.

While this chapter is focused on the 2014 national elections in India, the contest between populist and developmentalist politics has continued afterward. A party formed in 2013 called the Aam Aadmi Party (common person's/man's party), mainly on the promise of fighting corruption. They managed to form the government in the Delhi state (provincial) election. However, their rule was considered chaotic by many, and they resigned after forty-nine days to prepare themselves for the national election, in which they performed poorly. However, in the Delhi state elections of February 2015, they won all but three seats in a house of seventy.[11] The Aam Aadmi Party put forward a more populist appeal than the BJP in that election and trounced it. Many factors went into the victory, but in India's wealthiest state, the more populist appeal won decisively just eight months after the more developmentalist appeal won nationwide and even in Delhi.

Interest groups in Indian politics

Political competition in India has taken place within a society differentiated in multiple ways and undergoing transformation. This section will examine some of the important cleavages that divided voters or that political parties had to overcome to build coalitions. The national identity variant of each party had to appeal across cleavages to build a winning coalition.

---

[11] "BJP Trounced in Delhi by AAP in Big Blow for Modi," *Reuters* (February 10, 2015).

Between the 2009 and 2014 elections, there was a profound transformation of class patterns in Indian voting. The class composition of the electorate changed radically in this period, due to both rapid economic growth and a sharp increase in voter turnout among all but the poorest. The Center for the Study of Developing Societies applied the same criteria in the two elections to divide the electorate into four classes: rich, middle, lower, and poor. The share of the poor among voters in the two elections plummeted from 41 percent to 20 percent, while the share of the middle jumped from 20 percent to 36 percent.[12]

Voter turnout among the poor rose modestly, from 57 percent to 60 percent, while among the other three classes turnout in the two elections leaped from 57–59 percent to 67–69 percent. We can observe in the changing electorate both upward economic mobility due to economic growth and the decline of poverty as well as sharply increased political mobilization among the non-poor.[13] All four classes gave more votes to the BJP than to Congress, including the poor, who had been Congress loyalists until 2009. But the BJP's margin was only 4 percent among the poor, while it was 12 percent in the lower and middle and 21 percent among the rich.[14] Voters of all classes also responded that they favored infrastructure spending over antipoverty subsidies.[15] We can observe a qualitative transformation of the Indian political economy with the rise of a developmentalist electorate.

Gender inequality remains intense in Indian society, as demonstrated by the deterioration of the child sex ratio due to sex-selective abortions. Major gender inequalities in literacy and education persist, although primary school attendance has become nearly universal and thus nearly equal for girls and boys. No major political parties have advocated gender inequality. However, their candidates and legislators remain overwhelmingly male. Nonetheless, several prominent women have emerged as political leaders, even without being relatives of male leaders in the same parties. In the past, women's turnout in Indian elections was substantially less than that of men, but in 2014, 66 percent of eligible women voted as

[12] Eswaran Sridharan, "Class Voting in the 2014 Lok Sabha Elections: The Growing Size and Importance of the Middle Classes," *Economic and Political Weekly*, 49, 39 (2014), 72–76, 74.

[13] *Economic Times*, "Now, Only 22 Per Cent Indians below Poverty Line: Planning Commission" (July 24, 2013).

[14] Sridharan, "Class Voting in the 2014 Lok Sabha Elections."

[15] Eswaran Sridharan, "Behind Narendra Modi's Victory," *Journal of Democracy*, 25, 4 (2014), 20–33, 32.

against 67 percent of men. The BJP did suffer a gender gap, as it has for decades, winning only 29 percent of women's votes as against 33 percent of men's.[16] The improvement in women's voter turnout has been concentrated in the middle classes, and it does reflect the greater politicization of the middle class, aided by their access to social media.

Even as public caste discrimination has attenuated since independence, political caste identities have strengthened, particularly among the less privileged castes. In the early decades after independence, political leadership was concentrated among upper castes, and such leaders promised modest social liberation to the middle and lower castes. By the 1970s middle-caste political networks began to throw up winning politicians. In the 1990s lower-caste political networks made a decisive appearance, and from 2007 to 2012, a Dalit-centric party, the BSP, ruled India's largest state with an absolute majority in the legislature. Dalits formed only one-fifth of the state's population, and the BSP won by gaining upper caste votes.

By the 2014 elections, political leadership was no longer subject to caste privilege among Hindus, although Muslims remained overwhelmingly absent from the political class. The BJP in 2014 was more successful among the more privileged castes, winning 54 percent of upper-caste votes, 34 percent of middle castes, and only 24 percent of Dalit votes. Where the BJP broke the correlation with privilege was in tribal communities, which form 7 percent of the Indian population, among whom it won 38 percent of votes. Even among Dalits, the BJP got more votes than Congress.[17]

Muslims form 14 to 15 percent of the Indian population. Hindu–Muslim relations have been one of the most charged topics in Indian politics since independence in 1947. The Indian constitution stakes out a secular framework. All persons are awarded the same fundamental rights, although religious distinctions are made in personal law regarding marriage, inheritance, and aspects of taxation. The BJP has taken, to varying degrees over time, an explicitly Hindu nationalist position, defining religions originating historically in India as the natural religions of the land. This has rendered them highly unpopular with Muslims, who have often voted tactically to defeat BJP candidates, rather than strongly supporting any particular candidate.

---

[16] Rajdeep Sardesai, *The Election That Changed India* (Gurgaon: Penguin 2014).
[17] Sridharan, "Behind Narendra Modi's Victory," p. 24.

Congress and most other parties have taken a secularist position, defining India's culture as composite, tying together the Hindu, Muslim, and other religions. In practice, the secularist parties have competed for Muslim votes by aligning with conservative and even radical elements in the Muslim community and offering Muslims religious symbolic benefits more than economic gain. Although India has been ruled by secularist parties dependent on Muslim support for nearly all of the period after independence, Muslims have been surpassed by Dalits in educational achievement.[18] In 2014, Muslims continued to oppose the BJP, which received only 8 percent of Muslim votes.[19]

The Indian identity contest

In the 2014 elections, the Congress Party propagated its identity variant in its manifesto, speeches, and political actions. The Congress manifesto designates a national heritage in equating the Congress Party of 2014 with the independence movement and highlights the secular theme of "unity in diversity." Congress has had a longstanding heritage construct of "composite culture," in which India's culture is considered a well-settled and intricate admixture of Hindu, Muslim, and other influences. Sonia Gandhi said in an election speech, "The choice is between the Congress which believes in the Ganga-Jamuna culture [metaphor of the confluence of two rivers] that unites the country and the BJP which does not believe in cultural plurality or composite culture of India."[20]

Rahul Gandhi, who was the primary informal leader of the Congress campaign, highlighted his family history and his life story in his first television interview.[21] Since his family members have been leaders of the emerging Indian nation and then the established state since the 1920s, his family itself forms part of an Indian heritage construct. He emphasized his emotional reactions to the assassinations of his grandmother and father, tying himself into the emotional responses of the Indian nation to those two events. He tied his own life history to the Indian national heritage. In a major speech in 2013, Rahul Gandhi had mentioned that

---

[18] Sachar Committee, "Social, Economic and Educational Status of the Muslim Community of India: A Report," Prime Minister's High Level Committee Cabinet Secretariat, Government of India, New Delhi (2006).

[19] Sridharan, "Behind Narendra Modi's Victory," p. 24.

[20] *The Hindu*, "A Clash of Ideologies, Says Sonia" (April 10, 2014).

[21] *Times of India*, "Rahul Gandhi's First Interview: Full Text" (January 2014).

his grandmother's bodyguards, who assassinated her, taught him to play badminton.[22] He avoided direct responses in the interview to questions about the anti-Sikh riots that followed the assassination of Indira Gandhi.

The vanguard proposed in the Congress campaign included industrial capitalists as well as non-governmental organizations (NGOs) activists and prominent Muslim religious figures. In 2010, Sonia Gandhi convened the National Advisory Council, staffed by former bureaucrats and social activists, including some with views well to the left of the Congress government. This council played a key role in shaping social welfare legislation after 2010. In the 2014 campaign, Congress adopted the rhetoric of a "rights based economy." This reflected the outlook of social activists much more than that of capitalists. A month before the 2014 elections, Sonia Gandhi met with a delegation of Muslim religious leaders led by the imam of Jama Masjid, the largest mosque in India, and appealed to them to help ensure that "secular votes" do not split.[23] Congress was projecting these religious leaders as legitimate and authoritative moral leaders in the political sphere. The laggard group designated by Congress was the BJP Party and those who adopted a Hindu nationalist ideology. They were condemned as divisive and antidemocratic.

The danger Congress emphasized was that of national disunity based on Hindu–Muslim antagonism provoked by the BJP and other Hindu nationalist or communalist (sectarian) organizations. A major aspect of destiny was conveyed by the metaphor of river tributaries. Hindu and Muslim communities would continue to exist as socially distinct, as the tributaries, and would join in certain spheres of social interaction. The national destiny projected in the Congress campaign entailed a rights-based economy with major subsidies that would nonetheless remain capitalist. Congress envisioned a society more egalitarian with respect to gender and caste and projected new legislation as the principal means to that end.

The BJP projected an Indian heritage of a homogenous civilization and nation, in origin and up to the present. BJP's accounts of Indian cultural history made scant mention of specifically Muslim themes. While it also used the phrase "unity in diversity," the BJP's manifesto, for example, said of Indian history: "From the Vedas to Upanishads and Gautam – the

---

[22] Rahul Gandhi, "Speech by Rahul Gandhi" (2013), http://im.rediff.com/news/2013/jan/20_rahul_gandhi_Jaipur_Speech.pdf.
[23] *Economic Times*, "Sonia Gandhi Asks Muslim Leaders to Ensure Secular Votes Do Not Split" (April 2, 2014).

Buddha and Mahavira – the 24th Jain Tirthankara and then to Kautilya and Chandra Gupta and down up to the eighteenth century, India was respected for its flourishing economy, trade, commerce and culture."[24]

While the eighteenth century was a period of Muslim rule and great Muslim cultural influence, the sentence, as well as the document as a whole, downplays the Muslim role, specifically mentioning only pre-Islamic figures. It does, however, highlight figures from Buddhism and Jainism, which today are widely considered as religions distinct from Hinduism. The BJP has held that the term "Hinduism" should refer to all spiritual traditions of Indian geographical origin. The manifesto goes on to highlight the theme of civilizational and national homogeneity, saying that the leaders of the independence movement "had a vision to reconstruct the political and economic institutions of India as a continuum of civilizational consciousness, which made India one country, one people, and one Nation."[25]

The word "Nation" is capitalized in the original. It should be observed that what the BJP manifesto says of Indian independence leaders, particularly Gandhi, omits major themes from these leaders' own speeches. Narendra Modi also highlighted the concept of national homogeneity in his most watched television interview during the campaign. He was asked about charges he would "break the nation into pieces." He responded by criticizing the Congress government's aborted effort to get counts on the religions of soldiers: "Who created communal tension? For the first time, the [government] asked the army to provide [information] on the basis of religion." He continued "In Gujarat, I talk about 5 crore Gujaratis only. I talk of 125 crore Hindustani only. I have tried to avoid the sectarian terminology."[26]

The vanguard designated by the BJP included industrial capitalists and the urban middle class. The BJP's development agenda was strongly capitalistic, and Modi's track record of growth in Gujarat that was being sold to India as a whole was strongly associated with major family conglomorates. At the same time, Modi gave moral recognition to the "neo-middle class," as he called them, as not the winners of a rigged game

---

[24] Bharatiya Janata Party, *Election Manifesto 2014* (New Delhi, 2014).

[25] Bharatiya Janata Party, 2014

[26] A "crore" is ten million, and a Hindustani is an Indian; *India TV*, "Exclusive: Read Full Interview of Narendra Modi to Rajat Sharma in Aap Ki Adalat (Part 2)" (June 13, 2014), www.indiatvnews.com/politics/national/read-full-interview-of-narendra-modi-rajat-sharma-aap-ki-adalat-16533.html.

but as the pioneers of a future of the whole nation. He did this above all through use of social media. By 2014, cell phones had become near universal in Indian society, and their utilization for mass outreach by political campaigns did not have class-specific implications. But Internet social media, like Facebook and Twitter, were still restricted to the new middle class. Modi's unapologetic and prolific use of these Internet media conveyed a message of exoneration and congratulation to this class and on behalf of this class to the nation as a whole.[27]

BJP's destiny construct for India was one of prosperity, national homogeneity, and rectitude. These were pitched against the dangers of economic stagnation, corruption, and "pseudo-secularism." The opposition between the concepts of a homogenous nation and pseudo-secularism was propagated by a BJP spokesperson in criticism of Sonia Gandhi's appeal to Muslim religious leaders to help avoid a split of "secular votes." Prakash Javadekar said:

> Here is a new definition of secularism. We are seeking votes in the name of the country – for progress, for good governance. We are called communal. And those, everybody who seeks votes in the name of religion and caste, they are called secularists. This is absolutely a perverted definition of secularisms. They are not secularists, they are pseudo-secularists.[28]

BJP valorized only the country as a whole, devalued seeking votes in the name of religion and caste, and implicitly denied any legacy of injustice that could be rectified by such appeals. On other occasions, Modi did make emotional appeals against caste discrimination, particularly against himself. This statement conveys a destiny construct in its future orientation, in that each party is held to be promising a future course in exchange for votes in the present.

The identity variants of Congress and the BJP reflected and promoted two different assessments of the threats to human rights in India and of the appropriate remedies. In the Congress view, the human rights of religious minorities faced a distinctive threat, and thus opposition to religious majoritarian politics, referred to in India as "majority communalism," was a priority. In the BJP view, majority communalism was not a major threat, principally due to what they regarded as the inherently tolerant nature of the Hindu religion. They have supported instead

[27] Sardesai, *The Election That Changed India*.
[28] NDTV, "BJP Targets Sonia Gandhi over Reported Comments to Muslim Leaders" (April 2, 2014), www.ndtv.com/elections/article/election-2014/bjp-targets-sonia-gandhi-over-reported-comments-to-muslim-leaders-503480.

uniform rights for all citizens, without religious distinction. These differences are reflected in their debate about marriage laws. Currently, Indian Muslims may marry under provision of Islamic Law, adjudicated by regular Indian courts, and then be governed by Islamic family laws. Muslim opinion in India overwhelmingly supports the continuation of this system. The BJP has advocated a uniform civil code with gender equality.[29]

Social media and national identities

Social media played a significant role in propagating the national identity variants of both major parties to the upper middle class. The BJP campaign used social media far more vigorously and imaginatively than did the Congress campaign. But this was not the main factor in how social media shaped the election outcome. The main factor was that the use of social media added credibility to the BJP's variant of Indian national identity and subtracted credibility from the Congress variant. By using social media the BJP and the Modi campaign conveyed the message that members of the upper middle class had a legitimate right to use their superior access to communications technology to participate in democratic politics.

In terms of caste, the rich and middle-class voters formed more than triple the share of the upper castes in the population. Nonetheless, Facebook users formed a much narrower segment of the population and are likely to be overwhelmingly upper caste. However, the BJP did not become vulnerable to charges of elitism. The non-elite origins of their candidate Modi were certainly a factor in indemnifying the BJP from this accusation. But their indemnity was deeper than that. Their developmentalist message said to those who did not have Internet access that they would get this access in the future and that they had the same interests as those who did. This message had credibility, since those who did not have Internet access had acquired cell phones within the preceding decade; thus it was believable to them that they would gain access to other new technologies. The middle class and the upper middle class were projected by the BJP as a vanguard for the rest of society rather than as an unfairly privileged class. And this message was credible to large

[29] Zoya Hasan, "Religion, Feminist Politics and Muslim Women's Rights in India," in K. Kannabiran (ed.), *Women and Law: Critical Feminist Perspectives* (New Delhi: Sage, 2014), pp. 264–73.

sections of society due to the experience of economic growth and poverty reduction, as well as the rapid diffusion of cell phones.

The future

A few trends identified here are likely to persist. First, social media access is likely to increase. Smartphone prices worldwide are falling rapidly, so that trend alone will bring greater Internet and social media access in India. Among the poor and lower-middle classes, Internet and social media access will rise faster than incomes. The distinctive concerns of these classes with receive an airing. Political parties will use social media to address lower income groups. In 2014, the sheer use of social media conveyed an endorsement of the upper middle class. In the future, such use will convey a broader social message. Social media, then, are likely to emerge as more effective platforms for the realization and protection of social and economic human rights.

Second, the contest of identity variants is likely to persist. The Hindu-centric nationalism of the BJP is appealing to many but not all Hindus, and unappealing to most non-Hindus, who comprise a fifth of the population. The pluralist variant – projecting India as a confluence of Hindu, Muslim, and other streams – suffers from the disadvantage of projecting India as a fragmented nation and thus lacks the nation-centered emotion of the Hindu-centric variant. During the independence movement from the 1920s onward, the nationalism that emerged was secular and emotionally powerful, but contemporary secularist national identity gives greater weight to subsidiary minority identities. The disadvantages of each identity variant ensure the survival of the contest, without a decisive victory for either.

Third, fundamental quandaries in the definition and prioritization of social and economic rights are also likely to persist in India. The trade-off between poverty reduction and economic equalization is likely to persist. Given the vast scale of poverty in India and the limited effectiveness, worldwide, of direct government efforts at redistribution of income, poverty reduction will inevitably require market-driven economic growth. The scale and speed of employment generation required has been achieved in successful developing countries only through capitalist economic development. Capitalism has delivered miracles of poverty reduction in states across Asia. At the same time, there are strong dis-equalizing tendencies within capitalism, both in India and worldwide.

The incomes of upper strata, especially at the very top, are likely to outpace those of the poor and lower middle class, even as the latter rise.

The human rights quandary here is genuine. Poverty entails intense suffering even in the presence of collective knowledge on how to alleviate that suffering, so the state fails in its human rights responsibility if it does not act on that knowledge. The Indian state has reduced poverty but not as successfully as most other Asian states. And as many other states have drastically reduced poverty, the knowledge of how to do so has crystallized. Thus India's human rights failure in poverty reduction is intensifying over time. At the same time, the proven path of poverty reduction is capitalist economic development. That strategy frequently leads to greater economic inequality, which leads, beyond some point, to political inequality. And the doctrine of political and economic human rights strongly valorizes political equality among human beings. Thus human rights cuts both ways.

Fourth, the clash of developmentalist and populist rhetorics is likely to persist on social media. In particular, populist rhetoric is likely to persist in India despite its refusal to offer any strategy for poverty reduction and economic development that has worked in other countries. The disequalizing tendencies in capitalist development create the political opening for populism. Although a large bloc of voters rejects populism, as seen in the 2014 national elections, populism remains attractive to another large bloc, as seen in the Delhi state elections. The political viability of populism maintains the opportunity for members of the political class, social activists, and intelligentsia to attract people with the narrative simplicity and emotional power of populist rhetoric.

These four trends together foreshadow the content of political discussion on Indian social media going forward. Social media will host the clash of Hindu-centric and secularist identities, with varying degrees of ugliness. Simultaneously, social media will allow pluralism within religious blocs greater power of expression. Small groups within religious blocs, with views at variance with the majority in their bloc, will gain voice. This will facilitate cross-religious communities of agreement without the mediation of political parties and religious leaders. In the developmentalist-populist clash, there will be a competition between narrative frames in social media for the allegiance of the newly online lower middle class and poor. The lower middle class and poor will be invited by the two frames into two different roles. The developmentalist narrative frame will offer them a heroic role of valiant workers earning a promotion in their class stratum. The populist narrative will offer them rescue from their impending victimization by the business elites.

Conclusion

In the Indian political system, social media has had little impact on direct human rights observance or violations. The conditions of Mubarak's Egypt were absent in democratic India, so the Arab Spring analogy does not apply. However, social media has played a role in the contest of national identity versions that contain their own conceptions of human rights and of the challenges of upholding them in India. The rise of social media has contributed to the increased politicization of the middle class and in the spring of 2014 enabled them to pull India toward an identity of national homogeneity and developmentalism and toward a conception of human rights that was also homogenous, with less emphasis on specific considerations for religious minorities.

Social media served as one of the channels of communication to the middle class and was the conduit for competing national identity variants and their allegorical human rights norms. Modi's use of social media gave recognition to this middle class and legitimized its ascent within his national identity variant. This process enthused the middle class and gave an advantage to the BJP's identity variant and the conception of human rights contained therein. Going forward, social media will spread down the income scale. The contest of identity variants and political-economic rhetorics established in 2014 will persist and enter circulation in social media. But the rise of social media will also enable the formation of smaller communities, cross-cutting the major blocs of identities and rhetorics.

11

Promises to keep

The Basic Law, the "Umbrella Movement," and democratic reform in Hong Kong

MICHAEL C. DAVIS

In late 2014, Hong Kong youth captured the global imagination in massive protests challenging Beijing over failed promises of democratic reform. Thirty years earlier, Hong Kong and the world were confronted by the prospect that one of the freest, most developed cities on the planet was to be turned over to what was then one of the world's most hardline regimes, the People's Republic of China (PRC). As outlined in the 1984 Sino-British Joint Declaration, to preserve Hong Kong that regime promised the city all the ingredients of modern constitutionalism, including democracy, human rights, and the rule of law.[1] Hong Kong people were told to "put their hearts at ease." There would be "fifty years without change" (or as Deng Xiaoping said, maybe more), "a high degree of autonomy," and "Hong Kong people ruling Hong Kong." The required Hong Kong Basic Law completed in 1990 promised democratic reform and the "ultimate aim" of "universal suffrage."[2] More recently, in a 2007 decision, Beijing promised such universal suffrage could be fully realized for choosing Hong Kong's Chief Executive in 2017.[3]

---

[1] "Joint Declaration of the Government of the United Kingdom of Great Britain and Northern Ireland and the Government of the People's Republic of China on the Question of Hong Kong" (hereinafter "Sino-British Joint Declaration" or "Joint Declaration"), December 19, 1984.

[2] "The Basic Law of the Hong Kong Special Administrative Region of the People's Republic of China" (hereinafter "Basic Law"), adopted by the National People's Congress on April 4, 1990, effective July 1, 1997, articles 45 and 68.

[3] "Decision of the Standing Committee of the National People's Congress on Issues Relating to the Method for Selecting the Chief Executive of the Hong Kong Special Administrative Region and for Forming the Legislative Council of the Hong Kong Special Administrative Region in the Year 2012 and on Issues Relating to Universal Suffrage" (adopted at Thirty-first Session of the Standing Committee of the Tenth National People's Congress on December 29, 2007), para. 1.

Skeptical Hong Kong democracy activists in the summer of 2013 moved into action, forming a group called "Occupy Central with Love and Peace," promising to clog Hong Kong's Central financial district with 10,000 occupying protesters if genuine democracy was not allowed. This aggressive posture is the result of mistrust born of years of government foot dragging over electoral reform. Increasing Beijing interference in Hong Kong affairs has left the society fearful that the open rule of law-based society they know will increasingly be swamped by the authoritarian mainland political culture and its associated corruption. Democracy is sought in the hope that an elected government would better defend Hong Kong's interest.

The perception that the Hong Kong government rarely takes steps to defend Hong Kong's promised high degree of autonomy has meant that civil society has usually had to take up this role. Generally, this has meant organizing mass protest marches typically announced in both traditional and new media. Because Hong Kong is an open society with numerous social groups and traditional media, new social media tend to supplement and not displace traditional organizing activities as a driving force behind public protests.[4]

A group planning a protest might begin with an Internet signature campaign supporting a letter of protest against objectionable government policies. With a large number of newspapers and other publications in Hong Kong, this could typically be either published in the newspapers directly by the organizers or disseminated to the public through press conferences and reportage. When the protest date is near, both the Internet and smartphone texting services may get the word out to join the protest through various social networks. Traditional media will then cover the protest, supplemented by personal reports and testimonials through the Internet and other new media.

A decade ago, large protests of up to half a million demonstrators took place over proposed national security, secrecy, and sedition laws, to be enacted under Article 23 of the Basic Law.[5] The mobilization began with a press conference by the organizer, the Article 23 Concern Group, which was followed by the circulation of half a million pamphlets on the street and eventually Internet mobilization by the Civil

---

[4] Matthew Hillburn, "Social Media Documenting, Not Driving, Hong Kong Protests," *Voice of America* (October 1, 2014).

[5] "Article 23 Legislation: The Proper Way Forward," www.article23.org.hk/english/news update/aug03/0813Pamphlet_e.htm.

Human Rights Front.[6] The recent Occupy Central protest followed a similar pattern, but, as discussed below, this time the pamphlets were replaced by new media and online posters and announcements. When the police used tear gas, as discussed below, the same new media got the word out, bringing tens of thousands of protesters to the street.[7]

Hong Kong people have come to appreciate that maintaining basic freedoms without democracy is futile. A common Asian values argument has long been used to promote the idea that it should be possible to maintain human rights and the rule of law under authoritarianism.[8] The trouble with this argument, as Jon Elster eloquently put it, is that the dictator "is unable to make himself unable to interfere whenever it seems expedient."[9] Confidence that one could maintain the rule of law and human rights without democracy was particularly prevalent in Hong Kong during British colonial rule, as the colonial rulers in the postwar years generally applied the same rights protections afforded in the United Kingdom. A degree of Beijing constraint in the first decade after the handover may have resulted in some confidence in mainstream society that this condition of the rule of law without full democracy would continue.[10] With more and more mainland interference in Hong Kong affairs in recent years, doubts have been sown as Hong Kong people worry about the loss of autonomy and the consequent loss of the rule of law.[11] Democracy has become the sought-after vehicle to better secure existing freedoms that are slowly being eroded.

[6] May Sin-mi Hon, "Lawyers to Issue Pamphlets Outlining Article 23 Fears," *South China Morning Post* (November 16, 2002); "Civil Human Rights Front," *Wikipedia*, http://en.wikipedia.org/wiki/Civil_Human_Rights_Front.

[7] "Police Fire Tear Gas and Baton Charge Thousands of Occupy Central Protesters," *South China Morning Post* (September 28, 2014); Danny Lee, "The Role of Social Media in Occupy Protests, on the Ground and around the World," *South China Morning Post* (October 30, 2014).

[8] This argument has been widely challenged. Michael C. Davis, "Constitutionalism and Political Culture: The Debate over Human Rights and Asian Values," *Harvard Human Rights Journal*, 11 (1998), 109; Michael C. Davis, "The Political Economy and Culture of Human Rights in East Asia," in Sarah Joseph and Adam McBeth (eds.), *Research Handbook on International Human Rights Law* (London: Edward Elgar Publishers, 2010), pp. 414–39.

[9] Jon Elster, "Constitution-Making in Eastern Europe: Rebuilding the Boat in the Open Sea," *Public Administration*, 71 (1993), 169, 199–201.

[10] Michael C. Davis, "The Basic Law and Democratization in Hong Kong," *Loyola University of Chicago International Law Review*, 3, 3 (Spring 2006), 165–85.

[11] See Victoria T. Hui, "Hong Kong's Umbrella Movement: The Protests and Beyond," *Journal of Democracy* 26, 2 (April 2015), 111–21.

The initial pessimism about Beijing's intentions among democracy supporters proved to be justified. In the summer of 2014 a Beijing-issued White Paper accused Hong Kong people of a "confused and lopsided" view, and a National People's Congress (NPC) Standing Committee decision turned "universal suffrage" into a Beijing-vetted election.[12] The latter was widely viewed as fake universal suffrage. That Hong Kong's current government has become the chief proponent of Beijing's flawed model has caused great concern. Moderate proposals for compromise suggested during a public consultation were uniformly rejected.

Spearheaded by student activists and the full panoply of tools for modern social movements, in September 2014 the "Umbrella Movement" was launched as hundreds of thousands of protesters occupied major streets at protest sights in Hong Kong. Unlike the many protest movements that challenge entrenched regimes, demand regime change, and construct a new democratic order from scratch, these protesters launched their movement by demanding compliance with a constitutional script originally authored by the authoritarian regime itself. Basic freedoms and the rule of law were already in place as a colonial legacy. The Joint Declaration and the Basic Law promise their continuance.

Hong Kong's Umbrella Movement is the story of a social movement using the resources of civil society and modern communications to demand compliance with existing constitutional commitments. In this story, political ideas drive social activism. The ideas laid out in the Sino-British Joint Declaration and the Hong Kong Basic Law are now being challenged by mainland forces with habits of social and political control that are at odds with the basic liberal commitments made. With a local, purportedly autonomous government subservient to the mainland habits of control, a social movement, armed with traditional tools and modern social activism, was born. The special condition of a preexisting rule of law and an open society raises unique questions about the ideas that drive this movement and their survivability.

This chapter outlines the commitments made and the driving forces behind Hong Kong's Umbrella Movement. The following sections will

---

[12] "Information Office of the State Council, the Practice of the 'One Country, Two Systems' Policy in the Hong Kong Special Administrative Region" (hereinafter "White Paper"), June 10, 2014; "Decision of the Standing Committee of the National People's Congress on Issues Relating to the Selection of the Chief Executive of the Hong Kong Special Administrative Region by Universal Suffrage and on the Method for Forming the Legislative Council of the Hong Kong Special Administrative Region in the Year 2016" (hereinafter "NPC Standing Committee Decision"), August 31, 2014.

discuss, first, the constitutional foundations in the Joint Declaration and the Basic Law; second, the degree of noncompliance posed by Beijing's policies and associated rulings; third, the emergence and challenges of Hong Kong's Umbrella Movement; and fourth, the achievements of the movement and prospects going forward. At this writing the Hong Kong democracy movement remains a work in progress. It has enjoyed tremendous success in exposing failed compliance with China's commitments and international human rights standards, while its immediate democratic goals remain out of reach. By failing to keep its autonomy and democracy commitments, China has effectively constructed a resistance movement.

Constitutional foundations: the Sino-British Joint Declaration and the Hong Kong Basic Law

Sino-British Joint Declaration

Hong Kong's democracy movement is chiefly driven by efforts to promote compliance with fundamental constitutional commitments contained in the Sino-British Joint Declaration and the Hong Kong Basic Law. These commitments aim to achieve China's often-repeated promises of a "high degree of autonomy," "Hong Kong people ruling Hong Kong," and "fifty years without change." The perception that these commitments have been eroded and Hong Kong's autonomy is threatened by increasing interference from the Central Government is driving the democracy protests. While a "localist" movement that has become skeptical of ever achieving these promises has emerged from within the democracy movement to make more radical demands involving amendment of the Basic Law and more genuine autonomy, the majority of Hong Kong protesters appeared focused on demanding full compliance with the promises already made in the Joint Declaration and the Basic Law. Beijing's ultimate delivery on its original commitments may be the measure of the number of disaffected protesters to emerge.

The 1984 Sino-British Joint Declaration aimed to carry out the "one country, two systems" policy envisioned in Article 31 of the 1982 PRC Constitution. As stated by Deng Xiaoping, Hong Kong investors and, later, people in general, were encouraged to "put their hearts at ease."[13]

---

[13] Steve Tsang, *A Modern History of Hong Kong: 1841–1997* (London: L.B. Tauris & Co., 2007), pp. 219–24. Deng made it clear that Hong Kong would be handed back to China. His words of assurance became a general theme as to all Hong Kong people.

When the Joint Declaration was announced in late 1984, after several difficult years of negotiations, confidence in Hong Kong's future seemed assured.[14] The Joint Declaration was appropriately registered as a treaty with the United Nations. Anxiety about Chinese rule and associated emigration appeared to subside.[15]

It is doubtful that Hong Kong people would have been encouraged to put their hearts at ease merely based on some vague promises or policy commitments from Beijing without the solid foundation laid by an international treaty. China's track record in the decades before the agreement would certainly raise doubts in Hong Kong. Its treatment of other autonomous areas on the mainland in Tibet and Xinjiang offered little reason for confidence in mere constitutional or legislative guarantees of autonomy. Judging from Hong Kong's subsequent economic performance, international investors appeared assured by the agreement as well. International support no doubt further inspired Hong Kong confidence.[16] On balance, such confidence was likely based not so much on expectations that Britain, in case of a breach, would come to Hong Kong's rescue. Rather, it was simply that the agreement was in China's economic interest and its reputation was on the line over compliance with an international treaty.

The model outlined in the agreement was designed to protect Hong Kong from the intrusion of the mainland's socialist system. It guaranteed that Hong Kong would have a "high degree of autonomy, except in foreign and defense affairs." Promises of democracy, human rights, and the rule of law were elaborated sufficiently as to leave little doubt as to the fundamental commitment to Hong Kong's distinctive status. The future Chief Executive was to be chosen by "elections or consultations to be held locally," and the future legislature was to be chosen "by elections."[17]

The human rights guarantees were noteworthy for their liberal character. Fully half of the rights guaranteed were those generally categorized

---

[14] Recently declassified British files show that, starting from a large gap in perception, the agreement emerged after years of back and forth discussion where the Chinese side seemingly came to appreciate what was needed to assure the stability and prosperity of Hong Kong. Gary Cheung, "Signing of Joint Declaration Masked Deep Rift between Britain and China over Hong Kong's Future," *South China Morning Post* (December 30, 2014).

[15] Tsang, *A Modern History of Hong Kong*, p. 229.   [16] See generally ibid.

[17] Joint Declaration, supra note 1, para. 3, sec. 4; ibid., Annex I, para. I.

as freedom of speech, including press freedom, labor rights, academic research, and so on.[18] Human rights were further secured by continued application of the International Covenant on Civil and Political Rights (ICCPR) and the International Covenant on Economic, Social and Cultural Rights (ICESCR).[19] In 1991 the ICCPR, as applied to Hong Kong, was enacted into local law as the Hong Kong Bill of Rights Ordinance and is now routinely enforced by the Hong Kong courts.

To secure human rights and the rule of law the Joint Declaration provided that the existing laws, including the common law, rules of equity, local ordinances, and customary law, were to be maintained.[20] The courts were to be independent and final with the highest court of final appeal in Hong Kong.[21] Hong Kong people were to be allowed to challenge the acts of public officials in the courts.[22] All these commitments were stipulated to be included in the future Basic Law.

These commitments combined to lay a robust foundation for liberal constitutionalism in Hong Kong. Nothing less would serve as hedge against intrusion of the repressive mainland system. Being inside China but outside the mainland system, Hong Kong would be able to independently contribute to China's economic development and modernization. As one of the world's leading educational, financial, commercial, and cultural centers, it has surely done so. The success of such an autonomy model would depend on security for the liberal constitutional commitments, which inevitably involves empowering Hong Kong people to defend their separate system. Excessive intervention by a powerful central government would undermine this design.

Hong Kong Basic Law

The above commitments and other requirements from the Joint Declaration are for the most part faithfully included in the Basic Law. Armed with constitutional judicial review, such commitments are directly enforceable as constitutional requirements in the local courts.[23] There are substantial shortcomings in two areas: in provisions respecting the independence and finality of the local courts and in practice with respect

---

[18] Ibid., para. 3, sec. 5.   [19] Ibid., Annex I, para. XIII.
[20] Ibid., para. 3, sec. 3; Annex I, para. II.   [21] Ibid., Annex I, para. III.
[22] Ibid., Annex I, para. XIII.
[23] Ng Ka Ling v. Director of Immigration (1999), 1 H.K.L.R.D. 315, 318–19 (CFA).

to Beijing's interpretation of the democratic development requirements. These shortcomings very much predict the current impasse.

Hong Kong's rule of law under a common law system has long been put at risk by the ultimate power of amendment or interpretation of the Basic Law being vested in the NPC Standing Committee under Basic Law Articles 158 and 159.[24] This not only poses a risk to the promised independence and finality of the Hong Kong courts but also introduces a kind of nonjudicial precedent from a body that has traditionally taken great liberty with interpretation of legal requirements. The NPC Standing Committee often blurs the boundary between Basic Law interpretation and amendment, as occurred in the 1999 right of abode case[25] and again in the 2004 decision on changing the electoral method, discussed below.

That these NPC Standing Committee decisions are binding on the courts introduces the biggest challenge to the rule of law and protection of the basic human rights necessary to sustain Hong Kong's open society. The requirement that the NPC Standing Committee be advised by a Basic Law Committee made up of mainland and Hong Kong members has offered little constraint on this power due to the opaqueness of such consultation process. The further NPC Standing Committee acceptance of a power in the Hong Kong Government to directly make such referrals poses further challenge to the rule of law, creating an implicit threat the local government will run around a court decision when expedient. The saving grace up until the recent White Paper has been a degree of restraint at both governmental levels in using these powers.

---

[24] In an article that caused concern in Hong Kong respecting compliance with the Joint Declaration, Basic Law Article 158 provides that the NPC Standing Committee has the ultimate power to interpret the Basic Law. The local courts are also authorized to interpret when adjudicating cases essentially within the scope of autonomy. Article 159 assigns the power of amendment to the NPC Standing Committee but affords methods for amendment to be proposed by the local government. That the NPC Standing Committee has over the years exercised a degree of restraint in using this power has inspired some public acceptance. With the seeming abandonment of such restraint in the White Paper, there have been some calls for amendment of the Basic Law with respect to these and the democratic provisions; this included a minority of protesters burning the Basic Law during the commemoration on June 4, 2015.

[25] Ibid.; in *Ng* the CFA upheld under Basic Law Article 24 the right of abode in Hong Kong of certain children of Hong Kong residents. Finding the matter within Hong Kong autonomy the CFA had refused to refer the matter to the NPC Standing Committee, as it must do for certain matters of central authority and those involving local–central relations under Article 158. The Hong Kong Government then referred the matter on its own and got the substantive ruling as to the law overturned.

Beijing and Hong Kong Government foot dragging on democratic reform has been the primary Basic Law concern. Relying on Basic Law Article 45 language specifying "gradual and orderly progress" based on the "actual situation," the government has continuously deflected public demands for substantial democratic reform.[26] Basic Law Article 45 further provides, "The ultimate aim is selection of the Chief Executive by universal suffrage upon nomination by a broadly representative nominating committee in accordance with democratic procedures." A similar promise under Article 68 is made for the Legislative Council.[27] To date, only half of the Legislative Council is directly elected, and the Chief Executive's selection by a narrowly representative Election Committee would clearly fall under the category of consultations noted above from the Joint Declaration. For many of the legislative constituencies, corporate voting with no meaningful electoral contests prevails.[28]

Much of the recent debate has focused on the meaning of "universal suffrage." Given that Hong Kong is a party to the ICCPR and both the Joint Declaration and the Basic Law (in Article 39) require its continued application, the ICCPR offers a good source to clarify its meaning.[29] ICCPR Article 25 provides, "Every citizen shall have the right and the opportunity, without the distinctions mentioned in Article 2 (regarding discrimination) and without unreasonable restrictions: ... (b) to vote and to be elected at genuine periodic elections which shall be by universal and equal suffrage . . . guaranteeing the free expression of the will of the voters." The General Comment on Article 25 issued by the ICCPR Human Rights Committee (HRC) emphasizes that universal suffrage should enable the voters a genuine choice in a free and fair election.[30]

[26] Basic Law, supra note 2, Article 45 and Annex I.   [27] Ibid., Article 68 and Annex II.

[28] Thirty-five of the seventy legislative seats are elected by functional constituencies. Of these, twenty include corporate voters. These are small-circle elections with twelve of the corporate constituency representatives elected uncontested. Corporate voters participate in electing 570 of the 1,200-member Election Committee. Carine Lai, "Abolish Corporate Voting to Make Hong Kong Elections Fairer," *South China Morning Post* (November 14, 2014).

[29] Efforts by the Hong Kong Government to assert a forty-year-old colonial British reservation against election of the Legislative Council have been rejected by the ICCPR Human Rights Committee as no longer applicable after democracy has been initiated. The reservation did not include the Chief Executive election. Joyce Ng, "Human Rights Committee to Discuss Universal Suffrage in Hong Kong," *South China Morning Post* (September 10, 2014).

[30] International Covenant on Civil and Political Rights, General Comment 25 (August 27, 1996).

The prohibited distinctions mentioned in the article bar discrimination, among other things, for political opinion. The August 2014 NPC Standing Committee Decision has already been challenged as noncompliant by the ICCPR HRC in a follow-up procedure on Hong Kong's periodic report.[31] The Basic Law offers more assurances, guaranteeing in Basic Law Article 26 that Hong Kong residents have "the right to vote and the right to stand for election in accordance with law." Of course such law includes guarantees of freedom of expression and equality in the Basic Law.[32]

In a 2004 interpretation the NPC Standing Committee substantially amended the Basic Law process for electoral reform by requiring that the Hong Kong Government initially submit to the NPC Standing Committee for approval a report indicating that there is a need to change the method of electing either the Chief Executive or the Legislative Council.[33] Though the Basic Law requires NPC Standing Committee approval for changing the method of electing the Chief Executive, it requires reporting only "for the record" in respect of the Legislative Council.[34] Beijing now requires its advanced approval to initiate the process for either reform. This type of interference has caused grave concern about Hong Kong's autonomy.

In 2007 the NPC Standing Committee ruled that the ultimate aim of "universal suffrage" would be allowed for the 2017 Chief Executive and the 2020 Legislative Council elections in that required order.[35] This would also require the above-noted step of initial approval that there is a need for change. The 2007 NPC Standing Committee decision suggested that the required Nominating Committee for Chief Executive "may be formed with reference" to the current Election Committee.[36]

---

[31] Michael Forsythe, "U.N. Human Rights Panel Urges China to Allow Free Elections in Hong Kong," *New York Times* (October 23, 2014).

[32] Basic Law, supra note 2, Articles 25 and 27.

[33] "The Interpretation by the Standing Committee of the National People's Congress of Article 7 of Annex I and Article III of Annex II of the Basic Law of the Hong Kong Special Administrative Region of the People's Republic of China" (Adopted at the Eighth Session of the Standing Committee of the Tenth National People's Congress on 6 April 2004), sec. 3.

[34] Basic Law, supra note 2, Annex I and Annex II.

[35] Universal suffrage for the Legislative Council would be allowed only after it was achieved for the Chief Executive. "Decision of the Standing Committee of the National People's Congress on Issues Relating to the Method for Selecting the Chief Executive," supra note 3, para. 1.

[36] Ibid., para. 4.

The heavily proestablishment Election Committee used to select the first three chief executives has historically barely been able to nominate prodemocracy candidates under a 1/8 threshold. Democrats do not stand a chance in the actual election before the 1,200-member Election Committee. The Beijing suggestion, therefore, stirred a lot of suspicion that Beijing would manipulate the makeup of the Nominating Committee to control the election outcome.[37] This distrust prompted democrats to put forth proposals for public or civil nominations that would be binding on the Nominating Committee.[38]

Beijing has attacked the pan-democratic proposals as violating the Basic Law requirement of nomination by a "broadly representative nominating committee." The more serious violation of the Basic Law in Beijing's manipulation of the nominating committee to control the electoral outcome is given little regard. With the publication of the Beijing White Paper the die was cast for the massive Umbrella Movement that would stretch across the fall. As discussed in the following section, the blatant power-grab and disregard for Hong Kong's autonomy in the White Paper has shaken the very foundation of the "one country, two systems" model and threatens to undermine both the rule of law and human rights.

The White Paper, the Hong Kong reports, and the NPC Standing Committee decision

In the White Paper, Beijing asserted ultimate authority over Hong Kong, showing little regard for autonomy. The encouragement that Hong Kong people put their hearts at ease was effectively replaced with the assertion that Beijing is the boss. The twelve articles of the Sino-British Joint Declaration are characterized as twelve preexisting Chinese principles that "come solely from the authorization of the Central leadership," dismissing the international legal stature of these

---

[37] These suspicions were verified in a September meeting when a top Beijing official suggested the democrats were lucky they were tolerated to be in Hong Kong to even run for legislative seats. James Pomfret, "China Asserts Paternal Rights over Hong Kong in Democracy Clash," *Reuters* (September 11, 2014).

[38] The most prominent pan-democratic proposal was put forth by the Alliance for True Democracy, made up of the pan-democratic members of the Legislative Council. Their proposal involved both civil and party nominations. Alliance for True Democracy, "Composition of the Nominating Committee," reported in *Apple Daily* (January 9, 2014), http://hk.apple.nextmedia.com/news/art/20140109/18585320.

commitments.[39] Through this move, Beijing emphasized its full authority to interpret or amend the Basic Law as it chooses. Objection to this assault on Hong Kong's autonomy and rule of law was a driving force behind the massive democracy protest that followed in the fall. Democracy is widely understood as critical to protecting such Hong Kong core values as freedom, human rights, and the rule of law.

The White Paper aggressively condemns the liberal democratic view of the Hong Kong commitments as "confused or lopsided" and emphasizes that a "high degree of autonomy" is not "full autonomy."[40] Beijing's "comprehensive jurisdiction" over Hong Kong is likened to its direct control over other local administrative regions.[41] This is hardly a comforting prospect given the tradition of top-down control on the mainland. The White Paper credits the NPC Standing Committee with "comprehensive jurisdiction" and the power of "supervision" over local legislation.[42] The NPC Standing Committee is identified as the guardian of Hong Kong's rule of law.[43] Judges are required to be patriots and are described as administrative or governing officials charged with upholding national security.[44]

The White Paper largely confined its comments on democratic reform to an assertion that the above-noted rather unrepresentative Election Committee "is an expression of equal representation and broad representativeness."[45] It further specified that the Chief Executive must be a person "who loves the country and loves Hong Kong."[46] Hong Kong people have rightly viewed this as code for excluding the more popular pan-democratic politicians.

---

[39] White Paper, supra note 12, part I, para. 2. This interpretation of the White Paper position is borne out by a further statement by a Chinese diplomat in the United Kingdom that the Joint Declaration is void and was fulfilled upon the handover, a view also supported by the Hong Kong constitutional affairs minister. Joyce Ng and Peter So, "Hong Kong Minister Says China Alone Pledged to Keep City's Way of Life Intact," *South China Morning Post* (December 18, 2014); L. Gordon Corvitz, "China Voids Hong Kong Rights," *Wall Street Journal* (December 15, 2014). China even banned British MPs conducting a parliamentary investigation from visiting Hong Kong. George Parker, "British MPs Banned from Hong Kong Visit," *Financial Times* (November 30, 2014).

[40] White Paper, supra note 12, part V, sec. 1.   [41] Ibid.

[42] Ibid., part II, sec. 1, para. 1.   [43] Ibid., part V, sec. 2, para. 2.

[44] Ibid., part V, sec. 3. Beijing has increasingly invoked national security to justify its hardline approach. Gary Cheung, "Occupy Central Threatens 'Hong Kong Security,' Beijing Advisers Warn," *South China Morning Post* (November 7, 2014).

[45] White Paper, supra note 12, part III, para. 4   [46] Ibid., part V, sec. 4, para. 3.

After the public consultation over democratic reform in early 2014 two Hong Kong government reports initiated the reform exercise: the report on the public consultation and the report by the Hong Kong Chief Executive to the NPC Standing Committee on the need for reform. The latter report is required by the 2004 NPC Standing Committee interpretation.[47] These reports appeared to distort public opinion as supporting Beijing's designs for Hong Kong, ratcheting up even further the public anger over the direction the reform process was taking. With phrases like "mainstream opinion" or "relatively more views," the reports suggested that most Hong Kong people supported exclusive power to nominate in the Nominating Committee, requiring the Chief Executive to be a patriot, and that the Nominating Committee be based on the Election Committee, that a larger proportion of support be required to nominate, and that the number of candidates be limited to two or three.[48] The reports even suggested that people "generally agreed" not to reform the Legislative Council, this despite decades of protest over that body's slow pace of reform.

These conclusions were offered despite huge public demonstrations and nearly 800,000 people in a privately organized civil referendum endorsing genuine democracy in compliance with international standards and favoring a form of civil and party nominations. For this civil referendum registered voters could vote at polling stations or online after complying with verification software. The government reports were widely condemned for their failure to accurately convey Hong Kong public opinion. Academic studies of the consultative report noted that more than 90 percent of submissions were block submissions from the progovernment camp.[49] Subsequent Hong Kong Government reports published in January 2015 reporting to Beijing on the protests and launching a second-round consultation on democratic reform made no

---

[47] Hong Kong Government, "Report on the Public Consultation on the Methods of Selecting the Chief Executive in 2017 and for Forming the Legislative Council in 2016" (July 2014); "Report by the Chief Executive of the Hong Kong Special Administrative Region to the Standing Committee of the National People's Congress on Whether There Is a Need to Amend the Methods for Selecting the Chief Executive of the Hong Kong Special Administrative Region in 2017 and for Forming the Legislative Council of the Hong Kong Special Administrative Region in 2016" (July 2014).

[48] Ibid., pp. 8–11.

[49] Calvin Liu, Brian Yap, and Joyce Ng, "Consultation Dominated by Block Responses," *South China Morning Post* (August 18, 2014); Jeffie Lam, "Pollster Questions the Independence of Government's 'Public Consultation,'" *South China Morning Post* (December 1, 2014).

attempt to correct the earlier misrepresentations or seriously address public concerns.[50]

The NPC Standing Committee in lockstep embraced the Hong Kong Chief Executive's report, which had essentially functioned as an executive summary of the broader consultative report.[51] Beijing and Hong Kong officials further claimed there were no international standards for universal suffrage or that they are not applicable to Hong Kong.[52] Using its unfettered interpretive authority, "universal suffrage" was given an interpretation nobody but Beijing and its supporters would recognize. Going beyond the mere Central Government approval suggested by the 2004 interpretation, the decision approved the Chief Executive's request for change but imposed severe limits. Pan-democratic legislators immediately promised to use their one-third vote in the Legislative Council to veto any government bill based on these limitations – a promise they carried out in the June 2015 vote rejecting the ultimate government bill.[53]

The NPC Standing Committee decision, though expressing approval, effectively denies universal suffrage, by requiring the Nominating Committee to follow the makeup and formation of the Election Committee,[54] by imposing a 50 percent threshold for nomination,[55] and by limiting the number of nominees to two or three.[56] The decision also emphasizes that the Chief Executive must be a person "who loves the country and loves Hong Kong," generally perceived as code for excluding pan-democrats.[57] These requirements combine to guarantee that pan-democrats will have no chance at nomination before a heavily proestablishment committee.

---

[50] Hong Kong Government, "Report on the Recent Community and Political Situation" (January 2015); "2017 Seize the Opportunity, Method for Selecting the Chief Executive by Universal Suffrage" (January 2015); Tony Cheung and Peter So, "Hong Kong Government Submits Report Surrounding Occupy Protests to Beijing," *South China Morning Post* (January 6, 2015).

[51] NPC Standing Committee Decision, supra note 12, para. 5.

[52] Leading Beijing official Li Fei goes so far as to accuse democrats of misleading the public in asserting international standards. Chris Buckley and Michael Forsythe, "Beijing Rules Out Open Elections in Hong Kong," *New York Times* (August 31, 2014); Regina Ip, "The Logic of Beijing's Version of the 2017 Chief Executive Election," *South China Morning Post* (August 31, 2014); Tony Cheung and Joyce Ng, "Universal Suffrage for the 2017 Election Should Be Approved by Beijing on Wednesday" (August 26, 2014).

[53] "Pan-democrats Hoist Umbrellas as Carrie Lam Announces New Political Reform Consultation," *South China Morning Post* (January 7, 2015); "Hong Kong Reform Package Rejected as Pro-Beijing Lawmakers Walk Out," *South China Morning Post* (June 19, 2015).

[54] NPC Standing Committee Decision, supra note 12, part II, sec. (1).

[55] Ibid., part II, sec. 2.   [56] Ibid.   [57] Ibid., para. 7.

Elevating "one country" over "two systems," sovereignty and security are emphasized. The loyalty emphasis seems entirely unnecessary since the Hong Kong Oaths and Declarations Ordinance requires all prominent officials, including the Chief Executive, ExCo members, LegCo members, and judges to swear to uphold the Basic Law and "bear allegiance" to the Hong Kong Special Administrative Region.[58]

In further lockstep the Hong Kong Government in June 2015 put a bill exactly based on the NPC Standing Committee decision, without any effort at compromise, before the Legislative Council. The government argued this proposal completely fulfilled the requirements of Article 45, though the government proposal noted that further reforms in the future were possible.[59] Government arguments that the pan-democrats should "pocket" the proposal with the hope of further reform were rejected by the pan-democratic legislators, and the bill went down to defeat with eight votes for and twenty-eight against.[60] A last-minute walkout by progovernment legislators deprived the government of a majority vote, creating a particularly bad defeat. The excuse that the walkout was designed to deny a quorum and delay the vote did little to remove the egg from the government's face.[61] The veto of the bill based on the NPC Standing Committee decision leaves the current Chief Executive selection process by an Election Committee in place. The conservative NPC Standing Committee decision will presumably remain in place for any future reform exercise unless Beijing relaxes its requirements.

The electoral reform debacle is only the latest stage in Beijing's growing interference in Hong Kong. Systematic Beijing interference and responsive public protest have become a defining characteristic of Hong Kong governance. The more heavy-handed and undemocratic the governments are the more people protest, and the more they

---

[58] Oaths and Declarations Ordinance, Cap 11, Hong Kong Ordinances.

[59] Staff Reporters, "Hong Kong Government Sticks to Rigid Beijing Framework in 2017 Election," *South China Morning Post* (April 22, 2015); Tony Cheung and Lai Ying-kit, "Carrie Lam Says Reform Package Is No Endgame for Hong Kong Democracy," *South China Morning* Post (April 30, 2015).

[60] Michael Forsythe and Alan Wong, "Hong Kong Legislature Votes Down Beijing-Backed Election Plan," *New York Times* (June 18, 2015).

[61] "Hong Kong Reform Package Rejected as Pro-Beijing Lawmakers Stage Walk-Out before Vote," *South China Morning Post* (June 18, 2015); Tony Cheung, Lai Ying-kit, and Jeffie Lam, "Recriminations Fly among Pro-Beijing Camp over Bungled Legco Vote on Hong Kong Political Reform Package," *South China Morning Post* (June 20, 2014).

protest the more heavy-handed the governments become. Popular protests generally follow Central Government interference to advance its preferences. During the first fifteen years after the handover especially large protests of up to half a million people followed government efforts to enact Beijing-inspired national security and secrecy laws and efforts to initiate patriotic education. Both appeared aimed at controlling public knowledge and information in ways that are done on the mainland.

A local government that is made continuously subservient to the Central Government can hardly fulfill its duty to guard Hong Kong's high degree of autonomy in a responsible way. Hong Kong officials who represent and convey only Beijing's wishes can hardly encourage confidence that Hong Kong interests and concerns are represented. The resultant mistrust fueled the demands for democracy and the massive protest that emerged in late 2014.

Universal suffrage and public protests

Social movement

The 2014 debate over universal suffrage for the 2017 Chief Executive election got off to a raucous start as democracy groups anticipated foot dragging and manipulation of the above-noted official public consultation stretching across the first five months of the year. At the core of the movement, leaders of the newly organized "Occupy Central in Love and Peace" promised a civil disobedience campaign if the electoral model put forth by the government did not meet international standards. The June civil referendum, spurred by public contempt for the Beijing White Paper, conveniently launched the mass participation phase of the movement. Soon after the referendum half a million marchers showed up for the annual July 1 prodemocracy march.

Protest planning took shape much earlier in the democratic reform debate. A civil disobedience campaign promising 10,000 people to occupy Hong Kong's central financial district was announced in January 2013 by the newly formed Occupy Central. The three protest leaders who initiated this strategy included two professors and a minister. That such extreme measures were proposed so early is an indication of the complete lack of trust in the Beijing and Hong Kong governments after years of foot dragging on democratic reform. In this early phase the governments at both levels attacked the planned occupation as a threat to Hong Kong's economy, though the business community generally did not seem that worried about any significant impact.[62]

Civil disobedience typically involves intentional law breaking, usually of laws regulating public order, by a protester or a group of protesters to contest an unjust law. The protesters must generally be willing to accept the consequences of arrest and prosecution. Claims of freedom of expression may be used as a defense in the courts to mitigate punishment or even seek dismissal of the charges. That civil disobedience was announced so early in the Hong Kong reform debate worked effectively to articulate a clear expectation. At the same time it may have deflected the debate from the merits of democratic reform to the question of the legitimacy of civil disobedience. Civil disobedience is generally considered more justified when there is a lack of democracy, leaving no other channels to influence public policy. This early timeline made Occupy Central, rather than the government, the more frequent target of political attacks. Should such civil disobedience campaigns be announced so early or only late in the process as a last resort?

The civil disobedience campaign was planned in a very systematic manner. During the public consultation a series of deliberation days were used to come up with three democratic proposals that the movement would then submit to the public in the planned civil referendum. Many prodemocracy groups had uploaded their own proposals to the government's online consultation platform. The final deliberation day before the civil referendum discussed a number of these so-called moderate and radical proposals that were judged to meet international standards. The three top proposals would be presented to the voters in a privately conducted civil referendum. The so-called radical proposals were three proposals that called for either civil or party nominations. Since these were not primarily reliant on the Nominating Committee – expecting that committee to automatically endorse the candidates with the requisite public support – they were condemned by the two governments for violating the Basic Law. More moderate proposals generally accepted the required nomination by the Nominating Committee but argued for expansion of the electoral base of that committee and lowering the

---

[62] Toh Han Shih, "The Business Leaders Who Aren't Worried about Occupy Central," *South China Morning Post* (August 29, 2014). Seventy pro-Beijing tycoons visited Beijing in September to voice their support for the Central Government just after the NPC Standing Committee decision. Joyce Ng, "Beijing to Take a More Active Role in Hong Kong's Affairs, Hints Xi Jinping," *South China Morning Post* (September 22, 2014).

threshold for nomination, typically to one-eighth of the committee, so as to allow a pan-democrat to get nominated.

The three "radical proposals" won out in the deliberation day meeting and were selected to be voted on in the civil referendum. This limitation to three similar proposals was largely a consequence of university students from the Hong Kong Federation of Students (HKFS) and secondary students from a group called Scholarism dominating the deliberations. These two groups would later, in some respects, take over the civil disobedience campaign, bringing forward the occupation plans of the Occupy Central organizers in a less orderly manner. An antioccupy movement also took shape during this period, with a signature campaign to garner support and a telephone hotline for reporting on boycotting students. The occupy leaders branded the latter as "white terror."[63]

As the date set for the civil referendum approached in June 2014, there was some concern that the turnout would be low because of occupy fatigue after months of government attacks. Occupy organizers threatened to abandon their campaign if they did not attract at least 100,000 votes. Public objection to the extreme views in the White Paper, which was conveniently released at that time, saved the day, producing a civil referendum turnout of nearly 800,000 voters who voted to endorse the electoral model involving civil and party nominations, being the most conservative among the three "radical" proposals.

After a brief lull, the protests that became the Umbrella Movement began in mid-September just after the August 31 NPC Standing Committee decision. It began with a class boycott in the universities that eventually expanded to include secondary students.[64] Protests on campuses eventually moved to the government headquarters in the Admiralty district. After marches to the nearby Chief Executive's residence a large crowd gathered outside the government headquarters. The civic square there was fenced off after previous protests. After student efforts to climb over the fence to occupy the civic square were rebuffed with pepper spray and police batons, larger numbers gathered to defend those already there who had made it over the barriers.

Police efforts to block the arrival of protesters at the Admiralty site resulted in protesters pushing on to the public highway. The police rashly

[63] Peter So, "Anti-Occupy Group's Hotline for Reporting Student Strikes Branded 'White Terror,' *South China Morning Post* (September 8, 2014).

[64] Tony Cheung and Jeffie Lam, "Thousands Join Hong Kong Students' Democracy Protest as Classroom Boycott Begins," *South China Morning Post* (September 23, 2014).

resorted to using tear gas.[65] Such use of tear gas had not occurred in Hong Kong for decades, and a large crowd called forth by various social media quickly filled the streets, swelling to well over 100,000. It was the use of umbrellas in futile attempts to block the pepper spray and tear gas and the reports of this in the international press that gave the protest the name "Umbrella Movement."

As is often the case with public protests, government missteps largely created the Umbrella Movement. These ranged from Beijing issuing the unexpected White Paper and the excessively restrictive NPC Standing Committee decision to misleading local government reports and the use of tear gas. Early in the protest a parade of government missteps would reinvigorate the protest. When protest numbers subsided, typically something would be done by the police or even outside thugs that would attract more protesters to "protect" the youth who were already there. These activities ranged from pitched battles at the front line of the protest to pepper spray to attacks by alleged triads or thugs who appeared to go largely unpunished. By mid-October the government seemed to learn its lesson and took a more passive approach for several weeks, during which the protests appeared to subside. When the government's eventual efforts to clear the more volatile urban Mong Kok area met with some protester resistance, street confrontations and arrest again ensued.

Except for some minor scuffles during such protest-clearance operations the protesters themselves largely stuck to nonviolent discipline. Many protest leaders and core members had been trained in nonviolent strategies by the Occupy Central leaders early in the planning process. These efforts attracted global media praise by including a very orderly and tidy process, whereby early on, participants policed and cleaned the occupy areas, set up study areas for students, built barricades, and marshaled needed supplies.[66]

Occupy Central's leaders were cautious. They had planned to launch their occupy campaign as "grand banquet" at a square in Central Hong Kong on October 1, the Chinese National Day, figuring a holiday would be less disruptive. But the student class boycotts and the subsequent mass gathering (after the use of tear gas) launched a spontaneous occupy

---

[65] "Police Fire Tear Gas as Occupy Central Spreads and Ranks of Protesters Swell," *South China Morning Post* (September 28, 2014).

[66] "Police, Protesters in Tense Standoff Near Government Headquarters in Second Night of Clashes," *South China Morning Post* (September 27, 2014).

movement on the main highway and the area surrounding the government offices in nearby Admiralty. As networking via the Internet, Facebook, and smartphone applications brought massive crowds beyond the organizers' original estimates to the protest areas, the Occupy Central leaders came under pressure to move forward the start of the formal occupy movement that had originally been planned for October 1. Consequently they formally announced the launch of their civil disobedience occupy campaign in Admiralty in the early morning hours of September 27.[67] Though organized by the three groups noted in this chapter – Occupy Central, the HKFS, and Scholarism – the student leaders, building on their class boycott, effectively became the leaders of the resultant Umbrella Movement. Even when top government leaders met with protest leaders in a televised debate in late October, they actually met the HKFS officers rather than the original three Occupy Central leaders. Unfortunately, such televised meeting proved futile, as the government was unwilling to compromise.[68] As the movement eventually spread to two other remote districts in Mong Kok and Causeway Bay, social media and networking became critical to maintaining and coordinating a sustained movement over seventy-nine days.

Though the leaders promoted nonviolence, what had not been anticipated was the large numbers that showed up, with many not having received any briefing or training in nonviolence. Many commentators had encouraged withdrawal after the height of the protest when public support was greatest. But with so many uninitiated protesters the core leaders had questionable ability to orchestrate a withdrawal. As the protest dragged on, public support for the occupation, as opposed democracy itself, began to wane. Student protest leaders' last-ditch efforts to travel to Beijing to appeal to the Central Government were rebuffed by denying them entry to the mainland.[69] As a last resort, some student leaders engaged in a hunger strike as the occupation wound down.[70]

[67] "'Hong Kong Students Beat Us to It': Benny Tai Declares Start of Occupy Central," *South China Morning Post* (September 27, 2014).

[68] Joyce Ng and Gary Cheung, "Pan-Democrat Lawmakers Ready to Step Up after Student-Government Talks Stall," *South China Morning Post* (October 31, 2014).

[69] Lai Ying-kit, "Four More Occupy Student Protesters 'Barred from Entering Mainland China,'" *South China Morning Post* (November 17, 2014).

[70] "Hong Kong Student Leader Joshua Wong Begins Hunger Strike to Press for Political Reform," *South China Morning Post* (December 2, 2014); Chris Lau, "Hong Kong Students Bow to Continue Hunger Strike as Vomiting and Weakness Set in," *South China Morning Post* (December 3, 2014).

Many ordinary protesters were fearful their protest would die if they withdrew, but, on the other hand, continued blockage of main highways was causing protest fatigue and loss of public support, enabling the government to take a more inflexible stand. Eventually, the government relied on private civil injunction actions brought by transport businesses to get court orders backed by potential contempt proceedings to clear the protest areas.[71] The public response to these efforts was much more subdued than had been the reaction to the earlier aggressive tactics.

The mainstream press and social media

Beyond government misdeeds, the mainstream press and social media played major roles as driving forces in the Umbrella Movement. Despite foot dragging over democracy and increasing interference with autonomy, Hong Kong law continues to honor the basic principles of free speech and a free press. There is, however, darkness at the edge of town. Mainland influence and business interests have produced a chilling effect on the mainstream press, with reports of intimidation of reporters and editors, advertising boycotts of prodemocracy press, and self-censorship.[72] In the recent protests, at least twenty-four journalists were reportedly assaulted by either counter-protesters or the police, including a fire bombing of the Next Media offices, Next Media being owned by the leading prodemocracy publisher, Jimmy Lai.[73] Many local tycoons who publish newspapers are wary that too aggressive reporting may jeopardize their mainland business ties. In spite of this, with the city having approximately eighteen newspapers and a slew of broadcast media, strong media competition ensured that the mainstream press was bound to provide extensive coverage of the prodemocracy campaign, whether their slant was favorable to the government or the protesters. Such

---

[71] "Hong Kong's High Court Orders Protesters off Roads in Mong Kok and Admiralty," *South China Morning* Post (October 21, 2014); Thomas Chan, "20 People to Face Contempt Charges over Occupy Clearance in Mong Kok," *South China Morning Post* (January 6, 2015).

[72] PEN America, *Threatened Harbor, Encroachment on Press Freedom in Hong Kong* (January 16, 2015); Chris Buckley and Michael Forsythe, "Press Freedom in Hong Kong under Threat, Report Says," *New York Times* (January 16, 2015).

[73] Buckley and Forsythe, "Press Freedom in Hong Kong under Threat," Ibid.; Jonathan Kaiman, "Hong Kong Protests Bring Crisis of Confidence for Traditional Media," *The Guardian* (October 29, 2014); Danny Mok, "Firebombs Hurled at Home of Hong Kong Media Tycoon Jimmy Lai and Next Media HQ," *South China Morning Post* (January 12, 2014).

coverage included heightened hourly updates in several media and a rich trove of media commentary.

The condemnation of protesters in the progovernment media was at least matched by fair or openly supportive coverage and commentary on the other side. Jimmy Lai, the publisher of the openly prodemocracy Chinese language *Apple Daily* newspaper and *Next* magazine, actually joined the protest and camped out many days at the occupy site. He was eventually arrested along with other protesters during the clearance. A large contingent of international media also provided wall-to-wall, fairly balanced coverage. So the broader public debate was well reported in the mainstream press. Of course, the coverage in China was quite the opposite, rarely showing the protesters in news reports, with commentary supporting a crackdown, allegations of foreign influence in the protests, and allegations of a "color revolution."[74] Chinese officials and media have been especially fond of blaming the protests on foreign interference.[75]

In a modern city like Hong Kong, with high levels of personal freedom, social media have few constraints and were a vibrant factor in sustaining the protest movement. Protesters and their supporters could access more passionately supportive reports in social media. Voluntary reporting on Facebook-based news outlets quickly attracted 100,000 subscribers.[76] Such media could also be used to quickly bring supporters to the street. Another popular Web forum used by protest participants called HKGolden.com saw a ten-fold jump in page views during the height of the occupy protests in October, logging about 300,000 hits a day in its current affairs chat room.[77]

This boosted to 2.9 million page views per day after the police used tear gas. The site was used to provide participant updates on the occupy movement, share tactics, and encourage participation. That the police were monitoring messages being passed around among the protesters was evident from the arrest of a young man who posted calls for

---

[74] "Forget about Starting a Chinese 'Colour Revolution' in Hong Kong, People's Daily Blasts," *South China Morning Post* (October 5, 2014). The mainland firewall kept coverage to a minimum, and daring Internet entries would net arrests.

[75] Charles Hutzler, "Hong Kong Protests Fueled by Foreign Agencies, Ex-China Official Says," *The Wall Street Journal* (October 14, 2014).

[76] Some claim the Umbrella Movement "may be the best-documented social movement in history." Jonathan Kaiman, "Hong Kong Protests Bring Crisis of Confidence for Traditional Media," *The Guardian* (October 29, 2014).

[77] Phila Siu, "How Social Media Shapes Occupy: Web Forum HKGolden.com Takes Off," *South China Morning Post* (October 31, 2014).

protesters to charge at police and block rail lines. After such an arrest the site host encouraged users to not post calls for people to join the protest because they risked being charged with incitement to unlawful assembly or criminal use of a computer.[78] Protesters would still try to code their calls for support with words like "going hiking" or, after the Chief Executive called for people to support merchants in the cleared protest areas, by inviting people to "go shopping."[79]

During the early protest when cell phone services became overloaded in the protest areas, protesters would resort to offline apps such as FireChat, which works in a small area by creating its own open network outside the Internet.[80] On the Internet, prominent blogs have appeared to elaborate and explain the issues as they arise.[81] As known to the writer, at the end of the occupy phase there are several efforts at producing documentaries and even archival work in progress.

Technology was used not only to spread the word and facilitate communications but also to launch a cyberwar at a level never before seen in Hong Kong. Both protest supporters and the governments and their presumed supporters engaged in range of what analysts characterize as silent and violent attacks.[82] The antioccupy attacks, whether independent or under government influence, seemed the most substantial. Technical analysts described a variety of tools, including, among other tools, mobile applications with malware surveillance, distributed denial of service attacks, and phishing emails with advanced persistent threat.[83] One of the first attacks was on the civil referendum, using distributed denial of service to overload the system and disrupt online voting.[84] During the early occupation, smartphones were targeted for silent attack with what researchers call an mRat, which steals data when users clicked

[78] Ibid.
[79] Among these "shoppers" the Chief Executive is often referred to as "689" based on the number of votes by which he was elected in the Election Committee in 2012. Samuel Chan, "The Game Changes: As Occupy Sites Are Cleared, Hong Kong's Democracy Protesters Go 'Shopping,'" *South China Morning Post* (December 11, 2014).
[80] The service registered half a million downloads in the first week of the protest, with 1.6 million chat rooms created. Peter Shadbolt, "FireChat in Hong Kong: How an App Tapped Its Way into the Protests," *CNN* (October 16, 2014).
[81] A prominent blog posting many media reports and offering explanation of events includes "Hong Kong's Umbrella Movement," https://victoriatbhui.wordpress.com.
[82] K. P. Chow, K. K. Yau, and Frankie Li, "Occupy Central and Cyber War: A Framework of Cyber-Attack in Political Events," Proceedings of Ninth IFIP WG 11.10 International Conference on Critical Infrastructure Protection (March 2015).
[83] Ibid.   [84] Ibid.

on the popular WhatsApp messaging application.[85] Silent attacks targeted protesters and their supporters in a variety of other ways, including attacks on the websites of political parties and political organizations, phishing emails as an effective tool against university protesters, and cyberattacks on Apple's iCloud service.[86] Efforts to circulate news of the protests in China, especially photo sharing through Instagram, were blocked by the Chinese government.[87] Attacks went the other way as well, as a group called Anonymous officially announced a cyberwar against both governments by attacking government websites with a distributed denial of service tool that would overload the websites.[88]

Beyond technological tools, as widely seen around the world, the occupiers also built a tent city that remained in place even as the numbers dwindled. In this tent city on the pavement the occupy movement produced a flowering of protest artwork, posters, and message boards, sometimes even attracting mainland Chinese tourists to the occupy sights.[89] Public lectures in the evenings would often include prominent speakers from the pan-democratic camp and the supportive legal community.

In this open society where traditional social activism and social media are not much restricted, social media tend to play a supportive role to boost and spread the impact of the more traditional social movement strategies, including civil society organizations, public lectures, and street art.[90] The occupy movement and its constituent organizations took up disruptive actions, such as civil disobedience and class boycotts, and social media provided the tools to boost the message and convey the objectionable behavior of the police and government officials.[91] In this way, traditional strategies of civil disobedience, combined with outrage over government excesses, is channeled through social media to produce a massive social movement in support of human rights objectives. In the absence of the local government's commitment to Hong Kong's autonomy, such dynamics of

[85] Ibid.   [86] Ibid.   [87] Ibid.   [88] Ibid.

[89] Joyce Lau, "Rescuing Protest Artwork from Hong Kong's Streets," *Agence France-Presse* (November 14, 2014); Alice Woodhouse, "Pro-Democracy Groups Get Crafty in Occupy Central Aftermath," *South China Morning Post* (December 21, 2014).

[90] Robert K. Schaeffer, *Social Movements and Global Social Change: The Rising Tide* (New York: Rowman & Littlefield, 2014), pp. 211–12.

[91] See generally, Doug McAdam, Sidney Tarrow, and Charles Tilly, *Dynamics of Contention* (Cambridge, UK: Cambridge University Press, 2002), p. 62.

contention in civil society may prove critical over the long run to sustaining Hong Kong autonomy and the associated human rights and the rule of law. The challenge is to sustain the effort after the occupation subsides.

Postoccupy community-based political strategies?

After the clearing of the protest sights, appreciating that public support for the occupy strategy had waned,[92] protesters have shifted their strategies to more community-based outreach. Community education is seen as a way to keep the movement alive.[93] Early on the occupy organizers also launched a "noncooperation movement" urging people to pay their government rents and taxes in small bills and in small symbolic amounts.[94] Some have encouraged a boycott of the businesses of pro-Beijing tycoons.

For the final roll-out of the government reform package, a new series of protests and marches was launched. Protesters had vowed not to participate in the second round government consultation, and legislators promised to veto the government reform bill. These later protests targeted the government agenda but also aimed to ensure there were no defectors among pan-democratic legislators. One leading politician who holds a city wide legislative seat planned to trigger a citywide by-election after the veto of the bill as a referendum by resigning his seat.[95] Eventually it was determined that this would not be of much value at that stage, and the plan was abandoned. The walk out of the progovernment legislators during the voting on the bill proved to be a gift for the pan-democrats, undermining the ability of the government to attack them in future elections for undercutting the right of voters to choose their Chief Executive.

---

[92] Shirley Zhao, "More Than Two-Thirds Say Occupiers Should Go Home Now as Support Wanes: Poll," *South China Morning Post* (November 17, 2014).

[93] Peter So, "Helping Improve Hong Kong's Communities 'Could Keep the Spirit of Occupy Alive,'" *South China Morning Post* (January 11, 2015).

[94] Joyce Ng and Samuel Chan, "Occupy Groups to Start 'Non-Cooperation Movement' as Follow-Up to Mass Protests," *South China Morning Posts* (December 14, 2014).

[95] Peter So, "Beijing 'Won't Be Swayed' on HK's Political Reform Even if Albert Ho Triggers By-Election," *South China Morning Post* (January 11, 2014).

Arrest and intimidation

The bigger danger following the occupation was that the Hong Kong Government would use mass arrest and prosecution to intimidate the protesters and discourage further protests – what some protesters called "white terror." Initially this looked likely to be the case. Hundreds of protesters were arrested during the clearing of protest sites. In spite of this, most clearance efforts were relatively peaceful, with protest leaders calling for an end to the occupation and protesters not offering resistance to arrest, in compliance with their nonviolent strategy. Dozens of protest leaders were also ordered to report to police headquarters to "assist the ongoing investigation" of the civil disobedience campaign.[96] Many protest leaders voluntarily turned themselves in to police as a form of protest.[97] When they appeared, social media were again called into action to bring protest supporters to police stations where the protest leaders were reporting for arrest. Those who reported were then arrested and released pending possible prosecution.

Many efforts at prosecution ultimately proved futile, as several cases were dismissed in the courts for lack of evidence. Relatively few prosecutions, with clear evidence of confrontation with police, have gone forward. These typically resulted from confrontations with police, as pushing and shoving in volatile situations occurred.[98] This was often a consequence of the inability of the protest leaders to control the behavior of all protesters. There are also some charges of police abuse still under investigation and prosecution.[99]

---

[96] Stuart Lau, Chris Lau, and Lai Ying-kit, "Dates Set for Arrest of Three Occupy Central Leaders and Media Boss Jimmy Lai," *South China Morning Post* (January 9, 2015); Clifford Lo and Jeffie Lam, "'Report to Us' Hong Kong Police Tell 30 Key Occupy Central Figures Targeted for Arrest," *South China Morning Post* (January 5, 2015). Police have revealed that 1,000 people had been arrested during the occupation and over 900 had had their identity card numbers recorded. Samuel Chan, Alan Yu, and Joyce Ng, "Hong Kong Police Target Occupy's 'Principal Instigators' after All Sites Cleared," *South China Morning Post* (December 16, 2014).

[97] Joyce Ng, "Three Occupy Co-Founders Interrogated by Police for 'Inciting' Pro-Democracy Protests," *South China Morning Post* (January 24, 2015).

[98] Jeffie Lam, Stuart Lau, and Phila Siu, "Occupy Supporters and Police Clash as Protests Escalate," *South China Morning Post* (November 30, 2014). Efforts to target government buildings raised concern among some protest leaders. "Students Threaten to Target Government Buildings after Night of Clashes in Mong Kok," *South China Morning Post* (November 27, 2014).

[99] Emily Tsang and Ernest Kao, "Protesters Seek Legal Advice over 'Abuse' while Detained," *South China Morning Post* (December 8, 2014).

The government's use of civil injunctions to initiate the clearing operation raised the specter of the more serious charge of criminal contempt being added to the basic charge of unlawful assembly.[100] The use of court injunctions was of concern to protesters who were reluctant to ignore court orders. Those protesters who ignored court injunctions fueled government claims that the protesters were undermining the rule of law. This contrasts with the protester view that the two governments posed a greater risk to the rule of law by taking excessive liberties in their interpretation of the Basic Law. In the postoccupy period, hardline pro-Beijing politicians have even made calls for application of the draconian mainland national security laws in Hong Kong, a call that has been batted down even by moderates in the establishment camp.[101]

Conclusion: achievements and prospects

Since the demands of the protesters for Beijing to withdraw the August NPC Standing Committee decision were not met and the government ultimately put forth a bill that was vetoed by democrats, it would be easy to conclude that the protesters completely failed and the government won. This would be too facile a conclusion. While the protesters' demands have not been met, the local Hong Kong protests have shone a spotlight on Beijing's evolving failure to keep its Hong Kong commitments and on the failure of the Hong Kong Government to stand up for Hong Kong. This has left the reputation of both governments in shambles and their ability to govern effectively in doubt. That the government's reform bill failed so egregiously after nearly two years of intense efforts adds to the perception of incompetence and illegitimacy.

The protesters have every incentive to continue their campaign for genuine democracy. As government continues to flounder under the burden of Beijing's hardline distrustful policies, Hong Kong protesters will have ample opportunities to continue to shine a spotlight on the governments' disappointing track record. Protesters appear to appreciate that the occupation strategy has its limits, as public fatigue over disruptive behavior and a perception of government intransigence has set in. In the postoccupy period and after the failure of the government proposal, the movement's participants can be expected to embrace a variety

---

[100] Thomas Chan, "Department of Justice Granted More Time to Consider Mong Kok Criminal Contempt," *South China Morning Post* (November 28, 2014).
[101] Stuart Lau, "Mainland Think Tank on Hong Kong Affairs Forms Group 'To Safeguard National Security,'" *South China Morning Post* (January 24, 2015).

of traditional tactics, from community outreach to boycotts and political campaigns, to push their democracy demands and respond to future government policies. With a new generation of activists, we can expect the full range of social media to be deployed to get the message out. Hong Kong youth almost always have a smartphone in hand.

The occupy movement has given rise to a new generation of formidable political activists who have already run successfully for district offices and can be expected to enter the arena in future legislative elections. Unless the government is willing to roll up Hong Kong's open society, a variety of tactics will be available for democracy promotion, including online reportage, blogs and chat groups, media commentary, running for elective office, marching, artistic expression, teach-ins, and the use of multimedia for artistic and other avenues of expression. These creative activities will be disseminated through social media almost instantaneously on a daily basis as a new generation, after the Umbrella Movement, is drawn into Hong Kong politics. Government leaders and politicians will disregard public concerns at their peril.

The ability of the Beijing and Hong Kong governments to regain both local and international trust regarding their Hong Kong policies will depend on some clear sign of policy reform. That a variety of pan-democratic proposals for compromise have been uniformly dismissed shows a clear intention to exclude pan-democrats from leading roles in government. Policy reform would need to address this concern. Hong Kong people have long been prepared to work with China on fully carrying out the vision of "one country, two systems" but have not found a willing partner. Serious democratic development to afford them the avenue to uphold their end of the bargain would go a long way toward bringing the current sense of crisis to an end. Instead of lecturing Hong Kong people on their alleged mistakes in demanding fulfillment of the commitments made and accusing Hong Kong youth of being "triads" for their protest tactics, after the failure of the government initiative, there is a need for China's anointed government officials and supporters to offer an honest path forward.[102] The sorry path of misrepresentation and bullying that has occurred to date is clearly viewed with suspicion by many Hong Kong people. This mistrust has reached such a level that even the failure of civil society to turn out for future protests would signal government failure and that a sense of futility and hopelessness had set in.

---

[102] Peter So, "Pro-Beijing Activist Compares Organizers of Student Strikes to 'Triad Gangs,'" *South China Morning Post* (September 9, 2014).

12

Conclusion

The quest for human rights in the digital age:
how it has changed and the struggle ahead

MAHMOOD MONSHIPOURI AND SHADI MOKHTARI

The proliferation of information sources in the digital era that has accompanied the seemingly countless ways of conveying and exchanging information not only has made it easier to learn about the world around us but has created the digital environment for rapid change through activism and protest. Visual and interactive modes of information have enabled people to challenge, deconstruct, and even upend old authorities who once controlled the flow of information, in the hope of replacing them with new ones.[1] Digital technology and virtual platforms have changed how people relate to each other and how consumers have gained the power to generate content that transcends borders and localities. The convergence of "smart mob" technologies, to borrow a term from Howard Rheingold, has become inevitable.[2] Digital participation can translate into real power, but as Mirko Tobias Schäfer contends, talk of empowerment paints an abstract and fanciful picture of social progress attained through technology use often at odds with the stubbornness of practical reality.[3]

The debate over the power of social participation in the digital world has raised a key question: Will digital media, if properly safeguarded by privacy-protecting settings, flourish into new forms of communication, protest and resistance, the spread of knowledge, and a revitalized civil society? One pervasive view holds that in a digitally connected infosphere, gaining participatory media skills has become crucial to facing massive problems, from global warming to water-sharing conflicts,

---

[1] Bill Kovach and Tom Rosenstiel, *Blur: How to Know What's True in the Age of Information Overload* (New York: Bloomsbury, 2010), p. 24.
[2] Howard Rheingold, *Smart Mobs: The Next Social Revolution* (New York: Perseus Publishing, 2002), p. 215.
[3] Mirko Tobias Schäfer is quoted in Howard Rheingold, *Net Smart: How to Thrive Online* (Cambridge, MA: MIT Press, 2012), p. 137.

from mass collaboration to collective action, and from mediated barriers to face-to-face practices that can increase or drain social capital.[4] These technological developments, coupled with the flourishing of new civil society organizations, have empowered the powerless and voiceless, while at the same time rendering governments grudgingly more tolerant of diverse views and competing narratives.

Along this line, Joel R. Pruce's chapter aptly captures the effectiveness – and the essence – of the visual culture. As a prominent and pervasive platform for the conduct of information politics, the graphic realm is a contested space in which states, social movements, and nongovernmental organizations (NGOs) all attempt to shape public perception. Advancements in digital technologies permit and, indeed, compel actors to craft visual communication strategies because appearance and optics have become crucial sites of politics. Messaging, framing, and agenda setting are no longer confined to the words on the page, but instead have become a part of cross-platform campaigning.

An alternative view, however, underlines the extent to which context – both temporal and spatial – matters. In some cases, as demonstrated in this volume, the new forms of communication have had less direct bearing on the outcome of contentious politics. Rather, other factors, including traditional, political, and cultural variables, have had a much more decisive impact on the results of power struggles in the contentious politics than the utilization of modern technological tools. This explains why some situations, such as the Arab uprisings, have fallen back into well-established patterns: public discontent, followed by political instability and the return of the military to politics. In short, many political and cultural factors – both foreign and domestic – have come together to forestall attempts at confronting historical inequality and lack of power sharing. What we have found more clearly in this book is that given the multiplicity of sources brought by these new modes of communication, citizens are becoming more informed, yet more overloaded with information. The competing news sources and the rising interactivity with the audience could further reinforce this duality.[5] Consider, for example, the way in which the digital age has created a world of "digital citizenship" and the opposite side of human rights – that is, a new media nexus in which information technology through surveillance by authoritarian and democratic governments alike has facilitated a new avenue for control of

---

[4] Rheingold, *Net Smart*, p. 32.   [5] Ibid., p. 209.

the human rights debate. While the "digital citizenship" has led to shared innovation, interconnectivity, and intense cooperation through the Internet, state surveillance has become part and parcel of much broader concerns arising from the intrusive ways in which the state closely observes its citizens. These acts of electronic surveillance have raised numerous questions regarding the protection and promotion of an individual's rights to expression, access, privacy, openness, and collaboration as digital rights claims have gathered momentum.[6]

We problematize framing the debate solely in terms of a response to these concerns while lodging a main caveat: There is a wide spectrum of possibilities where technology can play an emancipatory role, but at the same time such technology may be used to intimidate and coerce citizens in some contexts into submission. The crucial point to note is that the way individuals participate, cooperate, organize, and coordinate forms of contention through modern technological means is what accelerates progress toward achieving human rights. Rheingold rightly notes, "Merely consuming the products of technology vendors is insufficient to better the human condition."[7]

From a different standpoint, some observers point out that a new kind of political subject, if not a citizen, has arisen from acting through the Internet. This political subject should be understood not as a "coherent and unified being but as a composite of multiple subjectivities that emerge from different situations and relations."[8] These political subjects make rights claims about the way in which their digital lives are configured, regulated, and organized by dissipated arrangements of corporations, states, and software devices, as well as programmers and regulators. How these routine acts come to produce a political subjectivity that has come to be known as digital citizens – that is, those citizens who make digital rights claims – merits particular attention.[9]

We argue in this concluding chapter – and throughout the book – that new digital tools mean new activism involving making new claims for rights. We also argue that grievances are more rapidly mobilized and hence could potentially boost the possibility of accomplishing the goals of both political redress and public protest. Our direction in this project is completely in sync with our thematic approach, namely, that the

---

[6] Engin Isin and Evelyn Ruppert, *Being Digital Citizens* (New York: Rowman & Littlefield, 2015), chapter 7, "Making Digital Rights Claims," pp. 159–85.

[7] Rheingold, *Net Smart*, p. 138.   [8] Isin and Ruppert, *Being Digital Citizens*, p. 4.

[9] Ibid., pp. 4–10.

application of digital media would likely lead to new changes in political contention, including contention over asserted rights claims. We also seek to dispel myths surrounding the notion that revolutions can merely be tweeted and in their own right be successful. The notion that revolutions can be "text messaged" or "instantly messaged" offers a misleading and overly simplistic account of what is indeed an extremely intricate and multidimensional issue.

The Internet is simply not beyond the power and the control of the state. Ronal J. Deibert and Nart Villeneuve argue that "Just as physical borders demarcate the boundaries of state power, states are seeking to create informational borders in cyberspace."[10] Technological mechanisms and practices, such as Internet blocking, monitoring of communications, surveillance, and content filtering, have been increasingly deployed to carve out spaces of control. Moreover, we argue that technology may accelerate protests but cannot solve deep-seated political tensions and social problems. With this caveat in mind, we turn our attention to the questions of why and when new technologies may help protect human rights.

ICTs' promising prospects

Numerous social movements in the digital age have completely failed to gain traction or any kind of presence offline by relying solely on the Internet, with their messages falling into the void. For some people the choice is a difficult one: Listen to those digital voices that transcend events and cities in pursuit of social justice, economic security, and basic freedoms, or to the voices of stability and predictability that cherish narrow nationalism and modes of traditional political action? It may be easier to mobilize protests than to change the outcome of political contestations. As Chapter 2 shows, despite the limitations of information and communication technologies (ICTs), such as the fact that the majority of the global population is not yet online, the digital age does hold promising prospects for social movements, activists, and organizations as they employ the connective tools ICTs offer. Arguably, the human rights movement is well positioned to take advantage of ICTs. The emancipatory power for human agency built into the ethos of the Internet goes hand in hand with the movement's emphasis on individual

---

[10] Ronald J. Deibert and Nart Villeneuve, "Firewalls and Power: An Overview of Global State Censorship of the Internet," in Mathias Klang and Andrew Murray (eds.), *Human Rights in the Digital Age* (London: Glasshouse, 2005), pp. 111–24; see p. 111.

rights. Increasingly, access to the Internet is seen as a human right in itself. Related to enhancing human agency, the Internet has also led to an expansion of political empowerment, which is vital to the promotion and sustenance of the human rights movement.

Perhaps more importantly, as Barry demonstrates, the social action networks that ICTs forge, also known as "network politics," are particularly suited for the human rights movement because of their ability to spread ideas rapidly across borders/distance and also due to their contributions to the idea of a "cascade of rights" leading to progressive realization of human rights.[11] In fact, the ability of ICTs to promote, protect, explain, and transfer human rights across borders through diverse networks accounts for a key explanation for the proliferation of human rights seen around the world since the early 1990s.

Liberation technology hits a stumbling block

From Tahrir Square to Kiev's Maidan, we have witnessed the potential for nonviolent change, reflected in the people's power on the street as well as in virtual spaces – a phenomenon described as "Revolution 2.0." Yet for many protesters who have participated in prodemocracy movements and human rights struggles, both online and offline, hopes for change and solidarity have remained but distant prospects. While in Tunisia, social media have led to greater political openness, grassroots organizing, and political development, in Egypt, collective action and mass protests have been preempted and ultimately curbed by the military and the return of authoritarianism. So the question that concerns us is, What is new about digital politics for human rights? The Arab Spring in Egypt and prodemocracy movement in Hong Kong were, for example, represented by social movements that successfully utilized social media to frame their narratives – at least in the short term – but it is not clear that social media made any long-lasting differences regarding the outcomes.

A skeptical view points to many stumbling blocks to the creation of a free society from Egypt to Ukraine to Hong Kong. The geopolitical

---

[11] This argument resonates with the three stages of the life cycle of norms – norm emergence, norm cascade, and norm internalization – advanced by Martha Finnemore and Kathryn Sikkink, "Taking Stock: The Constructivist Research Program in International Relations and Comparative Politics," *Annual Review of Political Science*, 4, 1 (June 2001), 391–416.

realities on the ground have come to overshadow the power of social media and the Internet to effect positive change, rendering Twitter and Facebook practically irrelevant. The message, one analyst observes, is that "Revolution 2.0 has failed. It is back to business as usual in Egypt and any gains that were made in the popular uprising have largely been swept away by a military power base reluctant to give up its long-held control."[12]

In Ukraine, by contrast, the protesters were keen to voice their demands for sovereignty in eastern Ukraine. The Ukraine crisis, where the overthrow of an existing regime arguably created a power vacuum in which uncertainty combined with prior grievances to stir up regional tensions, served as another reminder that ICTs are not enough for the realization of popular quests for substantial political change. Tellingly, as Bryon Moraski demonstrates, the resolution of Ukraine's political crisis has moved away from a discussion of democratic principles and reallocation of political power toward an escalation of violence with pro-Russian separatists backed by Russian manpower and weaponry. The enormity of the crisis in Ukraine has eclipsed the power of social media to make increased popular access to information possible and permit opponents of existing hierarchies to reach wider audiences.

In Chapter 4, Monshipouri, Whooley, and Ibrahim point out the difficulties the youth movement has encountered after the historic Arab uprisings. Transitional periods and processes raise essential yet unresolved questions regarding the viability of the democratic process. A long view of history demonstrates that combating authoritarianism, deeply embedded patronage, endemic corruption, and the mismanagement of economy in fledgling, frail democracies is no easy task and that the possibility of backsliding into a new form of illiberal democracy or traditional authoritarianism usually remains. The struggling democracies of the post–Arab Spring era, as in the case of Egypt and Tunisia, have found themselves entangled in such a historical trajectory.

Opportunities and uncertainties

While the uprisings in the Arab world were aimed at toppling the governments, in Iran, India, Hong Kong, and Turkey digital dissidence

---

[12] Mark Heley, "From Egypt to Ukraine: Revolution 2.0 Has Failed. What Next?," *Reality Sandwich*,   http://realitysandwich.com/217416/from-egypt-to-ukraine-revolution-2-0-has-failed-what-next/. Accessed on April 28, 2015.

was not directed at overthrowing their regimes. Rather, the intent was to bring about change, economic growth, reform, and social justice through using participatory politics as well as activism in virtual spaces and on the streets. Some attempts failed and some succeeded. Iran's Green Movement proved that increased popular access to new technological advances has permitted opponents of existing hierarchies to reach wider audiences. Nevertheless, a lack of central authority and of a robust strategy during the 2009 protests led to its defeat. But activists' effective use of social media, as highlighted by Elham Gheytanchi in her chapter, further proved that a new wave of social movement was in the making in Iran, in which human rights violations, arrests, and political repression exposed the insecurity of the Islamic Republic to the international community.

There can be no denying that Iran's Green Movement provided a fascinating case study for the experts working on the impact of networking, new media, and politics. Prior to the disputed 2009 elections, the growing number of Iranian websites and blogs offered new sources of information about many aspects of public life in the country, providing a robust link between activists and intellectuals in Iran, on the one hand, and these social forces and the opposition living in exile, on the other. The battle to control the Internet thus cannot be separated from these emerging, broader social movements embroiled in the ongoing conflict between the state and its internal and external opponents.[13]

These developments, however, have led some observers – wrongly, in our view – to depict the Green Movement as a "Twitter Revolution." In fact, Twitter functioned as a significant public space for reflecting solidarity messages from global voices backed up largely by the Iranian diaspora. Social media, the Internet, and YouTube became channels through which messages could be sent to international media organizations that had little or no access to domestic sources or any direct information about what was happening in Iran.[14]

Moreover, the Islamic Republic began to develop ways to police new media following the advent of the Green Movement. Perhaps the single most notable paradox of the digital age is that technology makes not only "an effective organizing tool, but also an ideal locale for

---

[13] Annabelle Sreberny and Gholam Khiabany, *Blogistan: The Internet and Politics in Iran* (London: I. B. Tauris, 2010), pp. 32–33.

[14] Ibid., p. 175.

surveillance and control."[15] In the end, the real action of dissidence and resistance had to be pursued on the Iranian streets in the face of repressive measures and state-led violence. Regardless, the blogosphere has increasingly emerged as a *substitute* for those political activities and traditional media coverage that have been subject to government control and censorship. Perhaps social media can be credited with keeping grievances alive and within public consciousness until opportunities for taking the fight back to the streets or political processes reemerge. This is especially true in the case of Iranian women, who, while generally excluded from key political positions, have resorted to blogs to express their views.

How social media has spurred the middle classes to participate in India's 2014 elections is best demonstrated by Sanjoy Banerjee (Chapter 10), who argues that India presents an interesting case in which the improvement in women's voter turnout has been concentrated in the middle classes, reflecting the greater politicization of the middle class, aided by their access to social media. This modern medium, according to Banerjee, served as one of the channels of communication to the middle class and was the conduit for competing national identity variants and their allegorical human rights norms.

The then-candidate Narendra Modi's use of social media gave recognition to this middle class in India and legitimized its ascent within his national identity variant. This process galvanized the support of the middle class and gave an advantage to the BJP's identity variant and the conception of human rights contained therein. Stable and secure economic growth – not economic equalization – appears to be the Modi administration's top priority. Modi and his advisers have astutely used social media to convey the idea that a policy of economic equalization may slow down economic growth, thereby undermining the development of the private sector. The latter seems to have been the main engine and driver behind India's amazing economic growth in the past decade.

In Chapter 11, Michael Davis rightly notes that protesters demanded respect for the constitutional promise of future free and fair elections. Their demands were produced and broadly reflected through social media that offered them an effective platform to vociferously voice their concerns. The Occupy Movement has indeed produced a new generation

---

[15] Narges Bajoghli, "Digital Technology as Surveillance: The Green Movement in Iran," in Linda Herrera and Rehab Sakr (eds.), *Wired Citizenship: Youth Learning and Activism in the Middle East* (New York: Routledge, 2014), pp. 180–94; see p. 191.

of political activists who will likely enter the arena in future legislative elections. If the government fails to fulfill its obligation to uphold Hong Kong's open society, democratic governance, and the rule of law, a variety of tactics will be available to promote these core values and Hong Kong's democratic development, including online reportage, blogs and chat groups, media commentary, running for elective office, marching, artistic expression, teach-ins, and the use of multimedia for artistic and other avenues of expression. These creative activities will be disseminated through social media almost instantaneously on a daily basis as a new generation of tech-savvy and digitally connected young men and women feel empowered – not despite but because of the Umbrella Movement – to shape the country's future politics. Hong Kong's political leadership faces a colossal risk in disrupting – much less strangling – Hong Kong's thriving open society.

In Turkey, as Ihsan Dagi astutely remarks, the Gezi movement challenged the status quo, denouncing both Kemalist and Islamic authoritarianism while representing social and cultural diversity. Ever since, the repression of media there has become part of an even more ominous trend. Today, Turkey is one of the strictest Internet censors in the world, as evidenced by the fact that the country's National Security Council (NSC) has listed social media as one of the fundamental threats to Turkey's domestic security, alongside terror groups such as the Islamic State in Iraq and Syria (ISIS) and the Kurdistan Workers' Party (KKP). Social media have increasingly been used as a campaign tool in Turkish politics.[16] President Erdoğan and the ruling AKP tried to use a crackdown on social media to boost their election chances in June 2015. The results of parliamentary elections indicated otherwise, as the ruling AKP won only 41 percent of vote, failing to muster even a simple 276-seat majority.[17]

From physical to virtual space

As discussed throughout this book, the new media have had significant implications for protecting and promoting human rights, perhaps none

---

[16] Jack Moore, "Turkey Lists Social Media as Top Threat in Leaked Document," *Newsweek* (April 7, 2015), www.newsweek.com/social-media-listed-top-threat-turkeys-national-security-alongside-isis-320186. Accessed on April 7, 2015.

[17] Constanze Letsch and Ian Traynor, "Turkey Election: Ruling Party Loses Majority as Pro-Kurdish HDP Gain Seat," *The Guardian* (June 7, 2015), www.theguardian.com/world/2015/jun/07/turkey-election-preliminary-results-erdogan-akp-party. Accessed on June 22, 2015.

more so than in altering the people's role from being consumers of information to active producers of knowledge. Technological changes have affected how the people negotiate an emerging but complex set of rights. But more important, this dynamic would likely transform how human rights can most effectively be monitored. Social media open up new opportunities for human rights organizations to provide evidence and thus better monitor human rights violations, possibly preventing further abuses in the future. The general value of social media lies in the ability to monitor and document human right violations instantly – a phenomenon epitomized by citizen journalism. The rise in citizen journalism and social media platforms has led to a growing and substantial evidence of human rights violations, with hundreds of potential crime scenes available to investigators online.

In 2006, a video clip of two Egyptian police officers torturing and sodomizing a minibus driver, Emad al-Kabir, unleashed a storm of comment on social media and led to the unprecedented conviction of each police officer to a three-year prison sentence. This and similar cases have encouraged many others to use their communications tools to "name and shame" perpetrators of crimes and corruption.[18] Similarly, in early December 2012, a gruesome video appeared on the Internet that depicted a child taking part in a beheading apparently in Homs. While in this case the video is unlikely to result in accountability for the crime evidenced, in other instances identifying the place and time of an incident can be crucial not only for establishing the extent of accountability but also for determining compliance with rights codes and norms. This was shown in 2015 in response to videos that showed a white police officer in North Charleston, South Carolina, shooting and killing an apparently unarmed African American while the man ran away. Thus, while it is important to underscore the importance of video, voice, and testimony expressed through social media, it is equally imperative to acknowledge the fact that digital voice and images do not determine outcome on their own.[19] Instead, a range of other political and situational

---

[18] Linda Herrera, "Youth and Citizenship in the Digital Age: A View from Egypt," in Herrera and Sakr (eds.), *Wired Citizenship: Youth Learning and Activism in the Middle East*, pp. 19–38; see p. 30.

[19] Brian Brivati, "Facebook Is like a Religion Around Here: Voices from the 'Arab Spring' and the Policy-Making Community," in Meg Jensen and Margaretta Jolly (eds.), *We Shall Bear Witness: Life Narratives and Human Rights* (Madison, WI: The University of Wisconsin Press, 2014), pp. 238–56; see esp. p. 242.

circumstances come into play in determining the ultimate impact of such media.

Increasingly, social media have created an opportunity to engage with civil society and grassroots organizations. There is a broad consensus that the networks and the Internet can mobilize groups with different compositions and identities to come together and lend their power to a common cause, while variously combining their agency to accomplish overlapping shared aims and projects.[20] To some extent, as experts point out, the Internet's value of open access to information and lived experiences of others across the globe has expanded the scope of recognition of the "other." The downside of this process is that it could just as well enable people to more easily hook up with groups that pursue exclusive strategies toward others (e.g., various hate groups), who are in the same way able to mobilize effectively online.[21]

One of the most difficult aspects of emancipatory networking is increasing encroachment of the securitization of the Internet. From the standpoint of informational privacy, the most problematic issue is the application of vast government security databases, which render the close monitoring of all online activities possible.[22] Well-founded and fair procedures that could safeguard some measure of a user's privacy and informational control are conspicuously lacking. Gaining informed consent regarding uses of information about oneself remains unlikely at best, to the extent that specific uses of information are concerned, but more particularly when "big data" is involved.[23] Edward Snowden's disclosures, along with data breaches at Sony Pictures, Target, and the insurance giant Anthem, have all clearly prompted some (arguably inadequate) level of public backlash in the United States, while at the same time empowering those in the United States Congress arguing for greater civil liberties and protection. These reactions likely prompted the Obama administration to end the bulk metadata collection program.[24] There is a broad sense in which these challenges have achieved very little substantively and that the encroachment that persists is significantly greater than any of the concessions made by the Obama administration.

---

[20] Carol C. Gould, *Interactive Democracy: The Social Roots of Global Justice* (New York: Cambridge University Press, 2014), p. 187.
[21] Ibid., p. 224.   [22] Ibid., p. 220.   [23] Ibid., pp. 220–21.
[24] Jonathan Weisman and Jennifer Steinhauer, "Patriot Act Faces Curbs Supported by Both Parties," *The New York Times* (May 1, 2015), pp. A1 and A17.

We have suggested in this book that modern communication technologies have profoundly altered not only what freedom of expression and information entails but also how to *protect the privacy and the freedom of Web users*. This has rendered the old rules of the preinformation revolution state of affairs outmoded and in desperate need of revision. The consequences of the technological revolution for domestic security, foreign policy, and freedom of information, including having unrestricted Internet access as a matter of human rights, are no less important.[25] Likewise, the WikiLeaks phenomenon is seen as one consequence of the information technology revolution, with its huge and cross-border empowerment of individuals and nonstate actors such as NGOs.[26]

In the case of human rights NGOs, as Pruce rightly argues, large media departments have emerged to scale up programs in visual communication through photojournalism, video production, and social networks. The graphic form presents new, unique opportunities to leverage traditional devices including storytelling, witnessing, and naming and shaming. However, as Pruce's chapter demonstrates, new media also expose human rights advocates to the challenges of expressing their work and their objectives within a rapidly evolving visual culture. For human rights organizations to maximize their impact in a digital age, they must articulate an identity that is resonant with the audience as well as consistent with the progressive principles at the heart of human rights claims.

The spread of graphic and implicit images has rendered people across the world increasingly aware of what is transpiring beyond their borders and easily mobilized to protest against their poor socioeconomic and political conditions, especially given that they can instantly compare their situation with that of their cohort outside. Access to the Internet and social media has combined to generate "electronic civil disobedience," a form of Internet activism and disruption bent on rendering digital rights claims through the Internet a legitimate demand on the part of hacktivists, activists, and bloggers. Freedom of expression inherently covers a freedom to access the Internet. Some observers have called for the right

---

[25] David Rothkopf, "Is Unrestricted Internet Access a Modern Human Rights?," *Foreign Policy* (February 2, 2015), http://foreignpolicy.com/2015/02/02/unrestricted-internet-access-human-rights-technology-constitution/. Accessed on March 25, 2015.

[26] Francois Heisbourg, "Leaks and Lessons," *Survival*, 53, 1 (February–March 2011), 207–16; see p. 211.

to digital self-determination broadly defined as the right to informational autonomy – or simply the right to privacy.[27]

Increasingly, the Internet has come to be seen as a fundamental aspect of the commitment to freedom and democracy, and the right to open access to information on the Internet is now widely regarded as a basic human right. The UN Human Rights Committee has noted that electronic and Internet-based modes of expression are and should be protected. The right to freedom of expression, the UN Committee adds, underpins the enjoyment of other rights, including education, cultural participation, scientific progress, and the freedoms of association and assembly.[28]

Yet to the extent that the Internet serves as an avenue for the application of the freedom of expression, the nature, intent, and scope of that freedom invites controversy from some quarters. Closely related to the issue of the limitations on freedom of expression is the protection of privacy. Of all social network challenges, privacy rights and protections are crucial for both users and social networks. Failure to provide a maximum privacy safeguard may have unsavory consequences for the popularity of such social networks and for the amount of information that social network users are willing to share. Social network sites must provide their users with wide-ranging support tools that align with users' perception of privacy.[29]

Moreover, there are so many other related ethical issues involving online networking and information politics – such as the potential for misuse, cyber-harassment, cyber-terrorism, and cyber-stalking – that are likely to compel governments and national legislatures around the world to enact laws intended to curb the growth of such threats to privacy and security. A right of Internet access, however, will need to be balanced against other rights and competing interests, such as privacy, intellectual property protection, ensuring public order, national security, and protecting vulnerable groups and minorities.[30]

---

[27] Simson Gurfinkel, "Stronger Internet Privacy Laws Are Necessary," in James D. Torr (ed.), *The Information Age* (San Diego, CA: Greenhaven Press, 2003), pp. 104–11.

[28] Stephen Tully, "A Human Rights to Access the Internet: Problems and Prospects," *Human Rights Law Review*, 15 (May 2014), 175–95; see esp. pp. 194–95; see p. 185.

[29] Elie Raad and Richard Chbeir, "Privacy in Online Social Networks," in Richard Chbeir and Bechara Al Bouna (eds.), *Security and Privacy Preserving in Social Networks* (New York: Springer, 2013), pp. 3–45; see p. 37.

[30] Tully, "A Human Rights to Access the Internet," pp. 194–95.

Social media's ability to simultaneously empower the populace as well as governments' capability to suppress basic freedoms, such as the right to the Internet, calls for an examination of the ways in which governments apply a wide range of control mechanisms. Social media and government functions are linked in a complex, contradictory manner. Both the government and social media vie for supremacy of the public sphere. While the rules are clear, it remains uncertain which side will prevail. Just as the capability of governments to monitor and mitigate the effects of social media has noticeably increased, so too has the capability of their security and intelligence apparatus to spy on their people and use counter-revolutionary tactics such as spreading disinformation.

The repertoire of protest in the digital age

Although social media have facilitated the connectivity and interactivity of individuals' aspirations, the need to fundamentally alter political and economic conditions and structures can be met only by an extraordinary commitment on the part of the protesters and their willingness to take on attendant risks. The lesson learned from the Arab Spring has shown that such uprisings may not necessarily yield fundamental structural changes. History and current events serve as a stark reminder that the foundations of despotism are deep and not easily uprooted.

Social media, which represent a mix of advantages and restrictions, are not the sole driving force behind protest movements and upheavals. Rather, they simply facilitate the operation of such movements. It is true that the growth of social media will culminate in new ways in which institutions, individuals, and groups, as well as political and social communities, interact, but the extent to which such interactions generate dramatically different attitudes and risk-acceptant behavior remains open to debate. It is not clear, for instance, precisely how social media interact with other systemic and contextual factors to support a widespread protest movement capable of unseating well-entrenched authoritarian regimes.

In Palestine, as Wesbrock, Monshipouri, and Ghannam argue, new digital tools mean grievances are more rapidly mobilized and hence could potentially boost the possibility of accomplishing the goals of both political redress and public protest. It is worth noting that the economic and social effects of a campaign for the Boycotts, Divestment, and Sanctions (BDS) movement, especially when supported by social media, are direct and effective. Again, it is also important to remember that unless digital activism, involving collaborative displays of collective knowledge, is complemented by many offline strategies that invoke collective action, the impact of such grassroots sanctions will be limited. This suggests that BDS and grassroots campaigns would not be enough to pressure Israel; rather, international pressure would still be needed. Grassroots sanctions may prove more effective if related activists can gain broader popular support.

Latin America's protest networks similarly illustrate both the promise and the limitations that digital media offer for protecting and promoting human rights. Social media, as Juanita Darling so aptly demonstrates in Chapter 7, can draw a great deal of attention to human rights abuses but cannot by themselves prevent those abuses. New technologies can be effective when they take the state by surprise, but over time, the state frequently learns to respond effectively. This is especially true in regions such as Latin America with deep digital divides that preclude many citizens from access and corporatist traditions that states adeptly use to co-opt leaders of dissident movements. As if states did not provide sufficient obstacles, human rights advocates also face opposition from violent, nonstate actors whose values and beliefs often undermine respect for human rights.

Thus, digital media have become a useful but not always decisive tool for promoting and protecting human rights. There is nothing inevitable about digital technology and its impact – in terms of speed and access – on the expansion of civil society activity and the progress toward achieving social change. In fact, as one expert has noted, the Internet has become "the best vehicle for the dissemination of hatred and potential crimes against humanity since the printing press and the availability of gunpowder – but also a tool for social justice in a radically decentralized information system."[31] Several key factors, including politics, human agency, the media, and the dynamic interactions between the government, NGOs, and technology companies, appear to be more powerful shapers of the public sphere than technology.[32]

A challenge will be to ensure that governments, NGOs, and private companies are held to new standards and contexts that are conducive to the rule of law, transparency, and accountability. Perhaps most far-

---

[31] William Thorsell, "Digital Diplomacy," in Janice Gross Stein with Colin Robertson (eds.), *Diplomacy in the Digital Age: Essays in Honour of Ambassador Allan Gotlieb* (New York: McClelland & Stewart, 2011), pp. 255–69; see p. 266.

[32] Michael Edwards, *Civil Society*, 3rd edn. (London: Polity, 2014), pp. 82–87.

reaching is the extent to which governments demonstrate real commitment to human security, democratic institutions, Internet freedom, and privacy, especially at a time when cyber security and state security have become inextricably intertwined in the face of rising terrorism. None of this means that the Internet has failed to grow in relevance, but it does require the existence of necessary institutional commitments, value-oriented perspectives, and corporate social responsibility that are unique to protecting and promoting human rights.

Digital and connective technologies undoubtedly have enabled civil society to operate more effectively and provided new platforms for protest and resistance to the public. The emphasis on communication technologies, however, should not undermine the importance of the notion that a range of issues relating to human security cannot be addressed without understanding the crucial link between human rights, democracy, and development.[33] To win the struggle for basic freedoms and democratic institutions is no mean task in the face of colossal structural and developmental obstacles, as well as the obvious, bitter reality of authoritarian regimes that are becoming increasingly adept at controlling and clamping down on what their citizens can do online.

Rethinking contentious politics

The Internet and social media have arguably made it more and more feasible to connect with, empathize with, and recognize others as equals – those in our local networks as well as those at a distance. New technologies have made these connections with others in cyberspace more meaningful and significant. These tools, however, neither replace activities and performances transpiring in physical spaces, such as streets and squares, nor do they resolve, as Marc Lynch rightly argues, "the debate about whether the weak ties generated by Internet relationships are more or less likely to promote contentious political action."[34] Similarly, it is not clear whether the Internet alone can play an important role in preparing

---

[33] US Department of State: Diplomacy in Action, "Internet Freedom: Promoting Human Rights in the Digital Age – A Panel Discussion" (March 4, 2011), www.state.gov/j/drl/rls/rm/2011/162490.htm. Accessed on May 19, 2015.

[34] Marc Lynch, "Media, Old and New," in Marc Lynch, ed., *The Arab Uprisings Explained: New Contentious Politics in the Middle East* (New York: Columbia University Press, 2015), pp. 93–109; see p. 98.

people for the transition to democracy; nor is it the case that the Internet will always promote democracy.

Our case studies have shown that no single theory or explanation can enable us to better account for the success or failure of collective actions. Rather, we have argued that addressing the challenge of existing political opportunities in the face of the online modes of communication and their impact in mobilizing and organizing protests should help us answer some important questions set out in the book's introduction. With ICTs becoming a key component of the public sphere, the link between local and global public spheres has intensified. Our emphasis on contentious politics, peaceful civil disobedience, cyberactivism, and offline activism has led us to conclude that for protest movements to achieve their objectives in the long term, contentious politics must be supplemented by institutional politics. Many studies support our argument that, despite new media platforms and other technologies that allow for the horizontal flow of information and decentralized communications models, powerful groups and institutions still hold sway over new communication venues.[35]

Many studies have shown that blogs have fostered the creation of new civil society activities or organizations with new functions, ushering in a period of change. For example, in Egypt, new NGOs have provided assistance and advice to female protesters about how to avoid sexual harassment. The role of the blog in increasing public awareness is largely attributed to the activities of these associations.[36] Egyptian human rights activists have noted that these blogs have led to a "paradigmatic shift" from the print media to a more expressive online platform, paving the way for the negotiating of new public spaces. This shift has vigorously energized civic engagement and citizen journalism by creating a more engaged and more politically receptive public inside and outside of Egypt.[37] But more specifically, these modes of communication have led to the reconstruction and reorientation of the participants' identities and their sense of community – both online and offline.[38]

Different governments, cultural perspectives, and local proclivities are likely to pose varying obstacles for the ways in which the Internet could

---

[35] Victoria Carty, *Wired and Mobilizing: Social Movements, New Technology, and Electoral Politics* (New York: Routledge, 2011), p. 91.

[36] Mohammed el-Nawawy and Sahar Khamis, *Egyptian Revolution 2.0: Political Blogging, Civic Engagement, and Citizen Journalism* (New York: Palgrave Macmillan, 2013), p. 201.

[37] Ibid., p. 202.   [38] Ibid., p. 215.

be utilized for human rights and democratic goals. It is important to realize that the struggle for human rights will be won on the streets through dissident speech and activism, and carried out by protests and demonstrations. The development of solidarity movements across borders facilitated by the Internet, supported by NGOs and advocacy groups, will contribute to furthering human rights. Internet groups, forums, or collaborative websites can play a crucial role in the pursuit of human rights worldwide.

The extent to which new modes of communication can contribute to the formation of coalitions on the ground and the promotion of critical consciousness for societal involvement will depend largely on how such activities are viewed by the people involved and whether or not key institutions and/or political structures support or oppose them. Some scholars suggest that throughout the world citizens have turned away from allegiance toward an unmistakably "assertive" attitude toward politics. They have become more skeptical of state authority, electoral politics, institutions, and representatives and are more willing to assert their own views and defy elites with demands from below.[39]

This transition from allegiant to assertive cultures is real and poses a new challenge to the seminal work of Gabriel Almond and Sidney Verba (1963), in which it was shown that civic culture in Western democracies supported democracy and that democracies expected their citizens to be supportive and largely quiescent. Such a pattern was seen as indispensable for democratic governments to function properly.[40] A growing and substantial body of evidence suggests that a wide spectrum of society is deviating from this pattern and has adopted more elite-challenging forms of nonviolent action, rendering protest an extension of conventional politics by other means. This increase in protest signals the rise of assertive mass publics.[41]

In less developed countries, where many individuals were presumably unaware of or at least unaffected by politics, these patterns have also transformed. People in developing nations have also become more

---

[39] Christian Welzel and Russell J. Dalton, "From Allegiant to Assertive Citizens," in Russell J. Dalton and Christian Welzel (eds.), *The Civic Culture Transformed: From Allegiant to Assertive Citizens* (New York: Cambridge University Press, 2014), pp. 282–306; see p. 305.

[40] Gabriel Almond and Sidney Verba, *The Civic Culture: Political Attitudes in Five Western Democracies* (Princeton, NJ: Princeton University Press, 1963).

[41] Tor Georg Jakobsen and Ola Listhaug, "Social Change and the Politics of Protest," in Dalton and Welzel (eds.), *The Civic Culture Transformed: From Allegiant to Assertive Citizens*, pp. 213–39; see p. 231.

connected to politics because of the forces of socioeconomic modern-ization and global communications. The fact that in these countries – as in established democracies – the model citizen today is more likely to be an assertive citizen seems to confirm this point.[42] These cultural changes have positive consequences but present new challenges for democracies by placing new demands on the political process and generating more contention and conflict. The rising assertive political culture empowers people to make their own decisions and to make their preferences felt and known. Most notably, societies that have success-fully made the transition from an allegiant to an assertive model of citizens, experts point out, are longstanding democracies with a high degree of regime legitimacy broadly defined in terms of *accountability* and *effective* governance.[43] This bodes ill for those developing countries that offer their citizens little in the way of either accountable or effective institutions.

Finally, the conceptual and theoretical directions taken to promote human rights in the digital age pose a series of different challenges. The debates in this book have forced scholars, practitioners, and activists to confront a dynamic array of issues and consequences for political redress in the wake of new technologies. It is essential to strategize new ways of thought and practice in light of this innovative and increasingly enmeshed atmosphere, characterized by digital advocates, norm entre-preneurs, and educators who harness technology to raise awareness.

Reemergence of authoritarianism

There is little doubt that ICTs and social media have expanded the role of dissident groups and civil society as the source of change into new domains. At the same time, discriminatory policies and hostile state actions remain widespread. Challenges to the continuation of the status quo and the established wisdom behind old policies and practices of the ruling parties in many countries in the Middle East and North Africa (MENA) region do not imply that the revolution in information technology can be expected to bring about structural changes in regimes with longstanding authoritarian institutions and political history.

Historically, a combination of many interconnected obstacles to democratization in the MENA region has helped explain decades of

---

[42] Welzel and Dalton, "From Allegiant to Assertive Citizens," p. 305.   [43] Ibid., p. 283

authoritarian endurance there. These include, but are not limited to, a set of institutional and symbolic strategies, the political economy of state formation under delayed development, and the effects of regional and international geopolitical factors.[44] Decades of authoritarian rule through suffocating civil society, stifling social movements and resistance, suppressing popular struggles for basic freedoms, and undermining development in some regions have created enormous state-building and socioeconomic challenges that would likely take precedence over democracy.[45]

Today, several different factors – such as political instability, deep societal divisions, chronic unemployment, and a continued lack of economic opportunity – in the aftermath of the 2011 uprisings in the MENA region have contributed to the reemergence of some forms of authoritarianism. A new path to a sustainable transition to democracy has become ever more complicated by the halting pace and slow progression – or even the absence – of reform. Most observers of democratic transitions in the region have warned against conflating the chaotic postuprising period with the drive toward establishing democracy – a tendency that sets unrealistic standards to achieve. Illiberal forces in the political arena will undoubtedly seek to blame democracy for the difficulties that invariably follow the forced dismissal of longstanding authoritarian regimes.[46]

The longstanding authoritarian regimes, often operating under a state of confusion and uncertainty in the immediate aftermath of the postupheaval period, face the remains of the old system forming hostile institutional settings that divert or upend the progress toward achieving democratic reform. Indeed, the transition narrative in these countries revolves around the issue not of how democrats can prevail but instead on how authoritarians seek to reconstitute themselves.[47] Some experts have described this pervasive sense of internal insecurity as the new normal. The new breed of postrevolutionary leaders appears to have been largely unprepared to meet the significant challenges that plague

---

[44] Rex Brynen, Peter W. Moore, Bassel F. Salloukh, and Marie-Joëlle Zahar, *Beyond the Arab Spring: Authoritarianism and Democratization in the Arab World* (Boulder, CO: Lynne Rienner Publishers, 2012), p. 288.

[45] Ibid., p. 300.

[46] Christopher Walker and Vanessa Tucker, "After the Arab Spring: The Uphill Struggle for Democracy," *Countries at the Crossroads 2011* (New York: Freedom House), https://freedomhouse.org/report/algeria/overview-essay#.VVVDekYYEew. Accessed on May 15, 2015.

[47] Ibid.

their countries from within and without.[48] The prevailing paradigm underpinning the new normal, in this sense, suggests that the reversion toward authoritarianism is justified in the name of prioritizing security and stability over democratic disorder.

The latest turn to authoritarianism in the MENA region, experts have shown, has proven to be adaptive and flexible, as the ruling elites have used limited openings, manipulated electoral systems and courts, and maintained their repressive capabilities through controlled liberalization or outright authoritarian strategies, while relying on the interaction of formal and informal modes of conflict resolution, coalition building, and bargaining.[49] Increasingly, as one analyst notes, the military coup on July 3, 2013, which deposed Egypt's elected President Mohamed Morsi, gravely vindicated the continued attention to the institutions and political forces of those old authoritarian regimes.[50] More critically, external support by regional and international powers for the military-led Egyptian state has proven to be equally instrumental in increasing the regime's temerity and tenacity. Saudi Arabia, the United Arab Emirates, and Kuwait together have given more than $42 billion over about twenty-two months to back the military takeover.[51]

Unable to avert the spread of new information technologies and satellite channels, authoritarian Arab regimes have contained new media with complex regulatory and monitoring mechanisms, including formal and informal modes of control. This goes to show, as most experts assert, "when it comes to the new media, old authoritarian habits seem to die hard."[52] Satellite stations have been used in a wide variety of proxy intra- and interstate conflicts, inflaming narrow nationalistic sentiments and sectarian tensions. Saudi-controlled media outlets have played an active role in stirring up a new wave of anti-Shiism in the region, while Qatar

---

[48] John Amble, "The New Normal: Instability after the Arab Spring," *War on the Rocks* (July 30, 2013), http://warontherocks.com/2013/07/the-new-normal-instability-after-the-arab-spring/. Accessed on May 12, 2015.

[49] Mehran Kamrava, "The Rise and Fall of Ruling Bargains in the Middle East," in Mehran Kamrava (ed.), *Beyond the Arab Spring: The Evolving Ruling Bargain in the Middle East* (New York: Oxford University Press, 2014), pp. 17–45; see pp. 27–28.

[50] Marc Lynch, "Conclusion," in Marc Lynch (ed.), *The Arab Uprisings Explained: New Contentious Politics in the Middle East* (New York: Columbia University Press, 2014), pp. 313–16; see p. 314.

[51] David D. Kirkpatrick, "Unflattering Leaks in Egypt Gain Credibility," *New York Times* (May 13, 2015), p. A7.

[52] Brynen et al., *Beyond the Arab Spring*, pp. 250–51.

has deployed Al Jazeera's reach to co-opt Islamist groups and audiences throughout the region.

Across the region, David Faris writes, digital media activists are grappling with disenchantment about the trajectory of the Arab Spring, while digital spaces have become sites for transnational contestation, including by the most successful challenger to the state system: the Islamic State in Iraq and Syria (ISIS).[53] In Egypt, some of the most vocal activists are in prison. In Jordan, they have returned to generating a kind of journalism that straddles tolerated and forbidden spheres. With the notable exception of Tunisia, no country in the MENA region is freer or more stable than it was in 2011, as optimism and resistance have largely given way to a turbulent and unsettled regional order.[54]

We may be witnessing, Faris notes, a period of experimentation when – unlike Western journalism – journalistic experiments in the MENA region are unfolding under the fog of authoritarian resurgence.[55] It is worth noting that the struggle between Arab protest movements and their authoritarian rulers is unlikely to end so long as political mobilization and contestation driven by the new Arab media pits the public against the persistent coercive capabilities of authoritarian regimes.[56] It is within this context that the relationship between new, highly interconnected agents of change and the old guard requires a critical assessment and timely warning.

Digital technology and human rights

Given that ICTs and social media have significant implications for human rights more generally, but especially for the right to privacy, freedom of information, and freedom of expression, addressing these rights would require seeking answers to the following questions: Can the effort to combat terrorism be conducted without violating human rights? How can the tensions between security needs and human rights be managed in a manner that the pursuit of security considerations need not necessitate the sacrifice of civil liberties? Do social media provide a new tool to enhance human rights? And finally, do social media bring anything new to the struggle for human rights? This volume has shown

---

[53] David Faris, "Multiplicities of Purposes: The Auditorium Building, the State, and the Transformation of Arab Digital Media," *International Journal of Middle East Studies*, 47, 2 (May 2015), 343–47; see p. 343.

[54] Ibid., p. 345.   [55] Ibid., p. 345.   [56] Brynen et al., *Beyond the Arab Spring*, p. 251.

that both traditional and nontraditional ways of thinking about human rights have much to contribute to the discussion, even in the digital age, realizing that it is important to operate within new avenues of thought, practice, and methodology, while reflecting on which past practices have been most successful. Theories of social action and communal empowerment, along the lines of self-directed practices – individually or collectively – can provide new answers precisely because they revolved around people and were rooted in antioppressive principles that underpin the new social movements of oppressed groups. These groups include, but are not limited to, differently abled persons, antiracist groups, and feminist, lesbian, gay, bisexual, transgendered, and questioning (LGBTQ) communities, to name but a few.[57]

At the center of this discussion is the individual. The demands for justice, inclusion, and political redress may have changed in character, moving from cafes and protest squares to online chat rooms and social media, but the claim for change remains the same. Echoing a similar sentiment, Annabelle Sreberny poignantly argues that citizen movements and political struggles for democracy and human rights in the MENA region did not originate with the Arab Spring, and neither did women's political activity. Online politics and actual social movements, Sreberny goes on to explain, "are not ontologically different activities but rather different modes of being political."[58] The presence of the ICTs together with the growing popular awareness of change, however, have generated a more conducive environment for women's political activities and hence for broadening the so-called "sphere of the political."[59]

Yet the fact remains that these new technologies can create new liabilities as governments become more capable of directly identifying protest agents through their Internet Protocol addresses and other data. A broad consensus holds that digital media technologies have enabled protest movements to an extent that would have been simply impossible without them. Such digitally enabled democratization, however, is effectively reversed when it comes to state power and security forces, which have used these communication technologies to pursue surveillance and repressive measures. Muzammil M. Hussain and Sonia Jawaid Shaikh

---

[57] Audrey Mullender, Dave Ward, and Jennie Fleming, *Empowerment in Action: Self-Directed Groupwork* (New York: Palgrave Macmillan, 2013), p. 37.

[58] Annabelle Sreberny, "Women's Digital Activism in a Changing Middle East," *International Journal of Middle East Studies*, 47, 2 (May 2015), 357–61; see p. 357.

[59] Ibid.

aptly summarized this liability: "The flip side of *digitally enabled democratization* is *digitally enabled repression*."[60] Challenging the governments under these circumstances is a daunting task. Nonetheless, so long as individuals are willing to seek change locally and globally, and so long as political change is allowed for and demanded in contexts around the world, human rights is a discourse increasingly used to put forth demands for greater quality of life and democracy. In the end, the success in these struggles turns, as Babak Rahimi argues, on the individual's ability to imagine politics, with or *without* technology, and pursue desires and visions for change.[61]

The debate persists over the conflict between geopolitical, ideological, and strategic economic interests, on the one hand, and the promotion of human rights and democracy, on the other. In response to the question of what is the most effective strategy for protecting human rights, especially during a period of profound change, crisis, and reform, some experts have underscored the importance of norm diffusion, while acknowledging the growing gap between the law on the books and the law in action. Much of the human rights legal system, Emilie M. Hafner-Burton notes, has descended into bureaucratic and political impasse. Many states that have signed international human rights treaties and conventions have done little or nothing to ensure that the provisions of human rights instruments have been enforced in domestic law. The international human rights legal system, Hafner-Burton warns, suffers from an array of deep problems, including broken commitments, vagueness of norms, downgraded capacity for deterrence of human rights abuses, and legitimacy.[62]

Others have emphasized the need to forge a practical and overlapping consensus on emerging standards. Today, as Jack Donnelly points out, the moral equality of all human beings is resolutely endorsed by most prominent comprehensive doctrines in all regions of the world.[63] While

---

[60] Muzammil M. Hussain and Sonia Jawaid Shaikh, "Three Arenas for Interrogating Digital Politics in the Middle East Affairs," *International Journal of Middle East Studies*, 47, 2 (May 2015), 366–68; see p. 367.

[61] Babak Rahimi, "Rethinking Digital Technologies in the Middle East," *International Journal of Middle East Studies*, 47, 2 (May 2015), 362–65.

[62] Emilie M. Hafner-Burton, *Making Human Rights a Reality* (Princeton, NJ: Princeton University Press, 2013), pp. 90–91.

[63] Jack Donnelly, "Universality," in David P. Forsythe (ed.), *Encyclopedia of Human Rights*, Vol. 5 (New York: Oxford University Press, 2009), pp. 261–70; see p. 265; see also Jack Donnelly, *Universal Human Rights*, 3rd edn. (Ithaca, NY: Cornell University Press, 2013), pp. 60–62.

advocating the formation of practical consensus on human rights, David P. Forsythe has argued that there is also morality or ethics beyond the human rights discourse and that peace and reconciliation can be prioritized over human rights.[64] Most analysts concur that human rights standards may *not* provide an appropriate device for handling every political and legal issue.[65]

In recent years, with increasing attention paid to nonstate actors, many observers have turned to transnational advocacy networks. A pioneer work by Margaret E. Keck and Kathryn Sikkink attempted to explain how transnational advocacy networks seek influence by using "the power of their information, ideas, and strategies to alter the information and value contexts within which states make policies."[66] These transnational activist networks play an important role in boosting accountability of powerful actors to their stated or past policies or principles, as well as promoting information politics by generating politically useful information and inserting it into the policy debate at crucial moments. These and many other tactics are greatly facilitated and even enhanced by modern communications technology.

Drawing on social movement literature and network theory, Keck and Sikkink explain the importance of norms, ideas, and shared values in producing positive change. "Modern networks," Keck and Sikkink write, "are not conveyor belts of liberal ideas but vehicles for communicative and political exchange, with the potential for mutual transformation of participants."[67] The concept of a transnational advocacy network, they note, is a key element in contemplating the changing nature of the international community and particularly in understanding the interaction between societies and states in the formation of international policies. No matter how central the role of states is in international arenas, advocacy networks provide domestic actors with allies outside their own states.[68] Keck and Sikkink, however, admit that a network's existence and its decision to focus on abuses in a particular case is a necessary but not sufficient condition for altering poor human rights

---

[64] David P. Forsythe, *Human Rights in International Relations* (New York: Cambridge University Press, 2000), p. 28.

[65] A. H. Robertson and J. G. Merrills, *Human Rights in the World: An Introduction to the Study of the International Protection of Human Rights*, 4th edn. (Manchester: Manchester University Press, 1996), p. 342.

[66] Margaret E. Keck and Kathryn Sikkink, *Activists beyond Borders: Advocacy Networks in International Politics* (Ithaca, NY: Cornell University Press, 1998), p. 16.

[67] Ibid., p. 214.   [68] Ibid., pp. 216–17.

situations.[69] The success of the human rights movements depends as much on such transnational and the wider world's networks as it does on internal activities and organizations themselves.

Still others note that human rights organizations should concentrate less on legal norms and connect more with social activism.[70] As noted throughout this book, the digital age has significantly contributed to social activism. Addressing the limits of what could and should be expected from technology can also help us better understand why and how cyberspace and cyberactivism may, under certain circumstances, be seen as an important source of civic engagement and collective consciousness. It has long been apparent, including to the governments that have spent more time controlling the flow of information, that today's assertive citizens are highly suspicious of the state's ability to perform effectively or even legitimately. Perversely, governments' efforts to shut down the Internet and contain or even suppress the use of social media have led to a surge in unrest and uprisings.

It is abundantly clear, as journalists on the ground frequently report, that the Internet has changed and is changing Iran as it has altered the world's social and political landscape. Iranians are avid users of social media, as they have learned how to dodge official firewalls by using illegal software that is widely available for purchase from Iranian websites that are not blocked. Much of the public debate transpires online. Young Iranians have muscled out some space for themselves where not much is legally allowed and yet, in reality, a great deal is possible.[71] Such cases demonstrate that despite the fact that digital media have not replaced face-to-face interaction, they have opened up new opportunities for much more direct and robust communication.

Modern technologies have profoundly altered the social contexts, allowing newer movements to penetrate deeply into the social fabric and mobilize new actors to become involved in social movements.[72] The growing use of social media has influenced the role of citizens in modern democracies, but as yet these new technologies have largely failed to determine the outcome of the political game, falling far short

[69] Ibid., p. 117.

[70] Smitu Kothari and Harsh Sethi, eds., *Rethinking Human Rights: Challenges for Theory and Action* (Delhi: Lokayan, 1991).

[71] Thomas Erdbrink, "Q & A: A Glimpse of Everyday Attitudes in Iran," *The New York Times* (May 24, 2015), p. 4.

[72] Jackie Smith et al., *Global Democracy and the World Social Forums*, 2nd edn. (Boulder, CO: Paradigm Publishers, 2015), p. 156.

of transforming the boundaries of state power. By providing effective tools for reaching large numbers of people, social media and new technologies have amplified the impact of connectedness, fostering social protests of staggering magnitude throughout the world. While new technologies can facilitate norm diffusion, including the diffusion of human rights norms in new and larger scale ways, as with any other medium for norm diffusion, they cannot necessarily produce long-term commitments to human rights protection and empowerment.

This concluding chapter has focused attention on several recurring themes running through the book, namely, the issues of political openness and privacy. Despite rapid advances in technology, the modern world faces daunting challenges of democratic governance, human security, and dignity rights. Without a robust system of checks and balances, however, the issues of mass surveillance and the widespread violations of privacy rights pose serious threats to individual freedoms. There can be no denying the fact that for new technological tools to be used to effectively influence electoral politics, stage peaceful civil disobedience and protest, mobilize efforts for any other democratic purposes, and offer a sense of promise, a variety of other conducive social and political circumstances must be in place.

SELECTED BIBLIOGRAPHY

Aboud, Brian, 2012, "Organizing and the Boycott, Divestment, Sanctions (BDS) Strategy: The Turn to BDS in Palestine Politics in Montreal," in Aziz Choudry, Jill Hanley, and Eric Shragge (eds.), *Organize! Building from the Local for Global Justice*. Oakland, CA: PM Press, pp. 202–15.

Aguilar Camín, Héctor, 1984, *Los Días de Manuel Buendía: Testimonios*. 1st edn. México City, D.F.: Océano: Fundación Manuel Buendía.

Anderson, Benedict, 2006, *Imagined Communities: Reflections on the Origin and Spread of Nationalism*. New York: Verso Books.

Anderson, Carol, 2003, *Eyes off the Prize: The United Nations and the African American Struggle for Human Rights, 1944–1955*. New York: Cambridge University Press.

Anderson, Lisa, 2014, "Authoritarian Legacies and Regime Change: Towards Understanding Political Transition in the Arab World," in Fawaz A. Gerges, ed., *The New Middle East: Protest and Revolution in the Arab World*. New York: Cambridge University Press, pp. 41–59.

Bakıner, Onur, 2014, "Can the 'Spirit of Gezi' Transform Progressive Politics in Turkey?," in U. Özkırımlı (ed.), *The Making of a Protest Movement in Turkey: #occupygezi*. Basingstoke: Palgrave Macmillan.

Balogun, Jumoke, 2014, "'Dear World, Your Hashtags Won't #BringBackOur-Girls.'" *The Guardian*, May 9, www.theguardian.com/world/2014/may/09/nigeria-hashtags-wont-bring-back-our-girls-bringbackourgirls.

Banerjee, Sanjoy, 1997, "The Cultural Logic of National Identity Formation: Contending Discourses in Late Colonial India," in Valerie Hudson (ed.), *Culture and Foreign Policy*. Boulder, CO: Lynne Reinner, pp. 27–44.

Bardhan Pranab, 2010, *Awakening Giants, Feet of Clay: Assessing the Economic Rise of China and India*. Princeton, NJ: Princeton University Press.

Barghouti, Omar, 2011, *Boycott, Divestment, Sanctions: The Global Struggle for Palestinian Rights*. Chicago, IL: Haymarket Books.

Barnett, Michael, 2011. *Empire of Humanity: A History of Humanitarianism*. Ithaca, NY: Cornell University Press.

Barrington, Lowell W., Erik S. Herron, and Brian D. Silver, 2003, "Research Note: The Motherland Is Calling: Views of Homeland among Russians in the Near Abroad." *World Politics* 55(2), pp. 290–313.

Barry, Jack J., 2012, "Microfinance, the Market and Political Development in the Internet Age." *Third World Quarterly*, 33(1), pp. 125–41.

Bob, Clifford, 2002, "Merchants of Morality." *Foreign Policy*, March 1, www.foreignpolicy.com/articles/2002/03/01/merchants_of_morality.

Brubaker, Rogers, 1995, "National Minorities, Nationalizing States, and External Homelands in the New Europe." *Daedalus*, 124, pp. 107–32.

Brynen, Rex, Peter W. Moore, Bassel F. Salloukh, and Marie-Joëlle Zahar, 2012, *Beyond the Arab Spring: Authoritarianism and Democratization in the Arab World*. Boulder, CO: Lynne Rienner Publishers.

Brysk, Alison, 2013, *Speaking Rights to Power: Constructing Political Will*. New York: Oxford University Press.

Budabin, Alexandra C., and Joel R. Pruce, 2014, "The Strategic Logic of Media Advocacy: New Modalities of Information Politics in Human Rights." Working paper.

Bunt, Gary R., 2012, "Mediterranean Islamic Expression: Web 2.0," in Cesare Merlini and Olivier Roy (eds.), *Arab Society in Revolt: The West's Mediterranean Challenge*. Washington, DC: Brookings Institution Press.

Cambanis, Thanassis, 2015, *Once upon a Revolution: An Egyptian Story*. New York: Simon & Schuster.

Carapico, Sheila, 2012, "Egypt's Civic Revolution Turns 'Democracy Promotion' on Its Head," in Bahgat Korany and Rabab El-Mahdi (eds.), *Arab Spring in Egypt: Revolution and Beyond*. Cairo: The American University in Cairo Press.

Carpenter, Charli, 2007, "Studying Issue (Non)-Adoption in Transnational Advocacy Networks." *International Organization* 61(3), pp. 643–67.

Carpenter, Charli, and Daniel W. Drezner, 2010, "International Relations 2.0: The Implications of New Media for an Old Profession." *International Studies Perspectives* 11(3), pp. 255–72.

Carty, Victoria, 2011, *Wired and Mobilizing: Social Movements, New Technology, and Electoral Politics*. New York: Routledge.

Castells, Manuel, 2012, *Networks of Outrage and Hope: Social Movements in the Internet Age*. Cambridge, UK: Polity Press.

Cole, Juan, 2014, *The New Arabs: How the Millennial Generation Is Changing the Middle East*. New York: Simon & Schuster.

Corrales, Javier, and Frank Westhoff, 2006, "Information Technology Adoption and Political Regimes." *International Studies Quarterly*, 50, pp. 911–33.

Dagi, Ishan, 2013, "Last Resort: Building Mosque in Taksim," *Today's Zaman*.

Davis, Michael C., 2006, "The Basic Law and Democratization in Hong Kong." *Loyola University of Chicago International Law Review* 3(3), pp. 165–85.

De Waal, Alex, 2003, "Human Rights Organizations and the Political Imagination: How the West and Africa Have Diverged." *Journal of Human Rights* 2(4), pp. 475–94.

Diamond, Larry, 2010, "Liberation Technology." *Journal of Democracy*, 21(3), pp. 69–83.

Donnelly, Jack, 2009, "Universality," in David P. Forsythe, ed., *Encyclopedia of Human Rights*. New York: Oxford University Press, pp. 261–70.

2013, *International Human Rights*, 4th edn. Boulder, CO: Westview Press.

2013, *Universal Human Rights*, 3rd edn. Ithaca, NY: Cornell University Press.

Doran, Michael S., 2011, "The Impact of New Media: The Revolution Will Be Tweeted," in Kenneth M. Pollack et al., *The Arab Awakening: America and the Transformation of the Middle East*. Washington, DC: Brookings Institution Press.

Drezner, Daniel W., 2003, "The Hidden Hand of Economic Coercion." *International Organization*, 57, Summer, pp. 643–59.

El Rashidi, Yazmine, 2013, "Egypt: The Rule of the Brotherhood." *The New York Review of Books*, February 3, www.nybooks.com/articles/archives/2013/feb/07/egypt-rule-brotherhood/.

Enloe, Cynthia, 1973, *Ethnic Conflict and Political Development*. Boston: Little, Brown and Co.

Erkan Saka, 2014, "The AK Party's Social Media Strategy: Controlling the Uncontrollable." *Turkish Review* 4(4), pp. 418–23.

Estrin, James, 2012, "When Interest Creates a Conflict." *New York Times Lens Blog*, November 19, http://lens.blogs.nytimes.com/2012/11/19/when-interest-creates-a-conflict/.

Faris, David, 2015, "Multiplicities of Purposes: The Auditorium Building, the State, and the Transformation of Arab Digital Media." *International Journal of Middle East Studies*, 47(2), pp. 343–47.

Fassin, Didier, 2011, *Humanitarian Reason: A Moral History of the Present*. 1st edn. Berkeley, CA: University of California Press.

Fisun, Oleksandr, and Anton Avksentiev, 2014, "Euromaidan in South-Eastern Ukraine." *Religion & Society in East and West*, 42, pp. 23–25.

Forsythe, David P., 2011, *The Politics of Prisoner Abuse: The United States and Enemy Prisoners after 9/11*. New York: Cambridge University Press.

2012, *Human Rights in International Relations*. New York: Cambridge University Press.

Fried-Amilivia, Gabriela, 2009, "Remembering Trauma in Society: Forced Disappearance after Uruguay's Era of State Terror (1973–2001)," in Noel Packard (ed.), *Sociology of Memory: Papers from the Spectrum*. Newcastle upon Tyne: Cambridge Scholars Publishers, pp. 135–58.

Furnivall, J. S., 1948, *Colonial Policy and Practice*. London: Cambridge University Press.

Gervasoni, Carlos, 2014, "Argentina's Democracy Four Years after Modernization and Bureaucratic-Authoritarianism," in Daniel M. Brinks, Marcelo Leiras, and Scott Mainwaring (eds.), *Reflections on Uneven Democracies: The Legacy of Guillermo O'Donnell*. Baltimore, MD: Johns Hopkins University Press, pp. 44–70.

Ghannam, Jess, 2011, "Health and Human Rights in Palestine: The Siege and Invasion of Gaza and the Role of the Boycott, Divestment and Sanctions Movement," in Mahmood Monshipouri, ed., *Human Rights in the Middle East: Frameworks, Goals, and Strategies.* New York: Palgrave Macmillan, pp. 245–61.

Gheytanchi, Elham, and Babak Rahimi, 2008, "Iran's Reformists and Activists: Internet Exploiters," in *Middle East Policy*, 15(1), pp. 45–59.

Ghonim, Wael, 2012, *Revolution 2.0: The Power of People Is Greater Than the People in Power: A Memoir.* Boston, MA: Houghton Mifflin Harcourt.

Gladwell, Malcolm, 2010, "Small Change: Why the Revolution Will Not Be Tweeted." *New Yorker,* www.newyorker.com/magazine/2010/10/04/small-change-3.

Gould, Carol C., 2014, *Interactive Democracy: The Social Roots of Global Justice.* New York: Cambridge University Press.

Hafner-Burton, Emilie M., 2008, "Sticks and Stones: Naming and Shaming the Human Rights Enforcement Problem." *International Organization* 62(4), pp. 689–716.

2013, *Making Human Rights a Reality.* Princeton, NJ: Princeton University Press.

Haran, Olexiy, and Petro Bukovskiy, 2014, "Before and after Euromaidan: European Values vs. pro-Russian Attitudes." *Religion & Society in East and West,* 42, pp. 13–16.

Hashemi, Nader, and Danny Postel eds. 2010, *The People Reloaded: The Green Movement and the Struggle for Iran's Future.* Brooklyn, NY: Melville House.

Herrera, Linda, and Rehab Sakr eds., 2014, *Wired Citizenship: Youth Learning and Activism in the Middle East.* New York: Routledge.

Hick, Steven, Edward F. Halpin, and Eric Hoskins, 2000, *Human Rights and the Internet.* New York: St. Martin's Press.

Hill, Symon, 2013, *Digital Revolutions: Activism in the Internet Age.* Oxford, UK: New International Publications Ltd.

Hillburn, Matthew, 2014, "Social Media Documenting, Not Driving, Hong Kong Protests," *Voice of America,* October 1.

Hoffman, Michael, and Amaney Jamal, 2015, "Political Attitudes of Youth Cohorts," in Marc Lynch (ed.), *The Arab Uprisings Explained: New Contentious Politics in the Middle East.* New York: Columbia University Press, pp. 273–95.

Hopgood, Stephen, 2006. *Keepers of the Flame: Understanding Amnesty International.* Ithaca, NY: Cornell University University Press.

Howard, Philip N., 2010, *The Digital Origins of Dictatorship and Democracy: Information, Technology and Political Islam.* Oxford, UK: Oxford University Press.

Howard, Philip N., and Muzammil M. Hussain, 2014, "The Role of Digital Media," in Larry Diamond and Marc F. Plattner (eds.), *Democratization and*

Authoritarianism in the Arab World. Baltimore, MD: Johns Hopkins University Press.

Hunt, Lynn Avery, 2007, *Inventing Human Rights: A History*. New York: W. W. Norton & Company.

Hussain, Muzammil M., and Sonia Jawaid Shaikh, 2015, "Three Arenas for Interrogating Digital Politics in the Middle East Affairs," *International Journal of Middle East Studies*, 47(2), pp. 366–68.

Hutzler, Charles, 2014, "Hong Kong Protests Fueled by Foreign Agencies, Ex-China Official Says," *The Wall Street Journal*, October 14.

Isin, Engin, and Evelyn Ruppert, 2015, *Being Digital Citizens*. New York: Rowman & Littlefield.

Jakobsen, Tor Georg, and Ola Listhaug, 2014, "Social Change and the Politics of Protest," in Russell J. Dalton and Christian Welzel (eds.), *The Civic Culture Transformed: From Allegiant to Assertive Citizens*. New York: Cambridge University Press, pp. 213–39.

Kamrava, Mehran (ed.), 2014, *Beyond the Arab Spring: The Evolving Ruling Bargain in the Middle East*. New York: Oxford University Press.

Kar, Mehrangiz, 2015, "Democracy after the Green Movement," in Abbas Milani and Larry Diamond (eds.), *Politics and Culture in Contemporary Iran: Challenging the Status Quo*. Boulder, CO: Lynne Rienner Publishers, pp. 69–90.

Keck, Margaret E., and Kathryn A. Sikkink, 1998, *Activists beyond Borders: Advocacy Networks in International Politics*. Ithaca, NY: Cornell University Press.

Khosrokhavar, Farhad, 2012, *The New Arab Revolutions That Shook the World*. Boulder, CO: Paradigm Publishers.

Kitzberger, Philip, 2012, "The Media Politics of Latin America's Leftist Governments." *Journal of Politics in Latin America*, 4(3), pp. 123–39.

Klang, Mathias, and Andrew Murray (eds.), 2005, *Human Rights in the Digital Age*. London: Glasshouse.

Korany, Bahgat, and Rabab El-Mahdi (eds.), 2012, *Arab Spring in Egypt: Revolution and Beyond*. Cairo: The American University in Cairo Press.

Kuran, Timur, 1991, "Now Out of Never: The Element of Surprise in the East European Revolution of 1989." *World Politics* 44(1), pp. 7–48.

Letsch Constanze, and Dominic Rushe, 2014, "Turkey Blocks YouTube amid 'National Security' Concerns." *The Guardian*, March 28.

Levitsky, Steven, and Lucan Way, 2010, *Competitive Authoritarianism: Hybrid Regimes after the Cold War*. Cambridge: Cambridge University Press.

Lotan, Glad, Erhardt Graeff, Mike Ananny, Devin Gaffney, Ian Pearce, and Danah Boyd, 2011, "The Revolutions Were Tweeted: Information Flows during the 2011 Tunisian and Egyptian Revolutions." *International Journal of Communication* 5, 1375–405.

Lust, Ellen, 2014, "Elections," in Marc Lynch (ed.), *The Arab Uprisings Explained: New Contentious Politics in the Middle East.* New York: Columbia University Press, pp. 218–45.

Lynch, Marc, 2012 *The Arab Uprisings: The Unfinished Revolutions of the New Middle East.* New York: Pacific Affairs.

Mihelj, Sabina, 2011, *Media Nations: Communicating Belonging and Exclusion in the Modern World.* London: Palgrave Macmillan.

Milani, Abbas, 2015, "Iran's Democratic Movements," in Abbas Milani and Larry Diamond (eds.), *Politics and Culture in Contemporary Iran: Challenging the Status Quo.* Boulder, CO: Lynne Rienner Publishers, pp. 217–58.

Moghadam, Valentine M., 2013, *Modernizing Women: Gender and Social Change in the Middle East.* Boulder, CO: Lynne Rienner Publishers.

Monshipouri, Mahmood, 2014, *Democratic Uprisings in the New Middle East: Youth, Technology, Human Rights, and US Foreign Policy.* Boulder, CO: Paradigm Publishers.

Morozov, Evgeny, 2011, *The Net Delusion.* New York: Public Affairs.

Motyl, Alexander J., 2010, "Ukrainian Blues: Yanukovych's Rise, Democracy's Fall." *Foreign Affairs* 89, pp. 125–37.

Mullender, Audrey, Dave Ward, and Jennie Fleming, 2013, *Empowerment in Action: Self-Directed Groupwork.* New York: Palgrave Macmillan.

O'Donnell, Guillermo, and Philippe Schmitter, 1986, *Transitions from Authoritarian Rule: Tentative Conclusions about Uncertain Democracies.* Baltimore, MD: Johns Hopkins University Press.

O'Donnell, Guillermo, 1993, "On the State, Democratization and Some Conceptual Problems." Kellogg Institute Working Paper, 192 (April).

Örs, Ilay Romain, 2014, "Genie in the Bottle: Gezi Park, Taksim Square, and the Realignment of Democracy and Space in Turkey." *Philosophy and Social Criticism* 40(4–5), p. 496.

Osman, Tarek, 2010, *Egypt on the Brink: From Nasser to Mubarak.* New Haven, CT: Yale University Press.

Pandey, Avaneesh, 2014, "Israel's Foreign Minister Urges Government to Encourage Departure of arabs to Future Palestinian State." *International Business Times*, November 29, www.ibtimes.com/israels-foreign-minister-urges-government-encourage-departure-arabs-future-1730716.

Pole, Antoinette, 2010, *Blogging the Political: Politics and Participation in a Networked Society.* New York: Routledge.

Portnov, Andriy, and Tetiana Portnova, 2014, "The Dynamics of the Ukrainian Eurorevolution." *Religion & Society in East and West* 42(5/6), pp. 9–12.

Poster, Mark, 1990, *The Mode of Information: Poststructuralism and Social Context.* Chicago, IL: University of Chicago Press.

Preeg, Ernest H., 1999, *Feeling Good or Doing Good with Sanctions.* Washington, DC: CSIS Press.

Pruce, Joel R., 2012, "The Spectacle of Suffering and Humanitarian Intervention in Somalia," in Tristan Anne Borer (ed.), *Media, Mobilization and Human Rights: Mediating Suffering.* London: Zed Books.

Putnam, Robert D., 2000, *Bowling Alone: The Collapse and Revival of American Community.* New York: Simon & Schuster.

Qumsiyeh, Mazin, 2015, "Evolution of Armed to Unarmed Resistance in Palestine," in Véronique Dudouet (ed.), *Civil Resistance and Conflict Transformation: Transitions from Armed to Nonviolent Struggle.* New York: Routledge, pp. 77–99.

Raad, Elie, and Richard Chbeir, 2013, "Privacy in Online Social Networks," in Richard Chbeir and Bechara Al Bouna (eds.), *Security and Privacy Preserving in Social Networks.* New York: Springer, pp. 3–45.

Rahimi, Babak, 2015, "Rethinking Digital Technologies in the Middle East." *International Journal of Middle East Studies*, 47(2), pp. 362–65.

Rheingold, Howard, 2003, *Smart Mobs: The Next Social Revolution.* New York: Basic Books.

Riabchuk, Mykola, and Andrej N. Lushnyky, 2014, "Ukraine's Third Attempt." *Religion & Society in East and West*, 42, pp. 29–31.

Rodriguez-Garavito, Cesar, 2014, "The Future of Human Rights: From Gatekeeping to Symbiosis." *Sur: International Journal of Human Rights* 11(20), http://conectas.org.br/en/actions/sur-journal/issue/20/1007380-the-future-of-human-rights-from-gatekeeping-to-symbiosis.

Sabea, Hanan, 2014, "Still Waiting: Labor, Revolution and Social Justice in Egypt." *International Labor and Working-Class History*, 86, pp. 178–82.

Sardesai, Rajdeep, 2014, *The Election That Changed India.* New York: Penguin Press.

Schaeffer, Robert K., 2014, *Social Movements and Global Social Change: The Rising Tide.* New York: Rowman & Littlefield.

Schock, Kurt, 2005, *Unarmed Insurrections: People Power Movement in Non-Democracies.* Minneapolis, MN: University of Minnesota Press.

Selnow, Gary W., 2003, "The Information Age Is Fostering the Spread of Freedom and Democracy," in James D. Torr (ed.), *The Information Age.* Farmington Hills, MI: Greenhaven Press.

Shapiro, Andrew, 2003, "The Information Age May Not Foster Democracy," in James D. Torr (ed.), *The Information Age.* Farmington Hills, MI: Greenhaven Press.

Shirky, Clay, 2008, *Here Comes Everybody: The Power of Organizing without Organizations.* New York: Penguin Press.

Shveda, Yuriy, 2014, "The Revolution of Dignity in the Context of Social Theory of Revolutions." *Religion & Society in East and West*, 42, pp. 20–22.

Smith, M. G., 1965, *The Plural Society in the British West Indies.* Berkeley: University of California Press.

So, Peter, 2014, "Anti-Occupy Group's Hotline for Reporting Student Strikes Branded 'White Terror.'" *South China Morning Post*, September 8.

Sreberny, Annabelle, and Gholam Khiabany, 2010, *Blogistan: The Internet and Politics in Iran*. London: I. B. Tauris.

Sridharan, Eswaran, 2014, "Behind Narendra Modi's Victory." *Journal of Democracy* 25(4), pp. 20–33.

Stepanenko, V., 2014, "Ukraine's Farewell to Post-Soviet Politics." *Religion & Society in East and West*, 42, pp. 26–28.

Tanguy, Joelle, and Fiona Terry, 1999, "Humanitarian Responsibility and Committed Action: Response to 'Principles, Politics, and Humanitarian Action.'" *Ethics & International Affairs* 13(1), pp. 29–34.

Thorsell, William, 2011, "Digital Diplomacy," in Janice Gross Stein with Colin Robertson (eds.), *Diplomacy in the Digital Age: Essays in Honour of Ambassador Allan Gotlieb*. New York: McClelland & Stewart, pp. 255–69.

Tilly, Charles, and Sidney Tarrow, 2007, *Contentious Politics*. Boulder, CO: Paradigm Publishers.

Torr, James D., 2003, *The Information Age*. San Diego, CA: Greenhaven Press.

Tully, Stephen, 2014, "A Human Rights to Access the Internet: Problems and Prospects." *Human Rights Law Review*, 15(2), May, pp. 175–95.

Waisbord, Silvio, 2011, "Between Support and Confrontation: Civic Society, Media Reform, and Populism in Latin America." *Communication, Culture & Critique* 4(1), pp. 97–117.

Warschauer, Mark, 2003, *Technology and Social Inclusion: Rethinking the Digital Divide*. Cambridge, MA: MIT Press.

Wilson, Andrew, and Sarah Birch, 1999, "Voting Stability, Political Gridlock: Ukraine's 1998 Parliamentary Elections." *Europe-Asia Studies* 51(6), pp. 1039–68.

Yahyanejad, Mehdi, and Elham Gheytanchi, 2012, "Social Media, Dissent, and Iran's Green Movement," in Larry Diamond and Marc F. Plattner (eds.), *Liberation Technology: Social Media and the Struggle for Democracy*. Baltimore, MD: Johns Hopkins University Press, pp. 139–53.

Yelegaonkar, Shrikant, 2014, "Media Effects on Political Elections." *Indian Streams Research Journal* 8(4), pp. 1–5.

Zelizer, Barbie, 2010, *About to Die: How News Images Move the Public*. 1st edn. New York: Oxford University Press.

Ziccardi, Giovanni, 2013, *Resistance, Liberation Technology, and Human Rights in the Digital Age*. New York: Springer.

Zirakzadeh, Cyrus Ernesto, 2006, *Social Movements in Politics: A Comparative Study* (expanded edn.). New York: Palgrave-Macmillan.

INDEX

Aam Aadmi Party, 228
activism, ix–x, 3, 7, 12, 14, 21, 24,
    50, 52, 56, 63–65, 69, 72, 74, 76,
    91, 94, 104–7, 110, 112, 115,
    119–20, 123–25, 131, 152–53,
    159, 179, 181, 190, 195, 242, 262,
    267, 269, 273, 278, 281, 283–84,
    292; *see also* human rights;
    social media
advocacy, 14, 38, 50, 52, 54–57,
    59–63, 65, 68–70, 72, 75, 104,
    109, 152, 161, 163, 172–73, 192,
    284, 291
agency, 6, 16, 36, 48, 74, 81, 91, 96, 210,
    216, 218, 270, 277, 281
Agha Soltan, N., 183–84
Ahmadinejad, M., 180–81, 183, 186,
    189
AKP leadership, 208–9
Alevis, 200
Almond, G., 284
Anderson, B., 130, 225
Anderson, L., 74
Anonymous, 171, 262
antiapartheid, 7, 112
anticapitalist, 201
anticolonial movement, 7
antiglobalization, 41
antioccupy movement, 256
antioppressive principles, 289
April 6 Youth Movement, 79, 93–94
Arab Spring, ix, xi, 11, 14, 23–24,
    31, 35, 39, 42, 74, 76–78, 80–81,
    89, 93, 97, 119, 130, 132–33,
    138, 193, 197, 200, 211, 223,
    238, 271–72, 276, 280, 286–89,
    295, 298

Arab uprisings, 5, 12, 14, 19, 73, 81,
    96–97, 268, 272, 287

Bahrain, 78, 90
Balatarin, 179, 181, 183–85, 187–88
El Baradei, M. 94
Bardhan, P., 227
Basic Law, 8, 239–43, 245–50, 253, 255,
    265, 295
Basijis, 179
Bayat, A., 3
Bharatiya Janata Party (BJP), 221–23,
    228–38, 274
Biafran famine, 66
Biko, S., 112
Black Lives Matter movement, 7
Block the Boat Movement, 119
blogs, 6, 8, 18, 24, 33, 54, 93, 115, 119,
    122, 130, 141–42, 148, 179–80, 183,
    188, 213, 261, 266, 273–75, 283, 296
Booth, K., 76, 78, 85, 97
Bouazizi, M., 35
Boycott, Divestment, and Sanctions
    (BDS) movement, 102, 105, 107,
    110–14, 118, 120, 125
Bremmer, I., 13, 129
Brysk, A. 7
Bunce, V., 73
Buycott, 105, 109–12, 125

Calderon, F., 171
Carapico, S., 14, 89, 132
Cardenas, S. 5
Carpenter, C., 14, 64
Castells, M., 4, 45, 128
Chavez, H., 133, 154, 159–60
El Chigüire Bipolar, 159–61

China, xv, 8, 47, 178, 227, 239, 241, 243, 245, 247–53, 255–64, 266, 294, 298, 301

civil disobedience, 5, 68, 76, 152, 181, 217, 254–56, 258, 262, 264, 278, 283, 293

civil liberties, 1, 28, 91, 277, 288

civil referendum, 251, 254–56, 261

civil society, 2, 9, 27, 35, 43, 70, 84, 91, 97, 103, 105, 112, 179–80, 194, 240, 242, 262, 266–67, 277, 281–83, 285–86

Committee in Solidarity with the People of El Salvador (CISPES), 166

contentious politics, 5, 8, 13, 268, 282–83

Crimea, 141–47, 150

culturism, 76

CyberBerkut, 143

cyberactivism, 283, 292

cyberspace, 1, 13, 17, 41, 73, 89, 129, 270, 282, 292

cyberstalking, 279

cyberterrorism, 279

de Waal, A., 63

democratization, 19, 32, 77, 84, 96, 127, 130, 149, 179, 285, 289

developmentalist, 221–22, 226–29, 235, 237

Diamond, L., 4, 9, 128, 130, 181–82, 192–93, 297–99, 301

digital media, ix, xii, 3, 14–18, 51, 75, 86, 98, 131, 151, 169–73, 267, 270, 281, 288–89, 292

digital revolution, 3, 9

digital surveillance, 1

digital text, 33

digital world, xiii, 6, 267

digitally connected population, 9

disruption, xv, 120, 278

Donnelly, J., 18, 77, 290

Dorraj, M., 193

Drezner, D. W., 14, 101, 295

drug cartels, 171

Egypt, ix, xiii, 8, 10–11, 14, 17, 47, 73–74, 79, 81–82, 84–95, 119, 131–32, 182, 200, 211, 238, 271–72, 276, 283, 287–88, 295–96, 298–300

El Salvador, 164, 166

el-Sisi, A. F., 89, 92

Elster, J., 241

emancipatory, xii, 2, 5, 7, 14, 48–49, 195, 269–70, 277

empowerment, 5–6, 10, 17, 31–32, 38, 48, 67, 74, 79, 104, 127, 152, 227, 267, 271, 278, 289, 293

Enloe, C., 140

Ennahda, 91, 93

Erdoğan, R. T., 196, 197, 199, 203–8, 210, 213, 215–19, 275

Euromaidan, 127, 135–37, 139, 141–44, 147, 296–97

Facebook, 13, 18, 24, 33, 47, 51, 75, 83, 86, 93–95, 107, 109, 114, 116, 118, 129, 132, 135, 138, 145, 149, 165–66, 169, 179–80, 183–84, 188–90, 192–93, 197–98, 211, 213, 215, 219, 223–24, 234–35, 258, 260, 272, 276; see also social media

Faris, D., 288

FireChat, 261

Five Broken Cameras, 104–5

Flickr, 33

Forsythe, D. P., viii, xii, xvii, 18, 75, 291, 296

freedom of the press, 152, 180

Gandhi, R., 222, 231

Gandhi, S., 222, 231–32, 234

Gaza, 106–7, 111, 117, 120, 122–23, 297

El General, 93

Gerges, F. A., 8, 73–74, 294

Gezi Park, 196–98, 201–3, 205–6, 208, 210–13, 218–20, 299

Ghonim, W., 12, 73, 94–95

Gladwell, M., 23–25, 36, 44, 47

globalization, 70, 151

Globovision, 156, 159–60

Göle, N., 200, 203

Granito, 162–63, 167

grassroots sanctions, 15, 103, 106, 110, 115, 120, 124–25, 281

Green Movement, 7, 12, 23, 79, 82, 119, 177, 181, 183, 185–86, 188–89, 192–94, 273–74, 297–98, 301

Guatemala, 162–64

Hafner-Burton, E. M., 61, 290
headscarves, worn in solidarity, 188
high politics, 8
Hill, S., 10
Hindu–Muslim, 230, 232
Hong Kong, viii, xiii, xvii, 7–8, 16–17, 239–62, 264–66, 271–72, 275, 295, 297–98
Hopgood, S., 12, 61
Howard, P., 179
human rights, viii–xiii, xv–xvii, 1–2, 4–6, 14–15, 17–19, 21, 23, 25–26, 28, 31, 35–38, 43–45, 48, 50–52, 54–55, 59, 61–71, 73–78, 80, 83–85, 91–92, 96–98, 103, 112–13, 116, 121, 133, 151–52, 155, 157–59, 161–66, 168, 170, 172–73, 177, 179, 183, 191, 194, 197, 221–22, 226–27, 234, 236–39, 241, 243–46, 249–50, 262, 267–71, 273–75, 278, 281–83, 285, 288–91, 293; see also civil liberties
Human Rights Watch, 38, 61, 71, 121, 171, 216
humanitarian, xiii, xv, 12, 50–52, 54, 57–58, 61–62, 65–68
humanitarianism, 50, 52, 54–56, 58, 61, 63–64, 66–69
Hunt, L., 74

identity, xi, 30–31, 51, 55, 61, 68, 86, 122, 140, 221, 224–26, 231, 234–36, 238, 264, 274, 278; see also national identity
Iguala, 151, 164, 168
imagery, 50–54, 56, 64, 66–68, 71, 84
impartiality, 58
independence, 13, 58, 61, 127, 141, 216, 230–31, 233, 236, 245–46
information and communication technologies (ICTs), 4, 15, 16, 18, 25, 26–49, 74, 84, 179, 194, 270–72, 283, 285, 288, 289
information technology, 8, 133, 149, 268, 278, 285
infosphere, 267
Instagram, 51, 148, 213, 262; see also social media

International Committee of the Red Cross (ICRC), xiv, 58
International Court of Justice (ICJ), 112
International Covenant on Civil and Political Rights (ICCPR), 38, 245
International Covenant on Economic, Social, and Cultural Rights (ICESCR), 38, 245
International Longshore and Warehouse Union (ILWU), 118
Internet, vii, xiii, xvi, 1–2, 4, 6–10, 12–14, 16–18, 23–26, 31–33, 36–42, 45–48, 73, 79, 83–84, 93, 95, 102, 110, 112, 115, 117, 120, 127–28, 130, 133, 139, 148, 151, 159, 163, 177–81, 185–86, 193–95, 215–16, 218, 224, 240, 258, 261, 269–70, 272–73, 276–79, 281–83, 292, 295, 297, 301; see also Facebook; Instagram; social media; Twitter; YouTube
intifada, 105, 109
Iran, x, xv, 7, 12, 16–17, 23, 31, 39, 47, 79, 82, 102, 119, 131, 133, 138, 177–86, 188, 190–94, 272–74, 292, 297–99, 301
ISIS, see Islamic State in Iraq and Syria
Isla Presidencial, 159–60
Islamic State in Iraq and Syria (ISIS), 79, 81, 197, 217, 275, 288

Johansson, Scarlett, 113–14
journalism and photography, 50

Kamrava, M., 287
Kar, M., 193
Karoubi, M., 179
Keck, M., 38, 59
Kefaya movement, 93
Kemalist, 220, 275
Khalid Said, 83, 132
Khamenei, A., 186
Kharkiv, 149
Khatami, Mohammad, 180–81, 185
Kullena Khaled Said, 94
Kurds, 200
Kyiv (Kiev), 127, 135–39, 141, 143–44, 146, 149

Latin America, vii–viii, 12, 15, 17, 30, 34–35, 41, 151–73, 281, 298, 301
leapfrog technology, 34
Levitsky, S., 145, 153
LGBT community/issues, 200, 289
liberation technology, 9, 128–29
Libya, xv, 8, 11, 47, 78, 82, 90
Listservs, 151, 165, 190
Lynch, M., 77, 79, 82, 84, 282, 287, 297, 299

Maidan, 136–37, 139, 143, 145, 147, 271
mainstream opinion, 251
mainstream press, 53, 259–60
majoritarianism, 219
McLuhan, M., 48
Médecins sans Frontières (MSF), 58, 61
Mexico, 151, 164–65, 167–68, 170–72
Meyer, D., 27
micropolitics, 8
Middle East and North Africa (MENA) region, xii, 3, 75–91, 285–89
Milani, A., 192–93, 298–99
Modi, N., 221–22, 226, 229–31, 233, 274, 301
Morayef, H., 92
Morozov, E., 14, 134
Morsi, M., 11
mRat, 261
Mossavi, M. H., 179
Mubarak, H., 11, 86–87, 94
multimedia blogging, 33
Muslim Brotherhood, 10–11, 87–88

Nabavi, E., 189
Nasser, G. A., 88
national cyberspaces, 178
national identity, vii, 122, 221, 223–26, 228, 235–36, 238, 274; see also identity
National Intelligence Organization (MIT), 216
National People's Congress (NPC) Standing Committee, 242
Nayem, M., 135
neoliberal views, 9
network politics, 3–4, 15–16, 26, 28, 31, 48, 271

"Network Society," 45
neutrality, 58, 167
new social movements (NSMs), 3, 26, 28, 49
nonactivists, 200
nongovernmental organizations (NGOs), 12–14, 38, 50–55, 58, 60, 62, 64–71, 91, 109, 163, 171, 268, 278, 281, 283–84
NISGUA, 163
nonmovement, 3
nonstate actors, xiv, 57, 152, 170, 172, 278, 281, 291

Occupy Central, 240–41, 250, 254–57, 261–62, 264
Occupy Wall Street movement, 5, 24, 42, 45
Orange Revolution, 31, 138, 141

Palestine, 15, 81, 101, 103–5, 109–12, 125, 280, 294, 297, 300
photography, 50, 52, 65
photojournalism, 52–53, 278
PKK, 197
postcommunist Europe, 73
postoccupy, 265
postrevolutionary leaders, 286
postrevolutionary societies, 90
preinformation revolution state, 278
privacy, 1, 17, 269, 277, 279, 282, 288
privacy rights, 279, 293
prodemocracy movement, 271
progovernment, 189, 211, 251, 253, 260, 263
progovernment camp, 251
Putin, V., 129, 137, 147
Putin administration, 11
Putnam, R. D., 10, 44

Qaddafi, M., 90

Rahimi, B., 180, 290, 297
reform, viii, 11, 36, 38, 52, 88, 90, 92, 98, 168, 180, 194, 204, 239–40, 247–48, 250–51, 253–55, 263, 265–66, 273, 286, 290

resistance, 3, 8, 14, 17, 55, 65, 101,
    103–5, 110, 124, 170, 202, 213, 243,
    257, 264, 267, 274, 282, 286, 288
Rheingold, H., 130, 267
rhetorics, 237–38
Richardson, S., 74
Rorty, R., 97
Rouhani, H., 192–94

Scholarism, 256, 258
security, x, 102, 148, 178, 184, 189, 215,
    217, 250, 265, 275, 279, 300
self-expression, 75
self-image, 51, 208
Selnow, G. W., 2, 129
Sepahis, 179
Shirky, C., 23–25
short message service (SMS), 130, 182,
    187–88
Sikkink, K., 38, 59, 64, 161, 291
slacktivism, 12, 46–47, 135, 169
Smart Mobs, 27, 130–31, 267
social justice, x, 55, 62, 76, 78, 115, 119,
    270, 273, 281
social media, 11, 33, 75, 93, 97, 106,
    109, 119, 124, 127, 151, 161–62,
    167, 172, 188, 197, 211, 213, 219,
    221, 223, 235–38, 273, 275–76,
    280–81; see also Facebook;
    Instagram; Twitter; YouTube
social movement, 3, 25–27, 29–31,
    35–36, 39, 42, 45–46, 48, 55, 63,
    151, 177, 189, 194, 242, 260, 262,
    273, 291
social networking, 16, 33, 73, 108–9,
    119, 177, 179, 194–95
SodaStream, 113–14, 124
SoundCloud, 215
South Africa, 7, 96, 102, 112–13, 115,
    118–19, 123
Sreberny, A., 273, 289
StopWTORound, 41
Supreme Council of the Armed Forces
    (SCAF), 87
surveillance, 1, 17, 71, 178, 197, 216,
    218, 261, 268, 270, 274, 289, 293
Syria, xv, 12, 47, 78–79, 81, 90, 275,
    288

Tahrir Square, 8, 14, 83, 87–88, 92, 119,
    131, 271
Taksim Square, 196, 198, 211–12, 219,
    299
Tarrow, S., 27, 29–30, 262, 301
technological determinism, 13, 47
TED talk, 163
TeleSur, 155, 160
Televisa, 168
terrorism, xiv, 2, 17, 282, 288
texting, see short message service (SMS)
third wave, 30, 96
Tilly, C., 27, 29–30, 39, 262
transformative impact, 70
transnational advocacy networks, 38,
    59–60, 64, 152, 161, 291
Trippi, J., 25, 31–32
Tufekci, Z., 197
Tunisia, xvii, 8, 11, 14, 17, 73–74,
    76–77, 79, 81–82, 87, 90–91, 93–94,
    97, 131–32, 200, 211, 271–72, 288
Turkish Telecommunications
    Authority (TIB), 215
Twitter, 18, 23–24, 33, 47, 51, 75–76,
    85, 109, 114, 116, 118, 129–32, 134,
    136–37, 149, 159–60, 164–65,
    179–82, 188–89, 193, 196, 198, 201,
    211–15, 217, 219, 223–24, 234,
    272–73; see also social media

Ukraine, x, xiii, xv, 8, 11, 15, 17, 31,
    127, 129, 135–37, 139–50, 271–72,
    296, 300–1
Ultimas Noticias, 156
ultranationalist, 200
Umbrella Movement, 239, 241–42,
    256–58, 260–61, 266, 275
unemployment, 78, 80–82, 93, 286
Universal Declaration of Human Rights
    (UDHR), xv, 37–38, 77, 78
universal suffrage, 239, 242, 247–48,
    252, 254

VahidOnline, 182
Venevision, 155, 160
Verba, S., 284
virtual revolt, 13
visual media, 50–51, 68, 70

Warschauer, M., 34
Way, L., 153
West Bank, x, 104, 110, 113–17, 121–23
White Paper, 242, 246, 249–50, 254, 256–57
WITNESS, 71
women's rights, ix, 91, 183, 190, 193

Yanukovych, V., 11

Yemen, 78, 82, 90, 94, 184
youth movement, 7, 15, 79, 86, 94, 177, 194, 202, 272
youth unemployment, 78, 80–82
YouTube, 33, 83, 93, 95, 132, 160, 166–68, 171, 181, 183–88, 197, 213, 215, 219, 273, 298

Zirakzadeh, C. E., 27

Lightning Source UK Ltd.
Milton Keynes UK
UKOW06n1410120616

276072UK00014B/63/P